BELIEF IN GOD

Belief in God

An Introduction to the Philosophy of Religion

T. J. MAWSON

CLARENDON PRESS · OXFORD

OXFORD

UNIVERSITY PRESS

Great Clarendon Street, Oxford OX2 6DP

Oxford University Press is a department of the University of Oxford.
It furthers the University's objective of excellence in research, scholarship,
and education by publishing worldwide in

Oxford New York

Auckland Cape Town Dar es Salaam Hong Kong Karachi Kuala Lumpur
Madrid Melbourne Mexico City Nairobi New Delhi Shanghai Taipei Toronto

With offices in

Argentina Austria Brazil Chile Czech Republic France Greece
Guatemala Hungary Italy Japan South Korea Poland Portugal
Singapore Switzerland Thailand Turkey Ukraine Vietnam

Oxford is a registered trade mark of Oxford University Press
in the UK and in certain other countries

Published in the United States
by Oxford University Press Inc., New York

© T. J. Mawson 2005

The moral rights of the author have been asserted

Database right Oxford University Press (maker)

First published 2005

British Library Cataloguing in Publication Data
Data available

Library of Congress Cataloging in Publication Data
Mawson, T. J.
Belief in God : an introduction to the philosophy of religion / T. J. Mawson.
p. cm.
Includes bibliographical references and index.
1. God–Attributes. 2. God–Proof. I. Title
BT130.M39 2005 210–dc21 2005020162
ISBN 0-19-928495-4 (alk. paper) - ISBN 0-19-927631-5 (alk. paper)

Typeset by Newgen Imaging Systems (P) Ltd., Chennai, India
Printed in Great Britain
on acid-free paper by
Biddles Ltd., King's Lynn, Norfolk

ISBN 0-19-927631-5 978-019-927631-8
ISBN 0-19-928495-4 (Pbk.) 978-0-19-928495-5 (Pbk.)

3 5 7 9 10 8 6 4

To my parents

*Without whom many would be less than they are and some
would be nothing at all*

Acknowledgements

TWO people have been more influential than any others in the development of my thought on these topics. The first is John Kenyon, my undergraduate tutor in Philosophy. The second is Richard Swinburne, my graduate supervisor. Later in life, I have had the privilege and pleasure of knowing each of them as colleagues and friends and neither has ever failed to improve my thinking in my conversations with them. The questions to which this book addresses itself were first put to me in a philosophically rigorous way by John; and he was the first to guide me to care about trying to answer them in a similar fashion. Anybody who is familiar with the work of Richard will recognize his influence on almost every page of this book: on starting points, we are often in complete agreement; on conclusions, less so. But in both their cases my debt is of course not for the conclusions that I reach but for the questions that I ask and the method by which I seek to answer them. If progress in Philosophy is marked not so much by an accumulation of answers as by the improvement of one's questions, then these two have helped me most in what progress I have been able to make.

Many of the ideas that I draw on in this book have appeared in more detailed form in articles in *Religious Studies*. I am grateful for comments on these articles by the editor, Peter Byrne, and by the various anonymous referees who have reviewed them. Others have appeared or will appear in more detailed form in the *International Journal for Philosophy of Religion* and *The Heythrop Journal*; again, I am grateful to the editors of these journals and their anonymous referees for their comments. Yet others have been discussed informally with members of the Natural Theology group that meets at the Athenaeum: Douglas Hedley, Dave Leal, and Mark Wynn. I am grateful to them for their insights. And most of the ideas that I draw on here have been tried out first on my pupils. In term time, almost every week sees me trying out some new idea or example in a tutorial with a pupil, safe in the knowledge that should I have overlooked some flaw that he or she spots, I shall be able to hide my embarrassment behind some Delphic utterance. If any pupil of mine reading this has ever wondered why I spent so much time in one of his or her tutorials insisting that he or she explain at length why some patently flawed argument does not work as if to someone who was so slow that they hadn't yet grasped it, now he or she knows the answer. A number of people have been kind enough to read the penultimate draft and offer suggestions for improvement. They are: Rodes Fishburne, Caroline Mawson, Richard Swinburne, and the two anonymous readers for OUP. For having extirpated a lot of worthless ideas from my thinking on these issues, all these people (as well as those whose only form of acknowledgement is that their work appears in the bibliography) must take credit; for those worthless ideas that remain, the blame falls solely on me.

Penultimately, I would like to thank those at OUP involved in the practicalities of bringing this book to publication, especially Rupert Cousens, Rebecca Bryant, and Sylvia Jaffrey.

Finally, I would like to thank my colleagues at St Peter's for providing me with the supportive environment in which I wrote this book. As I look back on my last five or so years here, I am reminded of the story of a man who, looking back at the end of a long life, commented that he had had a lot of troubles but that most of them had never actually happened. I have been unfortunate in having a lot of troubles in my time at St Peter's, but this has been more than compensated for by my good fortune in having as colleagues people who have ensured that none of them have ever actually happened.

T.J.M.

St Peter's College Oxford
4 January 2005

Contents

Introduction

I start with a—roughly speaking, psychological—claim that I venture is true of everyone reading this book. At some stage in your life, the physical world considered as a whole—the planet on which you live; the stars you see in the sky: the whole lot—has presented itself to your intellect as something close to a question. The physical universe has struck you as a phenomenon in need of an explanation. Some of you think that you've found the answer to that question. Perhaps question and answer came at once, in one psychologically durationless moment of realization as you now think of it. Some of you think that you've found that there is no need for an answer after all. You've decided that the feeling that the physical world as a whole is a question is illusory. And for the rest of you the physical world as a whole continues to strike you in your reflective moments as it did then, as a question to which an answer is required and yet sadly elusive.

To have the capacity to be puzzled by the fact that the physical world as a whole exists is a contingent feature of the human mind. And although common, it is not a universal feature. There are some who have never been puzzled in this way and who are thus completely unable to empathize with the speculations to which this puzzlement naturally gives rise. Such men and women cannot but find the philosophy of religion and a good deal of metaphysics pointless, a series of logic-chopping or vaporous attempts to smother non-existent problems in waffle and nonsense. But I venture that nobody reading this has never felt struck by the physical world as a whole in the way that I've just described. I venture that for a number of reasons, the most obvious and unexciting of which is that a selection effect has operated on those who find themselves reading books with subtitles like 'An Introduction to the Philosophy of Religion'. The prevalence of this puzzlement throughout time and across cultures explains the persistence of the philosophy of religion and metaphysical thinking: this puzzlement is, as Schopenhauer once put it, 'the pendulum which keeps the clock of metaphysics in motion'.

Because this puzzlement is a puzzlement about the physical world as a whole, if we allow it to keep the clock of metaphysics in us in motion, we will be led to think that the answer to the question of the physical world must lie outside it. An explanation cannot reside within that which it explains. Physicalism I define as the view that this puzzlement concerning the physical world as a whole is ultimately misguided, that there is nothing outside the physical world that accounts for it. Religions I define as those systems of thought that view physicalism as false, that claim then that there is something outside the physical world that accounts for it: there is something beyond the world that natural science describes and that something explains why there is a world for us to describe and why there is an us to do the describing.[1]

Physicalism has never been popular. It might be right none the less, but it's certainly never been popular.[2] The religious view has always been more popular. As a writer from antiquity summed his discoveries as to the diversity of the world's cultures: one can find cities without kings; without walls; and without coinage, but a city without gods has never been found. The religious view accepts the validity of this puzzlement. It accepts that the physical world is indeed a question in need of an answer. Specifically, the adherents of each religion claim that their religion provides the answer to this question.

What sort of thing do the various religions of the world say this answer is? Here we come to a great divide among the world's religions between, on the one hand, those—roughly speaking, Western—religions that view the sort of thing that is the answer to the question of the physical world as a personal agent and, on the other hand, those—roughly speaking, Eastern—religions that view the answer as an impersonal force. In this book, I'm going to be focusing on the central claim of the Western religions of Judaism, Christianity, and Islam, those religions that say that the answer to the question is a personal agent, namely God. The thought that the answer to the question of the physical world might be a personal agent is the pendulum that keeps the clock of Theology in motion, and it's that pendulum I'll be looking at.

I would encourage you to think of my ignoring the traditions of the Eastern religions as methodological humility rather than methodological narrow-mindedness. If I am to make significant progress in the space allowed by a relatively short book, I must concentrate on an area that I can reasonably hope to traverse in the amount of time such a format allows. So for this reason, which I admit is not a philosophical reason, I'm going to focus exclusively on the main philosophical arguments pertaining to the monotheistic religions of Judaism, Christianity, and Islam, and to the main claim of these religions, that there is a God.[3]

So I shall be looking at this claim:

There is a God

and be asking the following questions of it: What does it mean? Are there any reasons for thinking it true? Are there any reasons for thinking it false? What is the relationship between having reasons for thinking it true and having faith in God? I shall be asking these questions of it because they are all different aspects of the main question that interests me, Should one believe in God?

Those then will be my questions. How shall I approach them?

◆ ◆ ◆

He who has raised himself above the Alms-Basket, and not content to live lazily on scraps of begg'd Opinions, sets his own Thoughts on work, to find and follow Truth, will (whatever he lights on) not miss the Hunter's Satisfaction; every moment of his Pursuit, will reward his Pains with some Delights; and he will have Reason to think his time not ill spent, even when he cannot much boast of any great Acquisition.[4]

According to legend, when Alexander the Great first arrived in Asia, its rulers met with him and (hoping to avoid confrontation with his invincible armies) they offered him half their lands, palaces, treasures, etc., half of everything they owned. Alexander dismissed them instantly, telling them simply that he had not come to Asia with the intention of accepting from its leaders whatever it was they cared to offer him, but rather with the intention of leaving for them whatever it was he did not care to take. True philosophers are not beggars. They do not humbly accept whatever opinions are offered them by someone speaking to them from the front of a lecture theatre or from the pages of a book. They are conquerors. They take no pride in an opinion unless they themselves have won it by argumentation, and they deserve to be proud of what they win because the arguments that they use are ones they themselves have tested in the most intense fires that their minds and those of others could stoke. Of course they may be expected to take up weapons originally forged by others. But in testing them in dialectical battle they will fashion them to fit their own hands and purposes, adding their own experiences and intuitions to make a stronger alloy peculiar to them. It is in so conquering that philosophers' wars are always just and their victories righteous, for it is in so conquering beliefs that one can justify a claim to own them (genuinely own, as in have a right to them, that is) rather than merely happen to possess them. The best any philosophy book can hope to do is give a clear overview of the conceptual territory that needs to be conquered in this manner as it is seen from the point of view of its author, a point of view that will perforce be partial in the richest sense of the word. My only hope for this book then is that it will do this. As I travel across the territory, mapping it to the best of my ability, I shall be pursuing and chronicling my own campaign, travelling in a particular direction (i.e. towards a particular conclusion). But in doing so I shall do my best to indicate as I pass them the alternative positions that are or have been defended. In doing so, I hope to make it easier for you to assess the accuracy of my map; judge the wisdom of the particular course I have taken; and win the territory for yourself in the manner I have just described.

If no book can ever do philosophy, but rather only people can do philosophy, then in this sense no philosophy book can ever be more than an introduction to philosophy for the person reading it. But this book is intended to be an introduction to philosophy in the more usual sense too: it is written with the intention that every argument in it be understood by everyone who might read it, including those who start from a position of considering themselves to know no philosophy at all. Most philosophy books are not written with this intention. This one's being so means that, now and again, I'll take a moment or two to go over some terminological or other point in a way that those who consider themselves philosophers already will not find of benefit. My apologies to them for these delays. In fact, this tendency won't slow things down much. In this area of philosophy, unlike some others, one can make good progress without needing to master difficult technical ideas or symbolic structures. The ideas employed in the philosophy of religion are—contrary to what I find many people unexposed to this area expect—commonplace ones; the arguments, commonsensical. All are within the grasp of the average adult who finds himself or herself with a will to grasp them. This is not to say that all are within the grasp of the average adult. Sadly, the average adult has no will to grasp these sorts of issues or arguments at all. This widespread indifference is not peculiarly focused (if one may in principle speak of focusing indifference) on the philosophy of religion; it spreads itself to all philosophy. As Russell observed, most people would rather die than think; and of course most do. But happily, due to the selection effect to which I alluded earlier, you are very unlikely to be 'most people'. You will want to understand what I have to say and thus you will succeed in doing so.

Why do I have this optimism about the ability of the average adult who is willing to grapple with these issues to grasp them successfully? Why do I think that the human faculty of reason as it finds itself at work within the minds of normal people is up to the task of discovering the truth here and our faculty of language up to the task of expressing it? Shouldn't we humbly think that if there is a God, then he exists beyond the possibility of human thought and expression, that here our reach will always exceed our grasp?

Of course human reason is fallible. The best ideas and arguments any finite mind can come up with may be expected to fail to reflect perfectly the nature of an infinite God if there is such a being. But what should we conclude from this truism? Is it that we should not even *try* to use our reason to discern the truth about these matters and our language to express it? Or is it rather that we should proceed with caution, being careful, for example, to define what we mean by any important term before we use it; being careful, for example, to make each stage in our argument as clear as possible; being careful, for example, to proceed with our investigation as dispassionately as possible and, where our passions must needs enter in, being careful to consider how they might be misleading us? This book is written in the belief that it is the latter course of action that must commend itself to any enquiring mind.[5] I do not defend that belief here, except indirectly: if my arguments work, then this is a vindication of my 'working hypothesis' that, if we tread with care, we may reasonably believe ourselves to be using words in a meaningful way to talk about whether or not there is a God and using our reason to arrive at knowledge of the answer to this question (or at least knowledge of how we should go about answering it).

Not everyone believes in this working hypothesis. And not everyone is temperamentally able to suspend their disbelief in it for the relatively short period of time that it would take to explore imaginatively where it might take them, the exploration that this book undertakes. If you think that you don't share this optimism in the power of human reason to address these issues, I can say nothing that will better convince you to suspend your disbelief for the next dozen or so chapters than that which I might be able to persuade you to say to yourself by asking you to imagine this situation.

You are wandering alone in a vast and unfamiliar labyrinth. It is pitch black: you have no light to guide you, none at all, *except* that provided by the flickering and weak flame of the small candle that you carry. You are guarding this flame jealously as you tread your cautious and faltering steps. A man suddenly appears out of the gloom ahead of you. This man tells you that which you already know only too well, that your candle is a small one and its flame dim. Then he suggests that, in order to find your way more easily, you should put it out entirely. What would you say to him?

PART I
THE CONCEPT OF GOD

1

Personhood, Transcendence, Immanence

You may have heard the radio play; seen the TV series; and/or read the book *The Hitchhikers' Guide to the Galaxy*. In one incident in that story, a computer that has been working away—for thousands of years if I remember correctly—on finding the answer to 'the great question of life, the universe and everything' dramatically reports that it has found the answer but worryingly warns those who are speaking to it that they won't like it. Undaunted, they press on and ask the computer to reveal what is the answer to the great question of life, the universe and everything. The computer tells them—'42'. It adds, 'I told you you wouldn't like it.'

Judaism, Christianity, and Islam share the view that the answer to the great question of life, the universe and everything is God. God's not as amusing an answer as 42, but—and in part because—it's one that we can't help but think is prima facie more likely to be true. Jews, Christians, and Muslims differ over much else (as even a cursory examination of any newspaper will reveal), but these—often violent—differences should not obscure from us the even more remarkable fact that every Jew, Christian, and Muslim agrees on what each of them would say is overwhelmingly the most important fact to which the human mind can ever direct itself, that there is a God.

It will be handy to have a generic term for Jews, Christians, and Muslims, and, as the name of the conception of God that they share is usually referred to in the literature as the 'theistic' conception (from the Greek word for 'God'), so I'm going to call Jews, Christians, and Muslims simply 'theists'. So, my first question will be this: What does a theist mean when he or she says, 'There is a God'? This isn't, it will be observed, the question of whether or not what they say is true. Or at least, it's not directly that question. (If it doesn't mean anything to say that there's a God, then that entails it can't be true to say that there's a God.) It's the prior question of whether or not there's any common and coherent concept of God that theists have in mind when they use the term. Do they mean anything at all by saying it? At least initially, it appears that they do, that there is a common and coherent concept of God that they have in mind.

There is a traditional set of properties that all theists are agreed God has and that all atheists, that is to say those who believe that there is no such being, are

agreed that he would have had were he to have existed. Where atheists think that
it's logically possible that God exists (that is they think that the claim that he
does exist is not in itself inconsistent, in the way that the claim that a married
bachelor exists would be inconsistent), they agree with theists that these properties are 'co-possible', that is to say that there's no conceptual incoherence in
claiming that an entity with all these properties exists. Where atheists think that
it's not even logically possible that God exists, they think that, *pace* theists, these
traditional properties of God form a mutually incompatible set, they're not
co-possible. So what are these properties?

By believing that there is a God, theists believe that there is a being who
is personal; incorporeal/transcendent; omnipresent/immanent; omnipotent;
omniscient; eternal; perfectly free; perfectly good; and necessary. Furthermore,
they believe that this being has created the world (by which I now mean to
include anything else other than God that exists in addition to the physical
universe we encounter in our everyday lives—for example, souls, angels, other
universes, if there are any); they believe that he is the creator of moral and other
sorts of value for us; they believe that he has revealed himself to us; and they
believe that he offers us the hope of everlasting life.[1]

Not only do all theists agree that God has these properties, they also agree as to
their status: the first nine of these properties are held by theists to be essential
properties of God; the last four of these properties are held to be accidental
properties of God.

There are at least a couple of uses of the terms 'essential' and 'accidental' in the
literature. In this context we may helpfully say that a thing's essential properties
are the properties that of necessity that thing could not fail to have yet still exist;
a thing's accidental properties by contrast are those properties that it could in
principle fail to have yet still exist. For those who have not come across it before,
the distinction between essential and accidental properties so understood will be
easier to see if I give an example. So, let me take as my example of a thing the
particular book that you hold in your hands at the moment. (I'm assuming
you're holding it; if not, pick it up.) And let me pick out two properties that this
book has, one of them plausibly essential on this understanding and the other
accidental. This book has pages—that's an essential property of it—and at the
moment it is being held by you, its reader—that's an accidental property of it. If
you removed from the book the property it currently enjoys of having pages—
for example, by tearing them all out and eating them—then the book would
cease to exist. What would exist instead would be a tattered book cover and a case
of indigestion; and a tattered book cover and a case of indigestion do not—of
necessity—constitute a book. That shows then that having pages is an essential
property of this book—it's a property that of necessity the book could not fail to
have yet still exist. By contrast, if you removed from the book the property it
currently enjoys of being held by you—for example, by putting it down on a
table—then the book would not of necessity cease to exist. So being held by you

is not an essential property of the book; it's an accidental property. Being held by you is a property that the book could in principle fail to have yet still continue to exist.[2]

So—according to theism—God has the first nine properties on my list essentially. They're properties that of necessity he could not fail to have yet still exist. The last four properties of God on my list by contrast are seen by theists as accidental properties; they're properties that God could have failed to have yet still have existed. God, in virtue of his perfect freedom (a property I'll come to in due course), could have chosen not to create a world, in which case there would have been no us for him to create moral and other values for; there would have been no us to whom he could reveal himself; and there would have been no us to whom he could offer everlasting life.

In a moment, I'm going to start going through these properties in the order in which I've just given them, talking about the conceptual difficulties and philosophical issues that they raise. By doing so, I'll show—as I've already started to show—why it's no accident that all theists would agree that the first nine of the properties I give in my list are essential and that the last four are accidental; and I'll also show how the divisions within the first nine of these properties and within the last four of these properties are artificial. I should stress a consequence of this before I go on: my dividing the essential properties of God into nine, rather than dividing them into some other number, is at least somewhat arbitrary. As we shall see, at least some of the properties that I initially describe as distinct are conceptually entailed by others. Indeed, I shall later argue for what is sometimes called the Doctrine of Divine Simplicity, that is the theory that all the nine essential properties on my list are best seen as differing aspects of a single and simple property that constitutes the divine essence.[3] So, while I've divided the divine nature into nine essential properties at this stage for the purposes of making my explication easier, some might sensibly divide it into a different number or indeed not divide it at all. The same goes for my dividing the four accidental properties that all theists are agreed God has into four rather than some other number or not dividing it at all. Later, I'll consider and endorse (more contentious) arguments to the effect that that also is arbitrary: given that God's created a universe with people in it, then he must (of necessity) create value for them; reveal himself to them; and offer them everlasting life. The division between essential and accidental properties however, *that* is—without contention—not arbitrary. We'll further explore why in due course.

This caveat about the potential for disagreement on the precise number of essential properties and the number of accidental properties of God having been made, it is, as I say, a remarkable fact that all Jews, Christians, and Muslims are agreed that God has these properties and that this is their status. Of course, one can find a few Jews, Christians, and Muslims who will deviate from this orthodoxy, but they are *very* few and they are very far between. Go to your local synagogue, church, or mosque and try to find a Jew, Christian, or Muslim who understands what they are saying and sincerely denies that God has one of these properties. You will find that it is about as easy as finding a member of the Flat Earth Society at an astronomy convention. A consequence of this remarkable consensus on the divine properties is that the theistic concept of God cannot be an incoherent or vague concept unless the properties in terms of which theists define God are themselves incoherent (or incoherent when taken together [not co-possible]) or vague. It cannot be a term with little substantial content unless the properties that theists attribute to God themselves have little substantial content. I want to stress this consequence now in order to begin to meet a claim that is often made, that 'God' is a term with little, ambiguous, or only vague meaning attached to it. Of course there are deviant uses of the term 'God' in popular discourse, though they are usually indicated by a lack of capitalization—as when one speaks of the ignorance of the Greek god (NB no capital 'G') Zeus as to the identity of the person who will dethrone him. Nevertheless, in the theistic context, the term 'God' (capitalized) has a quite different and quite substantial set of properties associated with it. If the theistic understanding of the properties themselves is coherent and substantial, then the term 'God' thus has a very clear meaning; it isn't vague at all.

If we are going to understand what theists mean when they say that there is a God, we thus need to understand what these properties amount to and how they are related to one another; we need to find out whether the theist's understanding of these properties is coherent and substantial. My first task then will be to go through these properties in the order in which I've just given them and explain what theists mean by them. This is the task that will occupy me for the first five chapters. If a clear picture of God emerges as a result of this, we can then sensibly go on to investigate whether or not we have any reasons for or against thinking that there is anything like the picture we've thus painted. This is the task that will occupy me from Chapter Six onwards. From this description of my intentions, you can guess then the sub-conclusion I shall be arguing for on the issue of the coherence and substantiveness of the theistic conception of God: I shall be arguing that it is coherent and substantial. If it wasn't, there'd be no need for the second half of this book.

Without further ado then, let me start with the first divine property on my list: personhood.

PROPERTY ONE: PERSONHOOD

Theists pray to God; they ask him questions; they listen for answers; they ask him to do things; they suppose that by asking him to do things, they make it more likely that he will do the things they have asked him to do.

By way of illustration, let us consider an example of a purported conversation between God and the person whom Jews, Christians, and Muslims regard as the father of their faith, Abraham. As we join the story, Abraham is about to start arguing with God over God's plans to destroy the city of Sodom.

Abraham remained standing before the Lord. Then Abraham approached him and said: 'Will you sweep away the righteous with the wicked? What if there are fifty righteous people in the city? Will you really sweep it away and not spare the place for the sake of the fifty righteous people in it? Far be it from you to do such a thing—to kill the righteous with the wicked, treating the righteous and wicked alike. Far be it from you! Shall not the Judge of all the earth do right?'

The Lord said, 'If I find fifty righteous people in the city of Sodom, I shall spare the whole place for their sake.'

Then Abraham spoke up again: 'Now that I have been so bold as to speak to the Lord, though I am nothing but dust and ashes, what if the number of the righteous is five less than fifty? Will you destroy the whole city because of five people?'

'If I find forty-five there,' he said, 'I will not destroy it.'

Once again he spoke to him, 'What if only forty are found there?'

He said, 'For the sake of forty, I shall not do it.'

Then he said, 'May the Lord not be angry, and I shall speak. What if only thirty can be found there?'[4]

The discussion goes on in this vein for some time, Abraham bargaining God down until in the end, while God does in fact end up destroying Sodom, he sends some angels to ensure that Lot and his family—the only righteous people who are actually to be found in that city—have the chance of escaping. Genesis 19: 29 thus reads, 'So when God destroyed the cities of the plain, he remembered Abraham, and he brought Lot out of the catastrophe that overthrew the cities where Lot had lived.'

Now of course we cannot assume at the start of an investigation into the coherence of the concept of God that this story is true or thus non-problematically use it as 'evidence' of the coherence or properties of God, but we can use it as exemplary of the universal theistic practice of ascribing to God a certain property, the property of personhood. It may be that there is disagreement among theists about whether or not we should take this story literally and, even if we do, there are not many theists who would claim to have as intimate and conversational a relationship with God as it depicts, but all theists are agreed with the presumption of this and every other story that any of the religions of Judaism, Christianity, and Islam tell involving God's relations with humanity, that God is *not* simply an impersonal force, something which is either arbitrary or can be manipulated by certain actions that we can choose to perform. He is not a supernatural mechanism, something which is in certain non-belief-type states and that merely undergoes events or causes other things to undergo events. God is a personal agent, a someone not a something, a someone who has beliefs about certain things; who cares about certain things; whom one can thus reason with and please or displease by certain actions that one can choose to perform; and God himself performs actions in turn in order to affect the world as he sees fit.

So all theists see God as a person.[5] But can we come up with a systematized view of what it is that makes a person a person? In other words, can we find the essence of personhood? I think that we can.

> A person is a person in virtue of and to the extent that they are a something—
> or rather, then, a some*one*—who is rational; who has beliefs; who is to be
> treated as the object of moral respect; and who reciprocates that attitude in
> actions that he or she performs, actions that paradigmatically include verbal
> communication.

There are a number of properties in that list. They're not black and white—either you have them or not—properties, and my combining them into a statement of the essence of personhood where I leave it vague what it means for these properties to contribute to making someone a person ('. . . in virtue of and to the extent that . . .') makes things even worse. Although I'm about to try to remove this vagueness, justification of the theory will nevertheless remain a task largely unaddressed here. My excuse for not addressing it fully is of course that if I were to try to do so, I would take us well outside the field of the philosophy of religion. I hope to remove enough of the 'rough and ready' feel of the theory here to make it plausible for me to suggest that the property of personhood is not itself an incoherent or vague one, even if it admits—as do most concepts—of borderline cases;[6] and I refer interested readers to another philosopher who has offered a more detailed defence of a theory pretty much like mine.[7] One word before I do even this, to those metaphysicians reading this: given the composite nature of the essence of personhood as I've just sketched it, it is tempting to look for some underlying and unitary fact about persons from which this 'essence' may be derived. If we had time, it might perhaps be profitable to give in to this temptation. But if there is a necessity that, for example, nothing that is not a unit of non-physical substance (the usual name is 'soul') could have all these properties and—perhaps—that anything that is a soul must have these properties, the necessity is not a conceptual one. (It is not a contradiction in terms to describe a wholly physical robot satisfying these criteria for being a person.) So the 'derivation' of the essence of personhood from any underlying metaphysical fact would not be a conceptual one. Thus it is best for our purposes to rest content with a description of the essence of personhood that stays at this composite conceptual level.

◆ ◆ ◆

Why do I say that these properties constitute the essence of personhood? Nobody would deny that the sorts of persons with whom we're directly acquainted in our everyday lives—other human beings—have very many other properties in addition to these. They have the property of needing oxygen in order to survive;

they have the property of being sometimes rather mean-spirited; and so on. Why choose as the essence of personhood the properties I have? Well, plausibly these other properties are not essential to being a person: one could in principle fail to have one or all of these other properties yet still be a person. If extra-terrestrials visited us one day, we might find that, while undeniably persons, they did not need oxygen in order to survive; we might find someone here on Earth who was never mean-spirited; and so on. Even if we don't think that there are any extra-terrestrials or that there ever has been a person here on Earth who has never been mean-spirited, we understand that it is conceptually possible that there might be such persons. So we can see then that even a property that is universal among the persons we actually know or that there actually are need not be essential to personhood.

Those new to philosophy often find it difficult to appreciate the fact that a property that is universally held by tokens (that is to say instances) of a particular type of thing may yet not be of the essence of that type of thing. Let me therefore illustrate the point briefly with an example. If every book about the philosophy of religion happens to be humourless, then it is a universally held property of books about the philosophy of religion that they are humourless. But it is not an essential property of books about the philosophy of religion that they are humourless. If one wrote a humourless first draft of a book about the philosophy of religion and then (after it had been accepted by a respected academic publisher) one went through putting in humorous examples, one would not thereby of conceptual necessity—because of what the words mean—stop it being a book about the philosophy of religion. Of course any property that is of the essence of a certain type of thing will be universally held by all tokens of that type. It's the essence of books about the philosophy of religion that they address the issue of what reasons we have for believing physicalism true or false; addressing this issue is what makes a book be a book about the philosophy of religion. Therefore, while a book about the philosophy of religion may or may not be humourless, it cannot—of conceptual necessity—fail to address this issue. To work out what is essential to personhood then, we do not need scientific investigation; we need conceptual (and perhaps in the end metaphysical) investigation. We need to ask questions like the following: would we ever call anything a person which or who did not need oxygen in order to survive? Yes, so needing oxygen is not essential to being a person, even if it is a property that is universal among all the persons we have ever come across. Would we ever call anything a person which or who was never mean-spirited? Yes, so being mean-spirited is not essential to being a person, however universal some element of mean-spiritedness is among the people who actually exist. Would we ever call anything a person which or who did not have beliefs? Well, perhaps yes, if they happened to be in a dreamless sleep.[8] But something that *never* had any beliefs, never had any mental representations of the world whatsoever, we would not count as a person. So having beliefs—at least at some moments in one's history—is essential to being a person. To the extent that one has periods in one's life where one does not have beliefs, one conceptually undermines one's status as a person in the sense that were those periods to link up in an uninterrupted and unterminated fashion, one would—of conceptual necessity—lose one's status as a person. Reflection on various other properties mirroring the sort of reflection I've just undertaken for needing oxygen, being mean-spirited, and having beliefs would—I suggest, but do not have time to argue—reveal that the other essential properties of persons are as I have stated them. Exhaustive reflection would reveal that there are no other essential properties of persons.

One's understanding of how these properties constitute the essence of personhood should not then entail that there couldn't be persons who were sometimes irrational (e.g. when in a fit of pique). It shouldn't entail that there couldn't be persons who occasionally failed to have beliefs (e.g. perhaps when in periods of dreamless sleep). It shouldn't entail that there couldn't be persons who were—in extreme circumstances—not to be treated as the object of moral respect. (It's rather more difficult to find an example of this as on some metaethical theories no person could ever fail to deserve such treatment. On Consequentialism—the theory that the moral status of any action depends on the goodness of the consequences it brings about—if you travelled back in time and could slay the infant Lenin (not then known as such of course), he might be such a person.) One's understanding of how these properties constitute the essence of personhood shouldn't entail that there couldn't be persons who sometimes fail to reciprocate the attitude of moral respect in their dealings with others (e.g. when being amoral). And it shouldn't entail that there couldn't be persons who fail to perform any actions for some parts of their lives (again, dreamless sleep would be an example). But, equally, it should entail that to the extent to which someone fails to show any of these characteristics over an extended period, they conceptually undermine their status as a person, this conceptual undermining thus showing that these properties are of the essence of personhood.

This account has as a consequence that foetuses and severely mentally retarded human beings do not count as persons. This conclusion will strike many people as unacceptable and hence a reason to reject the view of personhood that leads to it. I incline to accept the conclusion and defuse our uneasiness with it by pointing out that many things that are not persons still count, morally speaking. If you own a dog, you think that you may not simply do with it as you would an inanimate object such as this book. For example, you have an obligation to your dog not to tear it into pieces for your amusement whereas—risky though it is to draw this to your attention—you do not have an obligation to this book not to tear it into pieces for your amusement. Your dog counts in a way that this book does not. If you could only save either your dog or your copy of this book from a fire that was engulfing your home, you should save your dog. Not only would you save your dog—feeling more psychologically attached to your dog than you do to this book—but you *should* save your dog; your dog not being consumed by fire is more important than this book not being consumed by fire. Your dog counts morally, yet it is not a person. Once we appreciate that things that are not persons may still count in this way, we appreciate that human-beings that are not persons may still count morally and so we can square all our moral intuitions about how we should treat foetuses and severely mentally retarded human beings (whatever these intuitions may be) with an account of personhood that has as a consequence that these human beings are not persons. In short, we cannot find the conclusion that foetuses and severely mentally retarded human beings are not persons morally objectionable unless we are assuming that persons are the only sorts of entities that need to be considered morally important, but we don't assume that persons are the only sorts of entities that need to be considered morally important in our dealings with animals, so we shouldn't be assuming it here. It would be wrong to cause a person needless pain; it would be wrong to cause a foetus needless pain; it would be wrong to cause a severely mentally retarded human being needless pain; it would be wrong to cause a dog needless pain. But the reason why all these things would be wrong is simply that pain is bad and needless pain a morally unjustifiable bad (that's what the word 'needless' secures). Whether it's pain occurring in persons; pain occurring in human-beings who are not persons; or pain occurring in animals that are not human beings isn't something we need to know before we can know that it is something about which we should not be morally indifferent.[9]

It follows from this sort of account of the nature of personhood that whether or not something/someone is a person may be indeterminate, something which some would also take as a reason to object to the account. Personally, I don't see it as such. It is very plausible to suggest that most concepts have 'borderline' cases, that is to say cases where the correct thing to say is that the concept neither applies nor fails to apply and so whether or not something falls under that concept may be indeterminate. Imagine an apple sitting on your desk. You spot it slowly turning orange in colour; at the same time, the shape is subtly changing. Over a period of five minutes it 'morphs' into an orange. Are we to suppose that within these five minutes there was one instant at which it was a rather odd apple and the next at which it was a rather odd orange, or that there was some 'in-betweeny' stage when it was neither an apple nor an orange but some third sort of fruit; and that there was a moment at which it stopped being an apple and became this third sort of fruit and one at which it stopped being this third sort of fruit and became an orange? Surely not. The correct thing to say is that it started as an apple and remained so for an indeterminate period; it finished as an orange and had been such for an indeterminate period; and in between, for an indeterminate period, it was indeterminate whether it was an apple or an orange. Now imagine a 'fully-fledged' person such as—let's say—your best friend and an obviously non-personal thing, such as a banana. Imagine your friend slowly 'morphing' from being a person into being a banana; at the start of the process, where he or she merely takes on a slightly yellowish hue and starts to lose perhaps just one or two mental powers, he or she is still recognizably a person, indeed your best friend. At the end of the process, no person remains; all that remains is a banana. Should we posit that somewhere in between there was a moment at which a person was there and then, a moment later, gone? No. It seems much more sensible to say that a person existed at the start of this process and survived for an indeterminate period; there was a banana at the end of the process and there had been one for an indeterminate period; and in between, for an indeterminate period, it was indeterminate whether or not there was a person or a banana.[10]

There are no doubt other objections one might raise to this theory, but as to defend it further would be to embark on an elongated diversion from my main topic, so, having stated it and drawn attention to some of its implications, I'm just going to hold it up for your approval and assume that it's right in what follows. I maintain then that in regarding God as a person, theists regard God as someone who is rational; who has beliefs; who is to be treated as an object of moral respect; who reciprocates that attitude towards us; and who performs actions, actions that paradigmatically include verbal communication. If this is right, then personhood as a concept is coherent and substantial and thus so is the theistic claim that God is a person.

According to theists, not only does God have these essential properties of personhood, he has them we might say 'maximally'. God is not rational in the more or less haphazard way that we are; he is supremely rational. He never does anything less than fully reasonable. God doesn't just have a finite number of beliefs, some true and some false; he has an infinite number of beliefs and they're all true. God is not just an object of moral respect in the more or less restricted way that individual human people are, exceptional circumstances perhaps occasionally necessitating that we fail to respect him for a moment or two. (Again, it should be noted that on some metaethical views no circumstances— however exceptional—should be taken to necessitate that we fail to respect any person, even for a moment or two.[11]) God, on any metaethical view, is the object of supreme and unconditional moral respect. We treat people more or less well and thus (that is, in, virtue of treating them badly) conceptually undermine, to some extent, our status as persons.[12] God, by contrast, reciprocates our faltering attitude of respect for him with perfect respect of his own for us. We can perform a variety of actions, but we are not all-powerful. God, by contrast, can perform any action; he is all-powerful. We can communicate verbally with those around us and even—by telephones and the like—with those far away; in speaking to them, we can convey much of what we wish to convey. God can speak directly to anybody anywhere and in doing so he can convey anything that the finite minds to whom he speaks can accommodate.

If I'm right about the essence of personhood, then—because if there's a God, then he has the essential properties of personhood that I have termed 'maximally'—if anyone is going to count as a person, God's going to count as a person. Essentially, if there's a God, then he is much more of a person than any of us. It's worth bringing this out because one quite often hears claims to the effect that God, if he exists, can't be a person in the same sense that you and I are persons. According to my argument, this sort of claim is mistaken. If there is a God, then he is certainly *more* of a person than we are, but he is equally certainly a person in exactly the *same sense* that we are persons. It is not, as Tillich said, that God is not a person, but he is not less than personal.[13] Rather, God is a person because he is more personal than any other person could ever hope to be. Indeed one might say—and I shall later argue that this is the central guiding idea within the theistic concept of God—God is the most perfect person possible.

◆ ◆ ◆

Because God is a person and all—or almost all—the persons we come across have one of two biological genders—they're either male or female—it's natural to assign God a gender; you'll notice I've already done so, slipping into the traditional habit of referring to God as a 'he'. Of course, no sensible theist has ever thought that God really did have a gender. But because God is a person, then it would certainly be more misleading to call God an 'it' than it would be to call him either a 'he' or a 'she'. Ideally, from a purely philosophical point of view, we would find some personal but non-gender specific word like 'he-she'. Sadly—no doubt because of the near universal binary nature of gender among humans—our language does not provide us with such a term, so we are stuck with having to chose between 'he' and 'she' if we are to stay within the confines of ordinary language yet want to be true to the theistic conception of God as personal.

Theists should thus be happy to admit that the choice between calling God a 'he' and calling God a 'she' is a matter of indifference philosophically speaking. Of course this is not to deny that certain accidental associations between the genders and certain other properties might well have been formed in people's minds, associations that will make referring to God as a he or as a she misleading for them if they're not conceptually clear-headed. For example, in either a patriarchal or a matriarchal society there will be power connotations accidentally associated with the genders, connotations that may make referring to God as a he more or less potentially misleading than referring to God as a she given another of God's essential properties, which I have yet to do more than mention, his omnipotence, his being all-powerful. In a patriarchal society, one factor that would make it less potentially misleading to refer to God as a he than as a she would be the accidental association in people's minds between the male gender and power. In a matriarchal society, one factor that would make it less potentially misleading to refer to God as a she than as a he would be the accidental association in people's minds between the female gender and power. Of course, nothing of substance in any argument would turn on a terminological decision to refer to God as either a he or a she in either of these societies and it would not be taken to do so by anyone who was able to recognize as accidental any association between gender and power that had grown up in their minds, which is to say it would not be taken to do so by anyone who was tolerably clear-headed. Nevertheless, given the sad fact that not everyone is tolerably clear-headed, it might not be a matter of complete indifference when speaking to someone who had grown up in a patriarchal or matriarchal society whether or not one referred to God as a he or a she. However, for us—who are tolerably clear-headed—while we should prefer to refer to God as either a he or a she rather than as an it (because of God's essential property of personhood), it should be a matter of indifference whether we refer to God as a he or a she. Given that nothing can turn on the decision one way or the other, I'm going to continue within the tradition in which I have grown up, calling God a he.[14]

So that's what it means to say that God is a person. To say that God is a person is to say that he is rational; has beliefs; is to be treated as an object of moral respect; and reciprocates that attitude in his actions towards us, actions that paradigmatically include verbal communication. By these criteria, God is— if he exists—more of a person than any of us could ever hope to be. And I shall be calling God a he rather than a she as it's a habit I've got into and it's not going to confuse any of us. So far, so good. Let's go on to look at the next property on my list.

PROPERTY TWO: INCORPOREALITY/ TRANSCENDENCE

The person who is God is supposed by theists to differ from the persons that we are in a more radical way than having neither a male body nor a female body; God is supposed not to have a body at all. He is supposed to be incorporeal. What do theists mean when they say that God is incorporeal?

Incorporeality (not having a body) and corporeality (having a body) are obviously two sides of the same conceptual coin: one is simply the opposite of the other. So I'm going to start by speaking about what it means to say that we have bodies. If we can understand that, we will have a handle on what it means to say that God, by contrast to us, does not have a body. I'm going to argue that actually theists should not think that God does not have a body; but the fact that they shouldn't doesn't show that their conception of God is incoherent as there's a property conceptually close enough to incorporeality to be plausibly what theists have in mind when they talk of incorporeality and which it is sensible to predicate of God. The net result of my argument will be then that 'incorporeality' isn't really the right term—'transcendence' is to be preferred. That's why I call this property 'incorporeality/transcendence'. Let me start on my argument by asking you to do something.

Look at a section of matter that is obviously a part of your body, say your right hand, and ask yourself, 'What is it about my right hand that makes it a part of my body rather than a part of the book that it is holding or a part of the chair on which I sit?' (I'm supposing that you're sitting on a chair as well as holding this book with your right hand.) Don't say, 'Well it's connected to *my* arm rather than the book or the chair', for that would just push the question of body ownership a stage back—'And what is it that makes an arm your arm?' would be the next question that I'd ask.

I'm asking you to look for the conditions that a particular section of matter must satisfy if it's going to be a part of your body and for those conditions that, if it satisfies, are sufficient for it's being a part of your body; I am asking you to look—in other words—for the necessary and sufficient conditions of a particular section of matter being a part of your body.

A necessary condition for something is a condition that must be satisfied for that thing to be the case. A sufficient condition for something is a condition that, if satisfied, will make that thing the case. For those new to this, the distinction is easier to see if we consider an example. (I'll use this example later in another context, so even those who are old hands would be best advised to read it.)

Suppose you are sitting a test with a pass mark of 50 or above and 100 questions each of which is worth one mark. If you get the first 60 questions right, then there's no way you're going to fail the test however badly you do on the remaining 40 (I'm ignoring the possibility that it might be mis-marked). We express that fact by saying that it is a sufficient condition for your passing the test that you get the first 60 questions right. But it is not necessary for your passing the test that you get the first 60 questions right; you might pass even if you don't get the first 60 questions right. We express that fact by saying that it is not a necessary condition for your passing the test that you get the first 60 questions right. A necessary condition for your passing the test is that you get at least 10 of the first 60 questions right. If you get to question 61 and you haven't yet got at least 10 right, then—no matter how well you do on the remaining 40—there's no way you'll pass. Getting at least 50 questions right is a necessary condition for passing the test that is also sufficient; there's nothing you need to do to pass the test over and above getting at least 50 questions right.

So my question is, what are the necessary and sufficient conditions for a particular section of matter to be a part of one's body? I'm going to discuss two possible answers to this question.

First, one might think that the answer is that what it is for a particular section of matter to be a part of one's body as opposed to a part of someone else's or as opposed to a part of an inanimate object is for one to know at least some of what is happening in that section of matter without being reliant on first finding out what is happening elsewhere. You can only find out where this book is indirectly, by light travelling from its pages to your eyes or by you feeling it with your hands. You can know what's happening in your eyes and where your hands are directly—that is without needing to find out something else first. So the book's not part of your body but your eyes and hands are. Thoughts such as this might lead one to say, 'One's body is that section of matter one can know about directly', understanding oneself to have stated by doing so the necessary and sufficient condition for a section of matter to be a part of one's body. This could be called the 'One's Body is that Section of Matter One Can Know about Directly Theory', but that's a bit clumsy, so let's call it the 'Direct Knowledge Theory'.

However, the Direct Knowledge Theory doesn't seem to have stated a necessary condition for some section of matter to be a part of one's body. Consider the fact that you could have your right hand anaesthetized, so that you could not know what was going on within it directly, just by feeling it, but rather had first to look at it or to feel it with your left hand or some such. Then your right hand would have become a section of matter that you could not know about directly. Nevertheless, surely we would say that it would, even if anaesthetized, still be a part of your body. So I conclude that being able to know about the state of a section of matter directly is not a necessary condition for that section of matter to be a part of one's body. It might, however, be a sufficient condition. I'll consider that possibility in a moment, after having talked about another theory that is sometimes advanced.

The second possible answer then, to the question, 'What makes a particular section of matter a part of one person's body rather than someone else's or no one's?' that one might consider is that a section of matter is a part of someone's body just if it is a part of the vehicle through which that person acts on the world. If you are to turn the pages of this book, you can only do so indirectly—via moving something else, such as your hand—but if you are to move your hand, there is nothing you need first (consciously) move. Thoughts such as this might lead one to say, 'One's body is that section of matter one can control by direct acts of the will', understanding oneself by doing so to have stated a necessary and sufficient condition for a section of matter to be a part of one's body. This could be called the 'One's Body is that Section of Matter One Can Control by Direct Acts of the Will Theory' but that's a bit clumsy, so let's call it the 'Direct Control Theory'.

However, the Direct Control Theory doesn't seem to have captured a necessary condition of a certain section of matter being a part of one's body either. One might think of the possibility that, instead of being anaesthetized, your right hand could have been paralysed so that you could no longer move it by a direct act of the will, i.e. you could not move it without first needing to move something else, e.g. your left hand. Surely though, it would still have been your hand.

The possibility of a long-term completely anaesthetized and paralysed person whom we would describe as nevertheless corporeal shows that any adaptation or combination of the two conditions I've discussed along the lines of making what it is for a section of matter to be a part of one's body its being a section of matter that one can *usually* either know about or control directly or by discussion of the spatial proximity with sections of matter that satisfy one or both of these conditions will still not capture a necessary condition for a particular section of matter to be a part of someone's body.

So, what conclusion can we draw? Neither being able to know about it directly, nor being able to control it directly are on their own necessary conditions for a section of matter to be a part of one's body; nor is their disjunction necessary for a particular section of matter to be a part of one's body. However, these conditions are—I'm about to argue—very plausibly jointly sufficient for a section of matter to be a part of one's body.[15] Let me argue that then.

Before I do so, I want to tell you something about the oldest museum in the world, the Ashmolean Museum in Oxford.

The Ashmolean contains, among other things, many statues. One of these is sometimes known as the Adonis Centocelle; if you go to the Ashmolean looking for it, you'll be helped to know that it's on the left of the main entrance. It's an approximately life-size second-century AD Roman depiction of Apollo, standing up with the remains of an arrow in one hand and—one presumes—of a bow in the other. It's quite lifelike, and—unlike most statues that have reached from antiquity—there are no missing limbs or even missing fingers to detract by their absence from the whimsy that one might find oneself entering into as one looks at it, that it is in fact not a simulacrum of a person carved in stone but a genuine person whose body just happens to be made out of stone.

Now I want to tell you a story about yourself. Imagine this: suddenly—from your point of view—the room in which you sit appears to dissolve: you no longer see this page in front of you; you are no longer conscious—if you were conscious of it at all—of the feeling of pressure from the seat of the chair in which you sit. The same goes for any smells or tastes of which you might currently be aware. Instead, you find yourself apparently looking out into a gallery, with some statues from antiquity lined up ahead of you. That's your visual field. Your auditory field now has some subdued conversations taking place around you. Kinaesthetically, you feel as if you are standing up, with pressure slightly more on your left foot than on your right, and as if your arms are by your side, each hand holding something roughly cylindrical. You're conscious of the smell of dusty air and a dusty taste. What has happened to you?

Well in fact—as you've probably guessed—what has happened is that you now know directly of the state of the section of matter that forms the statue that I was just talking about; and indirectly—through the light landing on its eyes, sound waves reaching its ears, etc.—you now know who is visiting that particular gallery in the Ashmolean that the statue is in. That you can no longer know directly what is happening wherever it is you were reading this book is—of course—somewhat startling to you. But that your locus of direct knowledge has moved to the Ashmolean is not the only startling fact to which you need to become accustomed; so has your locus of direct agency. This book has dropped to the ground as the limbs of what everyone had previously known as your body have gone limp; you are no longer able to control them by direct acts of the will. But at the same time, the limbs of the statue have becomes supple; you are able to animate them by direct acts of the will. When you will your right hand to rise, it is the stone right hand in the Ashmolean that does so. You direct your body to raise your right hand to your face and you see the statue's right hand move upwards in your visual field, accompanied by all the kinaesthetic sensations you would associate with its being your hand. As it moves up, you see that the thing being held is the remains of a stone arrow. You will yourself to squeeze this arrow and you see the stone fingers clench around it, while feeling the sensation of the pressure of your fingers on cold stone; and so on. In short, rather than knowing directly what's going on in a human body and being able to animate that body by direct acts of the will, you are now able instead to know directly what is going on in this stone body in the Ashmolean and animate it by direct acts of the will. Suppose all this were to happen, wouldn't it be that this statue would have become your new body? I think it pretty obviously would be. Remember, we're not interested in whether it is physically possible that this happen—if we were, we'd be scientists. We're interested in whether it's logically possible that this happen and what we'd say if it were to happen— we're philosophers.[16] And, I maintain, it's logically possible that this happen and if it ever were to happen, we'd say that the statue would have become your new body.

So, I've argued that were you to lose any ability to know directly of or control directly your current body, and were the Adonis Centocelle in the Ashmolean to become a section of matter that you could know about directly and at the same time were you to gain the ability to control it by direct acts of the will, this would be sufficient for this statue to become a new body for you. If that's right, then the Direct Knowledge Theory and the Direct Control Theory state conditions that, while not necessary (either alone or as disjuncts) for a particular section of matter to be a part of one's body, are jointly sufficient for a particular section of matter to be a part of one's body.

If it is correct that these conditions are jointly sufficient for a particular section of matter to be a part of one's body, then God's incorporeality—his not having a body—would thus require that there not be any part of the physical world that he knew about directly and could control directly. If a bit of matter were to be one he knew about and could control directly, then this would be sufficient for it to be his body (or a part of it, if other bits also satisfied these conditions). Just hold on to this result for now. We'll need it in a moment.

So, to sum up, I haven't got on very well in finding the necessary and sufficient conditions for a given section of matter to be a part of one's body. I have found two conditions that are jointly sufficient for a given section of matter to be a part of one's body. Let me turn to consider the third of God's properties, omnipresence. Then I'll be able to tie up all these loose threads, I hope.

PROPERTY THREE: OMNIPRESENCE/IMMANENCE

According to theism, while God is transcendent, he is also immanent. While God is not subject to the limitations of the physical universe, he nevertheless permanently pervades it with his mind and agency. We—human beings—are not present everywhere in the sense of able to acquire beliefs about everywhere directly and able to control what happens everywhere directly. We are somewhat-less-than-omnipresent: you're not actually in the Ashmolean as well as in whichever room it is you're reading this book; you're not simultaneously at the top of the highest mountain and at the bottom of the deepest cave. God—by contrast—is omnipresent. He's everywhere. Without needing to operate through any particular section of matter distinct from others around it, he can know what is happening anywhere and directly produce any effect he wants wherever he wants. So God's omnipresence entails that he is not anywhere in particular in the sense that by being there he is absent from somewhere else; he is not absent from anywhere as he is able to know directly about and directly affect everywhere.

We are now in a position to see a 'conceptual tension'—that's the nice way of putting it—between the property of incorporeality and that of omnipresence. God's omnipresence entails that he meets both the conditions that I have argued are jointly sufficient for the physical world as a whole to be his body (or a part of his body if there are parallel universes, i.e. collections of spatial objects not spatially related to anything in this universe). Each part of the universe is a section of matter that he can know about directly and each is under the direct control of his will. It seems then that because God is omnipresent we should say that, rather than his being incorporeal, the physical world as a whole is his body (or a part of it).

In short, because it is a sufficient condition of God's being corporeal that he can know about the state of some section of matter directly and can control it directly, then it is a necessary condition of his being incorporeal that he cannot do this for any section of matter; yet because it is a necessary condition of omnipresence that he can know about every section of matter that there is directly and control all of it directly, then it must be a necessary condition of omnipresence that he be corporeal. This argument seems irrefutable.

So, has our hero shown that the theistic conception of God is incoherent and thus that Judaism, Christianity, and Islam—with their shared claim that there is such a being—must be false? If he has, there's no need to read any further.

Perhaps sadly then, he has not. Theists have room for manoeuvre here. They can stop a tactical withdrawal becoming a rout. How?

Theists can claim that by describing God as incorporeal, they simply mean that there is no section of matter distinct from others that is especially privileged as that which God knows about more directly than he knows about others or over which he has more direct control than others; in other words, they can maintain that when they describe God as incorporeal they are simply saying that there is no particular place where God is in the sense that by being there he is absent from being somewhere else. They can then go on to say that when they describe God as omnipresent, they are saying that there is no section of matter that is not one he knows about directly or that is not under his direct control; in other words, they can claim that when they describe God as omnipresent, they are saying that there is no place where God is to any extent absent. God's incorporeality is his not being present anywhere in particular; his omnipresence is his not being absent from anywhere in particular.[17]

If we take God's being incorporeal as his not having a body distinct from other bits of matter within the physical universe and his being omnipresent as his nevertheless knowing directly what is happening everywhere and being able to act directly everywhere, then there is no tension between the divine properties of incorporeality and omnipresence. However, in taking incorporeality in this way I would argue that theists would be seizing on an accidental—albeit universal—feature of those corporeal beings that we know in our quotidian ways—that their bodies are distinct from other bits of matter and, more specifically, from other people's bodies—within space—and making that feature essential to the concept of corporeality from which incorporeality is defined. Why do I insist that this universal feature of the corporeal beings that we come across in our daily lives—that their bodies are spatially distinct from other bits of matter and, more specifically, from other people's bodies—is not an essential feature? Because we can make sense of the possibility of its not obtaining; one can imagine the universe 'shrinking' around one until it reaches one's skin, at which stage one's body would be coextensive with all matter. Indeed it's arguably not even universal. There are some mental states—some cases of what is sometimes known as multiple personality disorder—that seem best described as situations in which more than one person inhabits a single body at the same time.[18]

So is God spatial? In one sense yes and in another sense no. If what it is for a person to be spatial is for him or her to exist at a place and (as I've argued) it is sufficient for someone to exist at a place that he or she be able to learn about and affect that place directly, then every place within the universe is a place at which God exists and so in this sense then he is spatial. If what it is for a person to be spatial is for him or her to bear spatial relations to something else, then God is not spatial. Because the universe as a whole is his body (or a part of his body if there are parallel universes) and the universe as a whole is not spatially related to anything else (for otherwise, the thing to which it was so related would itself be a part of the universe), then God's body is not spatially related to anything else. There is no space at which God does not exist yet God does not exist within space.[19]

In conclusion then on the issues raised by the second and third properties of God on my list—incorporeality and omnipresence—I would say that 'incorporeality' is not the best word for the property of God that theists are seeking to pick out here. I would argue that it would *not* be incorrect to say that if there is a God, then the physical world as a whole is his body (or a part of his body, if there are parallel universes), for if there is a God, then the physical world as a whole satisfies with regard to him two conditions which are jointly sufficient for a section of matter to be a part of his body: every part of the physical world is one he knows about directly and every part is one he can control directly. I suggest that a better term than 'incorporeality' would therefore be 'transcendence'—God transcends the physical world as he is not in any way constrained within it. To pair with 'transcendence', one might therefore prefer the word 'immanence' rather than 'omnipresence'. God is immanent in the physical world as he is not in any way ignorant of it or unable to control it by direct acts of his will.[20]

◆ ◆ ◆

To sum up so far, I've looked at the first three properties in my list of properties that theists attribute to God: his personhood; his incorporeality or—my preferred term—transcendence; and his omnipresence or—my preferred term—immanence. I've argued that his personhood should be understood as his being rational; having beliefs; being treated as the object of moral respect; and his reciprocating that attitude in his actions, actions that paradigmatically include verbal communication. I've argued that if there's a God, then by these standards he's more of a person than any of us are. I've argued that theists should be indifferent over whether they refer to God as a he or a she. I've argued that God's incorporeality is a—somewhat misleading—way of referring to the fact that there is no section of the physical universe at which he is more present than he is at any other and his omnipresence is a matter of there being no section of the physical universe from which he is absent (sufficient conditions of a person's presence at a place being that he or she has the ability to know about and act there directly). These are alternative ways of referring to his transcendence on the one hand and his immanence on the other. So far then the theistic concept of God seems coherent and substantial. In the next chapter, we'll look at the next three properties on my list: omnipotence, omniscience, and eternality. Perhaps these will cause more difficulty.

2

Omnipotence, Omniscience, Eternality

PROPERTY FOUR: OMNIPOTENCE

God is the most powerful person there could be; he is omnipotent. The more powerful one is the more one can do, so one might suggest that we define an omnipotent being as a being who can do anything. This is a good starting point, but sadly we cannot rest completely content with this definition because there are questions over what exactly the word 'anything' should be taken to include. Consider these questions:

1. Can an omnipotent being make an object that is both perfectly spherical and perfectly cubical at one and the same time?
2. Can an omnipotent being make mistakes?
3. Can an omnipotent being commit suicide?

I'm going to look at these questions in the order that I've raised them with the intention of satisfying you that the answer to each of them is 'No', but that this doesn't reveal any inherent confusion in the concept of omnipotence. This is perhaps a bit surprising. One's first reaction to these issues might most naturally be that any 'Can an omnipotent being do X?' question must have a positive answer; that's surely what it means to be omnipotent. In fact, I'll argue, this is not the case.

◆ ◆ ◆

First then, can an omnipotent being make an object that is both perfectly spherical and perfectly cubical at one and the same time?

The indicative sentence 'God made an object that was perfectly spherical' makes sense. It succeeds in describing an action and asserting that God performed that action. So does the indicative sentence 'God made an object that was perfectly cubical.' Not every grammatically well-formed indicative sentence that purports to describe an action and assert that somebody performed it gets on so well. Let me assume that the word 'mumbojumbo' has no meaning. The sentence 'God made an object that was perfectly mumbojumbo' then does not make sense; it does not succeed in describing an action; a fortiori it does not succeed in describing an action and asserting that God performed that action. Saying 'God could make an object that was perfectly mumbojumbo' wouldn't be saying anything meaningful, so it wouldn't be saying anything that could be entailed by 'God is omnipotent.' Thus God's omnipotence should not be taken to entail that he could make an object that was perfectly mumbojumbo. If one asks, 'Can an omnipotent being do X?' and substitutes for X things that don't make sense, the answer to the question is 'No'. It's 'No' not because one's described something that an omnipotent being can't do, but because one's failed to describe anything at all.

Moving back towards the example in our first question then, God's omnipotence may be taken to entail that he could make it true that 'God made an object that was perfectly spherical'; and that he could make it true that 'God made an object that was perfectly cubical.' These are each grammatically well-formed indicative sentences that make sense. However—as with mumbojumbo—God's omnipotence should not be taken to entail that he could make it true that 'God made an object that was both perfectly spherical and perfectly cubical at one and the same time.' The sentence 'God made an object that was both perfectly spherical and perfectly cubical at one and the same time' is a grammatically well-formed indicative sentence *that does not make sense*: it does not succeed in describing an action and thus it does not succeed in asserting that God performed that action. It doesn't say anything that could be entailed by 'God is omnipotent' as it doesn't say anything at all.

The fact that God could not create a perfectly spherical object that is at the same time perfectly cubical can thus be seen to be no more of a limitation on God's power than the fact that God could not create an object that is perfectly mumbojumbo. The limitation lies with us in that we can form grammatically well-formed indicative sentences that purport to describe logically possible actions and states of affairs, yet that do not in fact describe logically possible actions or states of affairs at all. These sentences don't describe anything and therefore even if God could do anything, he still couldn't do anything that they describe. Even if there's a God, he can't make these sentences true because there is nothing that could make these sentences true because there's nothing that these sentences say. (They may sometimes appear to say something to us from our— *genuinely* limited—point of view.) So, even if God can do anything, he can't do the logically impossible because the logically impossible isn't anything—it isn't even a possibility. That's why we call it the logically impossible.

◆ ◆ ◆

Let's look at the second question I raised about omnipotence: can an omnipotent being make mistakes? There's no logical impossibility about making mistakes. We do it every day. So, if the concept of omnipotence doesn't entail that God could make mistakes, that must be for a reason other than one that parallels what I've just sketched for why it doesn't entail he could do logically impossible things like create perfectly spherical objects that are at the same time perfectly cubical.

Consider for a moment a mathematical question concerning an example I used in the previous chapter. This is the question: how many ways are there of getting 50 or more questions right on a test composed of 100 questions? So, getting the first 60 right and the next 40 wrong would be one way; getting the first 40 wrong and the last 60 right would be another; and so on. Do you have any idea how many different ways there are in total? Do you think that the answer *must* be higher than ten million?

I imagine that everyone reading this for the first time will answer that question, 'No'. You'll find that you are able to believe that the answer to this question might very well be no greater than ten million. So I might say of you that as you are reading this for the first time you have the ability to believe that the answer to my question might very well be no greater than ten million. I'm about to do my best to take this ability away from you. Don't worry; it's in your best interests.

The correct answer is in fact quite a bit greater than ten million. In fact, it's so much greater that the computer that was running the programme to determine it for me could only manage an approximation. The correct answer is approximately the number I give in this endnote.[1] (I didn't want to put it in the main text because I didn't want you to see it while working out whether or not you were able to believe that the answer might very well be no more than ten million.) Have a look at it now. Pretty large, isn't it? Nobody who hadn't studied these sorts of things in some depth would ever have guessed that the answer was that big in advance of being told it, so don't feel embarrassed if you—like me when I first put the question to myself—were way off.

But let me ask you to suppose for a moment that there had been someone who, when she was reading this book for the first time and had got to the point where I first posed the question, had said to herself that she wasn't actually able to believe that the answer might be less than ten million. Let's suppose her name was 'Jean' (second name: 'E'us-in-Mathematics'). Jean wasn't actually able to believe what the rest of us were able to believe because she had done something that my computer couldn't do. She'd performed the relevant calculations in her head and indeed been able to check them dozens of times so that she was absolutely convinced that the correct answer would have to be many times more than ten million. Jean was able to see the mathematical fact that the answer must be many times greater than ten million with such clarity that she could no more believe that the answer might very well be no greater than ten million than we would have been able to believe that the answer might very well be no greater than two. Jean would thus be someone unable to believe that which we were able to believe.

Would Jean (were she to have existed) have been a less powerful mathematician than the rest of us? Obviously not; just the opposite. But, someone might argue, we had a mathematical power that Jean would not have had; we had the power to believe that the answer might very well be less than ten million; Jean would not have had this power; so Jean would have been a *less* powerful mathematician than us. Someone might argue that, but we'd instantly see that they were wrong. Their confusion would have arisen from their describing as a power on our part what was in actuality more accurately described as a liability. That we could entertain as possible that the answer might be less than ten million wasn't an expression of strength; it was an expression of weakness.

What conclusion do I want us to draw from this example? The conclusion is that some abilities, which one might—if one was not thinking carefully enough or did not know enough—call powers are really more correctly labelled liabilities and the more powerful one is, the less of these abilities one will have, not the more. Our ability to believe that the answer to my mathematical question might be less than ten million was a liability, not a power. So, by telling you about the computer programme and getting you to look at the endnote, thus removing your ability (assuming you believe what I say in the endnote), I actually increase your power even though I take away one of your abilities. Taking away your ability to make a mistake doesn't make you less powerful; it makes you more powerful. Given that the ability to make mistakes is a liability not a power, so we can see that the answer to the question of whether an omnipotent can make mistakes is 'no'. Omnipotence implies no liabilities whatsoever.

Reflection on another mathematical example illustrates another point even more clearly, that it will be impossible for us, as finite minds, to tell with complete certainty of some abilities whether they are powers or liabilities. Consider the binary form of Goldbach's conjecture, that every even number is the sum of two primes. So far, nobody has found a counter-example to show that this is false; nobody has proved that it is true; and nobody has proved that it is impossible to prove that it's true. I don't know if anybody's tried to prove that it's impossible to prove whether or not it's possible to prove that it's true. Anyway, ask yourself this: is being able to believe that the binary form of Goldbach's conjecture is provable a power or a liability? We just don't know. An omniscient being would know. So our failure to be omniscient limits our capacity to understand fully what abilities are powers and what liabilities and thus to understand fully what is entailed by omnipotence. But even if our lack of omniscience prevents us from having a full understanding of what's entailed by omnipotence, we can, of course, still gain some understanding, in this case understanding of a 'disjunctive' sort: if the ability to believe that the binary form of Goldbach's conjecture is provable is a power, then if there is an omnipotent being, he has it. If it's a liability, then he doesn't.

We can make mistakes and an omnipotent being—should one exist—cannot, so there is something (indeed a class of things) that we can do that an omnipotent being—should one exist—cannot do (and a class of things the precise membership of which we, being less than omniscient, are ignorant of). This is why our first stab at a definition of omnipotence—a being is omnipotent if he can do anything—isn't quite right. Can we adapt it? A being is omnipotent if he has all powers that it is logically possible to have (and no liabilities) perhaps? This isn't quite right either, but allow me to leave it as a second stab at a definition for the moment and turn to the third question concerning omnipotence: can an omnipotent being commit suicide?

◆ ◆ ◆

To put my argument in a nutshell, committing suicide would always be a mistake for an omnipotent being, so the answer to this question is 'no' too; it follows pretty directly from the answer that I've just established for the question about mistakes. In the course of arguing this we'll see though the interesting fact that what abilities count as powers and what count as liabilities can vary from case to case and person to person, something that has relevance to our search for an adequate understanding of omnipotence. That's the argument in a nutshell. Now let me take it out of the nutshell.

Consider this argument: we very often have the ability to commit suicide. We are dependent on many things for our continued existence. If these things altered, we'd cease to exist and we usually have it within our power to alter many of these things. Is our dependency on these other things a sign of our strength—a power—or is it a sign of our weakness—a liability? Should we say, 'I have the power to be killed by lots of different things; I am therefore more powerful than Superman, who does not have the power to be killed by anything other than Kryptonite,' or should we say, 'I have the liability to be killed by lots of different things; I am therefore less powerful than Superman, who does not have the liability to be killed by anything other than Kryptonite'? Obviously, we should say the latter; to be dependent on something for one's existence is a sign of weakness. Superman can only be killed by Kryptonite.[2] So he is much more powerful than we are; but he still has a weakness. God, being omnipotent, would be stripped of *any* element of this liability—there would be nothing that could cause him not to exist, not even himself.

It's the 'not even himself' bit tagged on the end of this argument that might make one nervous about it. Someone might agree that to be dependent on something other than oneself is a sign of weakness, but insist that depending on oneself—or more accurately one's will—for one's continued existence is no liability; it's a power. And if God depends on his will for his existence, then that ought to be enough to enable him to commit suicide. There's something plausible about these thoughts. Is having one's existence within the scope of one's own will to determine a power or is it a liability? I shall argue that it could be a power for creatures such as ourselves (and that's where the plausibility of these thoughts originates), but it could only be a liability for the most powerful being that there could be.

Consider the story told by Seneca of a young Spartan boy who, having been disgraced by allowing himself to be captured during a battle, would say nothing to his captors except for repeating over and over again the words, 'I shall not be a slave.' True to his word, the moment they warily unleashed him and gave him an order, he ran headlong into the nearest wall and smashed his head open on it, killing himself instantly. Seneca concludes by asking, 'When freedom is this close, can anyone still be a slave?'

Seneca was a Stoic (he had to be; he was Nero's philosophy tutor) and Stoics were in the habit of cheering themselves with these sorts of tales; you might not find them so bracing. But you might nevertheless agree that the boy gained in power the moment he had the issue of his continued existence brought back within the sphere of influence of his own will. If so, you will think that having one's existence depend on one's will can be a power rather than a liability. But, as this story well illustrates, circumstances where the ability to commit suicide is a power rather than a liability are circumstances where the person for whom it is a power is already terribly limited by factors beyond his or her control, limited in ways that are much greater limitations than the power to commit suicide is an empowerment. Someone is in a terribly disempowered state if you can point out the most encouraging possibility open to them with the sentence, 'Look on the bright side: you could kill yourself.' Thus surely we would say that had the boy had the power to seize his captors' weapons; make his escape; and so on, then this would have rendered the ability to smash his head open on the nearest wall a liability once more; and he would have been much better off with these other abilities and without the ability to smash his head open on the nearest wall. That set of abilities would have been more power-granting. So, while the ability to commit suicide could indeed sometimes be a genuine power for beings who were constrained by forces beyond their control, it could never be anything other than a liability for a being who was unconstrained by any external power, a being such as the theistic God. We might say something like, 'An omnipotent being could commit suicide if he wanted to, but he could never have any reason to want to and—being perfectly reasonable—could thus never want to commit suicide,' but, given that he could never want to commit suicide, it would be equally true to say that he could never commit suicide. In either case, the answer to our third question is 'No'.

There are lots, indeed an infinite number, of other interesting questions one might raise about what abilities an omnipotent being might have and we'll come to some of them later in other chapters—e.g. 'Can an omnipotent being do an evil act?'—but, as all are amenable to being answered by the techniques hitherto elaborated (*mutatis mutandis*), we may safely leave things here.[3]

♦ ♦ ♦

So, how—at the end of all this—would I suggest we define omnipotence? As a third and final stab at a definition, I would suggest we define an omnipotent being as the most powerful being that it is logically possible there could be; an omnipotent being is a being with the most power-granting set of abilities that it is logically possible anyone might have. How are we to understand what being omnipotent in this sense entails, which abilities are in this set and which aren't? Here we must acknowledge that we will soon run up against limits imposed by our own finitude. But we must equally acknowledge that we can make some progress.

Whenever one is considering an ability to do something which—of logical necessity—disables one from doing something else, one will have to use one's intuition to decide which of these abilities is most power-granting, the answer thus leading one to decide which to ascribe to an omnipotent being and which to deny of him. Is it more power-granting for one to be able to create a stone so heavy that one could not oneself lift it or is it more power-granting to be able to lift any stone? Plausibly, our intuition tells us, it is the latter. Being able to create a stone so heavy that one couldn't then lift it would be a liability. If so, then an omnipotent being would have the power of being able to lift any stone and not have the liability of being able to create a stone so heavy that he himself could not lift it. Obviously, in using one's intuition in this way to understand what is entailed by omnipotence, one is making what is at least in part an evaluative judgement—which of these is it better to be able to do?—and evaluative judgements vary to some extent between people. Perhaps you think it would be better to be able to create a stone so heavy that one could not oneself lift it than it would be to be able to lift any stone. If so, you'll have a different understanding of what abilities are entailed by omnipotence from me. But this worry can be overemphasized in two ways. First, it is not a worry about the meaning of omnipotence, just a worry about how much agreement we are likely to be able to reach about what abilities are entailed by omnipotence. Secondly, evaluative judgements aren't completely different from person to person. We've already seen that we value true beliefs over false and thus we think that being able to make mistakes is an ability which in itself one would always be better off without. Thus an omnipotent being could never make mistakes. And even on questions such as the stone 'paradox', almost everyone's intuition is that it's better to be able to lift anything than to be able to create something one cannot oneself lift. Thus we may reasonably hope to be able to make at least some progress in understanding what is entailed by omnipotence in this ad hoc fashion. However, as we have seen, we must admit that there are two points that must ultimately curtail our complete understanding of the entailments of omnipotence.

First, as the example of the binary form of Goldbach's conjecture has shown us, our lack of omniscience means that we won't be able to tell of some abilities whether they are powers or liabilities. We'll know that they're one or the other, but we won't know which. Thus we won't be able to tell whether we should ascribe these abilities to an omnipotent being or not. Secondly, as Seneca's story of the Spartan boy has shown us, for some abilities at least, whether they count as powers or whether they count as liabilities depends on what other powers and liabilities one has. Ultimately, therefore, one would need—for a full understanding of what is entailed by omnipotence—to compare sets of logically co-possible abilities to see which set one's intuition told one is most power-granting. This sort of reflection I have not really begun and to finish it (requiring as it would exhaustive comparison of an infinite number of sets of abilities, each of which has an infinite number of members) is of necessity beyond anyone but God himself. Fortunately, as we have seen, we do not need to complete it in order to reach a satisfactory definition of omnipotence and in order to make at least some progress towards understanding what being omnipotent entails in the ad hoc fashion sketched above.[4]

The concept of omnipotence is clear even if some of its entailments lie beyond the grasp of anyone other than an omniscient being. In the terminology of Descartes, one might say then that we perfectly apprehend the concept, even if we cannot fully comprehend it and, to switch to a Kantian manner of speech, though we cannot fully comprehend it, we yet comprehend its incomprehensibility and this is the very best that could be expected of a philosophy that finds itself at the limits of human understanding. Despite this necessary limit to our understanding, we have reached a coherent and substantial definition of omnipotence and discovered certain truths about what an omnipotent being would be like. Such a being would not be able to do the logically impossible. Such a being would not be able to make mistakes. Such a being would not be able to commit suicide. In general, we may say that such a being would not be able to do anything that would in fact be an expression of weakness, e.g. feel fear, uncertainty, or doubt.[5]

This brings us to the next property on my list.

PROPERTY FIVE: OMNISCIENCE

Omniscience literally means 'all knowingness'. Anybody who has studied any philosophy will have noticed that there is no consensus over what knowledge is. We don't want to allow ourselves to take a diversion into epistemology (the branch of philosophy that deals with knowledge), but fortunately we do not need to find out exactly what knowledge is in order to go some way in characterizing omniscience, for we may say that a being is omniscient just if it is the case that for all statements, if a statement is true, then that being knows that it is true. A statement is, we may take it, whatever it is that is stated by a well-formed and meaningful indicative sentence as uttered or written by a competent language-user. As well as the notion of knowledge being in contention, there's also some argument among philosophers about whether or not statements so understood exist, but let's suppose that they do. It makes the explanation easier and we can as little afford to take a diversion into the philosophy of language as we can into epistemology.[6] There are more pressing issues.

Consider the fact that there are—or at least prima facie it appears that there are—some true statements about the future. For example, consider the possibility that having finished reading this book, you'll find yourself so impressed by it that you'll rush out and buy another copy, giving it to your closest friend. Indulge me by allowing me to suppose that that's the way the future will indeed develop. If so, then the following sentence, as it might be said by me of you, is now true: 'You'll give a copy of this book to your closest friend.' We might say then—if we believe in statements—that the statement expressed by the sentence, 'You'll give a copy of this book to your closest friend' as it might be said by me now is true. You'd make the same statement with the sentence, 'I'll give a copy of this book to my closest friend.' (That we don't want to say that there are two truths here, even though there are two sentences with two different meanings (two propositions), is one reason to believe in statements.)

We might have different views over whether or not any of us knows this statement to be true now, but I imagine we'll all agree that none of us knows it *infallibly* now. None of us can be said to know it infallibly even if it is true as none of us can be said to have ruled out all possibility of our having made a mistake about it.

Initially at least it looks as if there's a good argument for the conclusion that God will know it infallibly. Why? Well, God's omniscient, so of anything that is true, he'll know that it's true. Therefore, if it is true that you'll give a copy of this book to your closest friend (as we are assuming for the sake of argument it is), he'll know that it's true. OK, so he'll know it. But why think he'll know it infallibly? Well, he's omniscient, so of anything that is true, he'll know that it's true. It's true that he's omnipotent, so he'll know that he's omnipotent, so he'll know that there's no possibility of his ever making a mistake (as we've just seen, an inability to make mistakes is entailed by omnipotence), so he'll know that there's no possibility of him having made a mistake about your giving a copy of this book to your friend, so he'll know it infallibly. If it is true that you'll give a copy of this book to your friend, then God knows infallibly that you'll do so. Surely every theist would agree with that? Well, actually no.

Not all theists agree that God infallibly knows the future. The reasons for thinking that he doesn't are usually linked with viewing God's eternality as his being everlasting inside time. So, before I can wrap up exactly what omniscience means (or, given that there's disagreement among them, perhaps I should say 'should mean') to theists, I need to consider the next property on my list—eternality.

PROPERTY SIX: ETERNALITY

All theists are agreed that God is eternal in the sense that he has no beginning and no end within time, but they divide over whether this is because he is outside time or inside time but everlasting. The traditional and majority view among those theists who have considered the alternatives is certainly that God is eternal in the sense of outside time. On this view—let's call it the 'atemporal view'— God atemporally knows infallibly everything that will happen at times that are, from our point of view now, future, but he cannot be said to know *now* what will happen at times that are from our point of view and his future, because his point of view in contrast to ours is not a point of view within time. So, on the traditional atemporal view, the right answer to the question, 'Does God know infallibly that you'll give a copy of this book to your best friend?' is the one that I've already given, 'Yes'. However, many have felt some dissatisfaction with the atemporal view. Why? Well, there are various reasons people come up with, but I think the main one is understanding prayer (and, more generally, God's interrelations with his creatures). On the atemporal view, God's not affected in any way by his creatures; and this seems (to many, but not all) religiously unsatisfactory.

Remember the story of the conversation between Abraham and God that I quoted in discussing the divine property of personhood. The obvious way to read that story would be to see it as involving God changing his mind as a result of his discussions with Abraham. But for God to change his mind would entail that he is inside time. Only temporal things can change, for change requires being in one state at an earlier time and a different state at a later time. Theists who place a lot of emphasis on God's being able to change his mind in response to prayer (and, more generally, as a result of his interrelations with his creatures) thus depart from the traditional atemporal view and instead see God as being inside time. Let's call their view the 'temporal view'.

One thought that it would be natural to have at this stage is: surely if there were a temporal God, then, prior to any discussion with Abraham, he'd already have decided to do whatever it was that was best to do with regards to the destruction of Sodom. If it really was best to destroy it utterly, then he'd have known this in advance of talking to Abraham about it and nothing Abraham could have said would have changed his mind. If, on the other hand (and as seems to have been the case), it really was best to destroy it having provided an escape route for any good people who lived there, then he'd have known this in advance of talking to Abraham about it and again nothing Abraham could have said would have changed his mind. So, one might argue that even if we go for the temporal view of God's eternality, we shouldn't read this story as one of God's changing his mind in the light of Abraham's subtle ethical questioning. Rather, we should read it as one of God's revealing his pre-existent plan in the course of answering Abraham's several questions. God is omniscient, so he knew in advance of talking to Abraham that it was in fact best for him to send some angels to save Lot and his family. The angels in turn were sent not to discover on God's behalf a fact of which he started off in ignorance (whether or not there were any people worthy of being saved) but merely to extract those who were worthy and of whom God already knew. God's conversation with Abraham is best interpreted as affecting him in no way whatsoever. He started and finished the conversation with exactly the same information and intentions. Of course the conversation affected Abraham—it reassured him that God is indeed good; and this is a reason for both God and Abraham to enter into it. The general point though, surely, is that we should say that no petitionary prayer we utter (or relation we enter into with respect to God) affects God. So a proper understanding of prayer or our relations to God in general cannot involve them changing God; thus a proper understanding of prayer and these relations cannot provide any incentive to adopt a temporal understanding of God's eternality.

Personally, I'm rather sympathetic to this argument, but I report that many theists are not happy to rest with this understanding of prayer and creature–God relations in general. They want petitionary prayers and our actions in general to be able to affect God, not just us. Of course, these theists accept, God never does anything other than whatever it is that is the best thing for him to do.[7] In this respect, he is immutable. But what it is that is the best thing to do can itself be affected by what we've asked for and how we've behaved and thus God's general intention to do the best can be modified in the particular intentions it gives rise to by our prayers and actions; he can change.

To take an example of what the temporalist will see as a parallel process from human-to-human interaction: it is of course impolite to give a negative assessment of someone else's choices in works of art unless they have asked for one's 'honest opinion' (with an appropriate amount of stress on the word 'honest' or something equivalent). If they have insisted on an honest appraisal of the aesthetic merits of some recent purchase and one's honest judgement is negative, then one should offer it to them in the most sensitive way that one can. This being so, you might find yourself uncomfortably trapped in a conversation with someone about a work of art that they have recently purchased with the unchanging intention to do the best, namely tell them the truth as you perceive it (that it's hideously tasteless) if *and only if* they ask for it, an intention that would lead you in one of two different directions, depending on what they asked of you.

What do you think of this?
It's very distinctive.
Yes, but what do you think of it *aesthetically*? Give me your honest opinion. Really, your honest opinion. Don't hold back.
Well, it's hideously tasteless. On the plus side, it fits in rather well with the way you've decorated the room. I'll be leaving now. Please don't trouble yourself to show me out.

Similarly, a temporalist might argue, God remains unchanging in his intention to do the best that he can for us (thus retaining the essential property of perfect goodness—a property we will come to in a moment); his character, we might say, is immutable. However, how this character manifests itself changes from moment to moment depending on what we do and—perhaps especially—on what we ask him to do. Does this require God to change his mind? One might say that in a sense then, no, it does not. He always intends to do what is best. But one must also say that in a sense then, yes, it does. Of some things it's true that at one time he did not intend to do them (he only intended to do them if they were—as a result of various choices as yet to be made by his creatures—the right things to do by the time in question) and at another time this intention crystallized out into the intention to do them (once his creatures had made choices that made them, rather than something else, the right thing for him to do). If we persist in requiring God to be able to change in this way, then we will have to put him inside time. We will also have to limit his omniscience about the future.

Consider a case where God changes from initially intending to give you either X or Y (two otherwise equally morally good options), depending on which it is you ask for in prayer and you actually ask for X, crystallizing out his intention into the intention to give you X. On the temporal model, the answer to the question of whether God infallibly knew that you would ask for X rather than Y at the time when his intention was to give you either X or Y depending on what you asked for in prayer can't be 'Yes', for then we'd have to say that he intended to give you X right from the start. He couldn't have kept an open mind at the earlier time over whether or not he'd give you X if he knew then that X was what you were going to ask for and thus what he would end up having most reason to give you at the later time. For God to know (with infallible certainty) that he was going to intend to do something would be for him already to intend to do that thing. So, to preserve the claim that God genuinely changes in the light of what we ask for, we'll have to limit his knowledge of the future in some respects. There'll have to be some true statements concerning states of affairs that are to us (and him) future which he does not infallibly know are true and some of these will have to concern his own future mental life. This is the price one will have to pay if one requires God to be able to change his intentions in response to prayer; temporalists must posit some divine ignorance. Indeed, temporalists usually subscribe to an understanding of freedom that gives them reason to extend this divine ignorance to future free actions in general. This reason is given by the following argument.

If God were inside time and his omniscience were to entail that he infallibly knows now that when you've finished reading this book you'll buy another copy and give it to your best friend, then God would now have the belief that you'll do this. But, if you're going to be genuinely free to choose whether or not to do this when you get to the end of your reading, then at the time you finish reading you have to have it in your power either to do it or not to do it. But if you are going to have it in your power at the end of your reading either to do it or not, you're going to have it de facto in your power to make God's current belief that you will do it false. But if God's omniscient about the future, then you cannot ever be going to have the power to make a current belief that he has about the future false, so you cannot be going to have the power either to do it or not. If he now believes you'll do it, you'll have to do it. But if you won't have the power not to buy another copy of this book and give it to your best friend, then you can't really be going to be free when you choose to do these things. What goes for future decisions about buying books and giving them to people goes for all other decisions too. So if God is temporal and, as we might put it, 'totally' omniscient about the future, then nobody can be genuinely free.[8]

One natural thought to have at this stage might be the following, 'Why can't the temporalist simply say that you will have the power to do other than give a copy of this book to your closest friend; it's just that, if you exercise it, it'll make it the case that God believed something different from what he actually believes now?' The reason is simple: it just doesn't make sense, for it involves the incoherent notion of having the power to change the past. (I'm about to state this simple answer in a more complicated way; if you don't care to read me doing so, you may skip the rest of this paragraph and the next without loss.) To posit that you are going to have the power to make one of God's present beliefs different from whatever it actually is would be to posit that you are going to have a power such that until the moment you exercise it—at, let's say, t—there's one past (containing, let's say, God having the belief that you'll give a copy of this book to your closest friend) leading up to t and then, just after t, there's a different past (containing then God having the belief that you'll not give a copy of this book to your closest friend) leading up to t. But the world can only ever have one past leading up to t; an omniscient temporal God's now in one of these belief-states or the other; he can't be in both or neither (a sort of Schrödinger's God). Most who've wanted to say something like this, then, have sought to defend the claim that it's not a causal power over the past that they're positing, but rather what they call a counterfactual power and the pressure then is on them to show that the latter doesn't entail the former. The hope is that it might make sense to say that you will in the future have a power such that were you to have exercised it, God would have believed something different from what it is he actually believes now, while nevertheless not having the problematic (because obviously incoherent) power to cause him to have believed something different from whatever it is he actually believes now. Sadly, it is inevitable that this hope will be thwarted: there's no way for the temporalist to avoid impaling himself or herself on one or other prongs of the fork: will you, in the actual future, have the exercisable-in-principle-power to make the actual God's current belief that you'll give a copy of this book to your closest friend false (in which case, he won't have been infallibly omniscient) or will you have the power to make it the case that he didn't actually believe that you'll give a copy of this book to your closest friend (in which case it'll be the incoherent power to alter the past that one's positing)?

But isn't it the case, one might wonder as a result of these considerations, that the atemporalist then is going to be afflicted by whatever problems affect the temporalist here in that if the sentence, 'You will give a copy of this book to your closest friend' now expresses a truth, as we are supposing for the sake of argument it does, then that's a fact about it now, and facts about things now are facts that (as we've just shown) you won't have the power to change in the future on pain of having the incoherent 'power to change the past'? This tempting thought is based on a faulty assumption—it's not a fact about the sentence *now* that it expresses a truth even if it is true that you'll give a copy of this book to your closest friend. The fact that the sentence 'You will give a copy of this book to your closest friend' makes a statement that is true is rather what one might call a 'soft fact'; it's not a fact wholly about the sentence as it is now, it's a fact in part dependent on what happens in the future. The content of the belief that a temporal being might express by using this sentence—the proposition it asserts—is by contrast a hard fact, this fact is entirely determined by the grammar and meanings of the words used in the sentence at the time it is uttered. And it's precisely this observation that reveals why the temporalist faces the insurmountable problem sketched at the end of the previous paragraph: the contents of a temporal God's beliefs about the future are hard facts; whether the sentences he might use to express them make true statements or not are soft facts; and you can't be going to have power in the future to affect hard facts about the past, that's what hard facts about the past are, so, if you're going to have the power to do anything other than what he now believes you'll do, you're going to have to have the power to make some of the beliefs he now has false, to make some of the sentences he might have used to express beliefs that he held turn out to make false statements.

If God is atemporal, these problems simply do not arise. Just as God's infallibly knowing what is from our point of view (though not his) now past does not mean that we were not free in the past, so God's atemporally knowing what is from our point of view (though not his) future, does not mean that we will not be free in the future. We don't need to worry about whether you will have the power to make a belief that God currently has wrong if God's not in time and thus doesn't currently have any beliefs at all. While on atemporalism it's still true that if God atemporally knows that you'll do X at a time that is to you future, then you won't actually do other than X, that's merely because of the logical necessity that knowledge must be of truth; he can't—of conceptual necessity—atemporally know that you'll actually do X if you won't. On the view of free will operative here, all that has to be true for you to be free in the future in your choice to do X is that you have the power at that time to do something other than X and on atemporalism you can have this power—have the power to make God either have the atemporal belief that you do X or the atemporal belief that you don't do X—without having the power to make any belief he actually has false or alter the past.[9]

So, if one is a temporalist, one will 'dilute' the notion of omniscience somewhat relative to the atemporalist's understanding, seeing God's omniscience as requiring only that he infallibly knows that which it is logically possible that he infallibly know at the time that it is (for him) now. Let's continue to ignore the Theory of Relativity, for to understand God's really changing his mind in response to our prayers and actions God's now has to be pretty much the same as our now. Presumably then on any account God's omniscience entails that he knows infallibly all statements about what is now the past, but, if one is a temporalist due to wishing to see God as changing as a result of his relations with his creatures, one must say that it does not entail infallible knowledge of all statements about what is now the future. Additionally, a move temporalists usually make is to say that God's omniscience does not extend to him infallible knowledge about future free actions in general. This move may be presented as paralleling with regard to omniscience a move one makes with regard to omnipotence: an omniscient temporal being just has to know infallibly that which it is logically possible for an omniscient temporal being to know infallibly, and—the temporalist may insist—it's not *logically* possible for a temporal being to know infallibly the future actions of free agents. Thus—a temporalist might maintain—God not knowing infallibly what you are about to choose freely to do is no more of a restriction on his omniscience than his not being able to create an object that is mumbojumbo is on his omnipotence. Future free actions are, by definition, those that cannot be known infallibly by any temporal being, even God.

In fact, if they go this far, temporalists must extend this divine ignorance yet further, to the future of the world as a whole. Given that, on theism, the world's having a future at all depends utterly on God's freely choosing to sustain it from moment to moment (in virtue of a property of God we'll come to in due course: his creatordom), and given that a temporal God cannot know with perfect certainty that he will freely choose to sustain the universe in the future (for otherwise he wouldn't be free in doing it), God cannot have infallible knowledge that the world will even be here in a moment's time and thus he cannot have infallible knowledge of the future of the world *tout court*.

All theists are agreed then that God is eternal in the sense that he did not come into being at some moment in the past and neither will he cease to exist at some moment in the future. However, as I have discussed, they divide over whether this is because he is outside time or inside time but everlasting. This disagreement on the nature of divine eternality has knock-on effects for theists' understanding of omniscience. An atemporalist will see God as infallibly knowing all true statements, including those concerning times that are to us future. A temporalist will see God as infallibly knowing all true statements that it is logically possible for a temporal being to know infallibly at the time it now is; this then, the temporalist will usually say, excludes statements about the future actions of free agents and thus, I have argued, given God's freedom and the dependence of the world on him, excludes statements about the future of the world in general.

So what should we be, atemporalists or temporalists? I'm going to argue that we should follow the majority opinion among those who've considered the issue and be atemporalists.

◆ ◆ ◆

It seems that we should say that if God is atemporal, then that he is atemporal is metaphysically necessary and if he is temporal, then that he is temporal is metaphysically necessary; either way then, it is not that both an atemporal God and a temporal God are metaphysical possibilities and philosophical reflection on the requirements of divine properties such as omniscience, omnipotence, and perfect goodness can lead us to prefer one to the other as an actuality. Thus there is scope for thinking that the best way to argue for either atemporalism or temporalism about God's eternality is from quite general reflections on the nature of time. One might, for example, argue that the passage of time is real in that the closed past is profoundly different from the open future; all concrete objects—such as God, if he exists—must be temporal. Alternatively, one might argue that the difference between past and future is entirely perspectival and it is quite possible for a concrete object—such as God, if he exists—to be freed from any frame of reference from which a perspective on it might be had; he might very well be atemporal. But suppose that one is starting (as is surely the case for most, who haven't been brought up reading books on the philosophy of time) from agnosticism with regards to theories of time, but believing that there could well be a God who has the attributes of traditional theism; one will, it seems to me quite properly, start by thinking of both an atemporal God and a temporal God as prima facie equal contenders for being metaphysically possible and one will allow reflections on the requirements of divine properties such as omniscience, omnipotence, and perfect goodness to lead one to develop a preference for one over the other, ultimately perhaps using the resulting preference in one's judgements on the plausibility of various theories of time. There are various arguments in this vein that one might put forward in favour of adopting the atemporalist view.[10] I'm going to advance only one, built on our understanding of omnipotence as hammered out earlier in the chapter.

One could only have reason to be a temporalist generated from one's understanding of omnipotence if there were some things that a temporal being could do and that an atemporal being could not do and if these were more power-granting things to be able to do than their atemporal correlates, an atemporal correlate being the closest thing to the temporal action under consideration that it is logically possible an atemporal being could do. A similar point may be made 'in the other direction'. One could only have reason to be an atemporalist generated from one's understanding of omnipotence if there were some things that an atemporal being could do and that a temporal being could not do and if these were more power-granting things to be able to do than their temporal correlates. There are, it seems, some things that it is good—power-granting—to be able to do and which only a temporal being could do: learn important philosophical truths and fall in love would be two examples. However, it is far from obvious that the atemporal correlates of activities that we recognize as good temporal things to be able to do and which an atemporal being could not do are less power-granting things than their temporal correlates.

If James (but not God) can perform the task of learning (let us say) the truth about the simplicity of theism; and God (but not James) can perform the task of atemporally knowing (let us say) the truth about the simplicity of theism, it is natural to say that God can do a better thing than James. One might say that the fact that there's no possible world in which an atemporal God performs a learning action is obviously not an expression of imperfection in him given that there's no possible world in which he's not performing the atemporal knowing action that has as its object everything that it is logically possible might be the object of a temporal learning action. If I write an end of term report on a pupil of mine, Ros, stating that she cannot learn anything about philosophy, I am only safe in thinking this will be taken as a criticism given that I am safe in thinking that anyone reading it will assume that Ros doesn't already know everything there is to know about philosophy. If Ros *did* know everything already, then although having this knowledge would of logical necessity remove from her the ability to learn, it would not remove from her anything that could properly be thought of as more worth having than what she already had. What about falling in love? Similar considerations apply. If the man or woman of your dreams tells you one day that he or she cannot fall in love with you, should this be a source for dismay on your part? Not if the reason is that he or she is already in love with you. Falling in love is of course a very exciting process (arguably even more exciting than the process of learning philosophy), but being in love is even better.

Now of course the temporal correlate of atemporal knowing is not learning; it is temporal—but everlasting—knowing and the temporal correlate of atemporal loving is not falling in love; it is being everlastingly in love; and it's not at all obvious that these temporal states are worse than their atemporal correlates. But neither is it obvious that they're better. Indeed, it's pretty obvious that they're the same. While there are some things—learning; falling in love; everlastingly knowing; and everlastingly being in love—that temporal beings can do and that are good to do, these things are not better, more power-granting, things to be able to do than their atemporal correlates. If one knows atemporally everything that is a possible object of knowledge, then the fact that one does not, of conceptual necessity, have the ability to learn anything or temporally everlastingly know anything does not detract from one's perfection in any way at all. If one loves atemporally, then the fact that one does not fall in love or love everlastingly does not detract from one's perfection either. So far then, it looks as if an atemporal God and a temporal God come out 'evens' in power. But an atemporal God would have at least this ability that a temporal God would not have: he would be omniscient in a sense that entails that he atemporally knows (infallibly) all things that are logically possible objects of knowledge (including those statements concerning what is to us—from our point of view, now—future), a sort of omniscience that we have seen a temporal God could not have on pain of being unable to change his intentions and, for some items of knowledge on a certain view of the nature of freedom, renouncing his freedom and that of his creatures. The closest a temporal God could come to this sort of omniscience would involve him having very well-educated guesses as to what is—from his point of view, which would be pretty close if not identical to ours—the future.

Is this ability of an atemporal God to know more a power, a liability, or a 'neutral' ability relative to the correlate that a temporal God might enjoy of having very well-educated guesses? It is obviously a power. Being able to make mistakes, we saw earlier, is best seen as a liability. (Jean, were she to have existed, would have been a more powerful mathematician than us in virtue of her not being able to make a mistake that we were able to make.) If one does not infallibly know everything about the future of something, one has the ability to make mistakes about it—that's what not infallibly knowing everything about it means. Conversely, if one does infallibly know everything about it, one does not have the ability to make mistakes about it. Thus having infallible knowledge of all aspects of the future of something is a more power-granting ability than having very well-educated guesses concerning it. One's better off with infallible knowledge than with fallible yet very well-educated guesses. Thus this sort of omniscience (and therefore atemporal eternality) are properties that we should ascribe to God in virtue of his omnipotence.

But perhaps this argument has been going 'too quickly'—that is to say, going wrong. Not having infallible knowledge of the future does not entail that one has to be able to make mistakes about it. One might have a nature which unerringly avoided mistakes by suspending judgement whenever there was a possibility of error, as there would be for a temporal God for all statements about the future of the world.

Take an ordinary coin; toss it in the air; and—before it lands—ask yourself which side up you believe it is going to land. Very probably you will find that you neither believe that it will land heads-side up, nor believe that it will land tails-side up. You suspend judgement on this, believing instead that it is 50 per cent probable that it will land heads and 50 per cent probable it will land tails. A temporal God then, it might be argued, could suspend judgement on what will actually happen. A temporalist may claim that instead of having very well-educated guesses about what will actually happen (and thus being prone to mistakes), God knows things about the probabilities of all future happenings and suspends judgement on what will actually happen (by doing so rendering himself immune from mistakes).

One worry one must have with this counter-argument of the temporalist is that it doesn't seem so obviously right for probabilities other than 50 per cent and it seems pretty obviously wrong for probabilities that are very far from

50 per cent. Take the coin again; toss it in the air; and—while it is still in the air—ask yourself what you believe about whether or not it will land on its edge. You will find that the answer is that you believe that it will not land on its edge. Yet it is conceptually (and indeed physically) possible that it will, something you are surely aware of. It could be argued then that believing that something will probably happen (or perhaps probably happen with a relatively high degree of probability) is just the same as believing that it will actually happen. I have some sympathy for this view. But a temporalist might maintain that it's just a sign of 'weakness' on our part that we move from believing that something will probably happen (or perhaps probably happen with a relatively high degree of probability) to believing that it will actually happen and the fact that we do so does not show—what is false—that they're the same belief. God would not give in to this weakness. I have some sympathy for this view too. Fortunately, we can sidestep the issue of whether believing that something will probably happen (or probably happen with a relatively high degree of probability) is the same as believing that it will actually happen, for the temporalist has an insurmountable problem even if this one can be overcome.

On the temporalist model as we have now worked it out, God must have some beliefs about the probabilities that his actions will meet certain descriptions, but he cannot know—with infallible certainty—of his actions that they will meet any description that they will in fact meet, for whether or not they will meet any description depends on future choices by himself (and perhaps others). This opens then the possibility on a temporalist model for God's actions to fail to meet the descriptions under which he willed himself to do them, for him—as one might put it—to bodge things up. Now we've watered down his omniscience, his omnipotence is also inevitably diluted; and his necessary benevolence no longer necessitates his beneficence. Let me give an example.

Imagine a temporal God looking sympathetically on a pregnant Austrian woman at the turn of the century (the junction of the nineteenth and twentieth centuries that is); she was in danger of miscarrying and, knowing of her predicament, praying fervently to God that he save her unborn child. On this occasion, God intervened by performing a miracle, violating the laws of nature for a moment or two, ensuring that the woman gave birth to a healthy child and thus that there was much rejoicing in their household when her husband, a local customs official, returned home that evening. God's intention in so intervening was to save the life of the unborn child and thus increase the aggregate happiness of the world in general. This was all laudable stuff; he is after all omnibenevolent. Of course, God knew that it was just possible that the child would grow up into someone who would produce terrible harm (and thus that overall his action would decrease the aggregate happiness of the world), but he also knew that this was fantastically unlikely. Thus it was indeed fantastically unlikely at the time he acted that his benevolence in this situation wouldn't lead to his beneficence in the resulting situation. Had he known what was in fact to happen, that this boy would grow up to be—yes, you guessed it—the fascist leader of Nazi Germany, he would have allowed the child to die. However, he did not know this; he took a risk; and, this time, the risk did not pay off.

This sort of thing has to be possible on a temporalist model. If it ever happened, the temporalist might maintain that it wouldn't mean that God would have made a mistake in the sense that something would have happened that would have shown a belief that he had to have been false. For instance, in my example, God wouldn't have believed that the unborn child whose life he was saving would not become a fascist dictator, just that it was very unlikely that he would (which his nevertheless doing so doesn't make false). But it would be natural to describe God as having made a mistake in the sense that his action wouldn't have fully satisfied the description under which he willed it; in my example, it wouldn't have increased the aggregate happiness of the world in general. The temporalist cannot evade the possibility of this sort of case by saying that God cannot will himself to do anything under a description the truth of which depends on future free actions, given that he or she is committed to seeing the future of the world as a whole as depending on the future free actions of God, and thus this would be to prevent God from willing himself to do anything to affect the world at all. So, the temporalist has to say that God could in principle bodge things up like this. If he doesn't in practice, then this is just lucky. So we must ask, is it more power-granting to be able to bodge things up or is it more power-granting not to be able to bodge things up? Well, this is the sort of question which can, I have suggested, only be answered by consulting our intuitions, but, I contend, on it our intuitions speak clearly: it is obviously the latter. Being able to bodge things up is a liability, not a power. A God who is atemporal never bodges up in any logically possible world; a God who is temporal bodges up in some—indeed an infinite number of—logically possible worlds. Indeed there's arguably an infinite number of logically possible worlds where he *always* bodges up. If he doesn't ever bodge up like this in the actual world, then this is just a matter of luck.[11] God plays dice and he has to keep his fingers crossed not simply that he'll win in the end, but that he'll even play well. Of course the claim that God takes risks is not universally thought to be in itself indefensible or even undesirable. Consider Hasker, who asserts that God is a risk-taker, under an understanding of risk-taking whereby 'God takes risks if he makes decisions that depend for their outcomes on the responses of free creatures in which the decisions themselves are not informed by knowledge of the outcomes.'[12] But the claim that God is forced by his temporality to risk his own goodness (where goodness entails beneficence, not merely benevolence) would be, I suggest, a risk too far for most theists. That goodness should be understood to imply beneficence as well as benevolence will not strike those (as I would see it, unduly) influenced by Kantianism as plausible; they might posit that even a God whose interferences were always bodges would—were these bodges always well-intentioned—be in himself perfectly good. The sort of character usually played by the American actor Rick Moranis (well-intentioned buffoons, as in his *Honey, I Shrunk the Kids*) are, such a person would maintain, as good as equally well-meaning but ultra-competent and thus, in contrast to his characters, also well-*doing* people. Against such a person, one might shift argumentative ground somewhat by asking whether it is really plausible to think that a Rick-Moranis God would be as worthy of praise as the God of traditional theism. Could Rick Moranis plausibly represent the God of theism in a film entitled *Honey, I May Well Have Bodged the Universe (for All I Know)*?[13]

Thus, if we share the intuition that an omnipotent being ought to be considered to have infallible knowledge of times that are from our point of view future because a being who was in all other respects like an omnipotent being yet did not have this knowledge would, our intuition suggests, be less powerful than one who did in virtue of being able to—as I have put it—bodge things up, then this provides a reason for us to follow the traditional path and adopt the atemporal understanding of the divine property of eternality.[14] If we share the intuition that a God who was—at best—contingently good and dependent for whatever goodness he had on luck would be a less worthy object of faith and religious hope, then this provides another reason for us to follow the traditional path and adopt an atemporal understanding of the divine property of eternity.

We have seen then that (regardless of one's views on libertarianism) temporalism leads inevitably to a retreat from ascribing to God complete omniscience and (when combined with libertarianism and the claim that he and his creatures are free) it leads to a retreat from the claim that he infallibly knows anything about the future of the world at all. We have also seen that, having surrendered the ground of complete omniscience, the temporalist cannot but retreat from ascribing to God complete omnipotence; the temporalist must admit that his or her God might make mistakes, not—if the temporalist treads carefully—by having false beliefs, but by performing actions that he reasonably expected would meet certain descriptions but which nevertheless do not do so. This then makes whatever goodness (in the sense of beneficence, not just benevolence) God has a matter of luck. Temporalism is committed to a partially ignorant God, one who is subject to the vagaries of luck for the efficacy of at least some of his actions and for his goodness.

◆ ◆ ◆

Before concluding my discussion of the divine property of eternality and summing up, it will be helpful to draw a parallel between God's relation to time and his relation to space, for seeing this parallel is what distinguishes the atemporalist from the temporalist.

You'll recall that theists do not regard God as located at any particular point in space in the sense that by being there he fails to be somewhere else. Rather, he transcends space. Despite his transcendence, God is not absent from anywhere in space. Rather, he is immanent in space. I am arguing that theists should be atemporalists, which amounts to them holding a similar understanding of God's relation to time. God is not located at any particular point in time in the sense that he exists then but not at other times. Rather, he transcends time. Despite his temporal transcendence, he is not absent from any time. Rather, he is immanent in time. Let me 'unpack' this.

It is tempting to say that according to the temporalist, God transcends time in the sense that he exists at all times and according to the atemporalist, he transcends it in the sense that he exists at no times. But in fact, I am about to suggest, the atemporalist should join the temporalist in saying that God—in virtue of his immanence—exists at all times, even though—in virtue of his transcendence and *pace* the temporalist—he does not exist within time. The traditional thing for the atemporalist going down this route to then say is that God exists at all times 'simultaneously'[15], but this creates an immediate 'collapsing problem': if God exists at all times simultaneously, then all times are simultaneous; but then the entire history of the universe collapses into one instant.[16] So it is that I suggest that the atemporalist should abandon the traditional 'simultaneously' clause in his or her description of God existing at all times. Given that what then remains—'God exists at all times'—is a claim that atemporalist and temporalist will agree on, we must ask what can then distinguish the atemporalist from the temporalist. The answer is that the atemporalist believes that if God had not created a universe, he would have existed at no time for there wouldn't have been time, whereas the temporalist believes that even if God had not created the universe, he would have existed at times, indeed at all times, for there would still have been time.

Given that we may take it that all parties to this debate are agreed that the universe is of finite age and, let us suppose, that they all agree that it began with the Big Bang, we may bring out the distinction between atemporalist and temporalist more clearly by imagining their different responses to the question: 'Did God exist before the Big Bang?' The atemporalist will answer this question 'No', for there was nothing temporally prior to the Big Bang; there was no time 'before' what was *ex hypothesi* the first moment the universe existed. The atemporalist and temporalist will agree that space is not 'bigger' than the—*ex hypothesi* finite—size of the universe. Although the universe is growing in size, they will agree that it would be incorrect to describe the universe as expanding into anything; it would be incorrect to describe God as already being at places the universe has yet to expand into. When the universe 'gets there', God will be there, but he won't be there beforehand because there'll be no 'there' beforehand for him to be at. Similarly, the atemporalist will assert, time is not 'bigger' than the—*ex hypothesi* finite—age of the universe. God was not at a time before the Big Bang, because time, like space, came into existence with the Big Bang. If the universe one day ceases to exist, God will not be there afterwards: there cannot be an 'after the end of time' just as there cannot be a 'to the left of space'. The temporalist however will treat the issues of space and time quite differently, saying that God did indeed exist before the universe; time is in fact 'bigger' than the—*ex hypothesi* finite—history of the universe and God existed in it before the universe did. If the universe one day ceases to exist, God will be there after it too.

It is a sufficient condition of one's being at a particular place, I argued, that one knows what is going on there directly, that is, without first needing to find out what is going on somewhere else, and that one can act there directly, that is, without first needing to act somewhere else. We should make the parallel claim about time. It is a sufficient condition of one's being at a particular time that one knows what is going on at that time directly, without first needing to do something at some other time, and that one can act directly at that time, that is without first needing to do something at some other time. On this understanding, if there is an atemporal God, then just as in virtue of his spatial transcendence he does not exist to the left of my painting of The Grand Canal any more than he does to the right of it, so, in virtue of his temporal transcendence, he does not exist before it was painted any more than he will exist after it has been destroyed. However, just as in virtue of his spatial immanence he does exist to the left of my painting as well as to its right, so in virtue of his temporal immanence he did exist before my painting was painted and will exist after it has been destroyed (assuming it was created after the Big Bang and will be destroyed before the end of the universe as a whole). As we've seen, the theist should understand God as existing to the left of my painting of The Grand Canal and to its right because it is sufficient for a person to exist at a place that he or she be able to know about it and act there directly and God satisfies this condition for all places within the universe. So the theist should understand God as existing before my painting was painted and after it is destroyed as it is sufficient for a person to exist at a time that he or she know about and be able to affect what is happening at that time directly, and God satisfies this condition for all times within the universe. The theist should therefore understand God as existing at every moment in the history of the world and thus before and after any particular moment in its history, except the first and last (assuming there is a first and a last).

Pace the temporalist, had he not created a temporal world, then God would not have existed at any moment in time. As it is however, he did create a temporal world and thus exists at every moment in time. That God exists at every moment in time does not make him exist in time. Just as the universe as a whole does not exist in space (and so the fact that it is God's body—or a part of his body—does not make God exist in space) it does not exist in time (and so the fact that God knows about every time directly and can act directly at every time does not make him exist in time). God's having the spatio-temporal universe as his body doesn't make him spatial in the sense of existing within space and neither does it make him temporal in the sense of existing within time.

When I talked in the previous chapter of the properties of incorporeality or (as I preferred it) transcendence, and omnipresence or (as I preferred it) immanence, I concentrated on spatial transcendence and immanence. The discussion of eternality in this chapter must prompt us to consider the wisdom of developing a broader understanding of transcendence and immanence, one which takes in God's relation to time as well as his relation to space. With such an understanding, we could then view eternality as divine transcendence/immanence as it pertains to time and incorporeality/omnipresence as divine transcendence/ immanence as it pertains to space, thus reducing by at least one the number of essential properties we need attribute to God. And of course scientists are happy to talk of space and time as merely two aspects of a unity, space-time. With the concept of space-time as basic, divine transcendence/immanence with regard to the universe would be seen as a single property. It also seems as if we might view God's omnipotence and omniscience as simply consequences of his fully transcending and yet being fully immanent in anything that exists and we have seen that it is his omnipotence, properly understood, that entails his omniscience (to secure him from the possibility of bodging things up), which in turn entails his atemporal eternality. The properties I've been discussing hitherto aren't then, one might say, separate properties at all. They're just consequences of what it would be to be the most perfect person possible. This is a theme to which we will return at the end of the next chapter.

◆ ◆ ◆

So, to sum up what I have argued in this chapter: if there is a God, he is by definition omnipotent; omniscient; and eternal. He is omnipotent in virtue of having the most power that it is logically possible a being might have. This does not entail that he has the power to do the logically impossible (for it is not logically possible that any being have this 'power'). Neither does it entail that he has the ability to do anything that would be the expression of weakness, a liability rather than a power. He has the most power-granting set of abilities that it is logically possible to have, a set the precise composition of which we are— due to our not being omniscient—doomed to remain to some extent ignorant of. However, our intuitions about what abilities it would be better to have in various circumstances allow us to deduce various things about it, for example that it would not contain the ability to make mistakes or commit suicide. God is omniscient in virtue of infallibly knowing all true statements, including statements about actions and states of affairs that are, to us, future. He is eternal in the sense that he exists outside time. The theist should adopt the traditional atemporal understanding of divine eternality in order to be able to ascribe to God the most power-granting form of omniscience that is logically possible, one incompatible with performing actions that one believes will probably satisfy the description under which one willed oneself to do them, but which do not in fact turn out to do so, and one that preserves the necessity of his perfect goodness. Nevertheless, despite his atemporality, it remains true to say that there is no time at which God does not exist as long as we understand ourselves by saying this to be saying no more than that there is no time in order to know about which he first needs to do something at some other time and there is no time in order to act at which he first needs to act at some other time. Given this understanding of what is sufficient for a person to exist at a time, we atemporalists can actually agree with a lot of the things temporalists would like to say about God's eternality. For example, we can say that if there's a God, then he exists right now, at whatever time it happens to be. We can say that if there's a God, then how his character manifests itself changes from moment to moment, depending on what we do and—perhaps especially—on what we ask him to do. But of course, we will insist that any change in how God's character manifests itself is entirely in the eye of the beholder. If there's a God, then changes in how his character manifests itself are rather like changes in how a static work of art such as a sculpture manifests itself as one walks around it and—figuratively speaking— asks questions of it. God does not change *in himself.* In virtue of his existing outside time, God is, in every respect, immutable.

In this chapter we have seen that the concept of omnipotence is coherent and substantial, even if our own finitude prevents us from fully understanding all that is entailed by it and that, although subject to some dispute internal to the theistic community, the concepts of omniscience and eternality are also coherent and substantial. We have also started to see how these properties may be seen as entailed by a proper understanding of those we have already discussed, indeed how they are really all different facets of the one property of divinity. In the next chapter, we'll return to this theme having considered the last three properties on my list of the essential properties of God: his perfect freedom; his perfect goodness; and his necessity.

3

Perfect Freedom, Perfect Goodness, Necessity

PROPERTY SEVEN: PERFECT FREEDOM

As with knowledge, Philosophers are not at all agreed about what freedom involves. Fortunately, as with knowledge, we do not need to know exactly what it involves to make some progress in understanding the traditional theistic claim that God is perfectly free. Most would agree that freedom requires or perhaps simply is the power to bring about what one wishes to bring about.[1] So God's being perfectly free must entail him not being in any way constrained in his bringing about what he wishes. What then might in principle constrain someone in bringing about what they wish to bring about?

Picking up on the argument of the last chapter, one might suggest that the only things that constrain agents in this regard and thus make them less than perfectly free are their not being sufficiently powerful and their not knowing what it is they are doing. In other words, one might suggest that if the answer to the question, 'Did you wish to do that?' as posed of an action you have just performed is ever 'No', then that is either because you recognized that what you were doing was less than what you wished to do but simply did not have it within your power to do anything closer to what you wished or because you did not realize exactly what it was you were doing as you were doing it, you bodged up.

By way of two examples: why did Medea have her young brother Apsyrtus killed and his dismembered body thrown overboard from her ship as she fled from Æetes? Because she didn't have the power to slow down Æetes in his pursuit of her in any way other than by causing him to tarry to pick up the pieces of his son. Having her brother murdered like this was, from Medea's own point of view we may assume, far from ideal, but it was, she presumably believed, the least bad of the options that were available to her. Given that her overwhelming priority was her own survival, it was 'the only thing she could do'. Had she had the power to delay Æetes by throwing overboard bits of his favourite throne for him to pause to collect, we may presume she would have done that instead. So Medea knew what she was doing and she chose to do it; as such she was, we might say, fully morally responsible for her brother's death. But if we suppose her thinking to be as suggested above, she certainly wasn't as free in her choices as she would have been had her father had a great attachment to a throne that she happened also to have on her ship and thus could have thrown overboard in pieces instead. So she was not as free as she would have been if she had not had her options limited by circumstances beyond her control. Her lack of freedom stemmed from her lack of power. The second example (the archetypal bodge-up): why did Oedipus kill his father and marry his mother? It was because he did not realize exactly what it was he was doing. He knew that he was killing someone, but didn't realize it was his father; and he knew that he was marrying someone, but didn't realize that it was his mother. It would be somewhat misleading then to say that Oedipus freely chose to kill his father and marry his mother. While he freely chose to do actions of which these descriptions were true, he did not know of these actions that they met these descriptions and thus it wouldn't be right to say he freely chose to do these things under these descriptions. His lack of freedom stemmed from his ignorance.

God, as we have seen, is omnipotent, so he could never be less than perfectly free in what he chose to do as a result of not having enough power to do anything closer to what he wished to do. There are no circumstances beyond God's control that he would dearly like to change but finds that he cannot. And God is omniscient, so he could never be less than perfectly free in what he chose to do as a result of not knowing exactly what it was he was doing. There will never be any description that is true of any of God's actions that he does not know is true. (Of course, as we saw in the previous chapter, this wouldn't have been the case had he not been omniscient about the future—our reason to prefer the atemporal understanding of eternality.) There are none of the limitations on God's freedom that there are on ours. His ability to bring about what he wishes is unhindered by either a lack of power or a lack of knowledge; and it is in virtue of this that we describe him as perfectly free.

Theists believe that God is perfectly free. We are free to do bad things as well as good. Does God have the ability to do bad things? The traditional theistic answer to this has been that he does not have this ability: he cannot do anything that is less than perfect. Doesn't that make him less powerful than us then? No—the answer is given—for the ability to do less than is perfect would be a liability rather than a power for him. Let us turn then to the next property on my list, perfect goodness. Understanding it will help us further understand God's perfect freedom and how it differs in interesting ways from our imperfect freedom.

♦ ♦ ♦

Before we do so, I want to state explicitly an assumption that all theists are agreed on making, the assumption that forms the foundation for their understanding of God's perfect goodness (and much else): this is the assumption that there is in *some* sense *objective* goodness and badness. All agree that normative appraisal isn't simply a matter of how—subjectively—we feel about the world; it's a matter of how—objectively—the world ought to be. If you're not of this metaethical viewpoint, you won't have much luck understanding the divine property of perfect goodness unless you appreciate that theists radically disagree with you over your metaethical view. Now, needless to say, I don't have time to go into the merits or otherwise of this metaethical assumption in any depth despite its importance, *and it is crucially important.* I shall have to assume that it's right for the purposes of my explanation. But let me use one thought experiment to remind you that in fact you do share this assumption.

After the Second World War, many Nazis fled to South America. It is quite possible that some might have formed self-sufficient communities there in the jungles, preserving their Nazi culture down the generations until now there is a thriving Nazi society as yet to be discovered by the outside world. Let's suppose that this is indeed what has happened and that, while exploring with your friend one day, you wander deep into the territory of this society. You are walking along a road between two of their villages when you fall into conversation with a couple of their local policemen. All is going well, until you let it slip that your friend is Jewish. Suddenly, the two policemen jump on your friend and tell you that you must shoot him to death. You are given an opportunity to consult the society's legal codes, a copy of which one of the policemen carries with him. In doing so, you realize that your shooting your friend would be absolutely legal, indeed it is legally required of you. Being Jewish is an offence punishable by death by shooting and the law dictates that he or she who brings the existence of a Jewish person to the attention of the police has the honour of being the executioner, an honour which he or she may not refuse. You ask whether anyone has ever challenged this law. The policemen look disgusted at the thought, telling you that nobody has; nobody has ever wanted to do so. So it is that this law, which enjoys the unanimous and unreserved support of the local population, allows no possibility for appeal against the sentence of death by shooting, a sentence that must be carried out immediately. The two policemen explain all this to you. One of them enthusiastically presses his gun into your hands as the two of them hold your friend securely before you, pointing out parts of his body through which a bullet will most probably be fatal. The policemen look at you with a cheerful expectancy. Your friend looks at you too. He has different expectations from those of the policemen. What ought you to do?

Everyone who is reading this outside the context of a mental institution knows what the wrong answer to this question is. The wrong answer is, 'Shoot your friend.' But by what standard is this the wrong answer? Not the standard that is actually enshrined in the legal codes of the society in which you've found yourselves and which enjoys the support of that society. That standard dictates that you shoot your friend. By your own, internal, standard then? But we all know that being good isn't simply a matter of doing what feels good by one's own internal standard. We all acknowledge that individuals can go wrong in their moral assessment of actions. It seems, from our reaction to this example, that we think that a whole society can go wrong in its moral assessment of actions too. If this is indeed what we think, then we must be assuming that morality is independent not only of anyone's beliefs or attitudes, but also of any society's beliefs and attitudes. Is it independent of everyone's beliefs and attitudes? It seems that we think it is, for we may imagine a possible world in which the Nazis had won the Second World War and so now the culture which in my thought experiment is confined to the jungles of South America has spread to all corners of the globe. And we think that even if we lived in a world where *everyone* believed that shooting someone merely for being Jewish was right, we'd all be wrong (although of course we wouldn't then realize it), just as we think that even if we lived in a world where everyone believed that the Earth was flat, we'd all be wrong about that (although again of course we wouldn't then realize it). It seems then that we endorse the metaethical assumption of objectivity: morality isn't generated merely by how people feel.

Suppose that you're unconvinced by this argument. If you take the fact that you're unconvinced as reflecting some sort of philosophical achievement on your part, you'll have to think not simply that as a psychological matter of fact you've remained unconvinced by it but that you're right to remain unconvinced. You'll have to think that this argument *shouldn't* convince one of the objectivity of moral value. But the sort of judgement you'll then be making itself supposes some normative principle or principles that dictate what one should or should not believe on the basis of a certain argument. So you'll be tacitly relying on the falsity of extreme subjectivism about value when you judge of the merits or otherwise of any argument in favour of objectivism (rather than merely the effects that considering that argument has as a matter of fact had on you). You'll be thinking that there are at least objective standards determining what people should believe as a result of arguments.

Of course, it is possible to retreat from objectivism even here. Rather than saying of this argument that it *should* not convince, one might simply report as a psychological fact about oneself that it has not convinced. Rather than saying that if you believe that p and you believe that p implies q, then you *should* believe that q, one might rest content with saying that one—or members of one's society—tend to believe that q if they believe that p and they believe that p implies q. And so on. If one goes down this road, it is true that no one will be able to give one any reason to return, but that is only true because one will have abandoned precisely the harder path of advancing reasons for the having of one belief rather than another in favour of the easier path of merely observing what beliefs one (or one's society) actually has. The more philosophically defensible ('more' because at least capable in principle of being defended) path to tread on the issue of the objectivity of value accepts then that there are objective principles dictating how people should order their beliefs but maintains that there aren't any such principles dictating how people should order their actions.

Someone might say, 'There's epistemic normativity, but there isn't moral normativity. When thinking, we should follow the law of non-contradiction (for example) because it is impossible for contradictories to both be true and it's good to believe truths and avoid believing falsehoods. However, when talking to others about one's thoughts, it's not the case that we shouldn't needlessly mislead them because it's good to help them reach truths and avoid falsehoods.' 'But why?', one must ask of a defender of such a distinction. Surely if it's good to believe the truth and avoid falsehood, it's good to avoid needlessly leading people away from truth and towards falsehood. The person initially walking this path will, in the light of this need to switch, it seems, to claiming that there are objective principles dictating what it is good and bad for himself or herself to believe, but there aren't any dictating what it is good and bad for others to believe; there's only epistemic normativity for him or her. Thus could he or she say, 'When thinking, *I* should follow the rules of logic because it's good *for me* to believe the truth and avoid falsehood,' without committing himself or herself to the more general claim that it's good to believe the truth and avoid falsehood, the more general claim from which it would follow that one has good reason to avoid lying to people. But he or she would now be left without any way of explaining why it is good for him or her and no one else to believe truth and avoid falsehood. He or she wouldn't be able to explain why it is good for him or her to believe truth and avoid falsehood in terms of the more general fact that it's good to believe truth and avoid falsehood and he or she wouldn't be able to consider himself or herself reasonable in thinking of himself or herself as a special case, the only person to whom such objective principles apply. This is why I incline to think that the most convincing argument for objectivism will involve one's distracting one's opponent with an overly complicated analysis of Kant's discussion of the nature of freedom or some such prior to kicking him or her somewhere sensitive with all one's force and then politely asking of his or her prostrate self if he or she has any reason to *resent* one for one's actions. (Readers will be heartened to learn that I've never actually deployed what I believe to be the most convincing argument for objectivism, though I confess that protracted discussion with relativists often tempts me to do so.)

Accepting then that some form of objectivism about moral value is right, let me go on to look at God's perfect goodness as theists understand it.

PROPERTY EIGHT: PERFECT GOODNESS

Goodness is a matter of behaving as one ought in one's relations with other people—and creatures more generally—and perfect goodness is a matter of doing the best thing that one can for them whenever there is a best and doing one of the best things that one can whenever two or more things are 'joint best' for them, i.e. are equally good and none is better.[2] Of course none of us are ever perfectly good towards one another. This in itself does not make us blameworthy. One is blamelessly less than perfectly good for example when one tries but fails to do the best or joint best that one believes one can for someone, failing either due to lack of power or lack of knowledge (as long as one does not, by failing to do the best, or joint best thereby also fail to do that which one ought to do and one's failure is itself the result of one's negligence). And one is blamelessly less than perfectly good towards someone even when one doesn't try to do the best or joint best that one can for them, as long as one tries to meet one's obligations towards them (and again as long as any failure to do so cannot be put down to one's own negligence). If I owe someone a certain number of tutorials and I give him or her this number, then in this respect I do all that I ought. It might have been better were I to have given more than I owed, but I was not obliged to do so and so if I decided not to do so, no blame attaches to me. My duty is fulfilled. My conscience is clear. We have the freedom to do this, to refrain from good acts that are not morally required of us, what are usually called acts of supererogation.

As well as being blamelessly less than perfectly good to one another, some-times we are also blameworthily less than perfectly good to one another. Sometimes we do something that is not simply not the best or joint best that we could do for someone but something we know we ought not to do. If I owe a pupil of mine a certain number of tutorials and I could give him or her this number without any harm befalling anyone, yet I choose to go down to the pub instead of being in my room at the times we have arranged, then—assuming I am aware of my duties—I have chosen to do that which I know I ought not to do. I have chosen to do that the doing of which will make me blameworthy. Of course, I no doubt hope that nobody will actually blame me, that I won't bump into my pupil in the pub and he or she ask me what I'm doing there (if only to deflect me from asking the same question of him or her). But I have done what I needn't have done and knew at the time I shouldn't do: I have not simply failed to give my pupil what would have been the best I could give him or her; I have failed to give him or her that which he or she had a right to expect of me. My duty remains unfulfilled. My conscience is not clear. We have the freedom to do this too, to choose to fail to do what we know to be our duty.

If one is morally obliged to do something for someone in a particular situa-tion, then it should be the case that one would do that thing for anyone in the same situation. When one does something good for someone that goes beyond what one is obliged to do for them, it is not true that it should be the case that one would do the same thing for anyone in their situation. In the case of a supererogatory act, one cannot do it from a disinterested sense of duty; one can only do it for the sake of the person for whom one's doing it.[3] In virtue of this necessary 'directedness' towards the good of the particular people for whom one is performing them, it does not seem unnatural therefore to call acts of supererogation acts of love. God's perfect goodness then is his perfectly fulfilling his duties towards his creatures and, furthermore, whenever there is a logically possible best or joint best thing for him to do for them, his doing that too, his perfectly loving them.

So that's what theists mean when they say that God is perfectly good or perfectly loving. But why is it that they say that God is *necessarily* perfectly good? Why do they make his perfect goodness an essential property of his, not an accidental one? Why don't they see him as free to be less than perfect?

We should remember that we are all agreed that goodness is an objective property of some actions, states of affairs, or people and that an action's being good is an objective reason for one to perform it. Given this, it is obvious that one action's being better than another action that is incompatible with it is obviously a reason for one to perform the better action rather than the worse. Thus, it might seem, one is most reasonable when one does whatever it is that is the best action available to one. It might seem that way; and for God, I shall argue, it is that way. But it is not that way for humans. In order to see this, let me ask the question, Why do we—finite humans—fail to be perfectly good? And let me answer it: there are four possible reasons: we reasonably conclude that we don't have enough time/resources; we're unreasonable; we're ignorant; and/or we're selfish.

When we fail to go beyond our duty with regard to someone, this could be because we correctly judge ourselves to have fulfilled our duty and reasonably enough wish to spend what we judge to be our finite time and resources elsewhere. It would be good for my pupils to have extra tutorials and this fact gives me a reason to give them extra tutorials, but it would be good for me if I occasionally had the chance to have a drink. I recognize that I am under no obligation to give my pupils extra tutorials (that's precisely what their being 'extra' means) and also that to do so would deprive me of the chance of ever getting to the pubs before they close. I am therefore blamelessly less good than I could be towards my pupils if I decide not to offer them extra tutorials, but go to the pub instead. If I had more time available, I'd do both. But I don't. My action is certainly not altruistic, but it would be odd to call it 'selfish', for selfishness carries with it the implication of blameworthiness and, in that I have willingly fulfilled my obligations, I am not blameworthy. Perhaps we might best call such failures to be perfectly good 'reasonably self-interested' or 'expedient' failures.

What of when we fail to be perfectly good not just in the sense of not doing the most good that we could do for others but doing less than we ought to do for them? That, I suggest, must be due to one or a mixture of the following three reasons. First, it might be because we know what we ought to do, but are acted on by factors beyond our control, e.g. overwhelming desires, and in this respect are thus unreasonable. I might genuinely want to give my pupils the tutorials that are their due but find that as a result of my overwhelming desire for alcohol I am nevertheless unable to bring myself to stay in my room at the times I have arranged these tutorials as I know that the pubs are open then. To this extent

I am less than perfectly free: I am being acted on by forces that are beyond my control. (Of course I might still be blameworthy for not giving these tutorials if the fact that my desires are beyond my control is itself the result of negligent choices I made earlier in life, e.g. my refusing to listen to those who told me that I was starting to drink too much.) Secondly, it might be because we are ignorant—we just don't know what we should do. I am fully capable of staying in my room and giving my pupils the tutorials that are their due even when I know that the pubs are open, but I nevertheless often fail to do so as I have a terrible memory; I just forget that I've arranged tutorials and, in my ignorance of my obligations, go to the pub instead. (Again, I might still be blameworthy for not giving these tutorials if the fact that I have a terrible memory is my fault or I do nothing to mitigate the effects of my terrible memory, e.g. keep a diary.) Thirdly, we might be selfish. We could do our duty; we know we should; but we freely choose to do something else instead, something that we calculate will serve us better. I know that I should be giving someone a tutorial; I am fully capable of doing so; but I decide that I'll enjoy myself rather more in the pub and that I'm going to prioritize my own enjoyment over doing what I should. This sort of action deserves the name 'selfish' because it is straightforwardly the blameworthy (in contrast to blameless) pursuit of one's self-interest at the expense of another. I am not doing what is expedient for me within what I believe to be the parameters imposed by my duties to others; I am knowingly transgressing those parameters so that I might (as I think of it) more effectively pursue my own interests.

If the mere fact that it would be good for somebody if we did something for them disabled us from being able to refuse to do it for them, then it would seem that we would never be able to get any of our time or resources for ourselves. It's a power for us to be able to refrain from doing the best that we can for people given that we take ourselves to have less than infinite time and resources available to us. What of the ability not simply to fail to do the best that we can for people but to do what we know we ought not to do? Is this too a power for us? I think it is.

Consider this scenario: you are a student. One day, you are walking to your college—wondering how you are going to tell the Bursar that you don't have the £500 pounds he says he requires from you today if he is not to send the handyman round to 'kneecap' you. As you are about to go into college, you notice the White's Professor of Immoral Philosophy drop a wad of money just in front of you; he's not noticed this as he is busy slapping his chauffeur for being a few minutes late in picking him up in his Rolls-Royce. You must act quickly if you are to return the wad of money to its rightful owner as by now the professor is in his Rolls-Royce, shouting to his chauffeur to 'Drive over those worthless peasants!', referring to the group of primary school children who are—at the moment—in front of his car. As you pick up the wad of money, you notice that it is sealed by a tape that tells you that it contains exactly £500. As you look back to its owner you see that he has set light to an identical roll of money and is using it to light a large cigar. What is it overall most reasonable for you to do? What should you do?

I suggest that the answers to these two questions are very plausibly different. You would be overall most reasonable in keeping the money yourself; you *should* give it back to its rightful owner, this necessitating that you not keep it yourself. Where prudence and duty conflict, it can be, overall, reasonable to be prudent rather than dutiful.

Consequentialists (among others, no doubt) will remain supremely unimpressed by this example. If one is a consequentialist, it might seem obvious that you should keep the money yourself; the so-called rightful owner has no rights to it because he is not going to use it to produce as much good as you are. What you would be overall most reasonable in doing, and what you should do, are one and the same. If one does think that way, then this example will not work in the way that I had hoped that it might.[4] It will not strike one that I have managed to describe a situation where you would be, overall, reasonable in doing something other than your duty. This example will not work, but another will.

Consider a choice between, on the one hand, an action that will produce a net overall increase in good of a certain amount, an increase that will be so evenly distributed over such a large population that each person will benefit only negligibly from it and, on the other hand, an action that will produce a slightly smaller net overall increase in good, but produce it closer to home—let us say maximally close to home, merely to oneself. For example, you find yourself having won the lottery with a choice: either you can give all your winnings to a charity which will distribute the resultant benefits evenly across a large population or you can spend the money solely on yourself, by doing so fulfilling (let us say) a great many of your (in themselves harmless) desires. There is no third way, keeping some for yourself and giving some to the charity. There again, it strikes me, it is very plausible to suggest that you would be overall most reasonable in keeping the benefit closer to home, even if—on consequentialism— you should perform the action that will produce the greater overall good.

I suggest then that whatever metaethical theory one adopts, thought experiments can always be constructed that yield at the 'intuition level' the same sort of separation between what it is most reasonable for an agent to do and what they should do. Whatever metaethical theory one subscribes to, one will have to admit—not on pain of contradiction, but on pain of counter-intuition—that it could be overall most reasonable for one to do something other than what morality requires of one. And if so, one will have to view the ability—knowingly and without any weakness of will—to do what we know we shouldn't as indeed for us a power rather than a liability. It can't be a liability to be able to do that which one has, overall, most reason to do; it must be a power. So the ability to be less than perfect, both in the sense of knowingly failing to do the best one could for someone *and* in the sense of knowingly failing to do what one ought to do for them, are genuine powers for us; they're abilities that it is good for us to have.

Against this line of thinking, one might argue that the ability to be less than perfect in these two ways isn't really a power rather than a liability if there's actually no way that exercising it could be in our best long-term interests. And if there's a God, then there is actually no way in which it could be in our best long-term interests. It could be argued that I have been assuming a certain lack of epistemic access to the truth of theism to generate examples where it is as one might say 'subjectively' reasonable for one to conclude that it is in one's best interests to be less than perfect. On theism, I have not succeeded in generating examples of situations where it is *objectively* reasonable to be so, because on theism there cannot be any situation where it really is in someone's best interests to be so.

I think that the distinction between what one has most subjective reason to do and what one has most objective reason to do is a good one, and that it is true that I have been rather conflating the two in my presentation so far. But even when we separate them out, it does not affect the conclusion. It is a genuine power to be able to do that which it appears to one is most reasonable, even if it only appears to one most reasonable because one is suffering already from the liability of being less than omniscient. We have already seen that not every ability that would not feature in the maximally power-granting set of abilities is ipso facto a liability when it occurs in another set. (The boy Seneca told us about did have a genuine power to commit suicide by dashing his head against the nearest wall although his ability to do so counted as a power only because of the other liabilities he was suffering under at that time.) If this is right, then the abilities to choose to do what one knows is less than the best that one could do for someone and to choose to do what one knows one ought not to do could be genuine powers for us—finitely powerful and knowledgeable—creatures even if, as is the case on theism, it is never in our best interests to exercise these powers. They could be, but are they?

Consider this situation:

A friend of yours, Sylvia, has applied for three jobs, one with University A; one with University B; and one with the Quality Assurance Agency, the government body that inspects universities. You know that it would be morally good for your friend to work for either University A or University B and in fact equally good to work for either; each is pursuing the same worthwhile goals. You also know that Sylvia is morally obliged not to work for the QAA. It is inherently evil and one's just deluding oneself if one thinks that one might be able to reform it from the inside. It's like the Cheka in this respect, and others too. Furthermore, you know that Sylvia won't be truly happy working for the QAA; although they give out more important-sounding titles and pay better, in the end the intellectual and moral bankruptcy of the organization means that she would end up having a mid-life crisis if she worked for them. By contrast, you know that if Sylvia worked for either A or B, although there'd be less chance of an important-sounding title and less pay, she would realize that what she was doing was worthy and ultimately end up a lot happier. Don't ask me how you know all this; it's my example, so let me just suppose for the sake of argument that you do.

Now Sylvia—not having your level of insight into these organizations or into her own psychology—has made applications for all three positions and gone off on a short holiday, leaving you with authority to open her letters while she's away and a contact telephone number should she need to make any decisions. So it is that one day you open a letter from A; a letter from B; and a letter from the QAA, each of which offers your friend a job with their respective organizations, jobs which she needs to phone to accept within the next twenty-four hours. A failure to phone will be taken as a rejection of the job offers, the jobs thus being offered to someone else. Sylvia will—it seems—have to choose between these three jobs.

It occurs to you though that you could tell your friend the contents of the letters from universities A and B and simply fail to mention the QAA letter. If you do this, she will be so excited about the A and B offers that she won't ask about whether there's any letter from the QAA. She will phone and accept one of the A or B jobs, which—as you know—will mean that she fulfils her obligations; does something that is positively worthy with her life; and does something that will ultimately be in her own best interests. Let me suppose that you know that there's no way you could ever be found out in this ruse. You have a choice yourself then: preserve your friend's freedom to fail to do what would be ideal; to fail to do what she ought to do; and to fail to do what is in her own best interests, or remove this freedom. What should you do?

Most people's intuition is that there's at least something to be said in favour of your telling your friend about the QAA letter and thus preserving her ability to choose to do what is less than ideal; what she should not in fact do; and what is in fact not in her best interests. Why? Because having this sort of ability is in itself a good, i.e. a power, even though it's not actually in her best interests to exercise it.

It's also very plausible to suppose that the good of this sort of freedom is directly proportional to the importance of the choice at hand. To see this, suppose that on the same day as you open these letters from A, B, and the QAA, you also open a letter addressed to your friend asking her to phone within the next twenty-four hours if she'd like to prevent herself from being automatically transferred from the circulation list for hard copies of *Practical Tiddlywinker* to the circulation list for soft copies of the same publication. You happen to know that she should allow herself to be transferred: the soft copy has slightly less detrimental effects on the environment. But the difference is a very small one, so this is not a major moral issue. Would there be much to be said against your making an executive decision on your friend's behalf here by not mentioning this letter? I think not. To remove your friend's freedom to decide whether or not to continue to receive hard copies of *Practical Tiddlywinker* is not to remove anything near as good as you'd remove if you removed the freedom to choose which career path to take. So freedom to choose to be less than perfect and to choose between fulfilling one's obligations and not doing so (not just between different ways of fulfilling one's obligations) is in itself a good for us and it's a good for us in proportion to the importance of the choice at hand. That, one might think, could certainly be a reason why God in his perfect goodness would choose to give us this freedom and why he'd put us in a world where we faced choices which were often more important than whether we got hard or soft copies of *Practical Tiddlywinker*. I'll leave that thought with you for a moment; we'll return to it in a later chapter.

At the moment, it is sufficient to observe that we have more freedom if our knowing that a thing that we want to do is less than the best thing we could do does not in itself prevent us from doing it; and we have more freedom if our knowing that a thing that we want to do is something that we are under an obligation not to do does not in itself prevent us from doing it. That we have this freedom is in itself a good, a power, for us, even if exercising this freedom in the direction of doing less than is perfect is objectively a mistake (as it would be on theism). If we did know with absolute certainty that we would enjoy an everlasting life of perfect fulfilment in God's presence after our death, it would be obvious to us that it was a mistake to be less than perfect; it could not strike us as reasonable and expedient to 'conserve' our resources by failing to do for others all that we could or to think that we could pursue our own interests more efficiently at the expense of others.[5] If we did know these things with absolute certainty, then these abilities would be liabilities for us. But we don't know these things with absolute certainty and so it is a power for us to be able to choose to do that which we know is less than perfect and it is a power for us to be able to choose to do that which we know we ought not to do.

In this context, the crucial question in this: could these abilities ever reasonably be thought of as powers rather than liabilities for God? And the answer to that is 'no'.

We can see this by altering the example of your coming across a much-needed £500. Let me suppose that as you are reflecting on whether or not it would be most reasonable for you to give the rightful owner his money, you remember that you are only a part-time student. With the other half of your time you hold down the tricky job of being Governor of the Bank of England. (You're pretty busy.) In a surprise legislative birthday present, the Chancellor of the Exchequer has given you for this day only the right to print money for your own purposes. Happy Birthday. Would it now be overall reasonable for you to keep the White's Professor's money too? Surely not if—as I have been supposing—you ought to return it, then now you have no need of it, it certainly becomes unreasonable for you not to do what you ought to do. In other words, the ability knowingly and without any weakness of will to do what one knows one ought not do is only plausibly a power, an ability that it is good to have, when one is in a situation where one desires an outcome that one reasonably believes one cannot achieve without deviating from what morality requires of one. God's omnipotence assures him of being able to get whatever it is he desires without deviating from what morality requires.[6] What about the ability to refrain from doing the best or joint best that one can for someone? Again, this is only plausibly a power when one is in a situation where it is reasonable for one to think that one has finite resources available to one and thus that it is expedient to conserve them for other uses. And again, God could never be in such a situation. So, to ask the question whether God has the ability to perform an action that is less than morally ideal is to ask whether he has the ability to perform an action that of necessity there is good reason for him not to perform (it is less than morally ideal) and which—being omnipotent—he need not perform in order to bring about any other state of affairs he might wish to bring about. In other words, it is to ask whether he has the ability to perform an overall unreasonable action. To answer this question 'no' is then obviously not in any way to retreat from a claim that God is all-powerful; such an ability would for him always be a liability; it could never be a power.

In virtue of our not being omnipotent and omniscient, it is good for us—a power—that we can choose to do other than what perfect goodness demands. We can choose in our relationships with other creatures to do things that we know aren't the best that we could do for them and, further, we can choose to do things that we know aren't simply not the best that we could do for one another, but are actually things we shouldn't do to one another. In virtue of his being omnipotent and omniscient, it is good for God—an absence of a liability—that he cannot choose to do anything other than what perfect goodness demands. Our lack of omnipotence makes our freedom imperfect in that we can only do some of what we might reasonably wish to do, but it is a powerful freedom nonetheless in that we can do at least some of what we reasonably wish to do, even when what we reasonably wish to do we know to be less than the best we could do, and even something we know we shouldn't do. God's freedom is perfect in that he can do anything he wishes and thus he can only do what is perfectly loving towards his imperfect creatures. Power might corrupt, but absolute power perfects, absolutely.[7]

Let us turn to the final property on my list of essential properties, necessity.

PROPERTY NINE: NECESSITY

There are many sorts of necessity. There's conceptual/logical and mathematical necessity—if he's a bachelor then he can't be married; every number must have a successor. There's what's usually called metaphysical necessity—everything that begins to exist must have a cause. There's physical necessity—if it was a particle, then it couldn't have been travelling faster than the speed of light. There's moral necessity—you must make an effort to pay your debts. There's aesthetic necessity—by Act IV, it's impossible for Macbeth to live happily ever after. There are no doubt other sorts of necessity too. Each of them uses a sense of necessity—a 'must', a 'couldn't'—but each uses a different sense. In what sense of necessary do theists regard God's existence as necessary?

Some have held that God's existence is logically necessary, that one actually contradicts oneself—albeit perhaps in a non-obvious way—if one denies God's existence. Anselm thought this and (as we shall see in a later chapter) this thought forms the basis of his Ontological Argument for God's existence. It's even possible to extract from Kant the view that we must see God's existence as aesthetically necessary. But these have been minority opinions among theists. Most theists have understood the necessity of God's existence as some form of metaphysical necessity. Unfortunately, metaphysical necessity is notoriously difficult to elucidate. Most philosophers are agreed that there is such a thing as metaphysical necessity, but there is no consensus over how to understand it; there are different senses of metaphysical necessity in the literature and much disagreement about which of these senses make sense and which is best. Should we agree with most philosophers that there's metaphysical necessity?

Assume for a moment that it is true that there are no metaphysical necessities. There are no necessities that are not purely conceptual—like logical or mathematical ones; physical—like statements of scientific laws; moral—like statements of fundamental principles of practical reasoning; aesthetic—like the principles concerning the nature of tragedy; and so on. Is it just an accident that there are no metaphysical necessities? Could there have been some? If we say, 'Yes, there could have been metaphysical necessities,' then we are saying that it's not necessary that there are none. If we say, 'No, there could not have been metaphysical necessities,' then we are saying that it is necessary that there are none. In either case, we are making a claim that employs a notion of necessity. What sort of necessity are we using when we make this claim? It's hardly going to be plausible to maintain that it is a conceptual necessity that we're using: those who say that there are metaphysical necessities do not seem to be conceptually confused and those who say that there are not do not take themselves to be merely stating a conceptual relationship, something to be placed on the shelf alongside claims such as 'There are no married bachelors.' But then it's even less plausible to say that it's a physical necessity: the putative fact that there are not metaphysical necessities doesn't seem to be a fact which should be placed on the shelf alongside the laws of nature either. And it's even less plausibly a moral, aesthetic, or some other form of necessity. So it must be a metaphysical necessity that there are no metaphysical necessities or a metaphysical necessity that there could have been metaphysical necessities even though there aren't actually any metaphysical necessities, but either of these latter two claims is a straightforward contradiction. So we should accept that there are metaphysical necessities even if we're not quite sure how to elucidate the notion.

However, having pushed the boat out by saying that theists mean meta-physically necessary when they describe God's existence as necessary and having argued that we should accept a notion of metaphysical necessity even if we can't fully elucidate it, we are not completely at sea when it comes to further understanding what this metaphysical necessity might amount to in God's case. All are agreed that God's existence is necessary in the sense that if it is true that there's a God, then this fact is in no way dependent on any other fact. (Rather, every other fact depends on it.) According to theism, this world could have not existed. That's the thought that prepares the mind for religion. Of course it may be a wrong thought, but if it's a right thought, then it seems that there must be this crucial difference between the world and God in virtue of which the riddle set by the world can be answered by God. God must be necessary in the sense that he could not have not existed. So, God being metaphysically necessary is him not depending for his existence in any sense on anything, not being able not to exist. As I say, while all theists are agreed on this, there is some disagreement over how this 'ontological independence', this 'could not have not existed' property, is to be understood. Some say it's a logical necessity. Most say that it's a metaphysical necessity and, for reasons I'll explain more fully in discussing the failures of the Ontological Argument in due course, I think we should follow majority opinion here.[8]

To sum up then: God is perfectly free in that—perhaps inter alia—he can bring about whatever it is that he wishes, which entails that he must be perfectly good, never being able to do for his creatures anything other than the best action (whenever there is one) or one of the joint best actions (whenever two or more are equally good and there is none better). It is only because we are less than all-powerful and less than all-knowledgeable that it is a power for us to be able to be less than perfectly good; God's omnipotence and omniscience perfect his freedom, removing what would be for him the liability of being able to be less than perfectly good. God's omnipotence also entails that there is nothing on which he in any sense depends; in this sense, then, he is necessary. The properties of perfect freedom, perfect goodness, and necessity are coherent and substantial too. Further, they too seem to flow from the properties we've already discussed.

◆ ◆ ◆

As I have talked about the essential properties of God, then, you will have noticed that they are very far from being conceptually autonomous. As I got further on in my list of properties, rather than simply elucidating what theists understand by these properties, I started arguing why it is that God needs to have those properties, given the properties that I had already discussed. In this chapter, I argued that being omnipotent and omniscient entail God being perfectly free—these properties entail that there is nothing that constrains God's actions (no external power that can trump his will and no ignorance that can misdirect it). Given his perfect freedom, I argued, he cannot but be perfectly good, for he can never have any incentive to do anything less than perfectly good; his omnipotence entails that he can fulfil his obligations and do the best possible thing for his creatures (whenever there is one) or one of the joint best (whenever two or more are equally good and none better); and his omniscience that he knows what this is/these are. I might have argued in the other direction: in order to be perfectly good, God must be omnipotent—so that he will always be able to do what is morally perfect, and omniscient—so that he will always know what to do. This then could have led me back to transcendence and immanence. In order to be omnipotent and omniscient God cannot depend on anything—including any physical thing—for his knowledge; nor can any physical thing be beyond his direct control. He must be both transcendent and immanent in space and time. God's omnipotence also entails that everything depends on him for its existence and he depends on nothing for his, so he is in that sense necessary and if he's necessary, then again he must be eternal—there cannot be anything that could cause him to cease to exist so he must either be outside time or inside time but necessarily everlasting, the two different views theists have on the divine property of eternality.

In fact then, one might say that my argument has shown that God only has one essential property—his being the most perfect person that there could be—and the nine properties that I've been talking about are best seen as merely facets of this property of divinity. From a proper understanding of what it would be to be the most perfect person that there could be, one would be able to derive all the traditional essential attributes of God. One might add to this claim that the divine nature is unitary the claim that it is also in itself simple. Although I hope it won't, I fear that the fact that I endorse the view that God's nature is simple as well as unitary might come as rather a surprise. If the divine nature is so simple, why did I divide it up into nine aspects and take three chapters to talk about it?

Something's being unitary and simple does not entail that it will always appear unitary and simple when one writes or reads about it in a book. Rather, the sort of unity and simplicity in question is like that associated with beauty in metamathematics.

Imagine that, instead of reading this book, you'd decided to read an introductory book on Gödel's Second Incompleteness Theorem, as you'd heard that it might have some interesting applications in the philosophy of mind. So it is that you are sitting with this other book in front of you, reading someone going through the argument step by step. Unfortunately, despite this author's best efforts, it's all looking frightfully complicated to you. It's as if the whole argument lies beneath a mist, which only occasionally lifts over the section that happens to be being talked about by the author at the time. When it lifts, then—for an instant or two—you see that part of the argument that the author is currently talking about more or less clearly, but even then it still looks oddly complicated; you can discern how its parts relate to one another, but their purpose in a larger whole remains incomprehensible. Each time the author moves on, the details of the section previously discussed become fuzzy in your recollection and, by the time the fog lifts over the next section, it has well and truly closed over the previous one. You are about to give up and go back to reading my book; even it wasn't as unhelpful as this, you think. Suddenly however—perhaps as the result of a chance comment, example, or analogy that the author uses, or perhaps for no obvious reason at all—the mist lifts over the whole. The outlines of the whole argument become—maybe only for a moment—visible at once in your mind's eye and visibly the whole argument works. You see, albeit impressionistically, how the parts that seemed to you oddly complicated when considered in isolation in fact form a simple structure when you do that which previously you could not manage, consider them together. As you focus down on one section of the argument again, the rest clouds over once more, but you know now that you've seen the whole, albeit imperfectly and fleetingly, and that as a whole it is indeed—as the author insisted on telling you it was—simple.

The theistic conception of God is the conception of a being whose essence is unitary and simple. The first three chapters of this book have been an extended argument to the effect that it is only the partial understanding forced on us by our finite minds that introduces apparent complexities, apparent complexities that require the sort of philosophy of religion that I've undertaken in those chapters, the sort of philosophy of religion that divides this divine nature up artificially into more manageable sections; does its best to remove any confusions we might have in our understanding of these sections; and then seeks to put them back together again, it is hoped, enabling us to see them now as facets of the one simple property, divinity; enabling us to see the central theistic claim that there is a God clearly, and see that this claim is, in itself, a coherent, substantial, and simple one. Well, as I say, that's what I've been trying to do in the first three chapters. How successful I've been is up to you to judge. It's now time for me to move on.

4

Creator of the World, Creator of Value

You'll remember that as well as agreeing over the essential properties of God, theists are also agreed that he has these accidental properties: he has the property of being creator of the world (that is to say the physical universe plus any non-physical things (other than himself) that might exist, e.g. souls or angels, if there are any); he has the property of being the creator of value for us; he has the property of having revealed himself to us; and he has the property of having offered us everlasting life.[1] Theists view these properties as accidental properties of God in virtue of the essential property of God that is his perfect freedom: God might have chosen not to create a world, but rather have remained the sole existent thing, in which case he would not have had the property of being creator, although, strictly speaking, he would still have created everything other than himself. But had he not created a world, there would have been no one for whom he could generate value, so he would not have had the property of being the creator of value; there would have been no one to whom he could reveal himself, so he would not have had the property of being a revealer; and there would have been no one to whom he could offer everlasting life, so he would not have had the property of offerer of everlasting life. Despite their being accidental, all theists are agreed that God has these four properties, and in this chapter and the next I'm going to talk about each of them in turn, explaining what theists mean when they ascribe these properties to God and showing why it's no accident that all theists are agreed in so ascribing them. In this chapter, I'll be talking about God as creator of the natural world and the values within it. In the next chapter, I'll move on to look at God as revealer and offerer of everlasting life.

PROPERTY TEN: CREATOR OF THE WORLD

Theists see God as the creator of the world. The traditional theistic—as opposed to deistic—view is that God did not just create the world in the sense of starting it off, as someone might create a firework display by lighting the blue touchpaper and retiring. Rather, God creates the world in the sense of keeping it in being from moment to moment, rather as someone might create a dance by moving his or her body. Indeed, if what I have said about the world being God's body is right, the dance analogy is a very close one. God's creatordom amounts not simply to his being that without which the world could never have started. He is that without which the world—even had it started without him (as is of course impossible on theism) or had it been there for ever (as the current consensus among scientists suggests it has not)—could not continue to exist. The world depends ultimately on God's will for its existence and its character as expressed in the natural laws that govern the behaviour of its constituents. Were God to have willed that no universe exist, none would have existed; were he to have willed that a universe governed by different natural laws existed instead, then that universe would have existed instead.

On theism, whereas God is metaphysically necessary, in virtue of God's omnipotence, everything else must be metaphysically contingent. The property of creatordom states simply the relation that must therefore obtain between God (if he exists) and anything else that there might be. I am using the concept of creatordom here in a sense rather more restricted than it would be used in everyday life, one which might be captured by the phrase 'ultimate creatordom'.[2] For X to be the ultimate creator of Y is for Y to be dependent on X and nothing else more ultimately for its existence and character. Thus for X to be the ultimate creator of Y requires more than for Y simply to depend on X for its existence and character. You depend on your parents for your existence and (largely, through your genes and, in most cases, upbringing) for your character. But your parents in turn depended on a great many things for their existence and character, your grandparents for example. As such, we might call your parents 'non-ultimate creators'; your grandparents were non-ultimate creators too, though they were obviously more ultimate than your parents—your parents depended on your grandparents for their existence, but your grandparents didn't similarly depend on your parents. In virtue of God's omnipotence, any non-ultimate creator must depend ultimately on God for his or her existence and character and in particular for the 'creative' powers that he or she has; and thus nothing is ultimately created by anything other than God—in the sense of dependent for its existence and character on something other than God and on nothing else more ultimately. God himself, in virtue of his omnipotence, is dependent on nothing for his existence and character; a fortiori, he is dependent on nothing else more ultimately for his existence and character.

Given God's omnipotence, everything other than God must ultimately depend for its existence and character on his willing it; thus he must be the ultimate creator of everything other than himself. That God is in this sense creator is an accidental property of God in that God need not have created anything and had he not created anything, then he himself would have been the only thing that existed and thus nothing that existed would have had the property of ontological dependence, of being—in any sense—a creation. But, on theism, if anything other than God exists, it must have the property of being ultimately ontologically dependent on him (due to his essential property of omnipotence).

So, it is no accident that all theists believe that God has the property of being creator even though it's an accidental property. Given that there's a God (who's omnipotent), it's logically necessary that anything else that exists be ultimately created by him, even though given that there's a God (who's perfectly free) it's not logically necessary that there be anything else.

As well as living in a world that we discover through observation and experiment operates according to natural laws, we also live in a world in which we discover, through a rather different sort of observation and experiment, that certain things are good for us and certain things are bad and that in the light of this we are obliged to follow various principles of conduct. Of course, not every philosopher believes that there is objective value of this sort (and that it can be accessed in this way), but almost every non-philosopher does and, I have argued, we think they're right. The theist says that God is perfectly good, that he perfectly fulfils the moral ideal that these observations and experiments reveal more or less accurately to us. So should theists say that these moral principles, like the laws of nature, depend ultimately for their existence and character on God's creative will, that he perfectly fulfils an ideal that he himself has created? Or should they say that these moral principles are not ultimately dependent for their existence and character on his will, that he perfectly fulfils a standard that is not of his own creation? Most theists say the former and I'm going to argue that they're right to do so.

PROPERTY ELEVEN: CREATOR OF VALUE

We live in a world where some actions, objects, and states of affairs are more valuable than others, and they are valuable in different ways. Mussolini's son-in-law once wrote with some feeling about the beauty of a bomb exploding among a crowd of Ethiopians; and *Triumph of the Will* has moments of greatness. But whatever the aesthetic or artistic merits of these things, neither reveals any moral value; indeed they obscure it. Mother Teresa—though she certainly made mistakes—was perhaps the greatest person of our age, morally speaking. But she was not as beautiful as any of a host of Hollywood actresses. Beauty may be a symbol of the good, but it is not the same as or coextensive with it. So there is moral value and there is aesthetic value; sometimes these things go together and sometimes they do not.

Within the differing domains of moral and aesthetic value, there are differing axes of appraisal too. Sitting one's child on one's knee and reading to him or her is a nice thing to do; holding a disbelieving adult by the shoulders and telling him or her that his or her child has died and that doctors would like to use the child's organs to save the lives of others is not a nice thing to do. Both actions could be equally morally good, but if so they would be equally morally good for very different reasons. This is revealed (though not generated) by the fact that one would naturally (and should) enjoy reading one's child a story; one would not naturally (and shouldn't) enjoy telling someone bad news, however important it is for that person to know that news. *The Mona Lisa* is beautiful; Francis Bacon's *Three Studies for Figures at the Base of a Crucifixion* is demanding. Perhaps both works are of equal aesthetic value, but in any case what value they have is not generated in the same way: Leonardo's work has aesthetic value in part because of its calm beauty; Bacon's in part because of its terrifying ugliness. One could naturally (and should) enjoy looking at Leonardo's work; we wouldn't believe that anyone who claimed to have enjoyed looking at Bacon's work had actually seen them.

So we live in a world where there are numerous, complex, and very different sorts of values attached to actions, objects, and states of affairs. Reflection on this may make these value facts seem queer to us in at least one sense: these value facts cannot be measured or tested in the same way that facts of the sort that scientists deal with can be measured and tested. Of course, the same reflection might lead one in the other direction, as it were. Isn't it queer that facts of the sort that scientists deal with can be measured and tested by the means that scientists employ when value facts, to which we are exposed as directly in our everyday lives, cannot? When the differences between value facts and scientific facts are pointed out, rather than its being value facts to which I incline to attach the label 'queer', it's scientific facts. But it is I who am rather queer in this respect. Upon reflection, most people incline to think of value facts as the queer ones and however queer or non-queer they might seem, it is natural to ask the question of them: where do they come from?

According to theists, the ultimate answer to this question is God. You had to expect that it would be; according to theists, God's the ultimate answer to any question. I am reminded of the story of the Sunday School lesson where the teacher is asking her class what she thinks of as an easy question, but the children are just looking more and more puzzled as she tries to make the answer more and more obvious to them:

'Who's the person who delivers letters to your door each morning? Come on, you know. The person who comes up your garden path each morning and puts the post through your letter box. Let's suppose he's a man. So he's a man who delivers your post. He's a . . .? Think about it. If he was a man who delivered just letters, we might call him a 'Letterman', but he delivers post in general so we call him a . . .?'

One child's hand is finally raised.

'Yes, little Johnny, do you know?'

Little Johnny tentatively replies, 'Well Miss, it's Sunday School so I know that the answer must be Jesus, but it does sound awfully like the postman.'

As well as being the creator of facts of the sort that scientists deal with in the sense that were it not for God's willing them, none of the natural laws that scientists uncover would be as they are, so God is the creator of facts about value in the sense that were it not for his willing them, none of the moral principles that we believe we should live our lives by would be as they are; neither would any aesthetic facts be as they are. Without God nothing would be good or bad, beautiful or ugly, funny or humourless. If it's stylistically awkward of me to interrupt a philosophical discussion of God's relation to value by levering-in a rather simple-minded joke about a Sunday School lesson, then that's because God's made it so. If the joke's nevertheless a pretty good one, then that's because God's made it so too. A nice simple view then. Just as by his creative will God generates the natural laws that govern how atoms and the like behave, so by his creative will he has laid down the principles which govern how it is in various ways good for people to behave.

But this view seems to generate a problem. It seems to imply that had God's will been different (and there can have been no pre-existent principle ensuring that it would not be), he could have distributed values entirely differently from the way we actually find them distributed. But it seems that if that were true, he could have made our world be one where torturing small Labrador puppies by wiring them up to car batteries was morally obligatory. Without affecting any other fact, he could have just stripped the property of moral badness off torturing puppies and replaced it with the property of moral goodness. He could have made *Macbeth* a delightful comedy of manners, except for the Butler scene, which would have become, let's say, a sincere and serious exploration of alcoholism among the Scottish working classes. Leaving all the dialogue and stage directions as they are, he could have stripped out the property of being a tragedy and replaced it with that of being a comedy of manners. And these sorts of consequences of the view are implausible enough to be sufficient reason to reject it. We can just see that there's no possible world where torturing puppies is good and where *Macbeth* is a comedy of manners. So, we can't understand God as standing in a relation to value such that he could create such a world. That, in any case, is often presented as a reason to reject the view that God creates all value, the view that I'm advancing.

Another putative reason to reject the view that I am advancing is that the property of being good will, on this account, simply amount to the property of being how God wills one to be, so the claim that God is good will turn out to be the claim that God is as he wills himself to be, which doesn't seem a substantial enough fact to act as a reason for praising him. The same argument may be made for aesthetic value. In virtue of a property that I have yet to do more than mention, that God offers us everlasting life, theists are committed to thinking that some of us at least are destined to enjoy an eternity of bliss in his presence, appreciating what in Christian theology is usually called 'The Beatific Vision' (though the same idea appears under different titles in the traditions of Judaism and Islam); the idea is that after death we will see God 'face to face'. The Beatific Vision is supposed to be supremely beautiful in a sense that if not literally the same as one might use when describing a Hollywood actress is at least analogous to it. Indeed only thus can the promise of The Beatific Vision be a reason for unreserved hope rather than for—in part at least—resignation. We should look forward to it as something that will delight us with its beauty, rather than treat the prospect of it with aesthetic indifference. But if God creates what is beautiful by arbitrary acts of his will, then the claim that he himself will appear beautiful to us when we see him in heaven amounts to the claim that The Beatific Vision will be of God as he wills himself to be, which again seems necessarily true and thus hardly a reason for us to adopt any particular attitude towards it.

These two worries have been sufficient to drive many philosophers of religion away from the theory that most theists are pre-reflectively drawn to adopt, that God creates value. Should they have done so? Let's look at the obvious alternative, that things are good or bad, beautiful or ugly, independently of God's will. This looks even worse. On such an account, God is not the source of all value and thus he can no longer be thought of as that on which all other things depend. On this view, there is something—indeed presumably the thing of overriding importance—that is independent of him, value. Value is ontologically prior to God; not everything other than God depends on God's will; and thus 'God' is not the ultimate answer to every question. If we then persist with the natural tendency to ask 'Where do these values come from?', the answer won't be 'God', it will have to be something else, something that is in some sense more ultimate than God and to posit something more ultimate than God seems straightforwardly incompatible with theism. To say that they don't come from anywhere, that they too are ultimate, is to posit something as ultimate as God, which again seems straightforwardly incompatible with theism. Now this seeming straightforward incompatibility isn't fatal to the view in that, were it to turn out that a God with all the essential properties we have hitherto looked at existed but that this being did not in fact create fundamental moral truths, this wouldn't—it seems—be a sufficient reason for one to deny that this being is God; he would still have all the essential properties, after all. And so, this way out of the problem doesn't seem, upon reflection, barred to the theist. Nevertheless, let us return to the view that I'm suggesting theists should take, that God creates value, and let us focus on God's creation of moral value. The points I make could be applied *mutatis mutandis* to aesthetic value and indeed any other realm of value that one believes exists, but the issues are more clearly focused by thought experimentation if we concentrate on moral value.

◆ ◆ ◆

Some things that we say are good and bad we know to be such merely due to the nature of the concepts under which they are picked out—suffering, for example. Whenever there is suffering—whether in people; human beings who are not people; or animals who are not human beings—it is bad. We wouldn't call it suffering if it wasn't. Its badness arises of conceptual necessity simply by virtue of its being suffering. Inducing suffering might not be the worst thing that one could do to someone. If someone would benefit greatly from being told a painful truth, then telling them that truth might be the best thing to do, but that learning this truth would involve their suffering would in itself be a bad feature of what it was that it was best to do. One should in such circumstances 'soften the blow' as much as is compatible with still conveying the truth. Some things are good or bad for people as a conceptual necessity arising from the fact that they are people. The essence of personhood, as we have seen, involves the having of beliefs, and the concept of belief necessitates that persons want true beliefs. Of conceptual necessity, one cannot go about acquiring beliefs save by thinking that one is acquiring them in a way that makes them more likely to be true than false because beliefs just are those mental occurrences one takes to be true representations of the world. So it's not a logically contingent feature of people that we aim at true beliefs. We cannot but think that true beliefs are good for people. If this is right, then we cannot but think that it is of necessity always in itself bad to lie to people, i.e. try to get people to have false beliefs. Lying to someone might not always be the worst thing possible. If someone comes to your door asking after the whereabouts of a person whom you know they intend to murder and whom you also know is hiding in your attic, lying to this would-be murderer might be the best of the options available to you. But it would in itself be bad; ideally, you would have the power to tell the would-be murderer the truth, yet argue him or her round from murder. If you lie to someone, then, in that aspect of your relationship to him or her, you fail to fully respect his or her personhood; by deceiving someone you do something that in itself frustrates his or her flourishing as entailed merely by the fact that he or she is a person, and this is in itself of necessity bad.

So one can come up with concepts that apply to things that are bad of conceptual necessity. Suffering would be one example. One can come up with concepts that apply to things that are bad of conceptual necessity for people: lying; murdering; raping; and stealing from them would be examples. Badness (or badness for people) is part of the content of these concepts in the same way that maleness is part of the concept of bachelorhood. Things that instantiate these concepts are of logical necessity bad for people and thus they are bad for people in any universe in which they may be picked out by these concepts, just as things that instantiate the concept bachelor are of logical necessity male and thus they are male in any universe in which they may be picked out by this concept. Not even God could make a universe in which the things that may be picked out by these concepts are good for people for the same reason that not even God could make a universe where the people who may be picked-out by the concept of bachelor are female.

But as well as these sorts of moral concepts, some concepts pick out things that are bad for people via contingent features that people happen—universally but not essentially—to have. As it happens, all people in this world have the property of suffering terribly if a large amount of electricity is passed through their bodies; this being so, it is a universal truth that it's bad to pass this amount of electricity through people. Penultimately, some things are bad for people because of contingent features that they happen not universally (nor a fortiori essentially) to have. It is necessary that it is in itself bad to make people uncomfortable (that's what 'uncomfortable' means—a negative, i.e. bad, state of comfort) but it is contingent and very variable which ways of greeting people, for example, cause them to feel uncomfortable. What strikes people as an overly familiar form of greeting depends on culture and circumstance. One human society might construct the code that kissing someone full on the lips was an acceptable way of greeting someone one had not met before; another might construct the code that it was not, but that shaking hands was to be preferred. These, what are sometimes called, 'minor morals' are objective only in a weaker sense than that I sketched before when discussing objectivism: they are independent of anyone's beliefs or attitudes but not of everyone's beliefs and attitudes. As such, minor morals change with time, context, and culture. Finally, there are matters of personal preference. As it happens, I prefer leisurely and non-strenuous walks in the countryside to jogging. Thus it would be better for me were a group whose company I am somewhat socially obligated to keep to converge on the plan of spending the afternoon by taking a leisurely and short walk (ideally, to a pub for a beer) in the countryside, rather than spending it by jogging to a health club some miles away for a mineral water. (For this example to work, one has to push to the back of one's mind the relative benefits to my health that jogging and drinking mineral water might bring me, something I sadly find relatively easy to do.)

I have argued that (with the caveat concerning 'minor morals' and matters of personal preference just given) we see ethical statements about the world as true or false independently of facts about any and every person's attitudes. But it seems that they are not all true or false independently of facts about persons qua the biological organisms they happen contingently to be. And given that on theism persons exist as the biological organisms they happen contingently to be only as a result of God's creative will, then, on theism, any ethical statement of substance (i.e. one that uses a moral concept to say something about the world rather than to say something about itself) depends for its truth on God's will. For example, the truth of the statement expressed by the sentence, 'If there are organisms that have a constitution such that passing a certain electric current through their bodies causes them to suffer, then it is in itself bad to pass that electric current through their bodies' is not dependent on God's will, but this independence isn't any restriction on God's sovereignty—it's just a conceptual truth generated from the fact that suffering is by definition something that is in itself bad. Whether the antecedent of this conditional (the 'there are organisms that have a constitution such that passing an electric current through their bodies causes them to suffer' bit) is true does depend on God's will (he's entirely free over whether or not to create any such creatures). Thus all substantive moral truths (as opposed to conceptual necessities of this hypothetical form) depend on God's will in creation. An analogy will help us in drawing these strands together.

◆ ◆ ◆

Let us imagine that we are creating a board game. Supposing that we have already made the pieces and the board, there will still be decisions to be made about the rules. The same pieces and board might be used for several different games. However, if we have already made the pieces and the board, then the rules open for us to choose between will be to some extent constrained by their natures. For example, supposing us to have made only four pieces, we would not be able to choose the rule, 'The game must have at least six players, of whom each should start with an unshared piece.' This is a logical consequence of the number of pieces we have contingently made, not a contingent one. It is logically necessary that if there are only four pieces, then six people cannot have one unshared piece each. It is contingent whether there are only four pieces. The pattern on the board will similarly constrain our choice of rules. If in creating our game we are starting from scratch, with no pieces or board as yet, then the only principles constraining us are what might be called the 'bare principles of logic'—for example that cheating cannot be an acceptable way to win the game—and these principles are, I have suggested, not properly thought of as constraints at all.

Thus it was with God's creation of morality. Prior to the creation of humans and the universe, the pieces and the board, if we assume for the sake of simplicity (what is false) that there are no non-human people or animals that count morally, the only principles that constrained him in what morality he could create were the 'bare principles of logic', i.e. he was under no constraint at all. He couldn't create a world where terrible suffering was good, but that's because it's logically impossible that terrible suffering be good. Having created people as humans, with the contingent physiology that they have, this entailed that passing a certain electric current through their bodies would always in itself be bad as it would always produce terrible suffering (natural law-violating miracles aside), which is something that is in itself of conceptual necessity bad. Creating people as humans was his creating the fact that it's bad to pass a large electric current through them. This is analogous to the maker of a game who has created a certain number of pieces or a style of board that constrains the rules he or she might then choose in that it is a logically necessary consequence of a contingent fact. (It is logically necessary that if passing a certain electric current through people's bodies produces terrible suffering, then it is in itself bad to pass that amount of electricity through people's bodies.) When it comes to the minor-morals of the universe that he creates, God is in the position of the maker of the game who has made the pieces and the board and now can choose between a number of different rules. Thus, were he to want to, he could make kissing or shaking hands on various occasions obligatory for human people without performing natural-law-violating miracles or affecting human nature at all.

We are now in a position to see as misguided the objection that seeing moral truths as part of God's creation entails that God could make torturing puppies good. The account does not entail this. Torture is of logical necessity bad and thus not even God could make it good. Anything one can successfully pick out under the concept *torture* must be a bad thing, just as anything one can successfully pick out under the concept *bachelor* must be a male person. Demanding that we say that God could make torture good would be like demanding that we say he could make a female bachelor. God could certainly have made or could yet make passing an electric current of a certain amount—an amount that actually has always caused and will always cause excruciating agony in any creature—through a puppy's body good. Were God to have created puppies with a different biological construction or now change their biological properties by some natural law-violating miracle, then passing a large electric current through their bodies would have been or could become good, morally acceptable, or even obligatory. But then of course it would no longer be torture. There is nothing counter-intuitive about this. After all, a magician can make 'sawing a lady in half' good, morally acceptable, or obligatory (supposing him to have freely entered into a contract to 'saw a lady in half' as a part of his show) *if* he can make it not have the consequences it would usually be expected to have in humans. (Of course he couldn't make literally sawing a lady in half not have these consequences, which is why I needed the scare quotes; to do that he really would have to be a magician.) It's no accident that we applaud the magician who 'saws the lady in half' *only when* we see that the lady is alive and well.

What of the objection that such an account would rob us of the possibility of substantively saying of God that he is good and thus of the possibility of providing a reason for us to praise him? The argument here was that if one were to make the substance of morality contingent upon God's action in creation, as we have done, then to say that he is good would merely be to say that he acts as he acts, which would seem necessarily true and thus hardly a reason for us to hold any particular attitude towards him, such as gratitude rather than resentment or praise rather than blame.

We have seen that given that God created us as human people, there are some things that are contingently good and bad for us and there are some moral principles that dictate how, as a contingent matter of fact, we ought to act towards other people and how they ought to act towards us. One's freely choosing to be good in one's relationships with people, one's conforming these relationships to these principles, is what makes one worthy of praise. That God's perfect freedom makes him necessarily choose to be perfectly good in his relationships with people does not then in any way detract from our reasons for praising him. There is nothing insubstantial about a claim that the maker of the game is also the best, indeed a perfect, player.

If God creates all values, then it is true that prior to his creation, there are no substantive principles to constrain his choices. However, this does not mean that he could choose to create a world in which torture was good, for this would be logically impossible. Neither does it mean that he could choose to create a world in which persons were destined to be eternally frustrated in their flourishing: the maker of the game of Monopoly could not make Monopoly pieces that could not be used to play Monopoly. It follows from the understanding of personhood that I sketched in an earlier chapter that to view someone as a person is—of logical necessity—to view them as someone to whom one must show moral respect, which entails that one is obliged not to frustrate them unnecessarily in their flourishing, just as to view a given chunk of metal as a Monopoly piece is— of logical necessity—to view it as something one can only use in a particular way in the context of a game of Monopoly. Just as when the maker of a game perfectly plays that game, he or she must—of logical necessity—use the pieces in accordance with the rules he or she has freely created (to do otherwise would be to cheat or play a different game), so we may rest assured that if there is a God, a perfect player of the game he has created, he will not allow anything to frustrate people's ultimate flourishing.

This brings us to the final two properties on my list of divine properties, the property God has of being a revealer and the property he has of offering us everlasting life. We'll look at them in the next chapter.

5

Revealer, Offerer of Eternal Life

PROPERTY TWELVE: REVEALER

As well as believing that God created this world and indeed any parallel universes there might be, theists also believe that God has taken steps to ensure that we who exist in this world are not left in total ignorance of his existence and will; he has revealed himself to us in the world that he has created. While theists are all agreed that God has the property of being a revealer of truths, especially of truths concerning himself and his will, the proponents of the particular theistic religions disagree to some extent about what truths these are. Theists agree that throughout history, prophets, theologians, and institutions have been used by God to convey truths concerning himself and that God has directly spoken to individuals or groups of individuals, for example to Moses on Mount Sinai. The things theists largely (but not entirely) disagree on are who have been the prophets; who the best theologians; which the divinely appointed institutions; and when it has been God speaking. Is the Pope infallible when he speaks ex cathedra on matters of faith and doctrine? If you had the Reverend Ian Paisley and Cardinal Ratzinger in the room with you now, you would be listening to two very different answers, each being shouted with equal confidence.

Why is it that theists are agreed that God has chosen to reveal himself and his will to us? Fortunately, we don't need to look too far to find the answer to this. We have seen already that we think that to believe the truth is good for people qua people; in itself it aids their flourishing. And it is obvious that the goodness of a true belief is proportional to the importance of the truth in question. There's a truth about whether or not there are the same number of words containing the letter 'z' in this book as there are chapters. Let's suppose that there are. There's also a truth about whether or not reading this book to the end would advance you on the path to everlasting spiritual fulfilment. Let's suppose that it would. One of these truths—our intuition tells us—is more important for you to believe than the other. Why? At least a part of the reason is that one has more implications for how you should behave than the other. If it's true that there are the same number of words containing the letter 'z' in this book as there are chapters, that's not a reason for you to do anything. If it's true that reading this book to the end would advance you on the path to everlasting spiritual fulfilment, that's a reason for you to read it to the end. On theism, God has chosen to reveal himself and his will to us because it's important for us to know about them so that we will know how we should behave.

The theist is best advised to say that we can access some of the truths about what values God has created and thus how we should behave independently of the fact that it is God who has created them—'It's always bad to wire puppies up to car batteries' would be an example. This is equally obvious to atheists, agnostics, and theists. No revelation is needed because it's obvious that wiring puppies up to car batteries causes them terrible suffering, something which is obviously (because of obvious conceptual necessity) in itself bad. But according to theism some values we cannot access independently of revelation because there is nothing intrinsic to the actions in question that explains the value: these activities don't benefit or harm anyone due to any intrinsic property or properties they happen to have. These are the actions that it is good (or bad) to do only because subsequent to his act of creation God has commanded that we do (or not do) them. This naturally raises the question, why would God command that we do (or not do) them if there is nothing intrinsic in them to merit his doing so? The answer: as ways of showing gratitude to him.

It is good for people to show gratitude to their benefactors. This is a necessary truth deriving from what it is to be a person. Where a person has chosen to benefit us in some way, we would be failing to treat them as a person were we not to acknowledge this fact with thanks, and thus, given that persons are inter alia also those who show moral respect for other persons, we would be diminishing our own selves as persons were we not to do so. Most often, we may show our gratitude to our benefactors by doing something for them in return. Perhaps—especially when the benefit is relatively small—we simply say, 'Thank you'. When the benefit is relatively large, we might say a more elaborate thank you or seek to help them in turn with some project of their own that they will find easier with our assistance. If there is a God, then he's at least as great a benefactor as any human could ever be. If there's a God, then in virtue of the property of creatordom, he's ultimately responsible for our continued existence from moment to moment. So, if our lives are overall good enough for it to be reasonable for us to wish that they not end, we should be grateful to him; we should seek to express our gratitude to him in some way. So how can we express our gratitude to God?

Let's try to think of an analogous situation to help guide our intuitions. One problem is that there will be no worldly situation where someone has greatly benefited us and yet there is nothing that they need in return; there'll always be something that any worldly agent needs. But for many people one's parents will—at least at the early stages of one's life—meet this condition for all practical purposes, as they will be one's greatest worldly benefactors and yet there will be nothing they need that one can provide. Most people, as young children, have no resources save those that their parents provide. It would be good for one to show one's gratitude to one's parents for their love towards one, but there is nothing that would be good for them that one can in any way assist them in achieving. As a young child one can (if one has developed a sufficient competence in the right language) inform one's parents that one is grateful to them, but—beyond that—one cannot *do* anything to express this gratitude and it would be good for one if one did. Why? Because only so can one fully express oneself to them as a person, can one reciprocate their love. A great benefactor with no needs that one can oneself meet has therefore good reason to generate a way in which one can show gratitude to him or her. Were a great benefactor of yours to say, 'As a mark of your gratitude to me, sing songs on Sundays,' you should follow his or her command. Before he or she asked you to do this, it would have been morally neutral—I'm supposing—whether or not you spent some of your Sunday singing songs rather than, say, washing your car, but now that he or she has asked you to sing as a mark of gratitude, you should do so. It's good for you to show gratitude to your benefactors; this benefactor needed nothing from you; there was nothing that would be good for him or her that he or she did not already have; so he or she generated a means by which you could show your gratitude and thus do what was good for you: express yourself as a person in relation to him or her. If there were a God, he could and should generate value in at least this way in virtue of his being the ultimate benefactor, the person without whom no other benefits could ever be received. If there were a God, he thus would have good reason to give us avenues by which we can express our gratitude to him, and to give them to us he must reveal them to us. It might seem that he would not be perfectly respecting us as persons if he didn't.[1]

Now, this isn't, it might reasonably be suggested, a very *strong* reason for God to reveal himself to us, much less an overwhelming one. If God can come up with some arbitrary symbolic acts by which we may express our gratitude to him, so, in the absence of him doing so (or even merely obviously doing so), we could equally well come up with such practices; perhaps, we might think, many individual hermits do in fact come up with their own, very heterogeneous, ways of making their 'sacrifices' to God and God is going to find *any* such well-intentioned act (that does not itself violate moral principles) equally acceptable to those acts, if any, which he himself has explicitly sanctioned via revelation. Even the more minimal claim that God must, if we are to be properly motivated in generating such practices ourselves, at least let us know that he is ultimately responsible for the goods of our lives might seem questionable. In the human context, one can do a good for someone without being blameworthy if one deliberately keeps one's identity as their benefactor secret from them. But while questionable, I suggest that in fact parallels from human-to-human interaction fail to establish that in itself it is not always bad to hide one's identity as a benefactor from those whom one has benefited, even if they do establish that very often (on theism necessarily) there are good moral reasons for humans—reasons that may in practice amount to overall moral reason—for one to do this thing that is in itself bad. In so far as one could reveal one's identity as a benefactor to someone one had benefited without directly or indirectly depriving that person or others—including oneself—of other goods, so one should reveal oneself to that person as their benefactor as not doing so deprives them of the good of expressing their gratitude to a person who is deserving of it, oneself, something that would in itself be good for them to do. But of course someone's expressing gratitude to one increases the risk that one will become big-headed, something that in itself would be bad, and detracts (albeit, we might reasonably posit, not much) from the time and energy that this person will have available to express their gratitude to God, something that—on theism—it is even more important that they do. Thus it is no accident that finite humans are instructed by all monotheistic religions in the benefits of anonymous benefaction; thus the gratitude felt by the recipient is more likely to go straight to God, rather than lodge on the worthy-but-not-as-worthy human agent who acts in such cases as a conduit of God's goodness.

I've been arguing that if there's a God, then that he exists and that he has asked that we do this rather than that to express our gratitude to him is extremely important for people in assessing what is good for us, and so believing truths about it is consequently very good for us. Only if we know that God exists will we know that we should express gratitude to him as our ultimate benefactor. Only if we know how he has asked us to express this gratitude can we do so in the way that is best (or at least joint best—to cater for the 'hermit' point of the previous paragraph). And because there is nothing intrinsic to the ways in which we can express gratitude to him that tells us how we should do so, he needs to reveal that this is his will for us if we are to be reasonable in doing these things. This is why all theists must see God as a revealer. But this train of thought cannot but lead one to ask, 'Why doesn't God therefore make it more clear than he has done both that he exists and how it is that he has commanded us to show gratitude to him?' I've argued in the penultimate paragraph that the reasons God has to reveal that he exists and reveal how it is that he has commanded us to show gratitude to him aren't overwhelming reasons, but they're still reasons and, in the absence of counter-vailing reasons, he'd unambiguously act on them. So what countervailing reasons might there be?

◆ ◆ ◆

As we saw in discussing the property of omniscience as it pertains to perfect freedom, not believing the right things about what descriptions one's actions will satisfy reduces one's freedom in performing those actions—it means one might bodge things up. So freedom in choosing to do something requires a certain amount of true belief about that thing. But, as we have also seen, on theism, for creatures other than God and for freedom to choose to be less than perfect, it also requires ignorance of the truth of theism. To preserve this power of ours, God

must therefore ensure that there is some 'epistemic distance' between his creatures and the truth of theism and the nature of his will for us.

It would be good for God to reveal his existence and will to people (as these
are very important matters for us), but for him to make this revelation one that
was absolutely cognitively inescapable would be to remove our freedom to
choose to do less than is perfect, something that is also good for us. If tomorrow
we woke up knowing with perfect certainty—with not even a shadow of a
doubt—of God's existence and will for us at every instant, then we would no
longer be able to choose to be anything but perfectly good; we would no longer
have any freedom to choose to do that which we knew to be less than perfect.
Given that we would no longer be free to choose to do that which we knew to be
less than perfect, we would have lost something that was in itself good—a
power—for us to have had. But we would have gained something that is in itself
good, a perfect revelation of what we should be. One might think then that
the best situation for us would be for us to live successively in two worlds, one
where we are free to choose to do what we know to be less than perfect and one
where that freedom is eliminated but we get the good of perfect revelation
instead. We cannot have our cake and eat it at the same time; but we can have
our cake at one time and then eat it later. Once we'd lost the freedom to do what
we know to be less than perfect we—obviously—could not choose to regain it;
we'd have lost precisely the ability to make such a choice. It would therefore be
impossible to respect our freedom while giving us the world of perfect revelation
first and the world of this sort of freedom later. So, if God wants to give us both
goods yet respect our freedom, he can only do so sequentially, putting us first in
a world where there is epistemic distance between us and the truth of theism and
the nature of his will (and thus we have the good of freedom to choose between
good and evil) and then moving us to the world of perfect revelation, a world
where we lose this freedom in the face of a perfect revelation of his existence and
will, perhaps (we shall return to this point in a moment) making this movement
dependent on our freely choosing to seek it.

God could have created a world with no creatures in it at all, or creatures of
such a low level of mental sophistication that none of them were people or even
closely approximated people and thus such that it would not have been any good
for them to know of his existence and will. If so, then obviously he need not have
had the property of revealer. That God has the property of being a revealer is
then again accidental (in virtue of his perfect freedom in creation), but it's
logically necessary (in virtue of his perfect goodness) *given* that he's created a
world with people in it, people being creatures for whom his existence and will is
significant and who would thus benefit from being able to know of them. If God
creates a world with people in it, then he must—in virtue of his perfect goodness;
its being good for people to believe the truth about important matters; and its
being important for people to express gratitude to their benefactors—offer them
means by which they can come to know of his existence and will; he must reveal

himself to them. However, if he wants to give people freedom of the sort discussed above, then, given the impossibility of our having such freedom in the full presence of God, he must allow us to start from a position of epistemic distance from the truth of theism. If we choose to investigate theism further, he should respect our choice and thus offer us ever-increasing communion with him, even to the point where we can no longer choose to depart from his company, but rather must remain with him forever, no longer free to choose to be other than what it is best for us to be. This brings me to the final property on my list.

PROPERTY THIRTEEN: OFFERER OF EVERLASTING LIFE

Theists are agreed that God offers us everlasting life with him in Heaven. There is much disagreement among theists over how widely this offer is extended; what if anything one needs to do in order to take advantage of it; and whether we will all ultimately accept the offer. But these disagreements are not disagreements about the concept of God or the nature of the offer. All agree that, for some at least, death is not the end; rather, it is just the beginning of an everlasting and blessed afterlife. Within Judaism, Christianity, and Islam, there is also a remarkable consensus as to the nature of this afterlife. There are two points which, while not universally held among theists, are very common.

First, there will be a Resurrection and consequently our post-mortem exist-ence will not be a disembodied existence; rather, it will be a spatio-temporal existence. It may be one where the relations possible in space-time as we know it are augmented, but it is certainly not one where they are diminished. It is worth stressing this as the increasingly large proportion of people brought up outside the context of any religion often have a very confused idea of the traditional theistic picture of the life hereafter. According to theism, our life in Heaven will not be a disembodied one or one where we float around as ethereal ghost-like figures. It will be an embodied one, where we eat, drink, and sing. Of course there will be intellectual, moral, emotional, and spiritual fulfilment, but there will also be physical fulfilment. Closely related to this, the doctrine of the afterlife within theism insists on our survival as individuals. It excludes claims, in so far as any sense can be apportioned to them, such as 'The soul returns to God at death like a drop to the ocean' in that, whatever else such a view may be taken to imply, it suggests some post-mortem absorption of persons into one being (or absence of being?) in such a way that it would not be us, as individuals, who would be in this state. In contrast, the person is envisaged by theists, in the final consummation with the divine that is achieved at death, as experiencing a complete realization of his or her true self as a result of that communion.

So progress in this life towards this happy conclusion may be variously described as an elevation or intensification of the person, but never an elimination or diminishing of him or her. The first point of general agreement among theists, then, is that the future life is in no sense ghostly or depersonalized. The only immortality that really interests us is *personal* immortality and the theistic hope—in so far as it is of interest—is thus a hope that something will happen to each of us as individual persons, after our deaths, when we are still individual persons, physically and psychologically distinct from others and capable of entering into meaningful relationships with them, indeed into more meaningful relationships with them and our God than we are ever able to here.

The second point of consensus among theists is that there will be a Last Judgement. We will be held to account in some sense for what we have done while on Earth. Those who have done good unrecognized by others will receive the recognition that is their due. Those who have done wrong and hitherto escaped punishment will receive it. After the Last Judgement, there will be a final division between those who go on from it to everlasting life in God's presence, Heaven; and those who go on to 'everlasting death' in his absence, Hell. Just as Heaven is a place of complete fulfilment for mind, body, and spirit, so Hell is a place of complete agony for mind, body, and spirit. This too often comes as a surprise to those brought up outside the context of a theistic religion. 'Surely, theists don't really still believe in this medieval picture of Hell, do they?' The answer is: 'Yes, they do.' I shall argue that they shouldn't, but in doing so I shall be departing for the first time from what is the majority opinion within the theistic community.

So what philosophical issues are raised by the claim that after our lives here we will enjoy (or endure) an everlasting life hereafter? First, does it make sense?

◆ ◆ ◆

It is certain that we are all moving inexorably towards our deaths: whether we shall ultimately arrive at this common fate by a predicted and slow decline or by a surprising and sudden descent may vary between us, but we all know *now*, only too well, that arrive there we shall. We shall die, and the probability is that our bodies will either be lowered into the earth and gradually dissolve there or be converted by cremation into ashes, which are then increasingly widely distributed as the world moves on. In any case, the power of our minds to affect the universe intentionally will disappear. The first philosophical issue raised then is that in the light of these uncontentious facts it is not immediately clear what *content*, let alone justification, could be adduced for a belief that we can survive our deaths.

Some philosophers[2] have concluded that it is logically impossible that one could survive one's death and sometimes seem to be arguing for this conclusion merely from the purported linguistic fact that that's what the word 'death' means, that which one cannot survive. When reading, say, the history of the

Titanic's maiden voyage, in coming across a table of the passengers' names that divides them into two columns, those that survived and those that died, we do not turn the page wondering where the list of those passengers who *both* survived *and* died might be. Similarly, we can know a priori that if in a hundred years' time a list is drawn up by someone with access to the appropriate historical information giving the names of everyone who has ever read this, our names could then be divided into two mutually exclusive and exhaustive categories, 'survivors' and 'dead'. At that stage, a few of us perhaps would still be listed as 'survivors' but most of us, no doubt, would have to be listed as 'dead': in *two* hundred years' time, if a similar list were drawn up, all of us would need to be categorized as 'dead', necessitating that the survivors column be empty—there cannot ever be a third column listing those of us who are both 'survivors and dead'. Just as the grammar of the words 'bachelor' and 'husband' prevent anyone being both a bachelor and a husband, so the question of whether or not anyone could in principle survive their deaths can easily be answered, such philosophers would suggest, by saying that the grammar of the words 'death' and 'survive' prevents anyone from both dying and surviving: *ergo* it is logically impossible that one survive one's death; hoping that one might makes as much sense as hoping that one might remain a bachelor after one's married.

This, no doubt, will strike many as a surprisingly and implausibly quick result. After all, the belief that one *can* survive one's death is so widespread across cultures and times that it has justifiably been called universal. Looking to its murky origins in the depths of pre-history, one can discern a form of it as presupposed by the funerary customs of all those early societies of whose habits we have acquired any knowledge. And, in our own age, survey after survey reports the persistence of this belief among the majority of peoples and societies.[3] By and large, we continue to bury our dead with the, possibly vague but not obviously incoherent, belief that they journey ahead of us to an undiscovered country where we may one day join them. Even among those who do not share this belief, very few seem to regard it as logically impossible that they are mistaken. Is it really plausible then to suggest that belief in survival after death makes only as much sense as belief in married bachelors? Is it really plausible to suggest that the vast majority of people have been mistaken, not just about a matter of fact, but about the meanings of the words they use? Unfortunately for a speedy conclusion to our investigation, we must say that the answer to these questions is 'no'.

Let us distinguish two senses of the word 'death'. One—'clinical death'—is the cessation of brain function; the decomposition and dissolution of the body etc. The other—'final death'—is all of this *plus* the added logical implication that one cannot survive it. With this terminology in place, the philosophers who would claim that it offends against the grammar of the word 'death' even to raise the question of whether or not people might survive their deaths can be presented as suggesting that, in common discourse, the word 'death' functions as equivalent to 'final death'. I have briefly advanced reasons to suppose that the way discussion actually proceeds on the issue of a life after death makes this suggestion implausible. Rather, it seems that the word 'death' functions more like 'clinical death'. However, even if the counter-suggestion to mine were to be true, it seems that a believer in life after death, may, if there is thus a danger of his or her position being characterized as oxymoronic, simply rephrase it as the position that not all clinical deaths are final deaths. Thus in drawing up a list of our fates in two hundred years' time, it is possible that three columns *would* in fact need to be included for a full account. First, there would be the straight-forward (i.e. earthly) 'survival' column. Then there would be two columns (each coming under the importantly ambiguous categorization 'dead'), namely that column corresponding to those of us, if any, who are clinically dead but enjoying or about to enjoy a post-mortem survival and that column corresponding to those of us, if any, who are clinically dead without any prospect of post-mortem survival—i.e. finally dead. Whilst we have every reason to believe that no one in a position to fill in our name in such a list in two hundred years' time could correctly put our name in the first column, it is then an open question whether any or all of us would be correctly classed as clinically dead but enjoying or being about to enjoy a post-mortem survival, rather than as finally dead. Using the word 'death' now as synonymous with clinical death rather than final, the question, 'Could one survive one's death?' remains an open one; it is open at least pending an investigation into the persistence conditions of persons. If someone is going to be able to argue successfully that it is impossible that one survive one's (clinical) death, he or she cannot simply rely on the grammar of the words 'dead' and 'survive' to do his or her work for, but he or she must also import—and argue for—a particular thesis on the persistence conditions of persons and how these conditions cannot be met in any situation where someone has undergone (clinical) death. One might, for example, think that if one could show persons to be identical to their bodies (or a part of their bodies—say their brains) in some sense, then perhaps, as clinical death is by definition the (at least temporary) destruction of the body, persons could then be shown to be such that they could not survive their clinical deaths—i.e. given what it is to be a person, clinical death must be final death. My argument then will be that we have no reason to think that persons' persistence conditions are such that they could not—of necessity—survive the (at least temporary) destruction of their bodies, their clinical deaths. I shall argue that a person's surviving the (at least tem-porary) destruction of his or her (current) body is something that God, were he to exist, could bring about.

Roughly speaking, there seem to be two ways for me to try to make sense of the possibility that one might thus survive death.[4]

The first way is the rather obvious one: it is simply to suggest that one is not—or not essentially—one's body or any part of it at all. Such a position would most naturally be associated with Descartes: according to Descartes, the human being as we encounter him or her is a composite of two distinct substances—the soul, which is immaterial, and the body, which is material. The person is to be identified with the soul and so, in principle, could survive the destruction of the material of the body. According to this way out of the problem, what happens at death is that the body does indeed die, but the soul, and hence the person, goes on—either on its own indefinitely or (the theistic view) in combination with some new body or a resurrected old body at a later time. Substance dualism, could it be established, would then easily solve the problem of how it is that one might survive one's death.

The second way of making sense of the possibility that one might survive the destruction of one's body is to suggest that although one is (in some sense) one's body, and although one does indeed have good reason to believe that one's body is *temporarily* destroyed at death, one cannot know that it is *finally* destroyed—one's body (and hence oneself) could be reconstituted by a sufficiently powerful being at some later time. A slightly different theory would emerge were one to stress that although one is at some level of description entirely physical, one is one's body, the mental properties that constitute one's psychology and (thus) personhood, belong to another level of description, and form descriptions of one as a person that could in principle apply to another body later, after the final destruction of one's current body. Within the non-substance-dualist way of making sense of the possibility that one might survive one's death, two models thus present themselves, corresponding to whether one thinks it is more important that the matter of one's body survives or that the arrangement of matter—what might be called 'the form'—and perhaps the psychological properties that are generated by/depend on this form survive.

At the first extreme, an analogy suggests itself, that of the motor engine disassembled for repair and then reassembled. Let us say (what seems plausible) that a motor engine is an entirely physical thing—there is no soul around—and that its identity is entirely governed by the identity of its parts. Given these principles, imagine the following circumstance: I start with an engine composed, let us say, of 500 parts. I then strip it down, distributing some of the parts fairly widely over my garage floor and sending others off to specialists for reconditioning. As a result of this destructive process, I then have no engine, but merely a fairly widely distributed collection of engine-parts (some on the garage floor and some at reconditioning factories). Eventually the parts sent to others are returned in the post and the parts on the floor are collected together again by myself. I reassemble the engine; surprisingly, it works. The disassembly of my engine can thus be seen to be a case of the engine going out of existence for a period of time and then coming back[5]—I started with an engine; then I had no engine; then I had my engine back. The engine that came back into existence was the same engine as the engine that ceased to exist when I disassembled it—rather than an entirely new engine—in virtue of being composed of the same parts. It is, of course, only too easy to imagine how things such as my engine, once disassembled, might never come back into existence. A story at least equally probable to that which I have just told would involve my starting with my engine; the engine going out of existence as I disassembled it; my then having a collection of parts as a result; my then trying to reassemble them; my realizing that my technical knowledge and practical powers are not up to the task; my thus having a heap of scrap metal as a result. Without inter alia a sufficiently skilled mechanic, engines cannot, as a contingent matter of fact, be 'brought back to life' if they are once destroyed. With a sufficiently skilled mechanic, they can be.

What conclusion can we draw? Well, at least some entirely physical things, it seems, can survive temporal gaps in their existence. It could hence be suggested that human beings—although entirely physical in the way that engines are—are similarly items of the sort whose histories are or could be discontinuous in the way that engine existence sometimes is or could be, i.e. they can survive disassembly. According to such a view, what happens at death is that we—essentially corporeal persons—go out of existence as our body parts are disassembled by those physiological changes that constitute death and decomposition. If there is an omniscient and omnipotent God to act in the role of cosmic mechanic, then he could keep an eye on where all the parts—molecules, atoms, sub-atomic particles, quarks, whatever-they-may-turn-out-to-be—go and, one day, traditionally referred to as 'The Last Day', reconstitute them (or enough of them) in the correct way: at that stage, we would come back into existence.[6]

This analogy naturally leads one to think of the importance or otherwise of the continuity of engine parts for the identity of the reconstituted engine with that of the disassembled. Had the engine parts been lost, I could not have brought the same engine back 'to life', rather than perhaps create a very similar new one out of new parts. However, one might be struck by the thought that had only one part been lost—and the remaining 499 correctly reassembled along with a new replacement part (functionally equivalent to that lost)—the resultant engine could still have been correctly thought of as the same one as that destroyed during disassembly. Just what percentage of parts is essential? Let us label this question 'the percentage question' and leave it on one side for the moment unanswered, instead observing that one might doubt—in the case of persons—the importance of the survival of *any* of the matter that at any stage constitutes one's body for one's survival. After all, according to some accounts at least, the matter that now constitutes your body is entirely different from that which constituted it seven years ago. Perhaps, for persons, it is not the identity of matter that is important at all then, but rather the arrangement of the matter—what in Aristotelian terms might have been called the 'form'—and perhaps it is not the physical form the preservation and instantiation of which is important for a person to survive but the psychological form that is (on non-soul theories) in some way generated by, or at least to some extent dependent upon, that arrangement. At this other end of the 'matter' or 'form' spectrum then one might think of another analogy.

Consider a computer running a particular piece of software. Again, let us say that computers are entirely physical at least in the sense that they do not have souls. I wrote this on such a computer using *Word 6.0*. *Word 6.0* is, as you probably know, a word-processing package that has, among other things, a customizable dictionary; default printer; pagination settings; etc. Let us say that in the course of using the programme on my particular computer for the past few years I have now so customized it that it is unique. Let's call this version 'George'. Now suppose that I learn that the circuitry on my particular computer—the piece of hardware that currently runs George—is about to wear out. Wanting to save George, I might record the contents of my hard-drive onto a series of three-and-a-half-inch disks; buy a new computer; and transfer the data from the disks onto it. The old computer and disks may then very well be destroyed, yet George would survive. George would then have survived the destruction of the particular piece of hardware on which it was originally created and run. Some people have of course suggested that the relationship between our minds and our bodies (in particular our brains) is rather like that between software and hardware and thus that the person—while not having a soul—could nevertheless survive the destruction of the body he or she is currently dependent on, *even if none of the body parts are ever reassembled*, because the person is to be identified with his or her mind, rather than the body on which that mind happens to 'run' at any one moment. If there is a God, then he could 'upload', as it were, the software that is us at the death of our old hardware, our earthly bodies, or more specifically our brains, and reinstall it, download it, onto some new hardware, our resurrection bodies, at a later time.

Within the non-substance-dualist way of understanding how one might survive the (at least temporary) destruction of one's original body, then, there is room for some disagreement on the issue of whether or not persons should be understood as more like engines—as more like the hardware—or as more like George—as more like the software (or perhaps as some combination of both). But whatever the truth here might be (assuming that the truth is somewhere here rather than with the substance dualist view), the truth cannot be problematic for the claim that if there's a God, he could arrange for us to survive our deaths.

Continuing to assume for the moment that a non-substance-dualist view of some sort is true—i.e. not allowing ourselves the easy route out of our problem—let us consider the following imaginary situation to enable us to hone our intuitions with regard to the question, 'Am I my hardware; my software; or both?'

The year is AD 2500 and you wish to emigrate to a planet orbiting Alpha Centauri where there is now a flourishing colony. Being a student; your university fees now standing at one billion pounds per week; and the grant having been cut to fifty pence per annum, you obviously wish to travel as cheaply as possible. As your travel agent, I advise you of four options. (As I go through these options, one to four, consider whether or not you would *really* survive the procedures that I describe—i.e. whether as your so-called 'travel agent' I am describing genuine cases of your *travelling*.)

Option 1. The Space Shuttle. First Class. This is the most expensive way to travel. You will lie in your own personal (reclining) hibernation chamber aboard a spaceship, in appearance much like an old-style passenger aircraft but travelling at one-tenth the speed of light. Within your hibernation chamber you will be unconscious for the duration of the flight, in cryogenic suspension. Upon arrival at Alpha Centauri, you will be unfrozen and, although it will appear to you that you have dozed off for merely a moment or two, 'in reality'[7] forty years will have passed.

Option 2. The Space Shuttle. Second Class. This is the second most expensive way to travel: the operator saves money (and passes some of that saving on to you) by packing in more passengers per cubic metre. To do this, arms and legs are amputated and frozen and packed separately from torsos and heads. However, they are clearly labelled and medical technology is now so advanced that they can be reattached once passengers arrive and before they awake from their cryogenic suspension. There is no discernible scarring; loss of function; etc. In other words, if you were to elect to travel in this fashion, then upon arrival, apart from knowing that you only paid to travel second class, you would never know that your limbs had been separated during travel. Again it will simply appear to you that you have dozed off for a moment or two, when again in reality forty years will have passed.

Option 3. The Matter and Information Teletransporter—MIT for short. This is the second *cheapest* mode of travel. Matter and Information Teletransporting is a process whereby things placed in a 'sender' unit on one planet (in this case you on Earth) are vaporized during a process of *exhaustive* information collecting concerning them; the resultant information is then beamed at the speed of light to a 'receiver' unit on the appropriate planet (in this case the appropriate one orbiting Alpha Centauri) where it is stored (in this case for sixteen years) until the matter that composed the original object arrives—having been beamed in sub-atomic form at one-fifth the speed of light. The information is then used to rearrange this matter so that the original object is recreated—in this case, you. As a result you will step out of the receiver unit saying something like 'Haven't I left yet? Wow, I've arrived: it seems to me as if no time has elapsed at all,' although in fact you will have stepped into the sender unit on Earth twenty years before your arrival at Alpha Centauri.

Option 4. The Just Information Teletransporter—JIT for short. This is the cheapest mode of travel. Again, things placed in a sender unit are vaporized during a process of exhaustive information collecting concerning them; again the resultant information is beamed at the speed of light to the receiver unit. But in the case of JIT, in contra-distinction to MIT, this information is used immediately in combination with matter originating on the receiving planet to recreate the object. JIT could thus be described as destroying your old body on Earth but building you a new body on arrival at Alpha Centauri, one so similar to your old that you'll never notice the difference. Again, subjectively, no time at all will seem to have elapsed, although in reality four years will have passed between your stepping into the sender unit and your arrival at the receiver unit. Total journey time by JIT is reduced to four years because there is now no need to wait for the arrival of the actual particles that constituted your body on earth, before you can be recreated on Alpha Centauri.

So which is the cheapest way to travel?

If you think that option one is the only way, why? Obviously, one could survive travelling separately to one's little finger, say, if the latter were detached temporarily before transit, shipped separately, and then sewn back on upon arrival, so why not separate one's limbs from one's torso in general? And if one says this, why stop at option two? Why insist that this temporary decomposition can only involve, if one wants to survive it, one's body being reduced to components of a certain size (limbs and torso); why can't it involve the body being reduced to components of smaller sizes—its component fundamental particles, whatever those are (option 3)? Wherever one draws the line between options 1, 2, and 3, one will be drawing it, it seems, rather arbitrarily. Perhaps for this reason most people are fundamentally divided between options 3 and 4, depending on how important they feel the matter is—i.e. where they fall on the matter/form spectrum.

If you think that the identity of matter is important, if you went for option 3 as the cheapest way to travel, it's obvious that you could survive if you arrived on the planet but the matter that had constituted, say, your little finger had been lost in transit. One can survive the destruction of one's little finger. So, not *all* the matter of your old body needs to be transferred for you to survive. And transporting matter costs money.

Suppose, therefore, I say that as your travel agent I can cut you a special deal. I can send a certain percentage of your original matter (and cut a pro rata proportion from the full MIT price), and you can choose how great a percentage and from what area of your body I select this matter. The shortfall of matter will be made up in the manner of JIT, with matter originating in Alpha Centauri. What percentage of original matter would you choose as necessary for your survival and from what bits of your body—50 per cent? Less? More? One hundred per cent of the brain and 25 per cent of everything else? The figure and the area and extent of the organs decided upon seems rather arbitrary—the percentage problem again.

It you think that it's the form, not the matter, that's important, if you'd go for option 4 as the cheapest way to travel, again it's obvious that you could survive if the information pertaining to the shape and colour of your little finger was not successfully transferred. Any generic human little finger could be grafted on upon your arrival and your survival would not be threatened. So not all the information needs to survive for you to survive. And information itself is not free to transfer.

So suppose again, that—as your travel agent—I say that I can cut you a special deal. I can arrange to send a certain percentage of the information collected (at approximately that percentage of the overall JIT cost), the remaining information will be made up from generic human male or female stock. Just how much information need be sent across and what areas are more important than those pertaining to your little finger? Presumably there will be a strong temptation to go for the information pertinent to your psychology, rather than your physiology, the software not the hardware is what needs to be preserved. So long as *some* hardware sufficient for running the software is provided at the other end, e.g. some generic human-type body, maybe all that need be sent is your personality and memories. But here again the same question can arise. Obviously you could survive if the information pertinent to your memory of this particular paragraph was corrupted or lost, but just how much information with regard to your psychology needs to be sent across? For example, need I send 90 per cent of the memories? Sixty? Fifty? Again, any answer will seem rather arbitrary. Again we have the percentage problem.

In my experience, thought experiments of the teletransportation sort, when complicated with considerations such as 'what would you say if x per cent (x taking a value of between 0 and 100) of information/matter were successfully transferred?' prompt a philosophically interesting response for at least some values of x, namely the response 'I don't know what to say'. In tutorials, this response is usually accompanied by a wistful, if slightly desperate, glance towards the door.

This response is philosophically interesting as it can be understood in two different ways—either as 'I don't know what one *would* say' or as 'I don't know what one *should* say'—corresponding to two different philosophical theses about what it is one doesn't know when one reports oneself as not knowing the correct percentages. The first approach is to think that what one is being asked to do is to report a decision that one is making, or thinks most people would make, about how to extend a concept—in this case 'same person'—in an unusual situation, a situation the concept was not originally constructed to deal with. The second is to think that what one is being asked to report is a truth about an identity and that that truth is independent of what people may believe or incline to say about it, how they might choose to use any concept. I want to describe these two approaches briefly.

First one first: some would be inclined to say that, assuming all the information to be 'in' (collected) as to what happened to the original matter and its subsequent arrangement on Alpha Centauri, then, if we have to make a decision on personal identity at all, we can do so only by stipulation.[8] Those who take this view in the face of the above stories and question could be called anti-realists on the personal identity issue. Anti-realists with respect to personal identity are happy for the question of the identity of the person to be reduced to questions of the identity of person properties or parts and subsequent indeterminacy or stipulation. The percentage problem is to be met with the equanimity that comes with knowing that in the final analysis it will be up to us to decide where, if anywhere, identity lies. 'Facts' about person identity are linguistic constructs. If 100 per cent of the matter and 100 per cent of the information is successfully transferred, our concept dictates that we say the person survives and has travelled; if 0 per cent and 0 per cent, our concept of sameness of person dictates that we say the person has not survived and has not travelled. For some values in between these extremes, our concept of sameness of person is simply not defined, or at least not defined as yet. There may thus be no answer as to whether the person has survived or not, or, if there is to be an answer, it is up to us to create it by deciding to speak in one way rather than another. So that's anti-realism.

By contrast, others might maintain that, even once all the facts are in—even if one knows *exactly* how much and what matter and information has been transferred—there is still an important question remaining, a question that it is not open to stipulative decision to answer; neither is the matter indeterminate; it is the identity question. Facts about personal identity exist independently of our linguistic constructs. They are 'real' facts. I shall call such a position a realist position with regard to personal identity.

So, now there's the meta-question as it were: should we be anti-realists or realists on the issue of personal identity? When we're confused about what to say in various complicated teletransportation stories, are we confused simply because there's described a state of affairs that our concept of continuing personal identity doesn't yet cover, or are we confused because there's something we don't know about the world in the situations they describe? Is the percentage problem a *real* problem?

This is a very interesting question, in many ways the most interesting question about personal identity, and given that it's so interesting, you are to be forgiven for being rather dismayed to learn that it's not a question I'll be answering. But what I *do* intend to do is argue that whichever way one goes on this issue, there can't really be a problem of whether or not one could survive one's death, which is the problem that concerns us directly here.

Firstly then, in favour of anti-realism, it certainly seems that realism is unnecessarily ontologically extravagant for artefacts such as engines.[9] If we'd been talking about teletransporting merely an engine, I think we'd all have been happy to adopt an anti-realist account of any confusion generated by the percentage problem. Who cares what percentage we fix for numerical identity of engines? One engine is as good for all practical purposes as any other qualitatively identical one. Treating persons as similar to artefacts in this respect would thus have the virtue of parity of reasoning and, furthermore, it would be 'philosophically' attractive as it would imply that once we know all the facts about where the matter of our bodies has gone and what properties are instantiated, once we know the percentages, there's nothing we don't know about the world, there's maybe just something we've yet to decide about our use of words. Positions are 'philosophically' attractive in this sense if they remove reasons for scepticism.

Imagine then, as an anti-realist, this scenario:[10] the human race eventually comes to an end. God then creates, in a set of extended objects (i.e. Heaven), more or less[11] exact psycho-physical replicas of all previously deceased people who can and would then be identified by one another with these previously deceased people. For example, in so far as you now feel confident about who you are and what you have done in the past, so your post-mortem replica will feel confident in identifying himself or herself with you and what you will ultimately end up having done by the end of your earthly life, *ergo*, if anti-realism is right, the word 'replica' here as used in my description of the scenario is really a misnomer as such a person would actually *be* you. That we can know now that, if such a circumstance pertained, heavenly people would choose thus to identify themselves with the earthly people they seemed to remember having been shows that our concept of sameness of person already has 'built into it', as it were, such an extension in these circumstances. If anti-realism is right then, if enough people in Heaven say they are the same persons as previously existed, as they would do in this scenario, such people would be speaking the truth—they would have survived their deaths.

However, all of this may strike one as rather odd. 'Surely there's more to some future person's being me', you might say, 'than enough people saying that he or she is me.' Let us consider, secondly then, a powerful argument against anti-realism expanding this intuition.

Consider again your travelling to Alpha Centauri. Suppose that in the end I had offered you a bargain bucket deal. The cheapest way to travel turned out to be an option 5, to have one organ removed and frozen; shipped to Alpha Centauri; and then transplanted into the body of your genetically cloned twin, who will by the time that organ arrives have been grown ready to receive it. There is, I think, a common inclination to say that one goes where one's brain goes (as long as it continues to work in the right way), so let's say that that is the organ you've initially chosen as the one you want removed, frozen, shipped, and installed. Now let's suppose that you are a philosopher holding an anti-realist interpretation of the truth that one goes where one's brain goes—that's a fact generated by what we *mean* by person, and we mean brain. Here's what happens then.

Just before your brain removal on earth, your eye is caught by an opinion poll in a newspaper lying to hand which announces that most people use the concept of sameness of person to imply heart continuity and heart continuity to imply sameness of person—unlike us, they take heart survival to be necessary (and indeed sufficient) for personal survival. Across the universe, heart 'transplant' surgeons, as they previously called themselves, have shot themselves (through the heart) and the *Oxford English Dictionary* is being revised. Being the anti-realist you are, knowing that personal survival is a matter of linguistic convention, you know now that you will not survive unless the heart is the organ chosen. 'It wouldn't be me who would wake up after the operation if you shipped my brain, it'd be my clone—so remove my heart and freeze and send that instead,' you say. 'Okay, that's even easier,' the doctor replies. You slip into unconsciousness and he dutifully removes, freezes, and ships your heart.

Forty years later an Alpha Centaurian doctor unpacks your heart and fits it into the body of your clone. This person wakes; has no memories; no personality; and no language, although eventually, through learning to speak and in doing so consulting an edition of the *OED* and the appropriate medical records, this person discovers that the grammar of the word 'person' dictates that they say they are you. Your travel plans have worked. But they've worked in part because people have continued to talk in a certain way. If, in the forty years it has taken for the heart to be shipped to Alpha Centauri, enough people had changed their minds and decided to say things like, 'Brain identity is necessary and sufficient for personal identity; heart identity has nothing to do with it,' then this person waking up would have discovered that they weren't you, would have discovered that you had died on Earth forty years before to act as a heart donor for them.

But surely in fact persons continue if their brain continues (in the right way) and the heart really is nothing to do with it—people just *do* survive heart transplants—thus if your brain is not sent and hence does not continue in the right way in another body, then it's a fact that you will not have survived. And the fact that you'll not have survived won't be affected by people, however large a majority they may be, saying that you have. Whether it's the brain, the heart, or something else that 'carries the can', as it were, of your identity is a matter of fact, not just a matter of linguistic choice.

In the case of engine identity, it seems we can be anti-realists with no counterintuitive consequences; we can say there's no fact of the matter about engine identity that our concept of engine is trying to track and so we can legislate which percentages to choose without fear of going wrong because there is nothing to go wrong about. But in the case of personal identity it seems this thought experiment provides us with reason to be realists, there is something to go wrong about. Whilst it might be reasonable to assume that people go where certain bits of their bodies go, that assumption could always be wrong in that it is an attempt to track a continuing thing (a person) the identity of which it's not entirely within our power to determine by stipulation.

But if we are thus drawn to realism, then we must be struck by the following thought: if people could in principle go wrong in their judgements about personal identity even while knowing all the physical facts, what physical and psychological properties went where, etc., then that can only be because personal identity isn't reducible to these facts: if personal identity is indeed a matter of fact and if we could know all the facts about physical matter and physical and mental properties and yet not know *this* fact, then this fact must be a fact about a non-physical thing and a non-property thing. Question: What is not a physical thing? Answer: A spiritual thing. Question: What is not a property thing? Answer: A substantial thing. Therefore we have reason to believe in the soul of substance dualism, a spiritual substance. And in so far as we have reason to believe in substance dualism, we have reason to believe that the first non-problematic route out of the problem of how a person might survive the death of his or her body is navigable.[12]

In summary and conclusion then: on the one hand, if anti-realism is right in suggesting that once we know all the facts about where the matter of our bodies has gone and what properties are instantiated—once we know the percentages—then there's nothing we don't know about the world, just perhaps something we've yet to decide about words, then we would survive our deaths in the situation previously described where enough people in some heavenly realm decide to use the appropriate words in the right way, something very easy for God to bring about. On the other hand, if, in contrast, realism is right in suggesting that once we know all the facts about where the matter of our bodies has gone and what properties are instantiated—once we know the percentages—there's still something that we may not know about the world, then that must be EITHER (A) because there's more to the world—to us persons—than the matter of our bodies and what properties they instantiate, and this truth must thus be a truth about a spiritual substance, a soul, but then one can survive one's death just if this soul survives OR (B) because there really is a correct percentage of matter/form or perhaps a tiny particle or somesuch in one's brain that can't be destroyed finally if one is to survive, it's just that we haven't found it yet. Now option (B) seems to me even more implausible than substance dualism, but in any case one can certainly hold that God (as omnipotent and omniscient) can make sure the right percentages are instantiated in Heaven; keep an eye on where any such tiny particle goes; and arrange for it to get to Heaven; etc. So, whether one is ultimately drawn to anti-realism or realism on the 'meta-question', one cannot have reason to suppose that it is impossible that one survive one's death. Whether or not we actually *will* survive our deaths is another question, one the conclusive answer to which I hope we will discover together at some stage in the future.

Having shown that the offer of everlasting life in Heaven is a coherent one on any plausible theory of personal identity, I'm now going to consider why it is that all theists are agreed that God has made us this offer; then I'll consider how widely it is reasonable to believe God, were he to exist, would extend this offer; then I'll consider whether or not it is an offer that it is reasonable to believe that any of those to whom God would extend it would be able to avoid accepting.

◆ ◆ ◆

Sometimes our desire fixes on something because we recognize value in it; it is responsive to pre-existent value. You read the back cover of a book in a bookshop. It tells you that the book will address various questions in the philosophy of religion. You recognize these as important questions and—desiring to know more—you purchase and read the book. Your desire has responded to pre-existent value. When one's desire for something that is valuable independently of one's desiring it (e.g. knowledge of important issues) is satisfied, one's life goes better in that respect. It goes better even if one no longer actually desires the valuable thing. If this book is informing you about important matters, reading it is making your life go better for you in that respect even if you have by now lost any of your initial interest in it.

As well as responding to pre-existent value, sometimes our desire fixes on something that was in itself valueless and by doing so creates value. Some people collect miniature teapots. (If this claim sounds too implausible to you, please accept my word that I have seen an advertisement on the television for a magazine devoted to the hobby.) When a person who collects miniature teapots finds a miniature teapot that is unlike one he or she already owns, he or she will— I presume—desire to add it to his or her collection, his or her desire thus making this teapot valuable (to him or her). When we achieve something that is valuable only dependently on our desiring it, this in itself is not sufficient for our lives to go better in that respect; the value of miniature teapots lasts only as long as the desire for them. If the advertisement I saw on the television formed in me an immediate desire to own a miniature teapot, prompting me to phone my nearest miniature teapot emporium and tell them my credit card details so that they would send one to me, then if, by the time it arrives in the post, the desire to own it has entirely evaporated, its coming into my possession does not benefit me at all.

The same points that may be made about benefits may also be made about harms. When we are hampered in achieving something that is valuable independently of our desiring it, then this is in itself a harm, regardless of what we think about it. If, while you are reading this sentence, someone sneaks up behind you and knocks you unconscious, you will be unable to acquire greater knowledge of the philosophy of religion and thus a harm will have befallen you even though your becoming unconscious will have simultaneously removed your desire to acquire such greater knowledge. If someone prevents me from sending off for any more things for which I form a fancy having watched advertisements on the television, this too is in itself a harm to me, albeit a slight one. But if this person simultaneously removes from me the desire to purchase things that I would previously have formed fleeting fancies for having seen advertisements on the television by pointing out the fact that they are all rubbish, he or she has not harmed me at all. (Indeed, given that buying such things is a waste of money and I am a poorly paid academic, he or she has actually benefited me.)

Given these facts, we may conclude that if death were to be the permanent cessation of the person, it would be a great harm. If death were the permanent cessation of the person, it would destroy all flourishing both in the sense of achieving what is independently valuable and in the sense of achieving what is valuable in virtue of being desired. Death would always be a harm in the first sense and it would usually also be a harm in the second, for most of us will continue to have hobbies and projects on a par with collecting miniature teapots until we die. But it is important to stress that even when people die having lost all interest in life, if their deaths were the end of them, they would still be bad for them in virtue of depriving them of the possibility of those things the value of which does not depend on their continuing interest.[13]

One might recall the conversations in Lucian's *Dialogues of the Dead* between Charon and the people he's ferrying across the Styx who tell him that their time cannot be yet as they are busy with so many things. This is reprised—rather poignantly to my mind—in the Western *Unforgiven*. Just before Clint Eastwood's character kills Gene Hackman's (sorry if that spoils the film for you), the latter can't believe that it's going to happen; as he stares disbelievingly down the barrel of the gun that will kill him some of his last words are, 'I was building a house.' Hume, in reflecting towards the end of his life on what he might say to persuade Charon not to take him to the land of the dead, concluded that as he had achieved all that he had wanted he was content not to try to persuade Charon to allow him a longer life. But even if it were true that Hume had achieved all that he had wanted, were Hume's death to have been the end of him, it would still in itself have been bad for him in another respect, for he had not achieved all that was of value independently of its being wanted by him. Even the great Hume did not solve *all* the problems of philosophy. (Of course— somewhat ironically—it was precisely because he hadn't solved the problem of value that Hume was able to be so equable in the face of what he considered to be his imminent extinction. If he'd been a better philosopher, the prospect of his death might have worried him more.) If someone is denied the chance to consider further the problems of philosophy, this is bad for this person even if he or she no longer cares to consider them, just as it is bad for you to make people go blind, even if you do so by administering a drug that simultaneously removes from them the desire to see. So if death is the end, all persons' deaths are bad for them at least in the sense that they deprive them of the future possibility of achieving things that would be good for them to achieve, the goodness of which is independent of their desiring to achieve them. It follows then from God's perfect goodness that if there is a God, he will ensure that death is not the end, that all people have a life after death in Heaven.[14]

♦ ♦ ♦

This reasoning certainly applies to all persons. It also seems to apply to some higher animals that are not persons. If a lower animal dies of old age, we incline to think of the prospect of this animal's having no future as not in itself bad for it if it has lived a full life and has had its desires satisfied; indeed we might think that its permanently ceasing to exist is good for it if the only remaining desire that we attribute to it is the desire to avoid suffering, something that its ceasing to exist would perfectly satisfy. It is plausible to say that some lower animals find their flourishing simply in the fulfilling of their desires to reproduce and avoid suffering and so if these desires have been satisfied by the time these animals die, their deaths being the end of them is not bad for them. Nevertheless, we also think that some higher animals find their flourishing in doing things that per- manently ceasing to exist would frustrate and have desires that permanently ceasing to exist would frustrate. Dogs don't just try to avoid pain—something that might make permanent ceasing to exist an unalloyed good for them—they also seek pleasure; they play. Dogs have a robust enough conception of their own future to form desires about it, desires that are often frustrated by their deaths, for these desires are that the future contain them. It is natural, for example, to describe dogs as frequently burying bones not simply from instinct, but with the intention of coming back to chew on them later. Of course, this attribution of a certain level of sophistication and certain sorts of self-orientated desires to dogs is very speculative; it could be that dogs are in fact best described as always acting on blind instinct. Even when they bury bones and the like, they do so with no mental representations of the future and desires as to their place in it at all. But most of us do incline to attribute to higher animals the sorts of ends and desires that would make their permanently ceasing to exist bad for them and, if so, we should conclude that God, were he to exist, would have good reason to extend the afterlife to include them as well.

It also seems he would have good reason to extend it to at least some lower animals whose permanent ceasing to exist would not be bad for them, because it would be bad for us.

If Rachel has a desire to see her sadly deceased pet hamster again, then—even if hamsters do not have ends that their permanently ceasing to exist frustrates and are not sophisticated enough in the forming of desires for their permanently ceasing to exist to be in itself bad for them—it would be less than ideal for Rachel were she to find in Heaven that her hamster had not been brought back to life too. A Heaven without Rachel's pet hamster would be slightly less good, from her point of view, than a Heaven that was in all other respects the same and yet contained her hamster. Of course, by the time Rachel gets to Heaven her views might have changed in this regard. But I see no reason to think that they will have. There's nothing wrong in Rachel's wanting to see her hamster again. So I see no reason why if there were a God, he would not bring back Rachel's pet hamster for no other reason than that Rachel, as by then a resident of Heaven, wants him to bring it back. There's nothing of intrinsic value in the continued life of Rachel's hamster beyond the grave, but there would be something of value in satisfying Rachel's desire to see her hamster once more if it were indeed a desire that she continued to have.

The permanent ceasing to exist of animals of a certain level of sophistication (a level considerably below that of the average human being) would be bad for them and so if there is a God, they too will share in everlasting life. The permanent ceasing to exist of other animals that fall below even this level would be bad for those who care about them, so if there's a God, they too will share in everlasting life. Some humans, though, are well below the average level of sophistication, not just of humans but also of these lower animals. What about foetuses, severely retarded human beings, and children who die before they reach the level of sophistication necessary for their permanent ceasing to exist to be bad for them? Should the theist conclude that they too will share in everlasting life?

Every child who has ever been born has had a mother, someone who will almost certainly have formed the desire to see that child grow up into a fulfilled and happy adult. If this desire of hers has been frustrated by the child's untimely death then—even if this death occurred before the child had developed a level of mental sophistication sufficient for him or her to have as ends things that permanently ceasing to exist would deprive him or her of, or to form desires that the future include him or her, and thus before the child's permanent ceasing to exist could be in itself bad for the child—God would thus have good reason to arrange that this child grows up in an afterlife, where he or she will be reunited with his or her mother. What about those children who weren't the object of such desires even by their own mothers? Don't we want them to enter the afterlife? If any of us do (and most of us do), then they are the objects of desires (ours) that would make their not entering it bad and thus, if there were a God, he would ensure that they too enter it.

One might think that this all sounds 'too good to be true'. According to my argument, if there's a God, he'll arrange for all human beings who have ever been born (and many who haven't—dying unknown before birth) and, even more contentiously, many animals—including animals of little sophistication—to enjoy everlasting life with him, for it would be good for them and/or for those who care about them if their deaths were not the end. But in fact it's precisely because our intuition tells us that it would be best were this to happen, that we should infer that—on theism—it is true that it will happen. Rather than being too good to be true, it's too good to be false.

Of course, one might be reasonably suspicious that the above just represents my taking our moral imaginations on a holiday. One's intuitions about what it's like to be a dog are hardly the starting point for an irrefutable argument as to the nature of moral reality and the afterlife. But, just as we must start any argument from premises, so in accessing moral facts, we must start from our moral intuitions. If your intuitions are as I describe above, then they are like mine and like those of a lot of other people and if they're sound, we are safe in concluding that, on theism, given that God has created people, that is inter alia creatures for whom permanently ceasing to exist would be bad (and various other animals who are sufficiently self-conscious for their permanently ceasing to exist to be bad for them); and given that he has given us the ability to care about creatures including those who lack the level of sophistication to be persons or to care about themselves, he must extend to all such creatures an everlasting life.

◆ ◆ ◆

I have been suggesting that in virtue of its being best to live again in Heaven after death, if there were a God, he would ensure that all people do so (and he would also ensure that many creatures who are not people do so). But we have seen at a number of places in our argument already that there is another thing that is good for people, that they have the freedom to choose what is less than the best for them and this opens up the possibility for doubting that on theism all people will enter this afterlife.

Imagine yourself as a medical doctor, offering a patient—Mr A—a certain treatment that you know would be in his best interests. If, having explained it fully to him, Mr A nevertheless refuses to give you permission to so treat him, it's plausible to say that you ought not to so treat him. The good of respecting A's freedom outweighs the good of treating him. It's even plausible to maintain that it does so in the case of a life-saving treatment.

Could it ever be better for God to respect our freedom if we freely chose, let's say, to go to everlasting torment in Hell, rather than to go to everlasting bliss in Heaven? Of course it wouldn't really be in our best interests for us to choose to avoid an afterlife in Heaven with God so that we could go to Hell instead. But we can choose to do that which isn't really in our best interests and, as we've seen, it's a power for us to be able to do so when we exist in conditions of less than perfect knowledge of the truth of theism. But this last clause points us to a negative answer to our question, or rather it points us to the question having been badly put.

A perfect revelation of God's existence and will is an 'offer' that no one can freely refuse because to the extent that one learns it's being made to one (a condition that must be satisfied before one can freely refuse something is that one knows what it is one is refusing) one learns that it would be supremely irrational for one to refuse it. Persons, we have seen, are inter alia essentially rational; to the extent that one is irrational, one undermines one's status as a person. Of conceptual necessity therefore, no person can be supremely irrational for all eternity as they would be if—*per impossibile*—they were, with full understanding of their choice, to choose to reject everlasting bliss in Heaven and remain forever in Hell instead. A person choosing to reject everlasting bliss in Heaven is criterial of that person not having fully understood what it is he or she is rejecting. It follows then that if in the Last Judgement we will all be brought to a full understanding of God's existence and will, then none of us will be free to respond to the offer of an everlasting and perfect communion with him with anything other than wholehearted acceptance. And coming—joyfully or painfully—to such an understanding is precisely what constitutes being so judged. The very act of coming into God's presence at the Last Judgement will dispel any shadow of doubt about his existence and will; thus it will dispel any shadow of irrationality in our response to it. At this judgement, we will not then be able to refuse to accept him. Could he still refuse to accept us?

Some people have done things that are so terrible that they deserve terrible punishment, punishment they did not receive this side of the grave. Adolf Hitler and Joseph Stalin would be two obvious examples. But we cannot think that even these monsters committed such terrible crimes that only a punishment of infinite duration could be appropriate and, I suggest, the punishment inherent in their simply being brought fully into God's presence at the Last Judgement would in itself be all that justice could demand.

If you are familiar with Ibsen's *Peer Gynt* you may recall the reception given by the Voice in the Darkness to the prodigal on his return. The Voice states that as a result of the prodigal never developing a character entitling him to any reward in Heaven or incurring any debt requiring payment in Hell, his destiny is simply to be stripped of such personality as he has and melted down into raw material to be used in the construction of others. It is difficult to imagine how the attitudes entertained as possible for the father in Jesus' parable of the returning prodigal could be more different from this.[15] When we hear of the prodigal's decision to return home and throw himself on his father's mercy, we are led to consider the possibility that the father may well, in his righteous anger, refuse to admit him to his household *simpliciter*; or perhaps that he may, with a certain iron-fairness, agree to employ him as hired help until he has worked off his debt and thus raised himself by his own efforts to the level of the non-prodigal elder son. Throughout the story, one attitude is never entertained even as a possibility, namely that the father might not recognize in his son anything worthy of a response, might not recognize him as a son who has betrayed him and whose betrayal calls for some response on both their parts. In the end, of course, our expectations of the father are shown to be inadequate to his character. We learn that while the son 'was yet at a distance, his father saw him and had compassion, and ran and embraced him and kissed him'. Servants were called to get him the best robe; a ring was placed on his finger, shoes on his feet; and the most sumptuous feast the father could manage was prepared in his honour.

As with any repentance, the destitution and humiliation of the son at the moment of his decision to turn back towards his father is in exact proportion to the selfishness and vanity in which he has previously indulged and we may be assured—if not reassured—that the same fearful equation will operate on us in the searing furnace of self-knowledge that must accompany any last judgement. When we are exposed directly to God's glorious presence, the worse we are, the more hellish that refiner's fire will seem to us as it burns off our misplaced egotism and self-satisfaction. But as a recognition of one's faults is a necessary precondition of choosing to turn from them, so such an inescapable recognition of them as we stand before God on the Last Day may be expected to have in each of us that very effect. One is never in a better position to recognize and hence respond to unconditional love than when one realizes one's inability to meet any conditions on which love could be premised. To be stripped entirely naked and left justifiably humiliated by one's own wilful ignorance and actions in front of someone who nevertheless loves one is to be humbled in front of oneself; and to be thus humbled with regard to one's own assessment of oneself and yet see that one is regarded as infinitely valuable by a being of infinite importance, would, I suggest, be enough to turn anyone towards such a being.

Recall the result of the bishop's choice in Hugo's *Les Misérables* at the moment the gendarmes bring Jean Valjean before him for justice, having discovered him with the bishop's stolen cutlery. The bishop telling the gendarmes that the cutlery was a gift; feigning surprise that Valjean could have forgotten to take the candlesticks that were also a part of the gift; and thrusting these too into his hands, wreaks more terrible havoc on Valjean's hardened soul than any the gendarmes would have been able to inflict had the bishop acted as we cannot help but fear we would have acted, snatching the cutlery away and telling the policemen to do their worst. This is not the imperative of love usurping the demands of justice; it is the imperative of love *perfecting* the demands of justice. The tears that Valjean later wept at his having stood on the little boy's coin were more bitter—and better for him—than any he'd have been able to weep had the bishop handed him over to the gendarmes.

Perhaps, like the son as he turns back towards his father, we regard ourselves or others as worthy only of condemnation by God. Perhaps we think of ourselves or others as not yet having turned towards God at all. Perhaps we have some hope for ourselves or others that we are somehow capable of being forgiven and entering our father's house. But whether we regard ourselves as worthy of condemnation or destined for Heaven, I suggest that theists must fearfully expect and at the same time dare to hope that for all of us the truth is both. If theism is right, we're all Valjeans waiting to find ourselves in front of the bishop; some may have already turned towards him and for them this judgement may seem a momentary delight; others, rather like Valjean, will not be turned until they find themselves there and for them this meeting may seem close to a torturous eternity. But for each of us it will in fact pass, once it has done its irreversible perfecting work. And everlasting bliss awaits each of us once perfected on the other side.

No one is worthy to see the face of God and live, but that does not entail that no one can see the face of God and live. Rather, no one can see the face of God and, by seeing that it is the face of perfect love in full awareness of the terribly fallen nature of the person who is loved, not be so raised by it that they will live for ever.

And so my mind, bedazzled and amazed, stood fixed in wonder, motionless, intent, and still my wonder kindled as I gazed. That light doth so transform a man's whole bent that never to another sight or thought would he surrender, with his own consent; for everything the will has ever sought is gathered there, and there is every quest made perfect, which apart from it falls short. Now, even what I recall will be exprest more feebly than if I would wield no more than a babe's tongue, yet milky from the breast; not that the living light I looked on wore more semblances than one, which cannot be, for it is always what it was before; but as my sight by seeing learned to see, the transformation which in me took place transformed the single changeless form for me. That light supreme, within its fathomless clear substance, showed to me three spheres, which bare three hues distinct, and occupied one space; the first mirrored the next, as though it were rainbow from rainbow, and the third seemed flame breathed equally from each of the first pair. How weak are words, and how unfit to frame my concept— which lags after what was shown so far, 'twould flatter it to call it lame! Eternal light, that in thyself alone dwelling, alone dost know thyself, and smile on thy self-love, so knowing and so known! The sphering thus begot, perceptible in thee like mirrored light, now to my view—when I had looked on it a little while—seemed in itself, and in its own self-hue, limned with our image; for which cause mine eyes were altogether drawn and held thereto. As the geometer his mind applies to square the circle, nor for all his wit finds the right formula, howe'er he tries, so strove I with that wonder—how to fit the image to the sphere; so sought to see how it maintained the point of rest in it. Thither my own wings could not carry me, but that a flash my understanding clove, whence its desire came to it suddenly. High phantasy lost power and here broke off; yet as a wheel moves smoothly, free from jars, my will and my desire were turned by love, the love that moves the sun and the other stars.[16]

♦ ♦ ♦

This then completes my discussion of the accidental properties that all theists are agreed in ascribing to God. Given that there is a universe, on the truth of theism God must—of logical necessity—be its creator. Given that there are creatures within the universe, it cannot but be that some things will be good for them and some things bad as a result of the way God has—as a contingent matter of fact—created them; he must thus be the ultimate source of moral and other sorts of value for them. In virtue of their being people *simpliciter*, it cannot but be that believing the truth about significant matters such as God's existence and will is good for them and thus it cannot but be that God will reveal himself and his will, in this world, though only if they choose to seek it. One of the things that would be bad for people is their permanently ceasing to exist at death and thus he must offer everlasting life in Heaven with him to people and to any other non-personal creature for whom permanently ceasing to exist would be bad (either in their own right or in virtue of their being cared about by people or other creatures). Further, this offer of everlasting life in Heaven with him is one which no person will ever be able ultimately to refuse. Ultimately, the love of God is inescapable for in coming into his presence at the Last Judgement, his existence and will will become inescapable for us; it will be too late then for any exercise of freedom to choose to be other than perfect, to choose to do other than what will be inescapably the only reasonable thing to do, bow down and worship him for ever. For those who have not already 'turned to him'—committed themselves to seeking God's will and conforming to it—being forced to one's knees like this at the Last Judgement will be more or less hellish, but for none will this suffering be everlasting; and for all perfect fulfilment lies just beyond it. These four accidental properties are in other words all necessitated by the fact that God has created a universe with people free to be less than perfect in it. Once we add to theism the (contingent given God's perfect freedom) fact that there's a universe with people free to be less than perfect in it, these accidental properties all follow and thus could be said to be mere aspects of the one property of ultimate creatordom as it applies to the world God has actually created.

Just as we said at the end of Chapter Three that the nine 'different' essential properties of God were all entailed by and thus could be seen as aspects of the unitary and simple property of divinity, of being the most perfect person possible, so these four 'different' accidental properties are all entailed by the claim that the most perfect person possible has created a world with people free to be less than perfect in it. Given that nobody would wish to deny that there is a universe and that there are people free to be less than perfect in it, no theist who fully understands what they are saying will wish to deny that God has any of these accidental properties.

◆ ◆ ◆

We have then at the centre of the main monotheistic religions—Judaism, Christianity, and Islam—a coherent, simple, and substantial claim with coherent, simple, and substantial implications.

Believing that God exists is believing that the most perfect person possible exists, a being who is personal; transcendent; immanent; omnipotent; omniscient; eternal; perfectly free; perfectly good; and necessary. Believing that such a being exists gives us reason to respect the world in which we live as his body and creation; to seek out his will for us in this world and to conform our lives to it; to fear a Last Judgement when our shameful failures will be laid bare; and yet to hope to be clothed in glory thereafter to share in everlasting life with him.

If a loved one is travelling by aeroplane and one hears that the plane has crashed and that only one person out of the hundred aboard has survived, it is reasonable for one to hope that this survivor is one's loved one, but it is not reasonable to believe that it probably is; the odds are against it. If an evil dictator is travelling by aeroplane and one hears that the plane has crashed and that most of the people aboard have survived, it is reasonable to believe that he has probably survived, but unreasonable to hope that he has survived (assuming I make him evil enough and perhaps juggle some other details); the odds are in his favour. The nature of God and its implications for us should he exist are sufficient then for it to be reasonable for us to hope that God exists and unreasonable for us to hope that he does not exist. I say that the nature of God and its implications for us are such as to make it reasonable to hope that he exists and unreasonable to hope that he does not because, from the consistency of the theistic concept of God as we have been hammering it out, we may conclude that it is logically possible that he exists and, from the implications for us of a concept with that content's being instantiated, we may conclude that it would be maximally good for us if he did exist. What could be better for us as individuals or collectively than that after this life we be gathered up into an everlasting afterlife in which we find perfect fulfilment? Given that this is what the existence of God would entail for each of us, it is unreasonable not to hope that there's a God. If one hears that a plane carrying someone who holds the secret of everlasting and ultimate fulfilment has crashed, it is reasonable to maintain the hope that this person has survived for as long as there remains a chance that he or she has survived. Of course that it is similarly maximally reasonable to maintain the hope that God exists does not entail that it is maximally reasonable, or even more reasonable than it would otherwise have been, to believe that he does exist. And this being so, we must be careful.

When one—reasonably or unreasonably—hopes that a certain conclusion is true, this can lead to one's being somewhat careless in checking the credentials of arguments that would purport to give one reasons for supposing that it is indeed true, and dilatory in considering those arguments that would purport to give one reasons for supposing that it's not true. Given that it is maximally reasonable to hope that God exists, we might then be more than ordinarily careless in our critique of the arguments for and against his existence. But to have drawn attention to this danger is for us to have forearmed ourselves in dealing with it. All we need do is continue treading carefully, guarding the flame by which we make our faltering way as best we are able. That this is all we need do is fortuitous as it is all we can do.

We have looked at what the central claim of theism means and what it would mean for us if it were true. The question that now presents itself is thus simple and compelling: is it true?

To this question we now turn.

PART II

THE EXISTENCE OF GOD

6

Arguing for and Against the Existence of God

In the first five chapters, I've discussed the properties of God that all theists are agreed in ascribing to him. I've drawn attention to certain prima facie conceptual problems associated with these properties. However, my—admittedly brief—analyses of these have led me to conclude that the conceptual problems posed by the divine properties that all theists are agreed on are by no means insuperable and are certainly no greater than those associated with the properties of many other entities that we believe exist. Had I been writing a book on the nature of atoms, civilization, or beauty I would not have encountered any less conceptual problems than I have encountered in discussing the nature of God; indeed I would have encountered many more. So it is that I concluded that the sentence 'There is a God' has a clear meaning: it says something determinate and substantial and something that is indeed in itself simple.

That God, should he exist, is simple is important in connection with the arguments for and against the existence of God that I'm about to go on to discuss, given that it is a canon of rationality that *ceteris paribus* we prefer simpler theories to more complicated ones. Let me illustrate that.

Suppose that this morning you'd found a letter addressed to your neighbour lying on your doormat. This letter lying there would have been something that required an explanation. The explanation we would all agree was the most rational one for you to believe on this evidence would have been that someone had misdelivered it, mistaking your house for that of your neighbour. However, there would have been other possible explanations of the letter lying there. Here's one:

A team of Ninja monkeys trained by a ruthless criminal mastermind purposefully delivered this letter to you as the first part of a devilish scheme to generate in you an identity crisis, as a result of which the mastermind hopes to be able to gain access to your bank account, using its funds to further his diabolical plans for world domination.

That would be an explanation too in that were it true it would explain the presence of a letter addressed to your neighbour lying on your doormat. Why then is it that we'd think that someone who believed the 'Ninja Monkeys' hypothesis was less reasonable than someone who believed the 'Mistaken Post-man' hypothesis on the evidence actually presented, a letter to your neighbour lying on your doormat? It is, I suggest, because the Mistaken Postman hypothesis is simpler. One might argue that background evidence not related to simplicity is relevant here, e.g. evidence that in one's experience it's very tough to train monkeys in the ways of the Ninja. If so, perhaps an example where one is deciding between two hypotheses one of which posits a single entity and the other of which posits two entities of a given level of complexity and prior probability would be better, e.g. if—for some reason—one was forced to posit at least one Ninja monkey, one would regard it as an unjustified extravagance to posit more than one.[1] We take simplicity to be a guide to truth. In general, we need simplicity to get over a problem that is usually called the 'Problem of the Underdetermination of Theory by Data'.

◆ ◆ ◆

Imagine that you wished to investigate how property y varied with property x. So you measured y for various values of x and plotted these measurements on a graph. The sort of graph that you got is shown in Figure 1.

What hypothesis concerning the relation between x and y would you be most reasonable in believing on this evidence? It would be the hypothesis that x equals y.

But why not x equals Fy, where F is the function that would describe this curvy line though all the points (Figure 2)?

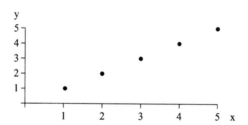

Figure 1

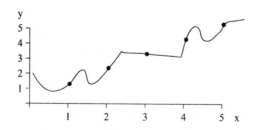

Figure 2

This line goes through all the points that constitute your evidence. In that sense it equally well explains your evidence. Does that make it equally reasonable to believe it on the evidence? We can see that if we said 'Yes' to that, then—because an infinite number of lines can be drawn through any finite number of points—we'd have to say that any evidence makes us equally reasonable in believing any of an infinite number of hypotheses. But that would obviously be absurd. When we decide therefore what it is most reasonable to believe on the basis of certain evidence, we look not just to an ability to 'explain' in the sense of conform to all the data, but for something else. What is this something else? Simplicity. We say that it's more reasonable to believe the hypothesis that x equals y on this evidence because that's the simplest theory that explains the evidence—a straight line is more simple than a curvy one.

Sometimes the draw of simplicity in a theory is so great that we allow it to lead us to prefer a theory that does *not* in fact even explain all the evidence and we consider ourselves rational in doing so. Consider a graph where there are thousands of data points on the line described by x equals y and only one off it. Would we not say that the most rational thing to believe in those circumstances would be that x equals y and that the result that can't be squared with this theory is mistaken, we just didn't measure x or y properly that time? I contend that we would. Even if we had no reason to believe that we had measured x or y incorrectly on that occasion other than the fact that the values we obtained for them couldn't be squared with the simplest theory, we'd still favour the theory that we had measured x or y incorrectly. So, in parallel with ability to explain our evidence, we take simplicity to be a guide to the truth of a hypothesis.

The hypothesis that there is a God is thus one that it is reasonable to hold to the extent that God's nature is simple *and* there's evidence that needs explanation that his existence would explain. I've argued that God's nature is simple. In a moment I'm going to go looking to see whether there is any evidence that needs explanation and that his existence would explain. If I find out that there isn't any such evidence, then the simplicity of the hypothesis that there is a God will become a moot point. Just as if in fact there was no letter addressed to your neighbour lying on your doormat this morning, the fact that someone misdelivering a letter is a relatively simple hypothesis is a moot point. On the other hand, if I find out that there is the right sort of evidence, then the simplicity of the hypothesis that there is a God will be crucial in eliminating as equally reasonable other more complicated hypotheses that might suggest themselves as equally well explaining that evidence.

So the question is: is there any evidence that provides a reason for believing that there is a God?

◆ ◆ ◆

Arguments are what purport to set out the evidence that gives us reasons to believe something and good arguments I initially define as those that do indeed give us reason to believe their conclusions. In a moment, I'm going to tinker with this definition of good arguments, but as a first stab it's pretty close and it's a good place to start.

I'm going to spend a moment or two describing the nature of good arguments. In doing so, I'm going to be setting up what sort of arguments I'm going to be looking for in going about answering the question 'Is there any evidence that provides a reason for believing that there is a God?', so, even though much of what I say will be familiar to those of you who've studied philosophy before, I'd encourage all of you not to skip the rest of this chapter.

The nature of arguments is to move from one or more claims—known as premises—to another claim—known as the conclusion. The premises state the evidence that forms the reasons for believing the conclusion. An argument is said to be a 'deductively valid' argument just if the conclusion follows from the premises in the sense that it is logically impossible for the conclusion to be false and yet the premises all true. In other words, telling you that an argument is deductively valid is just telling you that it cannot be leading from truth in the premises to falsity in the conclusion. There are definitely deductively valid arguments for the existence of God. This is one:

Everything the Pope believes as a matter of doctrine is true.
The Pope believes that God exists as a matter of doctrine.
Therefore, God exists.

This argument is deductively valid. Of course one might believe that the premises aren't both true, but the crucial point in assessing deductive validity is not whether or not the premises are as a matter of fact true but whether or not it's possible for them to be true and yet the conclusion be false. And it's not possible for the premises of this argument to be true and yet the conclusion false; thus this argument is a deductively valid one for the existence of God. Here's another deductively valid argument for the existence of God:

Cézanne painted Gauguin.
Cézanne did not paint Gauguin.
Therefore, God exists.

The premises of this argument contradict one another, so they can't both be true. It's not possible for both the premises of this argument to be true and the conclusion false because it's not possible for both the premises of this argument to be true. Thus this argument can't be leading from truth in the premises to falsity in the conclusion for it can't be leading from truth in the premises at all, so it must be deductively valid by the standard definition.

From these two examples, we can see that it's not simply deductively valid arguments for the existence of God that we're looking for when we're looking for good arguments for the existence of God. What else might be required?

An argument is said to be 'deductively sound' just if it's deductively valid *and* all its premises are true. Would deductive soundness alone be enough for an argument to be good? If there is a God, then there are definitely deductively sound arguments for the existence of God too. For example:

If you're reading this book, then there is a God.
You are reading this book.
Therefore, there is a God.

If there's a God, then whether or not you're reading this book there's a God, so it's certainly true that if you're reading this book, then there's a God. So if there is a God, the first premise is true. You are reading this book, so the second premise is true too. Finally, if there's a God, then the conclusion is true for the conclusion just says that there is a God. So if there is a God, then this argument does not have any false claims in either of the premises and it is deductively valid—for it has the structure 'if p, then q; p; therefore, q', which is a structure that can't be leading you from truth to falsity. So, if there's a God, this is a deductively sound argument for the existence of God.

But this argument is not what we would call good even if we think there is a God. This is because we are reluctant to call an argument good if we need to know the truth of the conclusion before we can recognize it as deductively sound. So, from this example, we can see that it's not simply deductively sound arguments for the existence of God that we're looking for when we're looking for good arguments for the existence of God. What we are looking for then—one might suggest—are deductively sound arguments for the existence of God that can be recognized as such without needing already to know that there is a God.

A deductively sound argument for the existence of God the deductive soundness of which was more obvious than is the existence of God would be a good argument for the existence of God. That sort of argument would be a deductive—airtight— proof that there is a God in the sense that it would be an argument that showed us that if we were to admit that the premises were indeed true, we would then contradict ourselves if we went on to deny that there is a God; and it would be an argument that employed premises and reasoning that were more obviously correct to us than was the truth of the conclusion that there is a God.

Is that the only thing that should satisfy us in our search for reasons for thinking that there is a God? No, it is not.

◆ ◆ ◆

We've just seen that there are many deductively sound arguments that are not good. There are also many good arguments that are not deductively sound. Consider this argument:

Andy was found standing alone in a locked room with the body of Bob, moments after Bob's death.
Andy had been heard to shout, 'I'm going to kill you, Bob' moments before a single shot had rung out.

Bob had been shot dead.
Andy had a smoking gun in his hand when he was found.
Andy's first words on being discovered were, 'I've just killed Bob'.
Therefore, Andy killed Bob.

That—I think we would all agree—is a very good argument. Anybody who accepted the truth of all the premises but denied the conclusion would be being very unreasonable indeed. Accepting the truth of the premises commits one—on pain of irrationality—to accepting the truth of the conclusion. However, it does not commit one on pain of *contradiction* to accepting the truth of the conclusion. The argument is not deductively sound even if all the premises are true, because it is not deductively valid. It is just possible that it could be leading you from truth in the premises to falsity in the conclusion—not likely, but just possible.

Consider this possibility: Andy intended to shoot Bob; he shouted this at Bob; and he pulled out a gun with the intention of shooting him. However, a certain Charlie—who had a silenced sniper-rifle trained on Bob through the open window from the garden outside—fired first, killing Bob. Andy—in frustration at having been denied the chance to kill Bob himself—fired his gun out of the window at Charlie, thus causing the sound of the single shot that was heard. When Andy was discovered with the smoking gun, he quickly decided that even though Charlie had denied him the pleasure of killing Bob himself, he wanted Charlie to be able to make good his escape, so Andy lied and claimed that he himself had just killed Bob.

This—though unlikely—is a possibility and so we must admit that the truth of the premises does not guarantee the truth of the conclusion. However, the truth of the premises makes it very improbable that the conclusion is false, so improbable that we would certainly call this a good argument for the guilt of Andy. Because this argument raises the probability of its conclusion on the truth of its premises so that its conclusion becomes more probably true than false, it deserves to have some sort of honorific name bestowed upon it; let's call it 'inductively valid', to pair terminologically with 'deductively valid'. An inductively sound argument then we could define as one that is inductively valid and has only true premises. An inductively sound argument for the existence of God that could be recognized as such without needing to rely on the assumption that there is a God would not be an airtight proof that there is a God, but it would be an argument that showed us that were we to admit that the premises were indeed true, we would then be irrational if we went on to deny that there is a God; and it would employ premises and reasoning that were more obviously correct to us than was the truth of the conclusion that there is a God. An inductively sound argument for the existence of God which could be recognized as such without needing to rely on the assumption that there is a God would thus also be a good argument for the existence of God.

There's obviously a crucial difference between an argument raising the probability of its conclusion to some extent, but not to the extent that its conclusion becomes more probably true than false, and its raising it to the extent that its conclusion does become more probably true than false. Consider this argument:

Andy hated Bob.
Therefore, Andy killed Bob.

This, we would incline to say, is not a good argument for (as well as, obviously, not being deductively valid) it does not have the property we are calling inductive validity: the truth of the premises—well, in this case there's only one premise—does not make the conclusion more probably true than false. But the fact that Andy hated Bob does in itself ever so slightly increase the chances that he killed him. If you hate someone, you're more likely to kill that person than if you don't hate him or her; the fact that Andy hated Bob does, we might say, inductively *support* the conclusion that he killed Bob. Of course, you're still much more likely not to kill than you are to kill someone you hate, and this is surely why we would say that merely drawing attention to the fact that Andy hated Bob is not on its own going to provide a good argument for the conclusion that he killed Bob, why the level of inductive support given by the premise to the conclusion is not so great as to make the argument inductively valid.

This all shows that my first attempt at a definition of a good argument—as one that gives one reasons for believing its conclusion—isn't quite right. Many arguments that would indeed have to be accepted as giving one reasons for believing a certain conclusion we would not call good because the reasons they give—though genuinely reasons—are not good enough reasons. They raise the probability of the conclusion—as I have put it, they inductively support the conclusion—yet the conclusion still remains less likely to be true than false on the truth of the premises. They are not deductively valid and neither are they inductively valid arguments. So a better definition of a good argument than the one I started with would be:

A good argument is one the premises of which make its conclusion more probable than not and the premises and reasoning of which are more obviously correct than is the conclusion.

This then would be a definition that included all deductively and inductively sound arguments for the existence of God that could be recognized as such without needing to rely on the assumption that there is a God.

Finally, a number of arguments that on their own inductively supported a particular conclusion but none of which considered in isolation raised the probability of this conclusion beyond 50 per cent and thus did not on their own count as inductively sound might, when taken together, raise the probability of the conclusion beyond 50 per cent and thus when taken together produce what could be called a 'cumulative case argument' for their conclusion that was inductively sound and thus good.

So that's what I suggest we should consider ourselves to be aiming at when arguing for and against the existence of God, good arguments. And that's what I suggest we mean by good arguments.

Now I want to speak about why we are interested in looking for good arguments for the existence of God (and, in due course, for his non-existence) and where I'll be assuming we're starting from in considering some putatively good arguments.

◆ ◆ ◆

Some of our beliefs are based on other beliefs by arguments that we take to be of the sort just sketched, these other beliefs stating the evidence that constitutes our reasons for the beliefs so based upon them. However, given that none of us (except God, if he exists) can entertain an infinite number of beliefs, which is what—*per impossibile*—would be needed were we to ground each of our beliefs in at least one other via an argument of one of these sorts, so it must be that some of our beliefs are 'unbased', they are basic. It is intellectually respectable (because it is intellectually inescapable) for us to have some beliefs without basing them on any other beliefs we have about there being evidence for them. It is thus natural to ask which belief or beliefs it is acceptable to have as basic; in other words, 'Which is or are "properly basic"?' In the context of our concerns in this book, it is natural to ask whether belief that there's a God might be properly basic. This is the question to which we'll address ourselves briefly now.

Some philosophers have certainly maintained that it could well be 'entirely right, rational, reasonable, and proper to believe in God without any evidence or argument at all'[2] and while I incline to agree with them in principle, I do not think that anyone reading this will be a person for whom belief in God can in this way be properly basic.

For some people in some cultures at some times, belief that there's a God has certainly been basic. We may imagine an orphan, brought up in a secluded monastery in the Middle Ages. He never hears of 'atheism' or 'agnosticism' as possibilities; he never has any argument for or against the existence of God presented to him for his consideration. Although he is ceaselessly told about God by his fellow monks, he does not take their testimony as evidence that what they are saying is true—he never uses the fact that they are saying these things as a premise in an argument for the truth of what it is that they are saying. He simply and uncritically believes what they are saying. His belief that there is a God is a belief that it has never occurred to him might be questioned or justified. For this orphan, belief that there's a God is thus basic.

So belief that there's a God could be basic; our only question then it might seem is, 'Could belief that there's a God be *properly* basic?' Of course, it is open to one to assert that it is properly basic to believe that belief that there's a God is always properly basic and thus that answering the question, 'Could belief that there's a God be properly basic?' affirmatively requires of one no argumentative effort at all. But if one does not avail oneself of this possibility, then in answering this question we will need to employ some criteria for proper basicality and give some arguments for why we should believe that the belief that there's a God satisfies these criteria generally or would do for someone in the right circumstances. If one deviates from the consensus among those who talk of belief in God as properly basic, and makes it a necessary condition for a belief being properly basic that it be true, any argument to the effect that belief that there's a God is or could be properly basic will then depend on establishing that there is a God, and thus the person who has a good reason for believing that belief that there's a God is or could be properly basic won't be the sort of person for whom belief that there's a God is properly basic—he or she won't be the sort of person who takes his or her belief that there's a God to be ungrounded on other, more basic, beliefs via some argument. But if one keeps with the consensus among those who talk of belief in God as properly basic, and fails to make a belief being true a criterion of its being properly basic, it becomes impossible to give a satisfactory account of what the 'propriety' of its basicality consists in. As *propriety* is a pro-concept—in this context it signifies a quality that it's good for a belief to have—and as our basic beliefs are precisely those that we have no reason to hold, the only potential good quality that our basic beliefs might have (in virtue of which we might bestow upon them the pro-concept of propriety) is truth. As it is therefore (*pace* the consensus among philosophers who discuss this issue most enthusiastically) plausible to make it a necessary condition of a belief's being properly basic that it be true, so on the issue of the propriety of taking the belief that there's a God to be basic we reach something of an impasse, but—for the readership of this book—we can see that the issue has become an irrelevance. Whether belief that there is a God could be properly basic for someone depends on whether or not it could be basic for them and belief that there's a God could not be basic for anyone reading this. Anyone reading this book will not be in a position analogous to the orphan brought up in a secluded monastery in the Middle Ages. They will have met theists; atheists; and agnostics. They will have heard of various arguments for and against the existence of God and thought about them. They will have started to place their belief in the existence of God; their belief in his non-existence; or their belief that they should suspend judgement on whether or not there's a God, in relation to other beliefs that they have about these issues, beliefs that they will regard as more basic. If they have the belief that there is a God (or that there's not) and are told that this belief might be properly basic, they will ask for arguments to suppose that it might be, arguments an understanding of which will—via the considerations just sketched—reveal that they themselves are not people for whom the belief is basic, a fortiori they are not people for whom the belief is properly basic. If belief that there is (or that there's not) a God could indeed be properly basic for someone, we are not such people. For better or worse, we need arguments if we are to proceed.[3]

As we have to proceed by argumentation, we need a clear idea of where we are starting from.

In colloquial use and indeed much traditional discussion, theists are those who believe that there is a God; atheists are those who believe that there is not; and agnostics are those who neither believe that there is nor believe that there's not. However, the etymology of 'agnostic' favours a deviation from colloquial use. We might say that agnostics are those who believe that they do not know whether or not there's a God; they may nevertheless believe that there is or believe that there's not. On this understanding of agnostic then, it is quite possible for theists or atheists to be agnostics. An agnostic theist, for example, would believe that there is a God but also think that his or her belief that there's a God did not have whatever it is that must be added to true belief to make it knowledge. Until relatively recently in the history of philosophy, this could have been taken to be the same as his or her believing that he or she didn't have adequate reasons for his or her belief that there's a God on the assumption that our agnostic was well up on (and subscribed to) the consensus view of the nature of knowledge. However, in recent times there has been some rethinking of the nature of knowledge as a result of which many would maintain that one might have knowledge of something without having adequate (or indeed any) reasons for believing it and one might have adequate (indeed overwhelming) reasons for believing something without knowing it even if it were true, so the position has become somewhat more complicated. We have just discussed one manifestation of this complication, the thesis that belief that there's a God might be properly basic. However, I have hazarded that everyone reading this will have thought about the existence of God before; everyone will have accumulated 'background knowledge' from his or her own experiences and those of others; everyone will have started to place their belief in God or lack of it in relation to this background knowledge and so will have started to deviate from what one might call the 'default position', in which one neither believes that one has good reasons for believing that there's a God, nor believes that one has good reasons for believing that there's not. Because this background knowledge and people's reflections on it are going to be very variable and I have to address to you in writing as a group rather than as individuals—when of course there would be no need for me to address you in writing at all (we could simply have a chat)—I have to choose a compromise starting point for my argument. I'm going to address myself directly then to a rather hypothetical readership, those who are still in the 'default position' in the following way: (a) they neither believe that there is a God, nor believe that there's not; and (b) they believe that there is no more reason to believe that there's a God than to believe that there's not and no more reason to believe that there's not than to believe that there is. While one could with precedent and reason call this 'agnosticism', because of the vexed issue of the nature of knowledge, I'm in fact going to call this the 'fifty/fifty position'. Take a coin. Toss it in the air. Let it land without looking at which way up it's landed.

What do you believe about whether it's landed heads-side up or tails-side up? What do you believe about your reasons for believing that it's landed heads-side or tails-side up? You will find that you neither believe that it's landed heads-side up, nor believe that it's landed tails-side up; you believe that it's 50 per cent probable that the coin has landed heads-side up and 50 per cent probable that its landed tails-side up because there are only two options—heads or tails (you've noticed that it's not landed on its edge)—and you recognize that you have no reason to think that one is more likely than the other. You're in the fifty/fifty position with respect to the claim that the coin's landed—let's say—heads-side up. The analogous fifty/fifty position with respect to the claim that there's a God is a position that, while probably not being exactly the point from which any of you are actually starting, will be one that minimizes the chances of anybody feeling left out by being too far away from me for what I say to be relevant to them.

If you are indeed starting from the fifty/fifty position, then any argument that inductively supports the conclusion that it is true that there's a God is, of course, in itself an inductively sound argument for the truth of theism. And any argument that inductively supports the conclusion that it is false that there's a God is in itself an inductively sound argument for the falsity of theism. If you have inductively sound arguments on both sides, you have to weigh them against one another to see what you have most overall reason to believe, if anything. (You might end up back in the fifty/fifty position.)

Let me go on, then, to start to tell you about the arguments I'm going to look at.

◆ ◆ ◆

In the history of thought, there have been a very great number of arguments that have purported to give us reasons for thinking that there is a God. Kant helpfully divided these arguments into three classes. First, there are those that begin from determinate experience (some particular feature of the world); secondly, there are those that begin from indeterminate experience (the mere fact that there is a world); and thirdly, there are those that begin from pure categories a priori (arguments that start simply from the concept of God). So, into the first class we would put those arguments for the existence of God that start with some feature of the universe, for example, that it is ordered; that it had a beginning; that it contains moral truths; that it contains the particular moral truths that it does; that it contains various miracles or reports of miracles anyway; that people have religious experience within it; and so on. Into the second class we would put the Cosmological Argument, beginning as it does from the mere fact that there is a universe. Into the third class, we would put the Ontological Argument, beginning as it does simply from reflection on the concept of God.

With the exception of the Ontological Argument, all these arguments for the existence of God can be presented as good in virtue of being deductively sound in ways more obvious than is the truth of theism; or as good in virtue of being inductively sound in ways more obvious than is the truth of theism; or as—while not in isolation good—having true premises and inductively supporting the truth of theism in a way more obvious than is the truth of theism, i.e. as positively contributing to what is potentially a good cumulative case argument for God's existence. The Ontological Argument can only be presented as purporting to be good in virtue of being a deductively sound argument that can be recognized as such without relying on the assumption that there is a God.

We've only got a finite amount of time available to us, so I've had to narrow my focus down to a manageable number of arguments. I've selected the arguments I'm going to look at on the basis of how prima facie plausible they seem to me. One can't look at every argument someone has or might in the future put forward; one has to engage in some sort of preselection by reference to one's philosophical 'gut instinct'. And if my gut instinct has led me to consider and yet ultimately reject arguments that your gut instinct would have warned you off even considering in the first place, my apologies for what you will see as unnecessary delay. If it's led me to ignore an argument that your gut instinct would have directed you towards, this is potentially a cause for more serious complaint. But I can also add now a point that will not be fully supported until the end: these sorts of omissions cannot affect the reasonableness of my conclusion. The arguments I am going to consider are sufficient to guarantee that.

I'm going to consider the Ontological Argument; the Argument to Design; the Cosmological Argument; the Argument from Religious Experience; and the Argument from Apparent Miracles as arguments that purport to give us good reason for believing that it is true that there is a God. Then I'm going to look at the Problem of Evil as an argument that purports to give us good reason for believing that it's false that there's a God. Each of these arguments will get one of the remaining chapters to itself. Finally, in my last chapter, I'm going to look at the relation between having the belief that there's a God and having faith in God.

7

The Ontological Argument

The Ontological Argument was first thought of by St Anselm almost a thousand years ago.[1] The essence of the argument can be stated very briskly.

1. **God, by definition, is a perfect being.**
2. **It is better to exist than not to exist.**

Therefore, God exists.

In an argument, one may define terms however one wishes, and premise 1 just reports one aspect—indeed, I have argued, the central one—of the theistic definition of God. So if anything goes wrong with the argument, then it must be in premise 2. But premise 2 looks pretty obviously right as well. Consider the question: which of these would be better for you: that you be vaporized now with a ray gun and thus that you cease to exist or that you continue to exist?

However small an amount of benefit or enjoyment you're receiving from reading this, I doubt if you'll really think you'd be better off if you didn't exist. Of course, we can all imagine a situation where someone's life was so bad that it would be better for them if they ceased to exist—maybe the Spartan boy I told you about in an earlier chapter was in such a situation. However, if the person in question was in all other ways well off, it would certainly be better for him or her if he or she existed rather than not; and God is obviously going to be maximally well off in all other respects, so it's obviously going to be better for him (and indeed us) if he exists. The claim that it's better to exist than not to exist seems then—minor and irrelevant quibbling aside—right.

Both the premises of the Ontological Argument seem to be obviously true; taken together they seem to lead in an obviously deductively valid way to the conclusion that God exists, which was something not so obviously true. If God's by definition perfect, then of course—given that it's better to exist than not to exist—he'll have to exist. It's impossible for the premises to both be true and yet the conclusion false and it's obvious that both the premises are true. So it seems as if we've got a deductively sound argument for the existence of God the soundness of which is more obvious than is the existence of God. The Ontological Argument then seems to satisfy our criteria for being a good argument. It seems to, but does it?

♦ ♦ ♦

It's easier to spot that something has gone wrong with the Ontological Argument than it is to describe what it is that has gone wrong with it. One way of seeing that something has gone wrong with the Ontological Argument is to consider that if it worked, one could generate parallel arguments ad infinitum that proved the existence of any sort of entity one cared to mention. Allow me to introduce one such parallel argument.

The Senior Common Room butler at my college is pretty good at keeping us all in order. For example, there was one occasion, early on in my membership of the Senior Common Room, when I was dining at High Table. The main course arrived—to be served silver-service style by the butler. I was one of the first to be served, and scooted one slice of whatever it was off the salver, then prepared to take a second. The butler leaned forward slightly and *sotto voce* advised me, 'One is usually considered sufficient, sir.' I was a bit miffed at this, but left the second portion on the salver, which proceeded in his hands down the table towards the end, where the Senior Tutor was sitting. As it arrived there, I noticed that there had been exactly the right number of portions on the salver to mean that the Senior Tutor—the last to be served—took the last one. Had I taken a second portion earlier on, then the Senior Tutor would have been left without any main course; the assembled eyes of the Senior Common Room would have then worked their way back along the table, unerringly seeking out where this problem had originated. Ultimately, they would have fallen on me, merrily munching my way through two portions. Were it not for the timely intervention of the butler, my career at my college might have been cut rather short.

So, as you can tell, my college's butler is pretty good at keeping people out of scrapes. But even he isn't the best possible butler; even he can't quite be a Jeeves to my Wooster, which is—one might reasonably hypothesize—more of a sign of how much of a Wooster I am than how little a Jeeves he is. In any case, reflection on this incident prompts me to think that it would certainly be rather handy to have a butler at one's side throughout one's life, ready to assist one in making one's way through the world with wise *sotto voce* advice. Let me define the term 'Jeeves' to mean the best possible butler for you. So, Jeeves will—by definition— always be on hand for you whenever you might need him.

1. Jeeves I define as the best possible butler for you.
2. If there is a better analysis of the Ontological Argument than this, it would be better for Jeeves to be right by your side now, handing you this better analysis.

Therefore, Jeeves must be right by your side now, handing you a better analysis of the Ontological Argument than this one.

This argument seems as good as the Ontological Argument for the existence of God. The first premise simply reports my definition of 'Jeeves', so there's nothing to be argued with there. The second premise reports the fact that if there were such a thing as a better analysis of the Ontological Argument than this, then, as it would be better if you were reading this better analysis, so a better butler would be one who was by your side with such an analysis. That seems to follow pretty obviously. Yet from these two premises it follows that Jeeves must be right by your side with a better analysis than this. Look for him. Is he there? No. The only way to escape the conclusion that he must be there seems to be to claim that this is the best possible analysis that one might attempt of the Ontological Argument. I might be happy to rest content with this conclusion, but I doubt that you are.

The objection that if the Ontological Argument worked, then my Jeeves argument and similar sorts of arguments would also work is sometimes called the 'Overload Objection' to the Ontological Argument; if the Ontological Argument worked, then we could overload the universe with all sorts of entities like Jeeves.

◆ ◆ ◆

So, something's gone wrong with the Ontological Argument. What exactly?

First, premise one is rather ambiguous. Is this premise using the term 'God' to pick something out and then attributing a property, albeit an essential one, to it, just as you might say that this book here—waving it around—is by definition something that has pages? Well, if so, we could not know that the term 'God' had secured reference without already knowing the conclusion of this argument, that there is a God, so premise 1 would not be one that could be known to be true with more certainty than we knew the conclusion, that there is a God. This would be sufficient to undercut any claim that the Ontological Argument— however deductively sound—is good. However, if premise 1 is not using the term 'God' to pick out something and then attribute a property to that thing, then it must mean something like '*If* there is a God, then he is by definition perfect', but if that's what premise 1 really means, then although it can be known to be true without first needing to know that there is a God, it cannot support the conclusion that God exists but only—at best—the conclusion that *if* there is a God, then he exists. This conclusion is a rather unexciting one. We all knew that anyway. So premise 1, despite my initial enthusiasm for it, is in fact deeply questionable.

Despite this being a sufficient reason to reject the Ontological Argument, for the sake of completeness if nothing else we must look at the second premise. The second premise is also the one on which most philosophical criticism has focused. The second premise is 'It is better to exist than not to exist.' What can be said against this second premise?

◆ ◆ ◆

One can beat around the bush for quite a long time here, but eventually one gets to the point that was first made by Kant: existence is not a predicate. Let me explain what Kant meant.

I talked earlier about this book and a couple of the properties that it had: one of these properties was that it was, I guessed, then being held by you. I'm guessing it's got that property again now. Kant's point would be that while it is indeed a bona fide property of this book that it is being held by you, it's not a bona fide property of it that it exists; saying that existence isn't a predicate is a way of saying that existence isn't a property that objects have. So, the following sentences as spoken by me are true (I'm supposing): 'This book is being held by you' and 'This book exists,' but—according to Kant—there's a crucial difference between these two sentences. The first really does predicate something of the book. It picks out the book and asserts of it that it has a property, the property of being held by you. The second sentence, despite its grammatical similarity with the first, does not—according to Kant—do this. It doesn't pick out the book and assert of it that it has a property, the property of existence. What does it do then? Answering that question is a bit more tricky. To do so I have to augment what Kant said with something said by a later philosopher, Gottlob Frege, and it's going to take a moment or two for me to set out all the ideas we need if we are to understand what Frege said.

First then, I want to introduce a distinction between what I'm going to call concrete objects and what I'm going to call abstract objects. Examples of concrete objects would be things like *this book*; *the chair you're currently sitting on*; and *your right hand*. Examples of abstract objects would be things like *the nature of education*; *the current government's misconception of the nature of education*; *its consequent policies with respect to universities*; and—to move away from my particular concerns—*the number five*. On what basis do we decide whether a given thing is a concrete or an abstract object; or indeed do we decide on any basis at all? (It may be that the distinction is a brute one—incapable of explication in terms of anything else.) This question is not an easy one to answer, but fortunately for my present purposes we don't need to answer it, assuming as I think it safe to assume that we all have a pretty good grasp on the distinction through the examples I've just given.

Armed then with the distinction between concrete and abstract objects, let's consider the concrete objects that are the chairs in the room in which you sit. Let me suppose for the sake of argument that there are three of them. It's natural for you to group the chairs in the room together in your mind for the purposes of discussion into one set, the set of chairs in the room. The set of chairs in the room is an abstract object the members of which are concrete objects. The abstract object that is the set of chairs in the room has properties that its concrete members do not have. It has the property of having a quarter of the number of members as the abstract object that is the set of chair legs in the room has (I'm assuming). The individual concrete objects that are the chairs in the room could not be said to have a quarter of the number of members as the set of chair legs in the room; that wouldn't make sense. The individual concrete objects that are the chairs in the room have properties that the abstract object that is the set of chairs in the room does not have; they each have upholstered seats (I'm assuming). The abstract object that is the set of chairs in the room could not be said to have an upholstered seat; that would not make sense either.

Now, consider the following two sentences as they might be spoken by you: 'The chairs in this room have upholstered seats' and 'The chairs in this room are three in number.' If one wasn't thinking too carefully, one might say that each of these sentences had the same subject—the chairs in the room in which you sit—and predicated different things of that subject, having upholstered seats and being three in number. But with Frege's help we can now see that the real subject of these two sentences is actually different, despite their similar grammar. The first sentence takes the concrete objects that are the chairs in the room as its subject; the second takes the abstract object that is the set of chairs in the room as its subject. The first is saying that the chairs in the room have a certain property, the property of having upholstered seats; the second is saying that the set of chairs in this room has a certain property, the property of having three members. With this in hand, we now have the tools to understand Frege's interpretation of existence.

Consider the sentence as uttered by you, 'The chairs in this room exist.' What is the true subject of this sentence? Is it the concrete objects that are the chairs in the room? No. Is it the set of chairs in this room? Yes. Saying that the chairs in the room exist is saying that the set of chairs in the room does not have zero members. Saying 'X exists' is not then actually saying anything about X. It's saying something of the abstract object that is the set of those things that's picked out by the concept of X and it's saying of it that it's not the set with zero members. So, according to Kant and Frege, existence is not a property of concrete objects; existence isn't something that objects do, like breathing, only quieter. Rather, when one says that X exists one asserts something, not about X, but about the set of Xs and what one asserts is that the set of Xs is not the empty set, the empty set being the set with zero members. If there is a God, then the set of Gods is not the empty set, but the fact that the set of Gods is not then the empty set is not a fact about God; it isn't a property of the concrete object that is God that the abstract object that is the set of Gods is not empty.

Once we've shown with Kant and Frege's help that existence is not a property of God even if he does exist, premise 2 of the Ontological Argument can be seen to collapse. If existence is not a property of God even if he does exist, then it cannot be a property that it is better for him if he has.

How then to explain our intuition that one's ceasing to exist would be bad? We have seen already that what would make one's permanently ceasing to exist bad for one is that it would frustrate one's flourishing and one's desires. Never having existed would not have frustrated any flourishing or desires, so even though it is not good for one that one was brought into existence, death would be bad for one if it was permanently ceasing to exist, which is why—as we've seen—if there's a God, he'll ensure that our deaths are not our permanently ceasing to exist. It's not bad for the brother that I never had that he never existed; it would be bad for the sisters that I do have if they permanently ceased to exist.

So, to sum up my conclusions with regard to the Ontological Argument: the first premise is true—on both interpretations of it—*if and only if* theism is true; it is false on the interpretation of it that would be necessary for the argument to be a deductively valid one for theism if theism is false. This is a sufficient reason for us to conclude that the Ontological Argument is not a good argument for theism. The second premise is false if existence is not a predicate, which it is not. This too is sufficient for us to conclude that the Ontological Argument is not a good argument for theism. The Ontological Argument fails in two ways then as a deductive argument and—starting as it does from pure categories a priori—it cannot be turned into an inductive argument. I therefore conclude that the Ontological Argument does not provide any reasons for believing that 'There is a God' is true.

◆ ◆ ◆

This is the 'classic' version of the Ontological Argument and one so central to the tradition that other 'versions', in so far as they differ from it, run the risk of not counting as versions simply by virtue of their doing so. However, if we think of the essence of the Ontological Argument as simply its proceeding 'from pure categories a priori', then there are arguments that are recognizably different from the classic version and yet deserve to be considered versions of the Ontological Argument. I'll close this chapter by discussing such arguments in terms of a rather generalized instance of them. It will be helpful, before I do this, to say a word or two about the notion of possible worlds as it is used in the presentation of arguments of this sort.

I began the book by using the word 'world' to refer to the physical universe as a whole, so that I might describe the perplexity that I claimed we have all felt at some moment in our lives when contemplating the world as a whole; the world as a whole raises in some sense a question to which we think God might be the answer. 'World' in this sense means 'universe'; in this sense of 'world', God himself could not then be a resident of the world; if he exists, he exists outside the world; he has to in order to explain it. The important point to note now is that the notion of worlds in play when we talk of possible worlds in this context is different. Possible worlds in this context are to be understood as ways that *everything* might be or might have been. Thus, at least prima facie, it seems logically possible both that there's a God of the sort we've been discussing in the first half of this book and also logically possible that there's not. Neither involves a contradiction in terms. If that's right, then—using this new notion of world— we might say that there's a possible world in which the physical universe (the world in my original sense) is as it is and there's a God on top and there's a possible world in which the physical universe is as it is and there's no God on top. God's a resident of the first world and not of the second. Theists think that the actual world is the first—the physical universe plus God (and perhaps various other supernatural beings)—and physicalists think that the actual world is the second—simply the physical universe as a whole.[2]

Consider then this argument:

1. It is possible that God exists, i.e. he does exist in some possible world.
2. If God exists in some possible world, then he exists in every possible world.

Therefore, God exists in every possible world, including the actual world, i.e. he actually exists.

The premises of this argument seem right. After all, we've just said that it is possible that God exists, which is the same as saying that he does exist in some possible world. And, even if it wasn't one of God's essential properties, given that it's obviously going to be better to exist necessarily rather than merely contingently, then, if there is a God, he's going to have that form of existence, he's going to exist in every possible world. So the premises seem right and the conclusion seems to follow deductively from them.

Again, perhaps the best way to see that something has gone wrong with this argument is to see that if this argument worked, then a parallel argument would also work, one that we won't want to say works. In this case, the reason we won't want to say that the parallel argument works is not because its working would 'overload' the universe but because we can't say that both arguments work as the second one working is incompatible with the first one working. This is the parallel argument:

1. It is possible that God does not exist, i.e. he does not exist in some possible world.
2. If God does not exist in some possible world, then he doesn't exist in every possible world.

Therefore, God doesn't exist in every possible world, including the actual world, i.e. he doesn't actually exist.

Surely we have no less (non-question-begging) reason to believe premise 1 of the parallel argument than we do premise 1 of the original argument. The first five chapters have established that the concept of God is internally consistent; it describes an entity that it is logically possible exists and that it is logically possible does not exist. So something's gone wrong with this version of the ontological argument. What?

The answer lies in the ambiguity of the word 'possible' and the notion of possible worlds. The first five chapters have established that the concept of God is consistent, so God's existence is logically possible, which amounts to there being no inconsistency in saying that God exists. This, we may say, is indeed equivalent to God's existing in some logically possible world, so let's take premise 1 of the original argument in this way: it is logically possible that God exists, i.e. he does exist in some logically possible world. As such, we may agree with premise 1. But that God exists in some logically possible world (indeed in an infinite number of them) does not entail that he exists in all logically possible worlds, as suggested by premise 2. Rather, God's non-existence is also logically possible; there is no inconsistency in saying that God does not exist. So God does not exist in some logically possible world, indeed he doesn't exist in an infinite number of them. So we may reject premise 2 and thus the argument. If we take the word 'possible' to mean metaphysically possible, then we must accept the second premise. If God does exist in some metaphysically possible world, then he exists in every metaphysically possible world because if there is a God, he's that on which everything else metaphysically depends. But then of course we have no (non-question-begging) reason to accept the first premise, that it's metaphysically possible that God exists. Whether or not we think that this is true depends on whether or not we believe there's a God. So this version of the Ontological Argument also fails as a good argument.

All versions of the Ontological Argument then fail to respect the categorical difference between manœuvring within a concept and discovering whether that concept, however understood, does or does not have an instantiation.[3] If we're going to find evidence of God's existence—a reason to believe that there's a God—we'll have to consider more than the mere concept of God. Where shall we look? The only place we can: the world that he's supposed to have created. We must see if he's left any evidence of his existence there. It has seemed to many that it's obvious that he has. Let us turn then to the Argument to Design.

8

The Argument to Design

Let me start by paraphrasing one of the most famous presentations of this argument, by a man called William Paley.[1]

Suppose that you and I happen to be walking across a heath one day and I pitch my foot on a stone. You ask me how I suppose that the stone happens to be there. I reply that it's probably been there since this part of the world was formed and—unless you knew quite a bit about geology—you find it rather difficult to know whether or not I'm wrong. We walk on. Next, I pitch my foot against a watch. In Paley's day this would have been a pocketwatch, but we can adapt his story slightly, so let me say I pitch my foot on a watch just like the one I'm guessing you're wearing on your wrist as you read this. Have a look at it now. Think about its construction for a moment or two, all the cogs and wheels it contains. You ask me the same question. How do I suppose that this watch happens to be there? It would hardly occur to me to answer for the watch as I had done for the stone. If I did, then—however little you knew about horology—you'd see immediately that I was mistaken. Yet why should not the same lack of explanation be equally appropriate for stone and watch?

The answer is that the watch, in contrast to the stone, displays evident marks of design; it is overtly a complicated mechanism constructed for some purpose. An intelligent being—even one who had never seen a watch before—would, if they stumbled across it, conclude that it was designed by a mind with some end in view. Now consider the universe as a whole. Is it more like a homogenous undifferentiated stone or is it more like a variable and complicated watch? The planets rotate on their own axes so that night follows day and they rotate around the Sun so that the seasons follow one another. The solar system itself is part of a galaxy, the Milky Way, which itself rotates and so on; wheels within wheels. Is this not rather like—suspiciously like—a watch? All are precisely adjusted relative to one another, adjusted then, one might think, for some purpose. And as surely as if there's a watch, there's a watchmaker, so if there's a purpose, there's a purposer. Should we not conclude then that the universe was designed by some supernatural agent of infinite power? We should. That—at any rate—is the Argument to Design.[2]

◆ ◆ ◆

The Argument to Design has a long history. There's arguably a version in one of the Psalms; St Paul seems to have endorsed a version of the argument in his letter to the Romans;[3] and even Kant, who rejected it, said that it was an argument that deserved always to be mentioned with respect.

I'm going to spend quite a bit of time talking about the Argument to Design as some of the points that apply to this argument equally well apply to others I'll come to later and that you'll come across in your own reading and thought. If I spend some time getting them straight now, you and I shall be able to make progress more quickly later.

The most significant critic of the Argument to Design is David Hume. Hume makes a number of points. I've divided them up rather artificially for the purposes of making my discussion of them easier. Here are four of the points Hume makes:

First, Hume points out that the Argument to Design is an argument from analogy, so the argument can only be as good as the analogy is close. And Hume argues that the analogy between the universe and human artefacts is not close: the universe just isn't that much like a watch; it's more like, say, a vegetable, something that one can't assume bears the marks of design on its face in the same evident way that a watch does.

Secondly, Hume argues that even if the analogy between the universe and human artefacts had been close, other hypotheses could equally well have explained the order in the universe. There might have been a committee of demigods creating this world; or this world might have been the first attempt of an infant deity, as yet not possessing the powers of the theistic God; or there might have been something rather like a giant spider that spun this world, somewhat like a web; or—well, you can go on inventing these hypotheses yourself. God might explain the order in the world, but there are an infinite number of other hypotheses that would explain it, so we could hardly be said to be forced to posit a God.

Thirdly, even if the existence of suffering in the world could be made compatible (or better, harmonious) with the existence of the theistic God—i.e. even if the Problem of Evil, which I have yet to discuss, did have an answer—it is still unreasonable to infer a perfect cause from an imperfect effect. You should only ever posit in the cause such properties as are strictly necessary to explain the effect you observe. The positing of a being who is omnipotent and perfectly good would thus be explanatory overkill. It would be rather as if, on the strength of my writing this, you were to conclude that I was the best philosopher since Socrates. The hypothesis that I'm the best philosopher since Socrates might be compatible with my writing this, but it could hardly be said to follow from it. (Feel free to disagree with the latter half of this opinion when discussing this book with others.)

Fourthly, the theistic hypothesis is useless as a hypothesis, for we cannot argue back from it to otherwise unknown features of the universe, for example the likelihood of answers to petitionary prayer and the likelihood and nature of a life after death.

What are we to make of these points? I think that the first one's good or at least can be polished up into something good and that the last three aren't good and can't be made so. Or at least that's what I'm going to start off by telling you I think. Later on, I'm going to endorse a point that might look a bit like a polished-up version of Hume's second point. For the moment though, let me look at the second, third, and fourth points to get those out of the way at least under some interpretations.

On my list, Hume's second point is the one that there are an infinite number of other hypotheses that could equally well explain the order in the world. Why is this not a good point? The answer comes in one word: 'simplicity'.

There are indeed explanations of the order in the universe other than the theistic one but—as my earlier discussion of the two explanations of a letter addressed to your neighbour finding itself on your doorstep showed—the availability of an infinite number of other explanations for some evidence doesn't make us think that it's not reasonable to believe the simplest explanation on that evidence. The hypothesis that there is a God is, I have argued, essentially simple—simpler certainly than the other hypotheses that Hume suggests. It is true then that we could hardly be said to be forced to posit a God; and this is indeed sufficient to show that the Argument to Design cannot be a deductively valid argument; a fortiori, it cannot be a deductively sound one. But then the Argument to Design need not be interpreted as purporting to be a deductive argument. It can be interpreted as purporting to be an inductive argument and if so interpreted it is an open question whether or not it might be inductively sound—i.e. show that it is more likely than not that there is a God—or whether, even if it did not live up to this standard, it might be an argument that could contribute something to an inductively sound cumulative case argument for this conclusion.

The same consideration of simplicity tells against Hume's third point, that to posit the theistic God is explanatory overkill. Contrary to Hume, it is not always rational to posit in a cause only such properties as are necessary to explain the particular effect we observe.

Do you posit that you yourself have only the power to be reading this book at the moment, that you don't have the power to put it down and go for a trip to the nearest shop instead? Of course not. You attribute to yourself all the powers that would be usual for a human being of your age and general level of health—even though vast numbers of these usual powers are not necessary to explain the particular effects you observe, your doing what it is you are actually doing. Why do you posit properties that are not necessary to explain the particular effects you observe? Because it's simplest to do so. Now one might suggest that in this case you know that you have various powers that you're not currently exercising because you remember having exercised those powers in the past; perhaps it strikes you as obvious that there are currently no barriers to your forming and acting on similar intentions and thus using those same powers again now. And while one should note, if only in passing, that this very induction would require the Principle of Simplicity to take you from the fact you've had these powers in the past to the fact that you've got them now (why not think you've suddenly become paralysed and not yet noticed?), it is true that if you came across something very different from anything you'd yet encountered and saw it displaying only one sort of power, you would not think yourself reasonable in ascribing to it other powers. But this diffidence is justified only because you know that creaturely powers are limited to a greater or lesser extent and in various ways by natural laws. Once one removes this background knowledge, as one must in the case of the creator of the natural laws, simplicity considerations will take one all the way to the God of theism. Rather than posit a being with just enough power to create this universe but no more and thus leave unexplained what it is that constrains this being in this way, simplicity dictates that one should posit no limit to this being's power. One infinite God is a simpler hypothesis than any hypothesis that posits another number of finite supernatural beings or mechanisms (or even one such being or mechanism).[4] The theistic hypothesis, I have argued, is simple. So, unless we have particular reason to posit that the explanation of the order of the universe is not omnipotent and perfectly good—which might indeed be provided by the Problem of Evil—it is *not* unreasonable to prefer the theistic hypothesis to other hypotheses as an explanation, just the reverse. So that's Hume's second and third points out of the way.

Hume's fourth point is that the theistic hypothesis once reached is useless in arguing back to otherwise unknown features of the world, e.g. the likelihood of answers to petitionary prayers and the likelihood and nature of any life after death. This seems—even if true (and, as we've already started to see, it isn't)—irrelevant. For it cannot be a good criticism of an argument that its conclusion does not allow one to infer various other interesting things.

Consider again this argument:

Andy was found standing alone in a locked room with the body of Bob, moments after Bob's death.

Andy had been heard to shout, 'I'm going to kill you, Bob,' moments before a single shot had rung out.

Bob had been shot dead.

Andy had a smoking gun in his hand when he was found.

Andy's first words on being discovered were, 'I've just killed Bob.'

Therefore, Andy killed Bob.

It's no criticism of this argument that the hypothesis that Andy killed Bob cannot be used to argue back to otherwise unknown features of Andy and Bob. What would you think as a jury member if, after the prosecution had convinced you of the truth of all the premises of this argument, Andy's defence barrister stood up and rested his whole case for the truth of the defendant's 'Not Guilty' plea on the fact that the hypothesis that Andy killed Bob did not allow you to infer anything concerning the 'vexing' issue of whether or not Andy and Bob had ever been clubbing together in Brighton? You'd think, 'That may be true, but it's certainly irrelevant.'

So, Hume's second, third, and fourth criticisms as I have given them on my list can, I suggest, be swept aside.

◆ ◆ ◆

This leaves Hume's first point. Hume contended that the universe does not in fact bear marks of design in the manifest way that a watch does. Is this plausible?

Imagine yourself for a moment as David Hume. You've just finished playing a game of backgammon—something that has taken your mind off troubling philosophical issues for a moment or two—when a man approaches you. He has the look of a religious enthusiast about him. You ready yourself for philosophical battle. But, before you can act, he lands the first dialectical blow by saying:

I suppose that you, Hume, would say that it is 'just lucky' that I have a couple of eyes; that it is just 'good fortune' that these eyes have lenses, which enable light to be focused on my retinas, retinas which 'by some coincidence' are at the back of each eye and 'by some fluke' are connected up to optic nerves, nerves which in turn are 'luckily' hooked up to the parts of the brain that are 'by some random chance' adjusted to process the sorts of information they provide. Come on, all this talk of luck and coincidence is madness. It's obvious that this sort of complicated structure resembles a machine constructed by an intelligence much more than it does anything thrown together by chance. If you don't accept it of the universe generally, then you have to accept it of our bodies—our bodies are obviously a lot more like watches than they are like stones. And if they're a lot more like watches, it's the height of irrationality to resist the conclusion that there must be something a lot like a watchmaker behind their creation.

Nowadays—in the twenty-first century—it's very hard to appreciate how devastating a blow this sort of claim would have appeared to one of Hume's contemporaries had they been watching the fight we're imagining. Of course not all this information would have been available to one of Hume's contemporaries, but even in Hume's day, when people put their hands on their hearts—figuratively or perhaps literally speaking—they did indeed feel compelled to admit that the human body resembled a machine much more than it did anything else and once one's done that surely the step to the machine-making mind behind the machine is irresistible. So you, as David Hume, stagger back under this blow.

It's time to give you a bit of help in our imaginary battle by time-travelling in for you a discovery that came along a bit later in the history of ideas—the Theory of Evolution by Natural Selection.

The Theory of Evolution by Natural Selection seems to show how something that resembles a machine much more than it does anything else could nevertheless result without the need for a machine-making mind behind it. As I assume the outlines of the theory are known to you, I shall not state it here.[5]

Had you as Hume heard of the Theory of Evolution by Natural Selection, you could have punched back with:

Bits of the universe—animals most noticeably—do indeed resemble human artefacts which, in our experience, have designers. That is true. Nevertheless, we now have a naturalistic explanation as to how this appearance of design could be generated in the absence of a designer—evolution by natural selection. Animals and plants reproduce themselves with the odd mutation here and there, mutations that, when positively adaptive, have a greater chance of getting passed down to the next generation, generating over time the appearance of design for the environment in which they find themselves without (necessarily) the reality of design. We think of evolution in the biological context, but similar sorts of considerations apply more widely; under the influence of gravity, a swirling chaotic mass will eventually condense into planets and the like. We can explain instances of natural order in terms of these natural laws; there is no need to posit a designer in virtue of them.[6]

This blow lands squarely on your opponent's chin; he reels back. Is he beaten? No, he is not. For to explain the order that is, for example, the human visual system in naturalistic terms one has to make reference to another instance of order, the laws of evolution or, more generally, the laws of nature.

Hume's first point, as I have now polished it up, admits that the stuff the laws of nature operate on is indeed ordered, but claims that that's because the laws of natural selection have operated on it, moving it from a relatively disorderly state into a relatively orderly one. The order that is expressed by these laws of natural selection is, we assume, capable of being explained in terms of biological laws; and the order that is expressed by these biological laws might be explained in terms of the order expressed by certain chemical laws; and the order of these chemical laws in terms of the order of other physical laws. But this process must stop somewhere, with the fundamental laws of nature. And the fundamental laws of nature will be expressions of order, order which, by the nature of the case (their being fundamental), cannot be explained naturalistically. That in terms of which everything else is to be explained naturalistically cannot itself be explained naturalistically. So, even after you as Hume have punched the proponent of the Argument to Design with your evolution roundhouse, there's still—and at the most fundamental level—order in the physical world that has no naturalistic explanation. You can't help but leave your flank exposed. The proponent of the Argument to Design has an opening. He launches himself forward.

According to theism, the order in the physical world is ultimately to be explained in terms of God. God had the idea of creating a universe like this and that explains the order that is the fundamental laws of nature. Having explained the order that is the fundamental laws of nature in terms of God, the rest of the order in the universe—the proponent of the Argument to Design might admit (at least for the sake of argument)—can be explained naturalistically in terms of these fundamental laws and their ramifications. As we've just seen, admitting this (at least for the sake of argument) means that the proponent of the Argument to Design can brush aside the Theory of Evolution as ultimately irrelevant. Sure, evolution may explain some order, but it does so in terms of natural laws, which are themselves instances of order. God is still needed to explain the order that is the fundamental laws of nature, the order that explains why naturalistic explanation is possible at all.

How would Hume have responded to this? Here we come to what I shall call Hume's fifth point.

Hume's fifth point is an instance of a sort of point that can be made in slightly different ways against many of the arguments for the existence of God. We could call it the 'How do you get your argument to stop at God?' point.

If it's order that needs explanation, as the proponent of the Argument to Design seems to think it is, then, while the order that is the fundamental laws of nature could indeed be explained in terms of God's having had the idea to create this universe, there'd still be some order left unexplained at the end of this story, the order that is the idea of this universe in the mind of God. On the principle that it's order that needs explanation—which is the principle the proponent of the argument relied on to take him or her from the universe to God—this idea in the mind of God (which must be at least as ordered as the universe to which it gave rise) must have an explanation. It could get one—one might think—from a super-God, who ordered the mind of God. But then there'd need to be a super-super-God to order the mind of the super-God to order the mind of God; and so on. It's obvious that the principle that order needs explanation would generate an infinite regress, with no justification for stopping at God rather than earlier. So we have to accept that there's going to be—in *any* story we tell—some unexplained order. That having been admitted, those who say that the mental order manifested by the divine mind requires no explanation are no better off, intellectually speaking, than those who say that the physical order manifested by the fundamental laws of nature requires no explanation. Indeed, they might seem to be worse off. If you're ultimately going to accept that some instance of order has no explanation, why go all the way to God before you locate that instance; wouldn't it be simpler to stop with the fundamental law(s)? However simple God is, a model that features him plus the fundamental law(s) must be more complicated than one which features the fundamental law(s) alone.

This seems—at least initially—a very powerful point against the Argument to Design and, *mutatis mutandis*, against a variety of other arguments. However, the proponent of the Argument to Design need not give up the fight yet. He or she has other moves which he or she might care to make.

One would be to claim that an infinite regress of explanation is not of necessity vicious; in the case of an infinite mind, it's quite acceptable. God's idea of the universe is a case of order explained by another idea in his mind and this idea is in turn explained by another idea in his mind; and this in terms of another; and so on ad infinitum. There's no need for a 'super-God' or some such; God's own infinite mind has all the resources one might wish for in order to provide an infinite chain of explanation. There is, after all, justification for stopping with an infinite God, rather than a finite universe.

An alternative move would be to claim that it is not order as such that requires explanation, but *physical* order. The fundamental laws of nature are an instance of physical order; the order in the mind of God is an instance of mental order; the former needs an explanation and the latter does not. What then, it behoves the proponent of the Argument to Design going down this route to explain, is this difference between physical order and mental order which means that the former needs an explanation whereas the latter does not?

The most promising way of defending the claim that mental order is less in need of explanation than physical order is to maintain that minds—in contrast to physical stuff—can be self-ordering. This is obviously not going to cut any ice with someone who does not think that minds are anything to contrast with physical stuff, so the defender of the Argument to Design going down this route will have to defend the further claim that minds are made of a different sort of stuff from physical stuff. Here, he or she can be seen to be moving outside the field of the philosophy of religion and into the field of the philosophy of mind. This is not the occasion on which we should allow ourselves to follow him or her. Let me just signpost the path and sketch one argument for why it is a path down which you might like to travel. Substance dualism is the view that you'd have to be convinced of on independent grounds before you could reasonably hope to meet the force of Hume's fifth point against the Argument to Design in this manner. We've already touched on some reasons people sometimes consider themselves to have in favour of substance dualism; here's another argument that purports to show that substance dualism is right. It's a reductio of the suggestion that we are entirely physical. I'll put it in the second person.

If you were entirely physical, then everything you did would be either the result of randomness, i.e. not have a cause at all, or caused by your preceding physical state and its interaction with the environment, your preceding state in turn being caused by randomness or its state a moment before that and its interaction with the environment and so on, backwards in time, to before your birth. So, if you were entirely physical, you could never be truly said to choose— genuinely choose that is. In every case of apparent choice, either randomness would be responsible; or physical circumstances beyond your control (for they originated before your birth) would determine you to behave in whatever way it is you end up behaving; or it would be a mixture of randomness and circum- stances beyond your control. You might think that you could have chosen to do other than whatever it is you did, but in fact the only way that you could ever have done other than whatever it is you did was if randomness had played a different part and then it wouldn't have been a result of your choice that you did other than what you did, it would have been the result of this randomness. So, if you were entirely physical, then you'd never have made any genuine choices. But it is just absurd to say that you've never made any genuine choices, so it is just absurd to say that you are entirely physical. You must have a non-physical bit, a bit that can cause itself and the rest of you—including your physical bit—to do things, in other words a self-ordering non-physical bit, a soul.

Of course one might resist this conclusion by taking what I described as the 'absurd' claim that we've never made any genuine choices 'on the chin'; one might say that this so-called absurd claim is true. But this is a hard blow for one's commonsensical chin to take. Think for a moment about whether or not you'd prefer to continue reading this book at the moment or interrupt your reading temporarily by doing something else, let's say a little dance. Consider the pros and cons of each option: the book might get interesting and it'd be better not to delay finding this out; the dance might be fun and the book's not going to go away if you take a couple of minutes off to do it. Now do one or the other; either continue reading straight away or do a little dance and then come back and resume you reading. Done that? Good. Whichever you did, can you really believe that you weren't able to choose and then do the other? Can you really believe that the fact that you did whatever it was you did do rather than the alternative was the result of randomness? Some people can believe these things, but most can't.

OK, so there's an argument for substance dualism. It may or may not be good. I'll leave it to you to think about.

I have argued that it's a necessary condition of your being reasonable in believing that the Argument to Design is a good argument that you have a solution to what I've called Hume's fifth point. This might necessitate that you have a good argument for substance dualism based on independent premises from those of the Argument to Design, but, if the first move that I canvassed is legitimate, then again it might not. Suppose that Hume's fifth point could be overcome in one (or—why not?—both) of these ways, should you then accept the Argument to Design as inductively sound or, failing that, as inductively supporting the theistic conclusion? Well, let's see. I'm going to approach an answer to this question via a little detour through a particular version of the Argument to Design that I've yet to mention.

◆ ◆ ◆

Sometimes the Argument to Design is called the 'Argument from Design'. I don't like that name, as it seems to me rather question-begging. If one admits that there is design, as one tacitly does when one allows the title 'Argument from Design', then it strikes me one cannot really deny that there is a designer, for design—as opposed perhaps to appearance of design—conceptually implies a designer. This is why one might reasonably prefer titles such as 'Argument *to* Design'. I want now to introduce another term. This term is 'fine tuning'. Rather like the title 'Argument from Design', 'Argument from Fine Tuning' or

'Fine-Tuning Argument' would seem to me rather question-begging. Unfortunately, as many would want to admit that there is the feature that I shall, in fact, end up joining the consensus in calling 'fine tuning', while denying that there's a fine tuner, and as, if one admits that there's been tuning, then one cannot deny—without it sounding as if one's contradicting oneself—that there's been a tuner (a fortiori fine tuning), so it's not obvious what name we should give to this argument. Unfortunately, there is no handy substitute for the name 'fine tuning' in the literature, so I'm going to stick with what strikes me as the less-than-ideal term 'fine tuning' and call this argument the 'Fine-Tuning Argument'. As long as we all remember that, apart from some slight linguistic infelicity, there's nothing immediately absurd in saying, 'I believe that there's fine tuning, but I don't believe that there's a fine tuner', we should be all right. Just as, apart from some slight linguistic infelicity, we have accepted the title 'Argument from Design' or 'Design Argument' and been all right saying things like, 'I admit that there's design, but I don't think there's a designer'. So what is this thing that, for better or worse, I'm going to follow standard practice and call 'fine tuning'?

Scientists have discovered that various features of the universe—let's call them boundary conditions—and of the laws of nature that dictate how the universe evolves within these boundary conditions needed to have values lying within a very small range if the universe was to be conducive to life in the broad sense that it is. For example, scientific consensus is that the universe began in a Big Bang some fifteen billion years ago (approximately). Scientists have discovered that the rate of expansion of the universe from that Big Bang had to fall within a very small range if it was not either to expand so fast that stars, planets, and the like never evolved, or expand so slowly that the same consequences followed. If stars and planets never formed, then life could never have formed. The exact figures for the ranges within which this and certain constants must lie if there is to be the possibility of life are not always agreed, but it is always agreed that they are very narrow; certainly, one in a million would not overstate the case. Of course scientists can't rerun the Big Bang or change the values of constants in the laws of nature in their laboratories—that, after all, is why they're called 'constants'. But they can perform computer simulations for differing values and, when they do so, they find that if—*per impossibile*—one *were* to alter any of these things by even a fraction of a fraction of a per cent, the universe would not be—in the broad sense that it is—conducive to life. The fact is that had the laws of nature and the initial or boundary conditions been even ever-so-slightly different from the way that they are, life could never have formed. In this sense then, the universe could be described as 'fine tuned' for life.[7]

Let me introduce the other idea, it's a principle of reasoning. In it's more worked out form it's called 'Bayes's Theorem'. We don't need to work it out in great detail to see the role it plays, so I'm going to give it in a slightly rough and ready way.[8]

Bayes's Theorem states, roughly, that if you find some fact—let's call it A—and A would be more likely if another fact—let's call it B—obtained, then you should conclude that you have some reason from A to think that B does indeed obtain and that this reason is proportional to how improbable A is in the first place; how much more likely B would make it; and how probable B is in itself. Let me reuse a previous example to show this principle at work.

Suppose that you'd found on your doormat this morning a letter addressed to your neighbour. Most mornings you don't find such things (I'm guessing). So supposing that it had happened this morning would be supposing that an antecedently unlikely event had occurred. An unlikely event calls for an explanation. What would it have been rational for you to believe on the basis of this evidence?

Let's apply Bayes's Theorem to this problem. You should consider those hypotheses that would have rendered it more likely that you would find such a letter on your doormat. There are as we have seen an infinite number of such explanations. One, though, must claim priority on our intellects: your postman got confused and delivered the letter to you by mistake. This is the simplest hypothesis that would explain this data; your postman getting confused (in the right sort of way, misreading the name; not realizing that he had this letter bundled up with another one that was indeed addressed to you; or some such) would make your finding a letter addressed to your neighbour on your doormat much more likely; and it's not in itself that improbable that your postman might have got confused in one of these ways. So, according to Bayes's Theorem, it would be rational for you to infer from the fact that you'd found such a letter that your postman had got confused in one of these sorts of ways, not infer it with certainty of course (Ninja monkeys cannot be ruled out), but infer it as the most probable hypothesis on the evidence. Of course, if your postman had been faultless in the past, this would decrease the prior probability of him having made a mistake on this occasion relative to what it would have been had he regularly made mistakes of this sort, but even if he had been faultless in the past, given that his making a mistake, albeit an unprecedented one, would still be—it seems safe to assume—more probable than any of the alternative explanations, Ninja monkeys et al., it would still be reasonable for you to believe it was the most probable explanation of the letter to your neighbour being on your doormat.

I suggest then that fine tuning is a fact and Bayes's Theorem is a principle of rationality. I'm not going to argue with either of them.

♦ ♦ ♦

Now let me lay out the version of the Argument to Design that utilizes these concepts most overtly.

The fine tuning that scientists have discovered shows that it is extremely unlikely in itself that the universe would be ordered so as to be conducive to life in the way that our universe obviously is. It would be considerably more likely to be so ordered if the process by which it came about was under the control of a

God. Therefore, from the fine tuning of the universe—via Bayes's Theorem—we have reason to believe that there is a God.

I want to consider three possible criticisms of this argument. (I'm not—you'll remember—going to call into question the fact that the universe is 'fine tuned' in the sense I've laid out or the fact that Bayes's Theorem is a principle of rationality.) These three possible criticisms are all closely connected, but it will be helpful to lay them out separately before drawing them together.

First, someone might say something like this:

Of course the universe is conducive to life, but that shouldn't be a surprise to us. We wouldn't be here to think about it if it wasn't. That which is a necessary condition of our being here cannot require explanation.

You may have seen the film *Pulp Fiction*. In that film, there's one scene where two hitmen are chatting to one another. Suddenly someone bursts in from an adjacent room with a large revolver. Before they have chance to react, he fires all six rounds at them from point-blank range. There's a pause. They look at him; they look at themselves and the wall behind them; amazingly, all the bullets have missed. They kill the man who's just tried to kill them. There then follows a discussion between the hitmen on the significance or otherwise of what has just happened for the rationality of religious belief.

I won't repeat that discussion verbatim here, for it is not conducted with the sort of rigorous adherence to the canons of terminological exactitude that one would expect from a book, even an introductory book, on the philosophy of religion. However, I shall tell you that one of the hitmen is inclined to brush off what has just happened as a fact that is not in need of explanation; the other is inclined to take it as needing explanation in terms of a God. Let me suppose that we all think that it is fantastically unlikely that six bullets fired at two people from point-blank range would miss them entirely. With which hitman do your sympathies lie (assuming you can have sympathy for any hitman), the one who brushes it off as not needing an explanation or the one who thinks it does need an explanation?

Before I tell you where my sympathies lie, I'll point out that this point is relevant to another argument for the existence of God. If your sympathies lie with the hitman who says that things that are a necessary condition of our being here thinking about them do not require explanation, then you're not going to have any sympathy at all with the Cosmological Argument, which asks for an explanation of why there is a universe at all. If your sympathies do lie with this hitman, you'll want to note this point now, as I won't be mentioning it again when I come to the Cosmological Argument in the next chapter.

My sympathies lie with the hitman who says that at least prima facie it *does* require some explanation. It is the improbability of the event that is the fact that requires explanation and that particular people—or even all people—would not be around to seek or decide not to seek an explanation for an improbable event had that improbable event not happened is an irrelevance.[9] Consider another example, which brings this out in a more clear-cut way than my hitman example and which I owe to Richard Swinburne:

A terrorist ties you up in a room where there is also a machine. The machine is linked up to a bomb that will, if it explodes, kill you. You see the terrorist put ten ordinary packs of cards into the top of the machine. He tells you that the machine will thoroughly shuffle these cards and then select ten at random and drop them into a little tray at its front. Only if the ten it dishes out are all aces of hearts will the bomb not go off. He leaves you. The machine whirrs away. The first card comes out—it's an ace of hearts; the second, another ace of hearts; the third, ace of hearts; and so on. In fact, all ten are aces of hearts. The machine goes silent; the worrying red light on the bomb turns to green. You have survived.

Would not this require some explanation? The chances of ten aces of hearts being dished out in a row if the machine worked as the terrorist said it did are fantastically small and the fact that something fantastically improbable has happened needs explanation—via Bayes's Theorem—in terms of something that would make it less unlikely, for example the machine selecting cards on a basis which actually gives it a preference for aces of hearts. If the terrorist came in and brushed off your survival as not needing explanation, as not being a fact which gave you a reason to suspect that the machine was not as he had described, you would give him short shrift, even shorter shrift than you would be inclined to be giving him qua terrorist anyway. Of course you could not have observed any other outcome, but there could have been another outcome and another outcome was—if what the terrorist told you was correct—immensely more likely. So, from the fact you have survived, you have reason to believe that what the terrorist told you was not correct.

So, I don't think this first objection to the fine-tuning argument works. The fine tuning is—if it is indeed in itself improbable—a fact that needs explanation. One point that we should register at this stage, though, is that given that it is true that we could not have observed a universe that was not conducive to life in the broad sense that ours is, so *unless we do have reason to think that such a universe is in itself improbable*, the fact that we observe such a universe should not require us to seek an explanation. To see this, consider the fact that if the terrorist had put all aces of hearts into the top of the machine, then your survival wouldn't have warranted you in believing that the machine didn't work as he had suggested. Consider also this, more probable, situation:

You suddenly find yourself lying on the ground in the street, with no recollection of how you got there; the last thing you can remember was walking happily along it. A man stands over you and announces that you fainted, but that he has been able to bring you round with the bottle of smelling salts you notice him waving under your nose. If what he's saying is true, you could not (if you were to recover at all) but have observed a universe where something such as this man had acted in a similar way to the way that he reports himself as having acted, a way conducive to your regaining consciousness. Of course, in place of the man there could have been a natural process of blood returning to your head as you lay recumbent; or a lady throwing water in your face; or one of a myriad of other possibilities, but, given that you awoke, you had to awake to a universe that was conducive to your awaking in some way or other. Given this, the fact that you regained consciousness to find nearby something (in this case a someone) which (who) appears to have acted in a way conducive to your regaining consciousness does not itself call for any explanation unless you have prior background evidence that would make it improbable that there would have been any such thing or a thing of this particular sort. Perhaps you do in the case of my example: just how likely is it that you'd find someone carrying round a bottle of smelling salts in the twenty-first century? Pretty unlikely, one might think. In any case, we can see that there is yet something of worth that may be extracted from this first objection to the fine-tuning argument. It's not the case, *pace* the objection as originally formulated, that that which is a necessary condition of one's observing it cannot itself be in need of explanation (it can, if it's in itself improbable), but it is the case that unless one has prior reason to believe that that which is a necessary condition of one's observing it is in itself improbable, it cannot be in need of explanation. Now this, even if granted, might be thought to leave the argument intact. (After all, it might be argued, the fact of fine tuning is precisely the fact that a very improbable (one in a million would not overstate the case) set of laws and boundary conditions has been alighted upon.) But in fact this point is crucial; we shall return to see why in a moment. First, let us turn to the second objection.

Why think that a universe fine tuned for life would be more likely on the hypothesis that there is a God than it would be on the hypothesis that there is not?

One problem for the proponent of the argument seems to be that it's not going to be possible to establish that a fine-tuned universe is in itself unlikely by the same sorts of methods that lead you to establish, for example, that finding a letter to your neighbour on your doormat is in itself unlikely. It's only as a result of the relative frequency in your experience of finding no such letter that it's obvious to you that it is in itself improbable that you find one. Given that your experiences over a large number of mornings have had a certain no-letter-to-my-neighbour-on-my-doormat character, you are indeed justified in thinking it unlikely that you would find such a letter and thus, when you nevertheless find one there, you are indeed justified in demanding an explanation in terms of a hypothesis that would make it more likely, your postman having got confused. How unlikely in itself is it that there be a universe fine tuned for life? It's not obvious that this question really makes sense, but someone might argue that one thing that is obvious is that even if it does make sense, you cannot have had any experiences that are relevant to justifying the answer to it that is needed if the argument is to get off the ground, namely 'Very'. As we've just observed, of necessity, you cannot have had any experiences of a non-fine-tuned-for-life character. However, perhaps this sort of worry is irrelevant here: we don't need the answer 'Very'; we just need the answer 'Relatively', for—as we saw—the mistaken postman hypothesis might still come out on top even if it was in itself pretty unlikely that he'd make a mistake; it just had to be relatively more likely that he'd do so than that any of the other possibilities that would otherwise equally well explain the data would occur.

Consider also this possibility: You arrive home and find that certain of the magnetic letters that you seem to remember having left randomly scattered on your fridge door since you bought them a week ago now read, 'Ceci n'est pas un frigidaire'. You consider two hypotheses, the first that the letters were, by sheer chance, nudged by you into this formation over the past few days; the second, that your friend—who visited you yesterday and was left unattended in the kitchen for several minutes—rearranged them thus. It's clearly reasonable for you to believe the second of these hypotheses on this evidence even though we may posit that it is in itself extremely unlikely that your friend would rearrange them thus; you've never observed him to do any such thing before. The fact remains that however unlikely it is that he'd rearrange them thus, it's *relatively* much more likely that he would do it than that they would have been formed into this pattern by random nudging. Why? Because there's at least some reason one can think of that your friend might have had to rearrange them thus, namely to amuse you when you spotted them. So it could be argued that before we're reasonable in believing this argument to be good we've just got to be reasonable in believing that if there were a God, he'd have at least some reason to create a fine-tuned universe rather than another sort of universe or no universe at all. But can we be reasonable in believing this?

Presumably the proponent of the argument will reply to this line of questioning by using analogies with cases of which we have more obvious experience, cases that illustrate that we value the creation of life as an end in itself. This having been established, he or she could then argue that if there were a God, he would be more likely to favour the creation of a universe that is conducive to life than one that is not or no universe at all; and thus establish that the hypothesis that there is a God increases the probability that a fine-tuned universe such as ours exist, the fine-tuned universe thus—via Bayes's Theorem—leading us to favour the hypothesis that there is a God. Is there something in the nature of goodness that would dictate that God would prefer to create a world with creatures such as ourselves in it rather than a world with other sorts of creatures in it; an uninhabited world; or no world at all?

Perhaps there are analogies or thought experiments that reveal that we think that it is in itself good to create a world capable of sustaining life—or perhaps (more specifically) intelligent, morally sensitive, free beings—rather than a world incapable of doing so. Perhaps there are, but, to reveal my hand early on, I've not found any.

Consider this situation: You are an astronaut. One day you are working on a distant planet rather like the Earth as it was several million years ago, with what biologists would call primordial soup swilling around under stormy skies. Conditions are ripe for the emergence of life, but as yet no life has formed. (The latest research would suggest that this is rather a simplification of the biology involved, but we need not worry about that.) You have a certain aerial, which you need to set up somewhere to send a signal back to your orbiting space ship. Two locations are equally suitable for sending the signal. You could set up your aerial in location A, where it would be more likely to be hit by lightning; conduct some electricity down into a pool of primordial soup; and thus assist this planet in developing life. (This lightning wouldn't damage the aerial in any way.) Alternatively, you could set it up in location B, on a rocky outcrop with no soup around. Each location is equally close to your current position; the aerial would work equally well in either place; and you would be perfectly safe whichever location you chose: the only difference is that if you put it up in location A, then—as a by-product of your sending your signal—you're more likely to create—with the help of the pre-existent conditions—life than if you put it up in location B. This life is likely, let us further suppose, to evolve over millions of generations into intelligent, morally sensitive, free beings, such as ourselves. Would you get any good feeling from thinking that you'd helped create this sort of life, rather than left this planet a barren rock, a good feeling that wouldn't be based on your assessment of yourself as having done what you had most reason to do? Let me suppose for the sake of argument that you would not; you find as you look into yourself that, pushing aside for a moment what sense of achievement you might get from feeling that you'd done what you had most reason to do, you would not feel any better having put your aerial at location A than you would do had you put it at B (or indeed vice versa).

Now with all these features of the thought experiment fixed: do you have more reason to site your aerial at location A than you do to site it at location B?

A positive answer is going to be needed to questions such as this if we're going to have a hope of being justified in thinking that if there were a God, he'd have a good reason for creating a fine-tuned universe and thus potentially be able to create a good argument from the fine tuning in this universe, using Bayes's Theorem, to the existence of God. You might have a different intuition about this from me, but I report that, personally, I think that the answer is 'No'. You have no more reason to put it at A than you do to put it at B. I'm not going to mount a protracted argument to persuade you into thinking about this my way, in part because I fear that we are here reaching the limits to which argument may take us. But before we leave this objection, we might consider three points, which seem to argue in support of my intuition.

First, we know of no other inhabited planet in the universe; there may be one; there may be billions, but we don't know of any. Let's fast-forward a few thousand years in time, to the point where we are travelling around in spaceships exploring the universe. Would we take every inhabited planet we came across as a bit of evidence in favour of theism and every uninhabitable one as a bit of evidence against? Surely not. No more than we took every inhabited or inhabitable island we discovered in the Pacific as evidence of his existence and every uninhabitable one as evidence against.

Secondly, suppose we meet a happily married couple one day and get chatting to them. They tell us various things about themselves, including the fact that they've chosen not to have any children. When we enquire whether this is to conserve their resources to, for example, increase the number or wellbeing of other people, we discover that it is not. Neither is it to enable them to pursue some project with which we disagree. Their decision not to have children has had, as far as we can tell, no effect other than to mean that there are less intelligent, morally sensitive, free creatures in the world than there could have been. Do we think less highly of them? Surely not.

Thirdly, what reason *could* God have to create anything (a lifeless universe; a universe fine tuned for life; a set of non-physical angelic beings; anything)? Being God, it's not as if any of these things could fulfil some previously unsatisfied need of his, and their not existing prior to his creating them means that they themselves could hardly be said to have previous requirements met by their being created. In short, it seems very hard to see what analogue to your friend's wanting to amuse you by rearranging the magnetic letters on your fridge door God could have had by way of reason for doing anything and indeed creating anything. This is not to suggest that God could not have created the world because it would have been positively *un*reasonable for him to do so. Sometimes, we do things for no reason at all and this doesn't make our doing them *un*reasonable. But it is to suggest that the best account on theism might well be that while God's free choice explains why this universe exists, that God made this choice, rather than another, is something for which there is no explanation.

You'd have to think that you could meet these points, that you do have good reason to put your aerial in location A rather than B, before you could hope to meet this challenge to the Argument to Design by establishing that creating life is in itself something that God would have a good reason to do. If, like me, you think that you have no more reason to put it at A rather than B, then it looks as if that's the end of the argument for you. Turning now to the third and final point that could be made against the Fine-Tuning Argument; this is the point that there are alternative hypotheses that could explain the fine tuning.

Now this point looks rather like Hume's second point, which I said earlier could be brushed aside simply by reference to simplicity considerations. I want to return to it and see if I can polish it up a bit by finding an alternative hypothesis to the theistic one that is at least as simple as it and that equally well explains the data. I think I can.

◆ ◆ ◆

I'm sure we're all familiar with the claim that if you give a monkey typing away at a typewriter enough time, then it'll eventually type the works 'of' Shakespeare, i.e. sentences that are type-identical with those in an edition of the works of Shakespeare. So, if we came into a room one day and found that there was a monkey sitting at a typewriter, and—among a vast pile of papers on the floor—we found a copy of the works 'of' Shakespeare, we shouldn't demand an explanation above and beyond the monkey one unless we had reason to believe that the monkey had not been there for a very long time indeed or the copy of the works 'of' Shakespeare was suspiciously close to the surface of the vast piles of papers. Of course, we *would* have a reason to suppose this. Monkeys have short life-spans relative to the amount of time that would be suggested as likely via random typing to result in a meaningful sentence let alone something akin to the lifework of a genius. But we may safely ignore this disanalogy. We may suppose for the sake of the analogy that we live in a world where we have no reason not to think that monkeys are everlasting or that there's an infinite number of them typing away at typewriters. On such a supposition, the discovery of a copy of the works 'of' Shakespeare wouldn't require us to seek any explanation other than the monkey one. Similarly, the fact that unless the boundary conditions and laws of nature had a certain character there could never have been any life should not make us demand an explanation in terms of God unless we have reason to believe that there aren't an infinite number of universes each with one of the infinite number of possible sets of boundary conditions and laws of nature. For an infinite number of infinitely variable universes would explain the existence of any universe with its particular set of boundary conditions and laws of nature in the same way that an infinitely long-lived monkey or an infinite number of mortal monkeys at typewriters could explain the existence of any 'work of literature'. So the hypothesis that there's an infinite number of universes each of which instantiates one of the infinite number of possible sets of boundary conditions and laws of nature would explain the occurrence of this universe as well as the theistic hypothesis.

The hypothesis that there are an infinite number of universes each of which instantiates one of the infinite number of possible sets of boundary conditions and laws of nature might seem prima facie much more complicated than the hypothesis that there's one universe and one God, but is it really more complicated? Simplicity considerations operate on types of entity as well as tokens of a type. Which then is the simplest hypothesis, one that posits an infinite number of infinitely variable universes or one that posits God and—let us say—this universe alone. The first is simplest on types of entity; there's only one type of thing, universes. The second is simplest on tokens of type; there's only two tokens, one each of two types of thing, the first God and the second the universe. Which is simplest overall? I would suggest that simplicity with regard to type is to be preferred over simplicity with regard to token and thus that the infinite number of infinitely variable universes hypothesis is actually a simpler hypothesis than the theistic hypothesis.

If you think you might disagree with me, consider this: you come across a room where, as far as the eye can see, monkeys sit at typewriters, typing away.

One person with you suggests the hypothesis, 'There's an infinite number of monkeys sitting at typewriters'; another, 'There's a finite number of monkeys and at least one non-monkey thing sitting at typewriters'. Which would you favour?

Surely, you would favour the former hypothesis, even though it posits infinitely more tokens than the latter, which posits one more type. Why, when each would equally well explain the data? It must be simplicity, mustn't it? Of course, again, my example is in danger of being let down rather by background information that we cannot help but import. You know that there can't actually be an infinite number of monkeys in this room because no room can be that big; every monkey takes up a certain amount of space and so the room would have to be infinitely large. So we must remember that we are assuming for the sake of argument that you have no reason to believe that such disanalogies hold; we posit then that you have no prior reason to believe that there couldn't in principle be an infinite number of monkeys sitting at typewriters in a room. The example then serves—if you share my intuition that we would prefer the infinite number of monkeys hypothesis to the finite number plus one non-monkey thing hypothesis—to illustrate that it is simplicity with regard to type that we prefer over simplicity with regard to token.

A more prima facie worrying reply to this line of thinking would play on the fact that we don't observe universes 'as far as the eye can see' or some such; we observe one universe (as far as the eye can see). So, someone might argue, our actual situation is much more like coming into a room and finding one copy of the works 'of' Shakespeare; one person with us suggesting on this evidence that there's an infinite number of monkeys sitting at typewriters; and another suggesting that there's one thing, an artistic genius. Suddenly the latter hypothesis looks much more plausible on the evidence before us, even when we sweep away as much as we are able of the background knowledge that 'prejudices us against monkeys'. But such a reply misses the point that we accepted in discussing the first objection to the Fine-Tuning Argument: we could not but have observed a universe conducive to life and so unless we have prior reason to think that such is improbable, the fact that our universe is conducive to life cannot require an explanation. On the 'multiverse' of an infinite number of infinitely variable universes hypothesis, each of these universes is equally probable (because each is actual). The situation is rather then analogous to us being unable to enter any room unless the door is unlocked by a doorkeeper who'll only unlock it if a work of literature is already in there waiting to be read by us. We find in the only room into which we are allowed by such a doorkeeper a work of literature waiting to be read by us. On this evidence, one person with us suggests that there's just this room, this work, and an author of genius behind it; and another suggests that there's an infinite number of rooms, each of which has some manuscript in it (produced, for all we know, by monkeys sitting at typewriters) and that it's just, of course, that, given the nature of the doorkeepers, we can't peer into those other rooms and see the gibberish typed onto the pages of the manuscripts they contain.

To revert to Swinburne's example, if the terrorist had in fact tried his card-shuffling machine on a huge number of people already, then the fact that it happened to work once would not need an explanation beyond the fact that he'd tried it so often; and the analogue to the background knowledge (e.g. that terrorists wouldn't be able to get away with trying such machines on a huge number of people) supporting the prior improbability of his having tried it a large number of times is just not there in the case of the universe. If the terrorist had tried his machine an infinite number of times, then of course someone would have survived it. If there's ultimately the multiverse of an infinite number of infinitely variable universes, then of course someone is going to find themselves in a universe conducive to life.

So, to sum up, if the order in the universe is a fact that is in need of explanation and hence one that it is indeed rational to take as pointing outside the universe as we know it, it is simplest to posit that it points to an infinite series of universes each of which instantiates one of the infinite number of possible sets of boundary conditions and laws of nature.[10] That hypothesis will be simpler than the hypothesis that there is this universe, or even any other number of universes, and a God. It posits more tokens—more universes—but it posits less types of thing; there's only universes. We can of course never collect any evidence against the existence of an infinite number of infinitely variable universes from scientific investigation conducted within our universe as, whatever natural features of our universe are discovered (that the boundary conditions and laws of nature are this way rather than that), the 'No God, but an infinite number of infinitely variable universes' hypothesis will, it seems, be able to explain them as well as a 'God plus this universe alone' hypothesis. It is not plausible then to regard the Argument to Design as raising the probability of the existence of God at all, so it is not plausible to regard it as a good argument and neither is it plausible to think that it can contribute to a good cumulative case argument for the existence of God. I conclude then that the Argument to Design does not provide us with any reason to suppose that there is a God.

Now someone might think that a 'No God but an infinite number of infinitely variable universes hypothesis' still wouldn't explain all that needs to be explained; why is there this sort of infinite number of universes, rather than an infinite number of universes all of which have sets of boundary conditions and laws of nature that are not conducive to life; or rather than no universes at all? Surely the existence of this infinite set of universes needs some explanation. Perhaps, but the fact that there's an infinite number of infinitely variable universes is no longer an instance of order, and so asking for an explanation of it is not asking for an explanation of order. In other words, this line of questioning takes us outside the field of the Argument to Design and into the territory of the next argument we shall look at, the Cosmological Argument.[11]

9

The Cosmological Argument

I'm going to start with a presentation of the Cosmological Argument given by Frederick Copleston in a radio debate with Bertrand Russell.[1] Here's the argument as Copleston puts it:

First of all, I should say, we know that there are at least some beings in the world which do not contain in themselves the reason for their existence. For example, I depend on my parents, and now on the air, and on food and so on. Now, secondly, the World is simply the real or imagined totality or aggregate of individual objects, none of which contain in themselves alone the reason for their existence. There isn't any world distinct from the objects which form it, any more than the human race is something apart from the members. Therefore, I should say, since objects or events exist, and since no object of experience contains within itself the reason for its existence . . . the totality of objects, must have a reason external to itself. That reason must be an existent being. Well, this being is either itself the reason for its own existence, or it is not. If it is, well and good. If it is not, then we must proceed farther. But if we proceed to infinity in that sense, then there's no explanation of existence at all. So, I should say, in order to explain existence, we must come to a being which contains within itself the reason for its own existence, that is to say which cannot not-exist.

There is something prima facie plausible about this argument to me. It seems to me intuitively obvious that the universe is contingent: not only might it have not been as it is, but also it might not have been at all. And whenever we come across something that might not have been as it is or might not have been at all, it seems that we can sensibly ask, 'Why is it as it is?' and 'Why is it at all?' and that—and this is the Principle of Sufficient Reason—we can require of reality that it provides an answer to our questions (even if we can't expect of ourselves that we'll always be up to finding this answer). The Principle of Sufficient Reason in its most general form (a form that, we shall see in a moment, the proponent of the Cosmological Argument actually has good reason to shrink from endorsing) says that for everything that is a certain way yet might have been otherwise, there's a sufficient reason why it is as it is and not otherwise. And this principle, I confess, seems—at least initially—a plausible one to me.

Sometimes, the 'Why is it as it is?' question that our following this principle encourages us to ask can be answered by the sorts of investigations into reality that are undertaken by scientists. However—as we have seen from our discussion of the Argument to Design—scientific explanation relies on laws of nature for which—at the most fundamental level—there is no naturalistic explanation. When we come to the end of scientific explanation of why the universe is as it is, we can either say that there is no explanation of these fundamental laws (they are the ultimate brute fact) or we can explain their being as they are in terms of an infinite number of infinitely variable universes (and then say that the fact that there's that set of universes rather than any other is the ultimate brute fact); or we can explain their being as they are in terms of God.[2] I have argued that the order in the world on its own, if it requires any explanation at all, compels us to think that explanation in terms of no God but an infinite number of infinitely variable universes is more rational than explanation in terms of God (because simpler) unless we have independent reason to believe that such a set of universes is less likely to be a brute fact than God. But—as I observed—any infinite number of infinitely variable universes hypothesis would still seem to leave us with an apparently sensible question: if the question, 'Why is there this universe at all?' gets its answer in terms of there being an infinite set of infinitely variable universes, then we may simply ask, 'And why is there this sort of set of infinitely variable universes at all?' That there's an infinite number of infinitely variable universes seems, if it's a fact, a contingent fact too. There could have been a finite number of universes; there could have been an infinite number of universes all of which were the same. Whichever way one cuts it, it seems that there's something left over at the end of any non-theistic explanatory story, something that needs explanation, an explanation that it could only get from one's telling a different sort of explanatory story, a theistic one.

What's to be said about this argument?

◆ ◆ ◆

The first objection I want to consider to the Cosmological Argument is a version of the 'How do you get your argument to stop at God?' objection.

The Cosmological Argument starts from the fact that the universe is contingent— let's accept that that is a fact for the moment—and then seems to argue from that fact using the most general version of the Principle of Sufficient Reason, the principle that wherever there's contingency there must be an explanation— let's accept that version of the principle too, at least for the moment—and thus the Cosmological Argument must end up with something that's not contingent if it's ever going to stop. This—the proponent of the argument says—is God. God by contrast to the universe is necessary. Fair enough, one might think. Necessity—as discussed in an earlier chapter—is one of God's essential properties. But we may ask of the theistic hypothesis whether or not the necessary being that is God necessarily created this universe. If he did, then as what a necessary being necessarily creates is as necessary as he is, so this universe is in fact necessary, contrary to the original premise of the argument. We need not in fact detain ourselves with this line of thought, as the theistic account—preserving what I argued in an earlier chapter is another of God's essential properties, his perfect freedom—has the necessary being that is God *contingently* choosing to create this universe. Thus the universe at the end of the theistic story is as contingent as it was at the beginning; God might have chosen not to create it. So far, so good then. But from this we can see that the traditional theistic story admits an element of contingency in God. And at this stage one might object that the principle that led one from the contingent world to the necessary being that is God was the principle that contingency needs explanation. So how can it be adequate to stop with a being that itself contains contingency? Surely, a super-God would be required; and a super-super-God; and so on. Here then, the proponent of the argument must make another move, paralleling one of the two that I have already rehearsed in discussing the Argument to Design. The proponent of the Cosmological Argument could point to the fact that in the infinite mind of God there are—*ex hypothesi*—the resources that there are not—*ex hypothesi*—in the universe to sustain an infinite chain of explanation. (Note: this would be to deviate from the spirit of Copleston's argument, which does not allow an infinite chain of explanation to count as an explanation and to require the extra premise that the universe is not itself capable of containing an infinite chain of explanation.) Alternatively, he or she could draw a distinction between contingency in physical stuff, which needs explanation, and contingency in mental stuff, which does not, or at least does not when it comes to free choices being made by bits of that mental stuff, minds. By now we are recognizably on the path that leads outside the field of the philosophy of religion and into the philosophy of mind. At this stage though, we need just observe that, one way or the other, the proponent of the Cosmological Argument can't endorse the Principle of Sufficient Reason in its most general form; he or she must accept that contingency in either infinite stuff and/or mental stuff needs no explanation if he or she is going to get the Cosmological Argument to stop.

◆ ◆ ◆

The Cosmological Argument rests on two premises then, that the universe is contingent (and possibly finite too, depending on which of the two ways the proponent goes in adapting the most general form of the Principle of Sufficient Reason so that the Cosmological Argument will stop) and that wherever there's contingency (in finite and/or physical stuff) there must be an explanation. I'm going to look at these two premises in order, first then the premise that the universe is contingent.

◆ ◆ ◆

That you are reading this book is, it seems, a contingent fact. There's no necessity that anybody ever read it. So—via the Principle of Sufficient Reason, which we may assume for the sake of argument at the moment—I may sensibly ask of anyone who finds themselves reading it why they are doing so. Why are you reading this? The Principle of Sufficient Reason ensures that I am reasonable in believing that this question has an answer. Let's suppose that you know the answer and that you write to me telling me; let's further suppose that everyone else who ever reads this writes to me with their answers. What would your reaction be if, having received all these different explanations, I then wrote back to each of you saying, 'Right, well that explains why each and every one of you considered in isolation read this, but there's a further question that reason assures us must have an answer and I now want you all to consider this question. This is the question of why all of you—considered as a totality—read it.' You would surely think that this question was not one that reason assured us had an answer over and above the answer that had already been given as to why each of you considered in isolation had read it; quite the opposite. As long as the presence of each contingent member of the set of people that constitutes the readership of the book is explained, *ipso facto* the whole set is explained. There's no fact 'left over', as it were, needing an explanation when each contingent member of the set has received its explanation (although we can of course ask other sensible questions, e.g. 'Why do people read books about the philosophy of religion at all?' and we'll come to that in a moment).

Now, armed with this result, let us accept for a moment that the universe is indeed composed of various contingent things as Copleston argues; the universe is an aggregate of contingent things. It would seem from my example and *pace* Copleston that it does not follow from this that there is a contingency with respect to the whole universe that needs explanation, even given the Principle of Sufficient Reason. If each contingent part of the universe were to be explained without reference to God, *ipso facto* the contingent aggregate that is the universe as a whole would be explained without reference to God. So the question is, '*Can* each contingent part of the universe be explained without reference to God?'

Well, some contingent parts of the universe certainly seem capable of more or less complete explanation without reference to God. We have just seen that your reading this is contingent and it might be explained in terms of something other than God, your wanting to read a book on the philosophy of religion perhaps. Your wanting to read such a book is also a contingent fact and as such—according to the Principle of Sufficient Reason—in need of an explanation (although not, of course, if one's accepted that contingency in mental stuff requires no explanation). But it might very well receive one, an explanation let me suppose in terms of your intending to learn about the philosophy of religion. Of course, that you intend to learn about the philosophy of religion is also a contingent fact. But it too might be explained, might it not? Perhaps in terms of your having a deep and abiding desire to reach the truth on matters of ultimate significance through educating yourself as best as you are able or perhaps, alternatively, in terms of your being required to sit some examination on the philosophy of religion. Does this process of explaining one contingent thing in the universe in terms of another always remain incomplete or ever need to stop? It might seem that it doesn't on one view. That view is determinism.

On determinism, the state of the universe at a later time—everything that is true of the universe at that time—can be explained in terms of its state at an earlier time and the operation of the laws of nature on it. Thus, if determinism is true, then every contingent thing that occurs—right down to the last detail—has a sufficient explanation of its occurrence and the character of its details in terms of the preceding state of the universe (and the laws of nature). Each member of the infinite set of contingent things that constitutes this universe is explained in terms of another member of this set; *ipso facto*, the whole contingent thing that is the universe is explained without any reference to a necessary being, God. One might think we'd need to add to determinism the thesis that the universe is of infinite age to secure this conclusion, but arguably this isn't necessary. Even if the universe is of finite age, it might still have passed through an infinite number of states, just as the current year is a finite number of days old yet has still passed through an infinite number of moments.

Now, one's first reaction on hearing all this might be to think that supposing that determinism is true and, if this is required too, that the universe is of infinite age, would be supposing one or more things that scientists are pretty much unanimous in telling us are false. You'll have heard of the Copenhagen Interpretation of various quantum phenomena and the Big Bang Theory. Now is not the time to go into these issues in detail. Fortunately then, we don't need to go into them as even a determinist who believes the universe is of infinite age can sensibly ask, 'But why is there a deterministic and infinitely old universe at all, rather than an indeterministic universe; a temporally finite universe; or no universe at all?' 'What about these boundary conditions and laws of nature?' They could have been different. It's not a logical necessity that the Big Bang started things off as it did (if we assume that it did) or that every massive body attracts every other with a force in proportion to the inverse square of their separation; and so on. 'Are the boundary conditions and laws of nature metaphysically necessary?' If we said, 'Yes' to this, the contingency would at last disappear, but then it would evaporate from everywhere else too—it would not be contingent any more that you're reading this; you couldn't but have read it, because the boundary conditions and laws of nature necessitated that you read it and they themselves are necessary. Assuming that one doesn't want to go down this road, then the fundamental question must surely remain. It can at best be postponed if we adopt the infinite number of infinitely variable universes hypothesis; that hypothesis would explain the existence of a universe with any particular natural feature—deterministic/indeterminisitic; infinitely old/temporally finite; gravity operating in one way rather than another; and so on in the following way: Question: Why does this particular universe exist? Answer: Because every possible universe exists. But even sweeping away with this broom must surely leave fundamentally the same question behind: Why is there *this* rather than nothing? Whether the 'this' takes the value of the particular universe we live in or an infinite set of infinitely variable universes, the question is still one that can, it seems, be sensibly asked because, it seems, the 'this' that we're left with is still a contingent this.

Perhaps, someone might argue, we're not in a position to realize that the universe in all its details; or its boundary conditions and laws; or perhaps the infinite set of infinitely variable universes, isn't contingent at all, it's necessary. Or at least—and this would be sufficient to resist this premise of the Cosmological Argument—we can have no non-question-begging reason for thinking that one or other of these things is not necessary. But, though someone might argue this, it is a hard thing to believe. The universe in its details just does seem contingent; to deny that it's contingent in its details runs contrary to our intuitions about every fact that we take to be contingent. You think that you could have failed to read this book; you think you could have failed to exist; and so on. I think these things too and, if the universe were necessary in all its details, then those thoughts and numerous other similar ones would have to be wrong. Of course one might say that it is the boundary conditions and indeterministic laws of nature that are necessary, everything else—the details—being (due to the indeterminism) contingent, but, while not as obviously wrong, this still seems wrong because it seems as if the boundary conditions and laws of nature could have been different too. Just as each of us can coherently think of the possibility of our never having existed, by imagining—for example—a possible world in which our parents chose never to have children, so we can coherently think of the possibility of our never having existed by imagining the boundary conditions and/or laws of nature being such as to mean that life could not form. Scientists do just that in discussing the fine tuning of our universe after all. Of course, if we have already decided that the apparent coherence of these 'possibilities' is in fact misleading as a guide to what's really possible, because the universe in all its detail and/or the boundary conditions and laws of nature are necessary— contrary to the theistic hypothesis that has it/them contingent upon (at least) God's creative will—then we'll take this appearance to be indicative of nothing more than confusion on our part. However, just as one cannot beg the question in favour of theism, so one cannot beg the question against theism. At this stage, one must take one's intuitions about what one can coherently think about as one finds them; and must take them as a guide to what's really possible (one has no other guide, after all). And so while, unfortunately for the proponent of the Cosmological Argument, there is no ultimately non-question-begging way of arguing this point, there does indeed seem to be quite a bit of pre-reflective intuitive support for 'this' being contingent, however big the 'this', whether it be the details of the universe; or it's boundary conditions or laws of nature; or even the infinite set of infinitely variable universes. All these 'thises' seem intuitively to have a contingency about them, a contingency assuredly that we will also find in God's decision to create 'this' if we ultimately adopt the theistic hypothesis, but a contingency nonetheless. Thus I conclude that there's quite a bit of pre-reflective intuitive support for the first premise of the Cosmological Argument.[3]

Let's turn to look at the second premise.

◆　◆　◆

One might deny the Principle of Sufficient Reason in the restricted form that is required for the argument. One can indeed sensibly ask the question why there is this universe or—if this is one's preferred starting point—why there is an infinite set of infinitely variable universes, but it does not follow from the fact that a question can be asked that it must have an answer. If we allow that there's contingency in the world, then ultimately, as we have seen, we must reach a brute fact on *any* explanatory account, a contingent fact that itself has no explanation. Perhaps there is no explanation of this admittedly contingent and finite universe or—if this is one's preferred resting point—of the admittedly contingent yet infinite number of infinitely variable universes. To think like this would be to reject the restricted form of the Principle of Sufficient Reason that the proponent of the Cosmological Argument needs, the principle that requires contingency in the finite aggregate of physical stuff that is the universe (or, if one's got as far as positing an infinite number of infinitely variable universes, the infinite aggregate of physical stuff that is the 'multiverse') to have an explanation. Is this then the way for the opponent of the argument to go? Well, one might wonder, 'Doesn't the principle that whenever there is contingency of this sort, there is an explanation, gain a lot of intuitive support from our everyday reasoning?' To look for explanations when something that is obviously purely physical happens that need not have happened is, one might think, the mark of a rational mind.

Imagine what you would think if suddenly, with a slight popping sound, a small banana appeared—apparently out of thin air—just between your head and this book. It hovered in the air for a moment or two, rotating slowly. Then it disappeared with a similar popping sound. Would you think yourself unreasonable in thinking that there must be some explanation for this contingent happening? Of course you wouldn't. Quite the opposite. You'd think that reason dictated that you believe that there was some explanation of it even if finding out what it was proved impossible. Of course, many things happen to us every day for reasons that are so obscure we never discover them and perhaps never could discover them (due to limitations in our powers of perception and intellect) but this doesn't persuade us that anything of this sort ever happens for which there is no reason. One might argue that while it may be very probable that the Principle applies to any given physical fact, this is compatible with its being very probable that it does not apply to every such fact or the 'big physical fact' that is the aggregate of all other such facts, but it seems to me that the proponent of the argument may respond to this by claiming that we apply this principle to any such fact we come across not because we judge it to be probable that the Principle is 'true', but rather because we take it that acting on the Principle is constitutive of rationality in our dealings with physical reality as such, large or small, finite or infinite. Denying the Principle of Sufficient Reason in the form the proponent of the Cosmological Argument requires is not then—it might seem—the way for the opponent of the argument to go. If this universe or— if this is one's preferred starting point—the infinite set of infinitely variable universes is contingent, then it needs an explanation.

But, one might equally wonder, 'Aren't there scientists who *would* deny that the Principle of Sufficient Reason applies to all physical stuff?' There certainly are; some—indeed, the majority—of those who specialize in Quantum Mechanics interpret it as telling us that, albeit at the sub-microscopic level and within the parameters imposed by certain laws, certain happenings are genuinely random. A certain atom decays at a certain time. 'Why did it do so then, rather than a couple of seconds earlier or later?', we ask. 'There's no reason', these scientists are happy to say. Now such a consensus among the scientists who study these phenomena most closely is not an insurmountable obstacle for those who would maintain the validity of the Principle of Sufficient Reason in this area. There's no obvious reason to think that scientists will make better philosophers of science than birds make ornithologists and there are 'hidden variable' interpretations of these phenomena available, such interpretations being ones that there is scope to argue could never—even in principle—be shown false, that's the thing about the variables they posit being 'hidden' (it must be admitted that there's also scope to argue that they can be—indeed, have been— shown false). But we can sweep all these issues aside in the present context, for the mere existence of this opinion among obviously cognitively well-functioning scientists is sufficient to show that it can't after all be constitutive of rationality that one thinks that the Principle of Sufficient Reason has universal scope in the realm of finite physical stuff. It may have universal scope in the domain of 'medium-sized dry goods' as one might call it, but not elsewhere. One might hope to go along with the consensus among scientists, yet save the Principle of Sufficient Reason 'for later use'. One might say something like, 'OK, there is genuine randomness in physical stuff at the quantum level, but why is the world in this way random? The various outcomes have probabilities associated with them and that's all that can be said to explain why any one of them happened, OK. But why those, rather than some other, probabilities? Why indeed any form of randomness rather than determinism?' These are, I suggest, sensible questions. But the point to observe in relation to them is that if one's already relinquished the universal applicability of the Principle of Sufficient Reason to physical stuff by saying that at the sub-microscopic level there are things to which it doesn't apply, then there's no need from consistency any more to suppose that these sensible questions that one is now raising have answers. If one's asking why the world is such that at the quantum level there are things to which the Principle of Sufficient Reason doesn't apply, one ought to consider the possibility that the fact that the world is such that at the quantum level there are things to which the

Principle of Sufficient Reason doesn't apply might itself be a fact of a type that one's already admitted, a fact about physical stuff to which the Principle of Sufficient Reason doesn't apply. So, despite the enthusiasm for it displayed in the previous paragraph, it's not at all indefensible to posit that the Principle of Sufficient Reason does not hold without exception in the realm of physical stuff. The appeal to size, 'But these quantum happenings are so very small and the universe as a whole is so very big,' need not detain us; the universe was very small in the past, very, very small at the Big Bang.

Schopenhauer criticized the proponent of the Cosmological Argument for treating the Principle of Sufficient Reason as a cab driver whom one is free to dismiss as soon as one arrives at one's desired destination. I have suggested that, although one might avoid the charge implied by this analogy simply by choosing the right cab driver for the journey (one might say, for example, that the Principle of Sufficient Reason is exceptionless only over the realm of physical stuff and rest confident that once one's reached God, this cab driver will dismiss himself), given that the cab driver one's then choosing is not in fact the one chosen by all rational people—the relevant principle is in fact explicitly denied by the majority of scientists working in a particular area of physics—so one's argument can hardly be rationally compelling. But in fact, matters seem even worse than this for the prospect of the Cosmological Argument being potentially a good argument for theism. On physicalism, the (we are supposing for the sake of argument) contingent and finite physical universe is all that there is, or perhaps there's an infinite number of infinitely variable such universes and that's all that there is; there *is* no explanation, sufficient reason, why this (whichever of these 'this' refers to) exists rather than something else or nothing at all; that's just what physicalism amounts to. Thus any principle that dictates that there *is* such a reason, an explanation-giving entity beyond physical stuff, is straightforwardly incompatible with physicalism. Thus any argument that starts from such a principle is begging the question against physicalism. One can't have a good argument against the view that physical stuff doesn't need any explanation premised on the principle that physical stuff does need an explanation.[4]

◆ ◆ ◆

So the Cosmological Argument cannot be a good argument for the existence of God for anybody. While it is plausible to suggest that the universe is contingent in its details and in its boundary conditions and laws of nature; and while it's plausible to say that an infinite set of infinitely variable universes would be contingent too, there's no rational compulsion, or even pressure it might seem, on us to take this contingency as one requiring an explanation. The Principle of Sufficient Reason in the form required to take us from collections of physical stuff to an explanatory entity outside such, which is the form the argument requires, is one that cannot be plausibly argued to be constitutive of rationality and one the adoption of which begs the question against physicalism. The

Cosmological Argument cannot be taken as inductively supporting the conclusion that there is a God; it is thus not a good argument and it cannot contribute to a good cumulative case argument for the existence of God. The Cosmological Argument does not provide us with any reason to believe that there is a God.

The feeling that the world as a whole is a question in need of an answer and an answer that only God could provide is a genuine feeling that many if not most people have had at least once in their lives. I hazard that all reading this will empathize with a comment of Darwin's, reported by the Duke of Argyll as having occurred after Argyll had said to Darwin that it was impossible not to infer a God from the world: 'He looked at me very hard and said, "Well, that often comes over me with overwhelming force; but at other times," and he shook his head vaguely, adding, "it seems to go away." '[5] Sometimes the feeling that the physical world as a whole is a question in need of an answer sweeps over us with overwhelming force; sometimes it seems to 'go away'. But at the very beginning of the book I hazarded that everyone reading it has had this feeling at some stage. When one considers the possibility that as well as this universe, there might be an infinite number of others, each of which instantiates one of the logically possible sets of boundary conditions and laws of nature, the tendency to this feeling does not disappear; it merely relocates itself. Answering 'Why does this universe exist?' with 'Because every logically possible universe exists' just prompts one to ask 'But why does every logically possible universe exist?' I hazard that anyone who feels puzzled by the contemplation of the physical world as a whole will feel similarly puzzled by the contemplation of an infinite set of such worlds. However, this feeling is not a reason for believing that the world or set of worlds as a whole needs an explanation of its existence in terms of a necessary God, unless, that is, a feeling that it does is itself a reason for believing that there is such a God. Even if one can't have a good argument against the view that physical stuff doesn't need any explanation premised on the principle that physical stuff does need an explanation, perhaps one could have a good argument for physical stuff needing an explanation premised on one's feeling that it did, if one's feeling that it did could itself be shown to be a reason to think that it did. To establish *that* point though would require a quite different sort of argument from the Cosmological Argument; it would require an Argument from Religious Experience. We'll consider that argument next.

10

The Argument from Religious Experience

I'd like to start by telling you the beginning of a fictional story.[1]

One day, a mountaineer, Nunez, who is climbing with a party of his friends high in the Andes, slips. His friends see him fall, and fall, and fall—down the mountainside and through the clouds, out of sight. They reason that there's no way he could have survived and there's no way to recover his body. Reluctantly, they give him up for dead and return home. Nunez however is not dead.

Trees and snow have broken his fall so that he has in actuality pitched up with only minor cuts and bruises at the bottom of the mountain in a deep and wide valley. He walks towards the centre of this valley and, as he does so, the trees thin out and he can see that it is surrounded by impassable mountains on all sides bar one, which in turn is cut off from the outside world by a large and obviously ancient rockfall. Further, he sees that he is not alone. In the centre of the valley there is a village, presumably isolated from the outside world for thousands of years. Roads come out from this village at regular intervals, like spokes on a wheel, and as he walks down one of these roads towards the village a man makes his way up the road to meet him. The two draw closer and Nunez is shocked to see that where the man's eyes should be there is just smooth skin; the man is obviously congenitally blind.

Nunez is about to speak when the man greets him; he has obviously heard Nunez's footsteps. With some difficulty, they make themselves understood to one another. The man—as Nunez thinks of it—speaks a corrupted version of his language; Nunez—as the man thinks of it—speaks a corrupted version of *his* language. Be that as it may, the man is friendly and accompanies Nunez into the village as they talk together. As they draw closer, other villagers, who Nunez notices also suffer from the same congenital blindness, emerge from their windowless houses to join them. Nunez asks the man if all the villagers are blind, but finds great difficulty getting the man to understand his question. Neither the man nor any of the other villagers seem to have the concept of sight or blindness; light or dark; and so on. Eventually, Nunez succeeds in asking if any of the villagers have eyes, a term which he manages to introduce by getting the man to touch his eyes. The man recoils in shock from these, but quickly apologizes for being so overtly disgusted by what is presumably an unfortunate deformity on Nunez's part. The man assures Nunez that nobody in the village has ever been unfortunate enough to have such oozing bulbous growths on their faces.

A meeting of the village is called for first thing in the morning, which Nunez is surprised to learn will be in about an hour. He is surprised to learn this as it is now dusk. As he discusses this with the man, he learns that the villagers treat what he—Nunez—would call night as their day and what he would call day as night, thinking it best to be going to bed for rest as things warm up and best to be getting up for exercise as things get colder. Given their blindness, that seems an eminently reasonable arrangement, he thinks. As the night closes in and Nunez awaits the so-called morning meeting, he remembers and ponders a saying he once heard in his youth, concluding from it that though he might never be able to escape from the valley, he will quickly be able to convince the eminently reasonable villagers that with his extra sense, he should be given a position of power within their community. The saying Nunez ponders is this: 'In the Country of the Blind, the one-eyed man is King.'

◆ ◆ ◆

The claim to have a sixth—spiritual—sense is not at all unusual. Research reveals that the *majority* of people in Great Britain would claim to have had at least one experience that they would describe as if of something supernatural, the most common type of experience being one as if of God.[2] I'm now going to consider what it might be reasonable for you to believe if it seemed to you yourself one day that you'd had such a religious experience. Would its seeming to you as if there is a God be a good reason for you to believe that there is a God? This seeming needn't be (though it could be) anything like the archetypal 'Vision of God', a glorious figure appearing in the sky or a booming voice speaking out of a burning bush. It could just be the difficult-to-articulate feeling that the physical world as a whole (and any set of such worlds) needs some sort of explanation, an explanation that the theistic God would best provide; or the even-vaguer feeling that it needs some sort of explanation that only something essentially dissimilar outside it could provide. Each of these are religious experiences as they are experiences that purport to point to a realm beyond anything like the physical world that we encounter with our five senses in day-to-day activity. Do religious experiences of any of these sorts provide us with any evidence that there is such a realm?

Richard Swinburne has crystallized out what seems to me to be the relevant epistemological principle in his book, *The Existence of God*.[3] He calls this principle the 'Principle of Credulity'. Roughly speaking, the Principle of Credulity states that:

> **If it seems to a subject that something is the case, then—all other things being equal—it is reasonable for him or her to believe that it really is the case.**

That isn't an exact quotation from Swinburne, but it's close enough.

The 'all other things being equal' clause is meant to take care of special considerations that make the subject overall more reasonable in believing that what prima facie seems to them to be the case probably isn't really the case, than in believing that what prima facie seems to them to be the case really is the case. That's a bit wordy; and it's not as confusing as the words make it sound. Let me give an example or two to make things a bit more clear. All other things would not be equal if one knew one had just walked through a door labelled 'Entrance to the Hall of Illusion' or if one knew one had just drunk ten Tequila slammers followed up by a Lysergic Acid Diethylamide—LSD—chaser. In the absence, though, of knowledge of these sorts of special conditions, i.e. conditions that one knows from past experience or testimony have been shown to have led to deceptive experiences, one should be credulous, one should believe that the world is as it appears to be. If it appears that there's a book in front of you, that's a prima facie good reason for you to believe that there's a book in front of you. If it appears to you that p implies q, then that's a prima facie good reason for you to believe that p implies q. And you should believe that which you have prima facie good reason to believe unless you have reason to believe that there are special considerations of the all-other-things-not-being-equal type.

So that's the Principle of Credulity.

I'm now going to ask, What reason do we have for thinking that we're most reasonable in collecting our beliefs according to the Principle of Credulity, rather than some other principle?

We could, it seems, collect our beliefs according to a more sceptical principle than the Principle of Credulity. One such principle would be:

If it seems to a subject that something is the case, then it is reasonable for him or her to believe that it really is the case if and only if he or she has a deductive argument showing that there's no way that he or she could be deceived, an argument that starts from indubitable premises and employs reasoning that not even an all-powerful demon could be confusing that subject about.

Those of you who've studied Descartes will have come across this sort of epistemic 'rigorism' before; and you'll have seen where it led, to solipsism of the present moment—the view that the only thing one can know is that one's own mind exists at the moment one's having that thought. The Principle of Credulity says in effect, 'Trust the world of appearance unless you've got reason not to do so'; Descartes said in effect, 'Don't trust the world of appearance unless you've got reason to do so.' It might seem that there's nothing to be said in favour of Swinburne's principle over Descartes's except that Descartes's makes progress in any area impossible. As Hume puts the point with respect to the general reliability of perception towards the end of the first *Enquiry*:

It is a question of fact, whether the perceptions of the senses be produced by external objects, resembling them: how shall this question be determined? By experience surely; as all other questions of a like nature. But here experience is, and must be entirely silent.

The mind has never anything present to it but the perceptions, and cannot possibly reach any experience of their connexion with objects. The supposition of such a connexion is, therefore, without any foundation in reasoning.

It seems then that the Principle of Credulity can't be non-question-beggingly argued for and it might be leading you astray (you might indeed be a brain in a vat being fed illusory experiences; scientists might be confusing you about even the simplest bit of reasoning you attempt), but even if one can suspend one's use of it for a moment or two in a discussion of various 'brains in vats'-type scenarios, for the purposes of everyday life one relies on the Principle of Credulity absolutely and one regards oneself as rational in doing so. And we should recall that the seeming that one relies on here is not merely perceptual seeming; if it seems to you that x is consistent (or inconsistent) with y, you have to take that as in itself good reason for you to believe that x really is consistent (or inconsistent) with y, otherwise you could never use what your experiences gave you (or indeed use anything else) in any form of argument.

If the philosophy of religion is not to become epistemology generally, then we must ignore the scepticism of those who would argue that there's no reason to believe that there is a God but whose only reasons for thinking this are the arguments that hyperbolic sceptics put forward for us having no reason to believe that there's anything exterior to our own minds at the present time. The lady who wrote to Bertrand Russell saying, 'I am a Solipsist and it's such a good philosophical position to hold that I'm surprised I don't find more people doing so' was not assisting him in his sceptical philosophy *of religion*. So, if we allow ourselves to 'divide through' as it were by the Cartesian sort of scepticism, we will in effect be accepting something akin to the Principle of Credulity. In that sense then, Swinburne is right to suggest, as he does, that the Principle of Credulity is a principle of rationality; even if in some exigent Cartesian or Humean sense one might be rational in not accepting it, in the practical day-to-day sense anybody who seriously doubted that most of the time the world is as it appears to be; that our reason can be trusted; and so on, would be irrational.

So it is that I suggest we should accept the Principle of Credulity.

◆ ◆ ◆

Given the Principle of Credulity, it follows that if it seems to you that you are having an experience of God, you have good reason in virtue of that experience for believing that there is a God unless you have reason to believe that all other things are not equal, that special considerations obtain. If it seems to you that the physical world as a whole must have an explanation in terms of something that lies beyond it, it's reasonable for you to think that it does have such an explanation, unless special considerations obtain. If, when reflecting on the possibility of an infinite number of infinitely variable worlds, you conclude that that too would be something in need of an explanation, then it's reasonable for you to think that it too would be something in need of an explanation, unless special considerations obtain. A word or two then about special considerations and whether or not we can have reason to believe that they always obtain in the case of religious experiences.

The majority of people who have experiences as if of God are very normal people: they raise families; they enjoy their food and the company of others; they are not what—for want of a better term—one might call 'religious nutters'. Other elements of these people's perceptual apparatus seem to equip them well for functioning in the everyday physical and social world. Why suppose that this—what they might think of as a sixth sense—does not put them in touch with a higher spiritual reality, but rather is some subject-specific, hallucination-inducing abnormality? The majority of people who have the intuition that there's something about the contingency of any set of universes that would need an explanation whereas there wouldn't be anything (or as much) about the contingency of a decision that needed an explanation are—from the rest of their lives, we would judge—as sane as those who would have the intuition that there's nothing about the contingency of, let's say, an infinite set of infinitely variable universes that needs any explanation. Why suppose that something's gone wrong with them?

Suppose that scientists were to discover a section of the brain that was different in those people who had experiences that seemed to them as if God was speaking to them. Tests revealed that scientists could remove this section of the brain without in any other way damaging the patient and, if they did so, from that moment on, no more such experiences were had. Would this show that the preceding religious experiences were not veridical? Not in itself. Nunez's eyes are ultimately regarded by the natives of the Country of the Blind as unfortunate growths that hamper him in engaging with reality by letting too much heat into his head. What would happen to Nunez's ability to have visual experiences if one day the medicine man of the village in the Country of the Blind removed his eyes? Obviously, it would disappear. This does not show that Nunez's eyesight was not veridical. If scientists were to discover some differences in the brains of those who have religious experiences of, let's say, the archetypal sort, the question of whether to label that section of the brain a sense organ or a subject-specific, hallucination-inducing deformity would not itself be decided simply by its discovery. What goes for finding a section of the brain goes for many of the other things that are often taken to be special considerations telling against religious experience tracking truth, for example that religious experiences often occur in those who are already members of a religious community; that they often occur after long periods of prayer; and so on. Unless those in these putative special circumstances had an inability to form correct beliefs by means of their other senses while in them, which characteristically they do not (fasting is perhaps the exception), then these so-called special considerations could not be non-question-beggingly taken to be such as to undermine the prima facie good reasons to believe that there is a God that these people's religious experiences provide for them. And again, we must remember that there is a sort of religious experience—a philosophical 'gut instinct' that the universe and anything similar needs an explanation in terms of a God or something similar—that can and does occur to many people when they are in what one might have thought of as ideal epistemic conditions—sitting back reflecting on what they've just read in a book about the philosophy of religion. Sit back now; reflect a bit.

♦ ♦ ♦

A more powerful argument against the veracity of religious experiences and thus the reasonableness of taking having had a religious experience as even a prima facie reason for believing what the experience seems to reveal would be provided if those who had religious experiences had a proven inability to form correct beliefs more often than incorrect ones by means of their spiritual 'sense'. And it's not unreasonable to think that there might be some hope of generating such an argument by showing that the diversity in the contents of the world's religions is so great that on the truth of any of them the majority of people who come to beliefs on the basis of their religious experiences must come to false beliefs.

Consider this situation: You are standing with some friends by the side of a deserted road to watch a car rally. After a few minutes, a lone car goes noisily by and it seems to you to be blue. This seeming to you is—via the Principle of Credulity—a prima-facie good reason for you to believe that the car is indeed blue, given that you have no reason to believe that all other things are not equal: it is broad daylight; you have an unobstructed view of the road, as do your friends; and so on. You therefore believe that the car is blue and think yourself reasonable for doing so. So far, so good.

You say to the gentleman standing next to you that you think that the blue car that has just passed is an original S-type Jaguar. He looks back at you somewhat startled: 'Well, it was a Jaguar all right, but it wasn't blue; it was bright red.' The lady standing next to him confirms his judgement, 'Certainly red'. Someone else chimes in, 'Of course it was red'; another says, referring to his judgement, 'That's right'.

What is it rational for you to believe now about the colour of the car? It would be rational for you to withdraw your judgement that the car is—probably—blue and replace it with the judgement that the car is—probably—red. To the extent that what seems to you to be the case is contradicted by the numerous and consistent testimonies of other independent witnesses, you have reason to believe that special considerations obtain (even if you can't see what they might be) and thus to be more sceptical about your original judgement; if the testimonies are sufficiently numerous, consistent, and independent, you should indeed withdraw your original judgement and replace it with the judgement of these others. If the testimonies of others are not quite numerous, unanimous, or independent enough for this, then you should suspend judgement altogether.

Let me alter the situation slightly to bring out this latter point. As before, it seems to you that the car that's just sped by was blue and when you say this to the man next to you he replies that it was bright red. However, the lady standing next to him says, 'Wait a minute, it was jet black.' Someone else says, 'It was yellow with pink spots'; another says, 'What car?' What is it rational for you to believe now about the colour of the car? To the extent that what seems to you to be the case is contradicted by the testimonies of others, you have reason to be sceptical about the veracity of your perceptions. However, if these testimonies themselves conflict with one another, then to the extent that they cannot be said to support any judgement more than any other, it is rational for you to stick by your original judgement as the one most probably correct among them while down-grading the probability that it is correct by some—perhaps considerable—margin, a margin so considerable that you should suspend judgement. If the collective testimony of your peers is worthless as a guide to the colour of the car—it is simply too various to support any particular judgement—then you are thrown back on the fact that (the reliability of one's own memories being assumed) it certainly seemed to you that the car was blue. (You can't be as certain that it seemed to anybody else to be the colour they report its seeming to them to have been.) While you should now be much more sceptical about this than you would have been before hearing your peers' testimony, you should therefore believe that it is more likely to be blue than it is to be any other particular colour (which is, of course, quite compatible with believing that it is more likely to be some other colour than it is to be blue). If you had to put your money anywhere, you'd put it on blue, but in putting it on blue you'd think that more likely than not you'd lose your money, and in this sense then you suspend judgement on the colour of the car. In the presence of testimony that conflicts with your experience yet is so mutually inconsistent that it—as it were—'cancels itself out', you are justified in sticking with your original judgement in the minimal sense of thinking it more probably true than any particular alternative, albeit downgrading your certainty in it to the extent that overall you suspend your judgement.

At this stage then the inductive soundness of what we might call 'the Argument from Having had Religious Experiences Oneself' depends on certain empirical contingencies concerning how numerous, variable, and mutually exclusive the contents of the testimonies of those who would claim to have had religious experiences are, a question that is not within the field of the philosophy of religion. It also depends on how numerous is the testimony of those who would claim to have had 'irreligious experiences', that is to say, experiences that seem to them to reveal that there is nothing exterior to physical stuff that accounts for it. If, when reflecting on the world as a whole or on the possibility of an infinite set of infinitely variable worlds, it strikes one that such is more like a self-explanatory whole than a question in need of an answer, one has had an 'irreligious experience', an experience that seems to one to reveal that there is no supernatural realm.

As well as religious experiences to be weighed in the balance, there are also then what I am calling irreligious experiences, experiences that seem to the subject to disclose that ultimate reality is merely physical. What is it that makes these experiences count as experiences of the absence of the supernatural rather than merely as the absence of experiences of the supernatural? If you have ever experienced separation from a loved one through their choice or death, you will know the answer. Your husband/wife, boyfriend/girlfriend has left you and you return to places that you knew together in happier times, places where his or her now-extinguished love for you was kindled. You feel his or her absence as you look around. Your parents have died. You go to their house to sort out their affairs. As you walk around their house, you experience a 'hole' that they would have filled. In each case, this isn't just a case of its not seeming to you that the person(s) concerned is (are) there; it's a case of its seeming to you that the person(s) concerned is (are) not there. There are certainly experiences like this in the religious sphere, but it is also true that they occur only to those who have previously had experiences of God: it is only those who have experienced God and believe in him who are then able to feel his absence, rather as it's only if you've been in love with the person who is now not with you at a place you once knew together, or known the parents who have died and in whose house you now are, that you will feel their absence. And, of course, this tends to make the people who do experience 'the absence of God' interpret these experiences as due to perceptual problems on their part, not as due to their gaining a better perception of the fact that God does not after all exist. But sometimes they do interpret these experiences in this latter way—in the darkest moments of their dark nights of the soul, as it were—and even if no one to whom these sorts of atheistic or irreligious experiences occur ever took them even initially to be evidence against the existence of God, it would still be conceptually possible that the same sort of experience might be had by someone who had not got the interpretative scheme of theism set up by previous experiences of God. If you gave me a vibrant enough description of your now-absent husband/wife, boyfriend/girlfriend, or now-deceased parents and then dropped me in the locations that made you feel their absence, it seems conceptually possible that I might report—and you have no reason to doubt—that I too had experienced their absence, not just failed to experience their presence. It seems then that there's the possibility at least of an argument from 'atheistic experience' against the existence of God and from 'irreligious experience' in general against the existence of a supernatural realm in general, i.e. in favour of physicalism. If the vast majority of people were to have experiences that they took to be revelatory of the non-existence of anything beyond the physical, this would be very good evidence for them—and indeed for any of the *ex hypothesi* rare people who were initially disposed to disagree—that there is no God. If upon contemplation of the physical world considered as a whole (or the possibility of a multiverse of infinitely variable such worlds), the vast majority of people felt that it was nothing like a question in need of an answer, it was much more like a self-explanatory whole, then that would be evidence that there was no supernatural realm. It's important to stress again that their just failing to be struck by the physical world (or the possibility of such a multiverse) as something akin to a question wouldn't be enough; that would just be the absence of an experience. They'd need to be struck by the physical world (multiverse) as a whole as something positively opposite to a question, as something akin to an explanatory whole or some such. But if these sorts of experiences occur, they too have to be weighed in the balance against the religious experiences of humanity.[4] And of course, the philosophical 'gut instinct' that this contingent universe, or a contingent multiverse of infinitely variable universes, is preferable as one's ultimate 'brute fact' to the God of theism making a free decision is one that many people will have had when reading the previous chapter.

Sometimes one cannot infer anything from a silence, but sometimes one can. When one shouts into a darkened room, 'Is there anyone there?' and silence is the only reply, this is in itself a bit of evidence that there's no one there. Of course, it's only such evidence on the hypothesis that any person who was there would have taken being asked to reveal himself or herself as a reason to do so, but—on theism—it is true that God will take being asked to reveal himself as a reason to do so. We've seen that he has reason to start us from a position of epistemic distance from himself, but we've also seen that he has reason to respect and reward our choice to seek him out. Merely asking him to reveal himself can't be an overwhelming reason for him to do so, which is why asking God to reveal himself and receiving only silence in reply can't be a proof that he doesn't exist. But given that being asked to reveal himself must give him *some* reason to do so, so our asking God to reveal himself and our apparently receiving only silence in reply must be *some* evidence that he doesn't exist. If, when you sincerely wish that if there were a God, he would reveal himself and his will more fully to you and—waiting of course to hear any answer—you appear to receive only silence in reply, then that's a reason for you to suppose that there is no God. Similarly, if, when in your most reflective and calm moments, you consider the physical universe as a whole (or a multiverse of infinitely variable universes), and it strikes you as not at all puzzling—more like an unremarkable and complete self-explanatory whole than a question in need of an answer—then that's a reason for you to suppose that physicalism is true and the religious point of view is false.

I must leave my conclusion rather hypothetical. If it seems to you that there is a God and the testimony against its being true that there is a God is not very great or mutually consistent in itself, then it could remain overall reasonable for you to believe that there probably is a God. If, on the other hand, there is numerous and unanimous testimony from others that—on the basis of their own experiences—you are mistaken, you should accept that you probably are mistaken and that—despite what appeared to you to be the case—there probably is no God. If the testimony of others is so mutually inconsistent that it neither supports nor undermines the claim that there is a God—if it, as I put it, 'cancels itself out'—then it could remain overall reasonable for you to believe that your experience raises the probability that there is a God to some extent. If, for some reason, you had to put your money somewhere, you'd be most reasonable in putting it on God.

Appearances can be deceptive, so no argument from your religious experience will ever be able to be a deductively sound argument for the existence of God. There'll always remain the possibility that it's leading you from truth to falsity; 'It seems to you that X' is always going to remain compatible with 'It's false that X' for the values of X we're interested in. But an argument from your religious experience—if you've had one—could in principle be a good inductive argument for the existence of God. Failing that, it could in principle inductively support the existence of God. Failing that, it could support the falsity of physicalism. Again, it is worth stressing that a very great many people have had what on my analysis is a religious experience, indeed I hazarded earlier that everyone reading this book will have had one: the feeling that the physical world or any set of such worlds considered as a whole is a contingency for which an explanation is more required than the right sort of supernatural contingency. This seems to reveal to those who have it that there is a supernatural realm beyond the natural one; it is an experience that in itself is a bit of evidence in favour of the religious outlook and against the physicalist.

◆ ◆ ◆

Now let me turn to consider what it would be reasonable for someone who hadn't had any religious or irreligious experiences to believe when confronted with the testimonies of those who would claim that they had, when confronted with what one might call the 'Argument from Other People's Testimonies to Having had Religious Experiences' or the 'Argument from Other People's Testimonies to Having had Irreligious Experiences'. If you'd never had an experience that seemed to you as if of God or as if of the absence of God, what would it be most reasonable for you to believe when one of the people who has had an experience as if of God told you about it or when someone who had had an experience as if of God's absence told you about that? I'm going to argue that the answer parallels the answer to the question, 'What does a person born blind have most reason to believe when they hear someone tell them that he or she—by contrast—has an additional sense, which has enabled him or her to discern various things about the world of colour?'

Nunez—as you have no doubt already guessed—finds much more difficulty than he initially anticipates in showing the inhabitants of the Country of the Blind that he does have privileged access to an aspect of reality of which they are ignorant. They quickly label him as 'mad'—albeit in a relatively confined area of his life—and ignore his, what are to them, largely meaningless jabberings. If you read the original story by Wells, I imagine that you will be struck by how reasonable, from their point of view (if you'll forgive the expression), their interpretation of his behaviour is. Their other senses are more refined than his and so his sight never seems to bring him any advantage over them. He just can't show them, in any way that is not amenable to reinterpretation on their part, that the words he uses do indeed pick out genuine properties of the objects they come into contact with. As it appears to them, he is awake in the night and sleeps in the day. He is incredibly clumsy inside buildings (their buildings, you will recall, have no windows and so are pitch black inside). And he has two physical deformities on the front of his head, deformities that their medical people assure them are the root of his mania, letting in too much heat as he runs around in the night, heat that addles his brain. Their lives by contrast seem to them to run perfectly smoothly without reference to this thing called 'colour', a thing spoken of by a solitary and apparently mad man who has fallen into their world.

Now consider the situation of those born blind in our society. They, by contrast with the natives of the Country of the Blind, do *not* dismiss the talk concerning this thing called 'colour' as meaningless jabbering. They *do* regard those around them as having privileged access into an aspect of reality of which they are ignorant. They quickly label them 'sighted' and accept on the strength of their testimony the truth of claims the terms used in which they cannot, we cannot help but think, fully understand. Those born blind in our society accept that skies are blue (sometimes); that grass is green; and so on, simply on the strength of the testimony of those around them. When you consider this, I imagine that you will be struck by how *un*reasonable they would be were they not to do so. For someone born blind in our society to insist that those who would call themselves sighted are—albeit only in a localized way—mad and that all their talk concerning colour is meaningless jabbering would be the height of irrationality.

So, what is the difference between the two cases, which makes it reasonable for those born blind in the Country of the Blind to ignore Nunez's testimony as to the existence of a world of colour and makes it unreasonable for those born blind in our society to ignore our testimony to the same effect?

I suggest that one important difference is that in the Country of the Blind, Nunez is the only testifier to the existence and character of the world of colour, whereas in our society there are numerous people who would describe themselves as sighted and—a second important point—not only are they numerous, but also they agree with one another as to the character of the world of colour. If we have but one witness to an event, we are more chary of accepting what they say as true than if we have several independent witnesses whose testimony is in essentials in agreement. Sheer weight of numbers of independent people who would describe themselves as sighted would not be enough on its own, for we can see that were a blind person to hear numerous *but conflicting* testimonies about the world of colour, he or she would be reasonable in suspending judgement.

But, as a matter of fact, in our society as well as being numerous, the testimony of sighted people is largely consistent. So, from this—if my analogy is apposite—it would follow that to the extent that there was a substantial number of people testifying in an essentially consistent way to the existence and character of a spiritual world, that would be a reason for those who had not themselves had any experience of this world to believe that it existed and had the character to which these people's collective testimony bore witness. Against this reason, one would of course have to weigh any testimony to the effect that the testifier had experienced the absence of a supernatural realm to see what it was one had overall most reason to believe.

There is one further caveat that I would like to introduce.

Consider this situation: you are watching television in your hotel room in the United States of America. You switch to a channel where a smart, if slightly flashily dressed, middle-aged man is speaking direct to camera. He fixes you with a rather arresting gaze and tells you: 'The Lord is telling me that you—yes YOU watching TV in your hotel room—should reach for your cheque-book right now and send me a cheque for ten dollars!' (Presumably he says 'check-book' and 'check', but let's not worry about that.) Momentarily startled, you are about to switch over when the camera goes to a wider shot that incorporates a huge gospel choir behind him, say two hundred people. They chant in unison to the tune of the Hallelujah chorus, 'Yes, God wills it. Yes, God wills it. Yes, God wills it. Send him a cheque!'

Let me suppose that before watching this television programme you had no views on whether or not there is a God or on the worth or otherwise of this person. What would it be most reasonable for you to believe now? You have two hundred and one people who are all testifying in an essentially consistent (indeed maximally consistent) way to the effect that there is a God and that he wants you to send $10 to whomever this chap is. In any other circumstance where the truth-value of a statement was a matter of epistemic indifference to you, you wouldn't demand 201 people to testify to its being the case before you believed that it probably was the case. Are you being unreasonable then if you ignore him and blithely switch to another channel? Of course not, and the reason why is easy to see. It's the same reason why one is reasonable in being suspicious of estate agents; they act on commission. This TV evangelist can reasonably be thought to have a non-truth-directed motive for saying what he is saying. Whether or not God existed or wanted you to send him a cheque for $10, this TV evangelist and his colleagues in the choir would have a non-truth-directed reason for saying that he did and wanted this.

So, I should nuance my conclusion by saying that to the extent that those in receipt of religious experiences are numerous among us and speak with a con-sistent voice as to the nature of the spiritual reality they describe, it is reasonable for those of us without religious experience or irreligious experience to take their collective testimony as reason for believing in the truth of what they say as to the nature of this spiritual world *unless* they may reasonably be supposed to have some ulterior non-truth-directed motive for persuading us to believe what they believe. This raises the question, how then can we remove the suspicion of an ulterior non-truth-directed motive? There seems to be one relatively simple way to ensure the absence of any non-truth-directed motive for a testimony, torturing the testifier to death.

If, under the serious threat of being tortured to death or—even better—if while actually being tortured to death, a testifier still persisted in testifying to the existence and character of a spiritual world, then—it might seem—we could rule out any non-truth-directed motive for his or her doing so. Of course, many people would withdraw claims they knew to be true if they were being tortured to death for maintaining them. You wouldn't have to torture me for long before I withdrew any claim you cared to specify. But the epistemically useful feature of torturing people to death is—it might seem—that nobody would persist with a claim that they did not believe with more certainty than almost anything else if they believed they were being tortured to death because they were testifying to it: torturing people to death may mean we fail to hear the testimony of many who would have been sincere witnesses to the existence and character of a spiritual world, but it will certainly mean we won't hear the testimony of any insincere ones. Or at least that's the way it prima facie seems. But we don't need to go into whether or not torturing people to death would be as epistemically useful as it prima facie seems, for those of even minimal moral sensibilities will have foreseen a potential objection to torturing people to death in order to further our investigation into the philosophy of religion, an objection that rather trumps any epistemic reason for doing so; it's not morally acceptable to torture people to death. Torture is in itself bad and our intuition tells us clearly that the good of increasing our epistemic access to truths about the philosophy of religion isn't great enough to justify it. So, morally, whether it would be useful or not, we can't do this. Of course, this doesn't stop us (or at least it doesn't without further argument) from considering the testimonies of those who have already and through no fault of ours been tortured and continued to assert various religious claims.

Some epistemic comfort to us as we mentally lay aside the tools of torture may be that (perhaps some TV evangelists aside) it's very difficult to see what non-truth-directed motive the people who testify to the existence and character of a spiritual reality or indeed its absence could have. There does not seem to be any reason why the epistemic worry as to the possibility of non-truth-directed motives should be greater in the field of testimony regarding religious or irreligious experiences than in the field of any other sort of testimony.[5] So it is that I conclude that to the less than perfect extent to which one can in practice rule out non-truth-directed motives; to the extent that one has not oneself had irreligious experiences; to the extent that one has a large number of independent witnesses; and to the extent that these witnesses testify in a consistent way as to the existence and character of a spiritual world, it is reasonable for those of us without the benefit of religious experience to take their collective testimony as reason for believing in the truth of what they say as to the nature of this spiritual world. To the extent that we cannot rule out non-truth-directed motives; to the extent that we ourselves have had irreligious experiences; to the extent that those who claim to be in receipt of religious experiences are few and far between; and to the extent that they speak with contradictory voices as to the nature of the spiritual reality they take these experiences to reveal, it is reasonable for those of us without the hindrance of religious experiences to take their collective testimony as a reason for believing that there is a relatively infrequent subject-specific hallucination-inducing (or metaphysical intuition-perverting) condition that we have been lucky not to have developed.

At this stage then, the Argument from Other People's Testimonies to Having had Religious Experiences is thrown back again on those things that philosophers are loath to engage with, empirical facts. To what extent are there large numbers of independent witnesses? To what extent can we rule out their having non-truth-directed motives? To what extent have we ourselves been in receipt of irreligious experiences? And to what extent do these witnesses testify in a *consistent* way as to the existence and character of a spiritual world; to what extent are these experiences distinctively theistic as opposed to being of some *imper*sonal spiritual world? To what extent are there irreligious experiences to weigh against them? To investigate these questions would take much introspection; take another book; and take us well outside the field of the philosophy of religion. In this context then, I must again leave my conclusion hypothetical. *If* the right sort of testimony were forthcoming, the Argument from Religious Experience construed as the Argument from Other People's Testimonies to Having had Religious Experiences could provide one with reasons for believing that there is a God. These reasons could never amount to a deductively sound argument for the existence of God, because what seems to people—even what seems to an enormous number of people—to be the case on this issue might not be the case; appearances can be deceptive. So it is that any Argument from Other People's Testimonies to Having had Religious Experiences to the existence of God could only ever be at most an inductively sound argument. But if the right sort of testimony were forthcoming it might very well be that and even if it wasn't quite that—if the testimonies were rather too minimal or inconsistent to raise the probability sufficiently for it to become more probable than not that there is a God—an Argument from Other People's Testimonies to Having had Religious Experiences could inductively support the theistic conclusion, i.e. raise the probability of its being true to some extent. As such, an Argument from Other People's Testimonies to Having had Religious Experiences could in principle form part of an inductively sound cumulative case argument for the existence of God. And of course, by parallel reasoning, an Argument from Other People's Testimonies to Having had Irreligious Experiences could inductively support the atheistic conclusion or form part of an inductively sound cumulative case for the non-existence of God.

◆ ◆ ◆

I've argued then that if you have an experience that seems to you to be of a God and in circumstances where no conditions obtain that you have reason to believe are likely to impair your perceptual apparatus in other regards, then it is reasonable for you to believe that there is a God if there isn't sufficient testimony from other people's experiences (or your own earlier experiences) to there not being a God. If your reflective philosophical intuition is that it's more likely that there be an unexplained contingency in the mind of God than in a universe or set of universes, then it's reasonable for you to believe that there's a God if there isn't sufficient testimony from other people's experiences (or your own earlier experiences) to their not being a God (or other 'defeaters' to your belief—that is to say, good arguments against the existence of God) and you think that there is contingency in the universe.[6] Even if you haven't had such a religious experience yourself, as long as you haven't had sufficient atheistic or irreligious experiences, if enough people whose integrity (i.e. truth-directedness) you have no reason to question testify in an essentially consistent and independent way to the effect that there is a God, it would be no more rational for you to withhold your assent to the claim that there is a God than it would be for a person born blind in our society to withhold his or her assent from the claims the rest of us make concerning the colours of objects (again in the absence of other defeaters). Of course, if you have had atheistic or irreligious experiences, you will have to weigh these against the testimony of any theistic or religious experience you subsequently have and against the collective testimony of humanity's religions. If there are other 'defeaters', e.g. an apparently inductively sound argument to the non-existence of God from the existence of evil in the world, you'll have to weigh that in the overall balance too. I conclude then that—depending on certain empirical contingencies—the Argument from Religious Experience might provide good reasons for one to believe that there's a God and the Argument from atheistic and Irreligious Experience might provide one with good reason to believe that there's not a God. Of course, if you are indeed starting from what I called the fifty/fifty position in an earlier chapter, then, as I've pointed out, any argument that inductively supports the conclusion that there is a God, however minimally it does so, is an inductively sound argument for you. These good reasons might make the Argument from Religious Experience a good argument for you (though overall, there might be more reason not to believe that there's a God, provided by even weightier defeaters). Similarly, the Argument from Irreligious Experience might provide one with good reasons to believe that there's no God. Which of these arguments that might be good in principle are good in practice? You must investigate and decide. But I close by referring to what would follow for you were your investigation to turn up the results that mine has.[7]

The collective testimony of the religious experiences of humanity is multitudinous relative to irreligious experiences. Far more people purport to have experiences as if of the presence of a supernatural realm than as if of its absence. But while relatively multitudinous, it is also relatively disparate. The commonalities among people's religious experiences—and here we must remember to include those of the adherents of religions that do not see the supernatural order as personal—is merely that there is some supernatural realm (of course, otherwise they wouldn't have got counted as religious experiences); that it is not malevolent; and that putting oneself in touch with it is of vital importance. As such, the collective testimony of humanity is not enough to give us positive reason to prefer any one religion over any other. Even then, though, it does (given that the testimonies to this effect are numerous enough and from people whose integrity we have no reason to question) give us reason to suppose that physicalism is false. We have reason to believe that there is a supernatural realm in addition to the physical, a supernatural realm that explains why there is a physical realm for us to describe and why there is an us to do the describing, a supernatural realm that is not opposed to our wellbeing and that indeed we need to orientate ourselves towards properly if we are to find our ultimate fulfilment. It is just that we can't, from a study of the collective testimony of humanity alone, conclude anything less vague about the nature of that supernatural realm and thus how it is that we may orientate ourselves properly towards it. We have reason to believe physicalism is false; we just don't have reason to favour any particular religion over any other as the most probable one.[8] But perhaps the testimonies of those who subscribe to one religion should be given greater weight than those who subscribe to another, not because these testifiers have greater integrity or are more numerous, but rather because there are peculiar facts that that religion being true would best explain or—even better—perhaps there are peculiar facts that *only* that religion being true could explain. This line of thinking brings us to the next argument we'll consider.

11

The Argument from Reports of Apparent Miracles

The Gospels tell us that Jesus was crucified, died, and was buried. So far, there's nothing particularly unusual about their story. But the Gospels go on to tell us something else: that three days later, Jesus was raised from the dead. Surely only God could have performed such a feat; and thus surely the Gospels give us reason to believe that there's a God; and indeed to believe that this God has endorsed one religion—Christianity—over and above the others. This is a version of the Argument from Reports of Apparent Miracles. Our friend David Hume is the most significant critic of this line of argument and in this chapter I'm going to be focusing on what he has to say.

First, we have what I'm going to call Hume's A Priori Argument Against the Rationality of Believing in Miracles on the Testimony of Others. Here Hume argues that no testimony could, even in principle, be good enough to make it reasonable to believe that a miracle had occurred. Secondly, we have what I'm going to call Hume's A Posteriori Arguments Against the Rationality of Believing in Miracles on the Testimony of Others. There are four of them, to the effect that the testimony we have to miracles having occurred is, in any case, not very good at all. I'll look at these arguments in order.

HUME'S A PRIORI ARGUMENT

The most detailed definition of miracles that Hume gives us is in a footnote[1] where he says:

A miracle may accurately be defined, *a transgression of a law of nature by a particular volition of the Deity or by the interposition of some invisible agent.*

This, one might think, seems reasonable enough. A merely unusual event, however fortuitous, would not properly be called a miracle. It is true that if we consider disasters in which many people are killed, it sometimes happens that one or two people survive against the odds and their survival is often called miraculous in popular reports of the events. However, we recognize that such a use of the term is strictly speaking incorrect, an exaggeration for dramatic purposes. To be rigorous, we would insist that only if their survival was caused not by a fortuitous something but by a benevolent someone and by a benevolent someone who acted not merely against the odds, but against the laws of nature, that we should call it genuinely miraculous. Hume's definition appears to capture these thoughts.[2]

In the main text preceding the note in which Hume defines miracles, he observes that wise people proportion their belief according to the evidence. Again, this seems sensible. If you believe to be true that which you have more evidence is false or you believe to be false that which you have more evidence is true, you are manifestly being unreasonable.

Having made this point, Hume goes on to define laws of nature as whatever uniform experience has established. Why do you think that it's a law of nature that water boils at 100 degrees centigrade (at sea level)? Because that's what you and thousands of other people have had uniform experience of having happened in the past. Laws of nature then, by definition, have uniform experience—maximally good evidence—in favour of their always holding. Otherwise they wouldn't be called laws of nature, they'd be called things like 'rules of thumb' or 'pretty good generalizations'.

With these points in the bag, we now have all the materials we need to construct Hume's A Priori Argument Against the Rationality of Believing in Miracles on the Testimony of Others.

A report of a miracle is on Hume's definition—among other things—a report that a law of nature hasn't held. That is what makes it a report of a miracle rather than a report of a rather unusual and fortuitous event. So, a report of a miracle is a report of something that were it to have happened would have gone against that which you have maximally good evidence for believing. When you proportion your belief according to the evidence therefore, when you are a wise person, you must believe that any report you hear that a miracle has occurred probably isn't true, that the miracle probably did not occur.

As Hume himself puts it:

A miracle is a violation of the laws of nature; and as a firm and unalterable experience has established these laws, the proof against a miracle, from the very nature of the fact, is as entire as any argument from experience can possibly be imagined.

◆ ◆ ◆

There are a number of things that might worry one about Hume's argument. I want to start by drawing attention to how parallel arguments are obviously wrong. The first point I'm going to make against Hume's A Priori Argument is rather analogous then to the Overload Objection to the Ontological Argument.

Consider the scenario: you are the Nolloth Professor of Bananas at Oxford University. You've been experimenting on bananas all your life and in your life you've never seen a straight one; you have firm and unalterable experience then—as Hume might have put it—that bananas are always bent. As Nolloth Professor of Bananas, you often act as a reviewer for articles submitted to your professional journal, *Top Banana*. One day, *Top Banana* sends you an article for review. It is written by respected banana experts at another institution; you've reviewed their papers before and they've almost always been truly excellent. You read the article and the substance of it is a claim made by these scientists that they've found a *straight* banana. The article looks scholarly (lots of footnotes and acronyms, things like that); the scientists at this other institution, when you contact them, pledge their sincerity; and so on.

What—according to Hume's argument—should you believe? Well, a straight banana is for you something that contravenes a law of nature, for laws of nature are—according to Hume—just whatever your firm and unalterable experience has established and your firm and unalterable experience has been that bananas are always bent. Thus, you should believe that these people are mistaken in their judgement or deliberately out to deceive you. You should screw up the article and throw it in the bin. But that seems unduly narrow-minded. If you couldn't sometimes be reasonable in believing those who told you something that was contrary to your experience, then science as a collaborative exercise could never exist. No scientist could ever be reasonably shaken in his or her prejudices by the reports of others, for in so far as these reports contradicted those prejudices he or she should simply dismiss them. So, something's gone wrong with Hume's argument. What?

One thing that may have been troubling you is that Hume has defined laws of nature as whatever uniform experience has established, but surely laws of nature are whatever laws nature actually follows and what uniform experience establishes are ideas in our minds about what these laws are.

Let us distinguish then between what I shall call 'objective laws of nature' and what I shall call 'subjective laws of nature'. Objective laws of nature are the laws that the universe really follows (unless God or some supernatural agent intervenes[3]) and that scientific theories approximate, and indeed seem, with each generation, to approximate more and more accurately. The subjective laws of nature on the other hand are, roughly speaking, the laws 'established' by taking the simplest law that can be made to harmonize with what has been our firm and unalterable experience to date; the subjective laws are our scientific theories about what the objective laws are.

Once we've distinguished between subjective laws and objective laws, Hume's definition of miracles, mentioning as it does simply laws of nature, must strike us as chronically ambiguous. Having made this distinction, we must seek to 'tidy up' Hume's original definition of miracles by asking whether a miracle should be understood as a transgression of an objective law or the transgression of a subjective law. It seems that we would have to say the former. To be a bona fide miracle, in contrast to an event that might very well be taken for a miracle, an event has to transgress what is in reality—independently of what anybody thinks about it—a law of nature, i.e. it has to be an event that transgresses an objective law.

Why think that it's objective laws that should feature in a 'tidied-up' Humean definition? There are two reasons. First, subjective laws change from person to person; day to day; and in general as science progresses. We don't want the status of an event as a miracle to be this variable. Secondly, many things that we would not wish to describe as miracles transgress subjective laws—whatever it is that forces us to abandon previously well-supported but now obviously over-simple scientific theories.

◆ ◆ ◆

Given what I have argued to date, one might thus think that the only problem with Hume's argument is that we need to tidy up his definition of miracles:

> A miracle may most accurately be defined as a transgression of an objective law of nature by a particular volition of the Deity or by the interposition of some invisible agent.

However, once we've tidied it up like this, a problem seems to be revealed. It's impossible to know with complete certainty whether or not any event counts as a miracle on this new definition. Epistemically speaking, we only have access to subjective laws—remember, our subjective laws are our best guess at what the objective laws really are—and so we could never tell with complete certainty whether or not a particular event satisfied the description of miracles specified in the revised definition.

However, this consequence isn't fatal to Hume's argument. There are all sorts of things one can form reasonable beliefs about without certainty; and—I'm about to argue—this is one of them.

As a matter of fact, one can distinguish between an event that, were it to occur, would be contrary to all that one has had experience of to date and yet that would not, one reasonably suspects, be a miracle, e.g. a straight banana, and an occurrence that, were it to occur, would not only be contrary to all that one has had experience of but would also, one reasonably suspects, be a miracle, e.g. a resurrection. How can one do this?

There are two parts to the answer to this question. Part of the answer to this question lies in the fact that one takes simplicity of hypothesis to be a guide to truth and the hypothesis 'There's a God plus simple objective laws of nature' might be simpler overall than the hypothesis 'There isn't a God, but there are much more complicated objective laws of nature.' Another part lies in the fact that one can come to some reasonable beliefs about what sorts of events God, were he to exist, would have good reason to bring about.

Let me look at the first part first and let me turn to the case of the Gospels' reports of Jesus' resurrection. If these reports are of a sufficient quantity and quality (and of course that's a big 'if') to justify one in believing that the events they describe probably did occur, then one is faced with a choice: either believe that the subjective law 'when you're dead, you're dead'[4] is probably not indeed an objective law, but rather has to be modified and thus complicated: Jesus was resurrected, but that's a naturally explicable fact. Or believe that it is indeed an objective law that when you're dead, you're dead, but there's a God or some other supernatural being who intervened on this particular occasion to break it. If the Gospel accounts are of sufficient quantity and quality, then which of these one should believe will depend on balancing how well supported the subjective law of nature is and how simple the hypothesis that there's a God or some other supernatural being is. There's another complication here, unfortunately, that what counts as sufficient quantity and quality will depend on the prior probability one's assigned to the existence of God. To keep things simple, I'm continuing to suppose we're all starting from the fifty/fifty position.

The subjective law of nature that when you're dead, you're dead is extremely well supported by experience. God—I have argued—is in himself a relatively simple entity to posit, certainly simpler than any other supernatural person. So, when dealing with the Gospels' accounts of the resurrection of Jesus, one is dealing with testimonies to an event that, were it to have happened, would have contravened a subjective law for the accuracy of which there is a great deal of evidence. It is thus rational to think that if the Gospels are of a sufficiently high quantity and quality for it to become reasonable for one to believe that the events they describe occurred, one should stick with the simplest law—when you're dead, you're dead—and see the event not as evidence that one's experiences to date have not been sufficiently wide to get one's subjective laws sufficiently close to the objective laws, but rather as evidence that there is a God, something that is not intrinsically so complicated as to reduce the overall probability of one's working hypothesis below that of the hypothesis that the objective laws of nature concerning death do not have the form when you're dead, you're dead.

Asking why this might be the case with resurrections and not straight bananas brings me to the second part of the answer. One can be reasonable in believing that if there were a God, he'd be more likely to perform miraculous resurrections than miraculous fruit-straightenings. I won't argue for this; rather, I'll just give a name to the difference between the two cases, it's as I am going to put it, a difference of 'existential significance'. Existentially significant events are those sorts of events that God—were he to exist—would be more likely to find reason to bring about. It is not easy to articulate exactly what existential significance amounts to, but this does not much matter for the purposes of our investigation, for we all have a clear understanding of when it would be there and when it wouldn't be there. A straight banana would not in itself be existentially significant; a man who had claimed to be God and who had been dead for three days coming back to life would be existentially significant. When dealing with testimonies to an event that, were it to have happened, would not have been existentially significant—for example, the finding of a straight banana—it would be rational for one to think that if the testimonies do reach a sufficiently high standard for it to become reasonable for one to believe the event occurred, it is reasonable for one to think that the simplest law 'bananas must be straight' is not in fact an objective law. When dealing with testimonies to an event that, were it to have happened, would have been existentially significant, such as the resurrection of Jesus, it would be rational for one to think that if the testimonies do reach a sufficiently high standard for it to become reasonable for one to believe the event occurred, one should think that the simplest law 'when you're dead, you're dead' is indeed an objective law, but God has intervened to suspend it. A supernatural agent is more likely to perform an existentially significant violation of an objective natural law than an existentially insignificant one.

◆ ◆ ◆

Some of what I've said about Hume's A Priori Argument has been rather involved. I've been trying to juggle a number of conceptual balls at once and it wouldn't be surprising if you'd lost track of where some of them were when I had the others in hand. What I thought I'd do therefore was put the gist of my argument in an analogy:

You've been watching teams of people play a particular game. To help you visualize it, let me tell you that it's rather like football, but has even more fantastically complicated rules. Now, to keep things relatively simple for the moment, I stipulate that there is a device called an 'Illegality Inhibitor', which is worn by every player and stops players ever making any illegal moves. You know with absolute certainty that every player always wears an Illegality Inhibitor. (Don't ask me how you know this; it's just an artifice to make the analogy work.)

You've watched hundreds of matches and on the basis of what you've seen you've been coming up with theories as to what rules the players are following. You've been jotting these theories down in your notepad and then amending them in the light of your experiences of subsequent matches. What you have written in your notepad now, then, are what we might call your subjective rules of the game. The subjective rules of the game that you've written in your notepad aren't just your best guess at the rules that the players must accord with given that they're wearing Illegality Inhibitors, e.g. 'Don't touch the ball with your hands,' they're also your best guess at the rules that they're *following*, e.g. 'Try to get the ball into the opponent's goal,' and you've been able to formulate this sort of rule because you know you've always watched well-motivated teams, i.e. teams composed of people each of whom has been trying to do everything within his or her power to make his or her team win. Don't ask me how you know you've always been watching well-motivated teams either. It's just another stipulation to keep the analogy going. These rules then form for you a pretty good guide as to what will happen from moment to moment; they help you predict patterns of play and so on pretty accurately. This then is the analogue to scientists developing, by experiment and observation, a set of subjective laws of nature that allow them to understand—to a large extent—the past and predict—to a large extent—the future.

Not being Hume, you've not confused your subjective rules of the game with the objective rules of the game, the rules that the players are really following. You know that your subjective rules of the game, while a pretty good guide to the objective rules, are likely to be mistaken in at least some details.

Now you discover four old newspapers, each of which contains a report of a particular match. In fact, though the four reports are ostensibly written by different authors, you notice some suspicious similarity in phrasing between them—perhaps one or two have copied, you think. This is rather obviously the analogue with coming across the four Gospels. The four newspaper reports tell a pretty consistent story—though they do differ over some minor details—and they talk a lot about one particular player and what moves he made during the particular match that they report on. The reports state that he made many moves, that—you realize as you compare them to the rules in your notepad—would square with your subjective rules. But the reports also agree with one another in stating that this player made a substantial number of moves that you realize you can't square with your subjective rules. If your subjective rules are right and the reports are right, then this player would have to have been making illegal moves (which you know is impossible, given that all players wear Illegality Inhibitors). So, for as long as you stick with the assumption that all players must always wear Illegality Inhibitors, there are only two options for you: either you must believe that the reports are mistaken, the player did not perform the moves in question, or you must believe that your subjective rules are mistaken; if your subjective rules are mistaken, the player could have performed the moves yet not done anything illegal. Of course, you could go for explanatory overkill and believe both, but let's ignore that.

What should you believe? Hume's A Priori Argument is to the effect that you should disbelieve the reports. I've argued though that the question, 'What should you believe?' cannot be decided a priori: it all depends. On the one hand, you will have to consider how mutually consistent and yet independent the reports seem on closer inspection to be and what if any exterior evidence supports (or undermines) their story; and, on the other hand, you will have to consider how well confirmed by your observations are the subjective laws that the reports say were violated. If the reports are very consistent, largely independent, and supported by great exterior evidence, and if the subjective laws they testify to a violation of are not very well confirmed by your observations, you should believe the reports and consider your subjective laws to be wrong. If the reports are rather inconsistent, seem largely dependent upon one another for what consistency they do have; are not supported by much if any exterior evidence; and if the subjective laws they testify to a violation of are extremely well confirmed by your observations, then you should believe your subjective laws are right and the reports are wrong.

Now let me return to consider the Illegality Inhibitor, the device that prevents players making any illegal move. This was the analogue to there being no supernatural force that could trump whatever were the objective laws of nature. If I relax my previous supposition that you know with absolute certainty that every player always wears an Illegality Inhibitor, what is it then that you are most reasonable in believing when you read the reports? This is analogous to relaxing the assumption—which Hume seems in some incautious moments to be relying on in his argument—that you know with absolute certainty that there cannot be a God. If I relax this assumption, you have three options rather than two when you read the reports: as before, you could believe that the reports are mistaken, the player did not perform these moves, or you could believe that the reports are right and it's your subjective rules that are mistaken. But you also have the option of believing that the reports are not mistaken, the player did indeed perform these moves; your subjective rules are not mistaken either, these moves were indeed illegal ones; and it's just that the player was not wearing an Illegality Inhibitor. This player could break the rules of the game. Could it ever be rational to go for the last of these options? It could; again, we cannot rule this out a priori. Again, it will depend on how mutually consistent and yet independent the reports are; what if any exterior evidence is available; and how well confirmed by your observations are the subjective laws of nature that the reports say were violated. If the reports are largely mutually consistent yet independent; if there exists some credible exterior evidence in support of them; and if nevertheless the subjective rules that they testify to a violation of are very well confirmed by your observations, then rather than these facts pushing in opposite directions, forcing you to do some delicate balancing and decide between either disbelieving the reports or disbelieving your subjective rules, it becomes rational for you to believe both. You should believe that the reports are largely accurate; your subjective rules are largely accurate on the point in question too; and it's just that the player in question could break the rules; he or she was not wearing an Illegality Inhibitor. The analogue is of course that if the Gospel reports are largely mutually consistent yet independent; if there exists some credible exterior evidence in support of them; and if nevertheless the subjective laws of nature that they testify to a violation of (for example, the law that when you're dead, you're dead) are very well confirmed by your observations, then rather than these facts pushing you in opposite directions, forcing you to do some delicate balancing and decide between either disbelieving the Gospels or disbelieving your subjective laws of nature, it becomes rational for you to believe in both. You should believe that the Gospels are largely accurate; your subjective laws of nature are accurate on the point in question (it really is an objective law of nature that when you're dead, you're dead) and it's just that the person in question could break the laws of nature.

It seems then that Hume's A Priori Argument Against the Rationality of Believing in Miracles on the Testimony of Others fails. If it is irrational to believe in a given report or set of reports of a miracle, this will be for a posteriori reasons peculiar to that report or set of reports. In a moment then, I'll turn to look at Hume's A Posteriori Arguments Against the Rationality of Believing in Miracles on the Testimony of Others. First though, I want to say a word more about the notion of exterior evidence, because it's a notion that I've just made use of in my discussion and I didn't explain what I meant by it.

◆　◆　◆

What did I have in mind when I spoke of exterior evidence? Let me give an example.

Suppose that the match reports had talked about one of the moves that the player in question had made—a move that would, if your subjective rules are right, have been an illegal move—marking the goalposts with a significant and peculiarly shaped dent. You go out and look at the posts and you find that there's a dent just as described in the reports. Now, of course, lots of other things could have caused a dent of this sort, so the dent is by no means proof of the reports' truth, but it does to some extent inductively support the reports. The dent supports the reports to the extent that there aren't credible alternative explanations of it. Recall Bayes's Theorem. When we look for exterior evidence that would support let's say the Gospels' account of the resurrection we need therefore to look for facts that are more obviously facts than is the fact of the resurrection, and facts that gain their best explanation from there having been a resurrection such as the one the Gospels describe. One fact sometimes presented as meeting these criteria is the existence of the early Church, which in this context may be taken to mean a significant group of people who claimed that Jesus had been resurrected and were prepared to suffer and indeed die for maintaining this belief relatively quickly after the putative event. (Recall the potential epistemic value of testimony maintained under torture.) To investigate such arguments would take me into all sorts of areas other than the philosophy of religion. In this context, it is sufficient for me to point out that it's these sorts of facts that I had in mind when I spoke of exterior evidence that might potentially be available to support, or the absence of which might undermine, a given piece of testimony.

Let me turn then to Hume's a posteriori arguments.

HUME'S A POSTERIORI ARGUMENTS

Hume has four a posteriori arguments against the rationality of believing in miracles on the testimony of others. I'll deal with them in the order he presents them.

First, and to quote Hume, 'there is not to be found, in all history, any miracle attested to by a sufficient number of men, of such unquestioned good-sense, education, and learning, as to secure us against all delusion in themselves; of such undoubted integrity, as to place them beyond all suspicion of any design to deceive others'.

But of course there's not to be found in all history *any* event—even the most mundane—attested to by a sufficient number of people of such qualities as to *secure* us against—in the sense of render entirely impossible—falsehood. Hume's point then, if it's not to be the rather obvious one that we're reliant on testimony when it comes to judging ancient history and that testimony can in principle mislead, must be that the witnesses to miracles having occurred have *less* qualities of good sense, education, learning, and integrity, than the witnesses to other events and that this is a reason to be more suspicious of their testimonies than we are of the testimonies of these other witnesses. There are two questions one might raise over this. In no significant order, they are, first, whether the qualities that Hume picks out as relevant to the assessment of the reliability of witnesses really are ones that it is plausible to regard as such and, secondly, whether it is plausible to suppose that those who testify to the occurrence of miracles are under-endowed with the sorts of properties that make for reliable witnesses relative to those who testify to the occurrence of other, more mundane events. Let me take the first question first.

A friend of mine was recently telling me about his appearance in a magistrate's court. His car and somebody else's had been involved in a crash; he'd said it was her fault; she'd said it was his. There'd been no other witnesses and he'd won his case. I asked him what argument his lawyer had used to convince the magistrate that his word was to be believed over hers. 'Well,' he said, 'surprisingly, the consideration that weighed most heavily in the magistrate's mind was the fact that I was a GP whereas she was a hairdresser.'

One might think that if one was a magistrate one would oneself have judged that GPs were less likely to make mistakes over matters concerning the Highway Code etc. and perhaps less likely to deceive wilfully than hairdressers, but it's not obviously anything other than snobbishness that would make one think anything like this. What of Hume's list of qualities that credible witnesses would have to have; are they reasonable or are they a sign of a certain snobbishness on his part?

When considering what makes for a good witness Hume talks first of good sense, which seems unarguably a good thing to have: good sense must be the sort of sense that makes one reliable in one's judgements, otherwise it wouldn't be called '*good* sense', it would be called 'bad sense' or some such. So Hume's surely right here, but only trivially so. There's nothing of substance yet in Hume's characterization of good witnesses. We get to something substantial as he implies that a good witness would have to have education and learning. This is a substantial claim, but is it a credible one?

I'm a member of a university and in that context I've come across many people whose education and learning cannot be doubted, yet at the same time whose testimony as to some matter outside their field of specialism I would trust less than that of a hairdresser. I'm thinking of people like the stereotypical don who knows everything there is to know about some obscure academic subject, yet doesn't know what day of the week it is. Whether or not education and learning are relevant to the reliability of a witness depends a lot on what they're witnessing to and, in the case of miracles, I suggest, the sorts of things being witnessed to are not the sorts of things for which education and learning are terribly relevant. For example, it doesn't need much education and learning to spot that someone has died and increased education and learning doesn't dramatically improve one's ability to classify people correctly as either dead or alive. Admittedly, the right sort of education and learning—medical education and learning—might enable one to decide more accurately whether someone is dead or alive in borderline cases, but the majority of cases are not borderline cases and thus education and learning are largely irrelevant. So—although it pains me to admit it, as someone who's devoting his life to education and learning—I find unconvincing Hume's implicit claim that good education and learning are necessary for witnesses to be reasonably taken to be reliable when they testify to miracles.

What about integrity, to guard against the witnesses wilfully deceiving us? This, by contrast, seems unarguably right, but only in the same way that good sense was. Integrity in this context must be understood as placing a premium on conveying the truth in so far as one knows it (having truth-directed motives); as such—trivially—it is a property that reliable witnesses will have. So, Hume's list of qualities that add to the credibility of witnesses are either vacuous—good sense and integrity—or dubious—good education and learning. Hume's first a posteriori argument amounts to the claim that the witnesses to miracles tend to be less reliable than witnesses to more mundane happenings. To defend this claim he must point to some feature of the witnesses to miracles that gives us reason to believe this, and he's failed to do so.

On then to Hume's second argument.

◆ ◆ ◆

Hume argues that the emotion of wonder that arises from our contemplating miracles is an agreeable one and that it's so agreeable that it gives us a non-truth-directed tendency towards belief in reports of miracles. In other words, people want miracle stories to be true because their being true would make them feel better and the fact that they want them to be true tends to lead them to give miracle stories more credence than they deserve. I'm going to argue that there is—generally speaking—the emotion that Hume speaks of, but that it doesn't—generally speaking—have the detrimental epistemic effects he describes.

Consider this: there was a boy at my school who went on holiday to Thailand. In the middle of the night there he woke up to find a huge spider biting his forehead; he threw it off; local Thai people told him the spider was not a poisonous one; his wound soon healed over; and he returned to the UK. Apparently, all was well. Apparently. After a few days, the bite started to swell and, on the morning he was due to go to the doctor to have it looked at, he was standing in front of his bathroom mirror when he squeezed the swelling and it burst: dozens of baby spiders fell out.

That's a story I was told by a school chum many years ago; when I was told it, it was certainly presented to me as true—indeed the boy was named as someone who'd just left the school a couple of years above me. But I confess that I have no real idea whether it's true or not. Nevertheless, I got more pleasure from telling you the Thai spider story just now as if it was true than I would have got from telling it having prefixed it with 'Here's a story a friend of mine once made up,' or telling you instead a story I know to be true concerning how I arranged my car insurance last week. So—as an autobiographical claim, but one that I think will chime with most people reading this—I report that Hume is right: I do get a certain sort of pleasure from contemplating wondrous tales, something that gives me an incentive to contemplate and tell them regardless of their truth. This all leads me to agree with Hume that, generally speaking, we have a love of wondrous tales, something that might potentially lead to our being somewhat epistemically dilatory in checking their credentials. It'd be a disappointment to me were I to learn that the Thai spider story is false, so I can't help but hope that no one will tell me it's a biological impossibility, a hope that endangers me epistemically as it may very well edge over into being the hope that no one will tell me it's an impossibility even if it is. So far then, I'm with Hume. But while, generally speaking, we have this love of wondrous tales, it is by no means a universal psychological feature. Hume seems to have been someone who had the opposite, a hatred for them; the evidence for this is present on every page of section X of the *Enquiry*. Nor is this love overpowering in the majority of those of us who have it. Though we do get a peculiar sort of pleasure from contemplating a wondrous story and this pleasure is diminished to some extent if we know the story isn't actually true, our epistemic processes aren't generally corrupted to any significant extent by this. It's psychologically quite possible that even though one would gain a great deal of pleasure from believing a certain thing, one remain epistemically diligent in assessing the reasons for and against believing that thing and indeed—I contend—this psychological possibility is an actuality for the majority of people. I haven't ever investigated the biological plausibility of the Thai spider story because nothing of significance has ever depended on whether or not it is true. If anything of substance turned on whether or not the Thai spider story is true, I'd be quite capable of impartially investigating its credentials. Consider the fact that past the age of, say, 8 not many of us believe in Father Christmas, although it would undoubtedly give us a lot of pleasure to do so.

So, while I agree with Hume that most people do have the love of wonder he describes, I do not think that it is as corrosive of the possibility of an objective assessment as he suggests. Indeed, it seems to me that its effect is likely to be negligible.

◆ ◆ ◆

Let me turn to Hume's third a posteriori argument. Again, I'll quote him: 'It forms a strong presumption against all supernatural and miraculous relations, that they are observed chiefly to abound among ignorant and barbarous nations.' Hume goes on to talk of how tales of miracles grow thinner with every turn of the page of history, as we advance nearer and nearer to what he calls 'the enlightened ages'.

This third a posteriori argument of Hume's is tinged with a similar snobbery to that evident in his first, but we can see past that to what I think we'll have to admit is a reasonable point. We'll have to admit that our ancestors were indeed—relative to us—ignorant of the way the natural world works. Things that we now have no difficulty explaining naturalistically would have defied naturalistic explanation for them, their subjective laws of nature being less good approximations to the objective laws than ours. Although it's not a necessary truth, we would expect that as a civilization's subjective laws got closer and closer in their approximations to the objective laws, fewer and fewer events would contravene them and thus be available for interpretation as contravening the objective laws, for while it's contravening an objective law that's necessary for something being a miracle, it's contravening a subjective law that's necessary for it being noticed as potentially miraculous. So, without being in any way snobbish, it seems we may say that our ancestors are to be expected to have, understandably yet mistakenly, regarded as miracles things that we would not now regard as miracles (and perhaps now and again conversely, though I shall not dwell on this). Thus we would expect there to be more miracle tales in the history of the more ancient past than in the history of the nearer past; and, in the present, we would expect there to be more among those with less-developed natural science than ours. This, as I say, I think we have to admit is a reasonable point. However, this reasonable point goes only so far.

Some things that would have defied naturalistic explanation in the past and thus have been reasonably thought of as having been miracles, do not defy naturalistic explanation now and thus when we read the accounts of them that reach us from the past it is rational for us to reclassify them. We should give these events (if we think we are reasonable in believing they occurred at all) the naturalistic explanation we now have available to us. However, other things that reports from the past state occurred continue to defy naturalistic explanation and, further, plainly will always defy naturalistic explanation. Thus, we should continue to give these events (if we think we are reasonable in believing they occurred) a supernaturalistic explanation. We now know a lot more about psychosomatic illnesses (and how they can in principle be cured by psychotherapy) than we did several hundred years ago. So it is that some events we hear of from many centuries ago that the contemporary witnesses described as being instances of demons being exorcized by miraculous intervention, we should (if we think they occurred at all) think of as instances of rather compressed psychotherapy. We also know a lot more about death than people hundreds of years ago, and thus a lot more about how quickly irreversible damage to the brain can be caused by oxygen starvation: it's a matter of minutes after one's heart has stopped pumping that one's brain becomes irretrievably damaged. So it is that an event that a contemporary witness described as being an instance of a man being raised from the dead after three days (if we admit it occurred) is an event that we still cannot find a naturalistic explanation for. Further, given what we now know about the speed with which the brain is irretrievably damaged once the heart has stopped pumping, it is reasonable for us to suppose that we will never be able to explain such an event naturalistically. If we stay within physicalism, we must believe that it never occurred; if we believe it occurred, we must abandon physicalism. Thus it's going to be relatively easy for us to sift out stories of events that were reasonably taken to be miraculous at the time but which we can now see as capable of naturalistic explanation from events that were incapable of being explained naturalistically then; are incapable of naturalistic explanation now; will be incapable of naturalistic explanation in the future; and thus are, if they occurred at all, genuine miracles.

◆ ◆ ◆

Hume's fourth argument is that, to quote him once more, 'in matters of religion, whatever is different is contrary; and . . . Every miracle, therefore, pretended to have been wrought in any of these religions . . . as its direct scope is to establish the particular system to which it is attributed; so has it the same force, though more indirectly, to overthrow every other system.' The reports of miracles made by the adherents of different religions are claims of what Hume calls 'contrary facts'; they undermine the credibility of one another; they 'cancel one another out'. This fourth a posteriori argument of Hume's is often called 'Hume's Contrary Miracles Argument'.

The crucial suppressed premise in this argument is that the supernatural order—perhaps specifically a theistic supernatural order—cannot be such as to allow genuine miracles in the context of a variety of religions.

Presumably, Hume's argument for this premise would be that God would know that miracles would reasonably be taken as supportive of the doctrinal claims of the particular religions in the context of which they occurred and if one religion was more true than another, God would wish to confine his miraculous activity to the context of this religion so as not to mislead people unnecessarily. Angels and any other such supernatural beings would similarly be constrained in their operations, being allowed by God to perform miracles that were always supportive of his particular favourite religion. Further, the adherents of each religion are committed to believing that one religion—their own—is more true than the others, is God's favourite.

This is not a manifestly unreasonable train of thought. However, one could justifiably alight from it at a number of stations before it arrived at its destination. One might posit that God did not in fact see overwhelming reason to confine his miraculous interventions to the context of the most correct religion; allowing people to be misled in their religious views might be a price worth paying for the benefits that some miracles might bring. We've seen already that starting us in a position of some ignorance of his existence and will is a price that God might indeed think is worth paying to give us freedom to choose to do less than the best that we can for one another and to choose to do what we know we ought not to do to one another. Scattering miracles across a number of religions might be one way of achieving this, and presumably a way that produced many side-benefits. Alternatively (or in addition), one might posit that the miracles of some religions are performed by bad angels, intent on leading people away from the true religion, God not constraining them despite this being actually contrary to his will as he respects their free-will too. One might even suggest that the conception of one of the monotheistic religion's being more true in important ways than another and thus being God's favourite is misguided. In fact, the various monotheistic religions are all equally good paths to the one true God.

Any of these moves would allow one to escape from Hume's Contrary Miracles Argument and all are viable. But they all come with a price attached; it becomes impossible for one to argue (as Hume's contemporaries often did) that any *particular* religion may be shown to have particular favour among the right elements of the supernatural realm simply by the miracle reports that attend it in contrast to the dearth of miracle reports attending others. If, for example, one becomes a rather liberal-minded pluralist sort of Christian, not allowing the miracle claims associated with one religion to undermine those associated with one's own for, as one might put it, 'there are many paths up the same mountain', then it becomes impossible for one to argue that one's own religion can reasonably be believed to be the most direct path to God as a result simply of its being founded on the report of a resurrection. If one goes down this route, one buys the rationality of believing that Jesus was resurrected only by trading in the belief that believing he was resurrected is terribly important for salvation, *unless*, that is, one can defend the claim that the Gospel accounts of the resurrection are more numerous, consistent, and better supported by external evidence than the miracles stories associated with other religions.

Overall then, I conclude that Hume's many-pronged assault on the Argument from Apparent Miracles has secured him at least the potential for a limited victory. He has shown that, unless the miracles associated with one religion are attested to by better witnesses and/or have better exterior evidence in their favour than those associated with another, it is not reasonable to prefer one religion over another on the basis of the frequency of the miracles it purports occurred. Hume has *not* shown that it is always irrational to believe in miracles on the testimony of others. His A Priori Argument fails and his a posteriori concerns, though to a greater or lesser extent legitimate, could in principle—unsurprisingly, their being a posteriori considerations—be met. Whether or not they are met depends, of course, on facts beyond the scope of this book to investigate. As with the

Argument from Religious Experience then, I must leave my conclusion in a hypothetical form.

We can never hope that an Argument from the Reports of Apparent Miracles will be a deductively sound argument for the existence of God. Even allowing that the event in question occurred and that it was indeed a genuine miracle on Hume's revised definition, it could always be that there was a supernatural agent other than God responsible for it. However, an Argument from the Reports of Apparent Miracles could in principle be an inductively valid argument for God's existence; and, even if it did not reach this standard, it could in principle contribute something to an inductively sound cumulative case argument for the existence of God. Whether it does so in practice depends on the considerations that I've outlined above. If it does well enough in this sense, it might even be sufficient for one to move beyond having reason to believe physicalism false and thus some religious view true, to the point of favouring one religious view over another.

◆ ◆ ◆

We've now come to the end of our investigation of the arguments in favour of the existence of God. It may be appropriate then for me to sum up what I think I've established to date; in any case, I'll do so.

I started my investigation by arguing that the concept of God shared by the monotheistic religions is coherent. The claim 'There is a God' is the claim that there exists the best possible person, a person who is transcendent, immanent, omnipotent, omniscient, eternal, perfectly free, perfectly good, and necessary. He created the world; he is a source—indeed *the* source—of value for us; he has revealed himself to us in the world; and he has offered us everlasting life. I argued that while there are some apparent conceptual difficulties surrounding these divine attributes, they're not by any means insurmountable. In fact, upon investigation, they dissolve very readily and the claim that there is a God may be revealed to be a simple one; prima facie, it could be true; it could be false. If it were true, it would have certain implications for how we should live: we should respect the natural world as God's body; those of us who lead lives that are good enough for us to wish that they continue should seek out his will for how we might best show our gratitude to him for the gift of continuing life; we should expect a Last Judgement at which our failures to be perfect will be laid bare; yet we should expect that after this perfecting judgement we will share in everlasting life with him in Heaven. The consistency and content of the theistic concept of God is such as to make it maximally reasonable for us to hope that he exists. Having argued this, I went on to look at whether or not there is any evidence for believing that he does indeed exist, any evidence that this hope can be justified.

I started by discussing why it is that the simplicity of God argued for in the first five chapters is important in assessing the worth of any argument for his existence. We take simplicity of hypothesis as a guide to truth when deciding between competing hypotheses that equally well explain—in the sense of conform with—the evidence. I then went on to define what it is that I suggested we should consider ourselves to be looking for when looking for such evidence, good arguments. A good argument, I argued, is one the premises of which make its conclusion more probable than not and the premises and reasoning of which are more obviously correct than is the truth of its conclusion. Even if there might in principle be someone (other than God) for whom belief in God is properly basic (i.e. appropriately not based on any argument), I argued that nobody reading this is such a person; we need good arguments. With this understanding in mind, I went on to look first at the Ontological Argument.

It soon became apparent that the Ontological Argument failed to be a good argument on this understanding in two ways. As I formulated it, its first premise could not be known to be true on the interpretation that would be necessary for the argument to be valid without one's already knowing its conclusion, that there is a God, and the second premise could not be known to be true because it supposes that existence is a property, something that is false. Other 'versions' of the Ontological Argument, which trade on the notion of possible worlds, also fail to be good, relying on the ambiguity of the notion of possible worlds in this context. I thus suggested that if we are to find any evidence of God's existence, we must turn from merely contemplating the concept of God to looking at the universe which on theism he is supposed to have created. Has he left some evidence of his existence there?

The Argument to Design, which articulates one way of giving the affirmative answer to this question, did not, I concluded, in actuality give us any more reason to suppose that there's a God than did the Ontological Argument. I argued that there are a number of points at which one might object to the Argument to Design, but a reason why it fails even to support inductively the claim that there is a God is that, even if all the other objections could be overcome, it would actually make it more reasonable for one to believe in there being no God but an infinite number of infinitely variable universes, as this is a simpler hypothesis than the theistic hypothesis (that there's this or a lesser number of universes and a God) with no less power to explain the natural orderliness of the world. As I observed, this might still leave one wondering what would explain the existence of an infinite number of infinitely variable universes. However, in that the putative fact—the existence of an infinite number of infinitely variable universes—that one would be wondering about then would not be an instance of order, one would have moved outside the field of the Argument to Design and into that of the Cosmological Argument, the argument that sees the mere existence of any universe at all—or, if this is one's preferred starting point, the existence of an infinite number of infinitely variable universes—as evidence of God's existence.

I therefore went on to look at the Cosmological Argument. Again, I argued, one could object to the argument at a number of places (the most significant being that the Principle of Sufficient Reason on which it relies is not in fact accepted by significant numbers of scientists). Thus, I concluded, that the Cosmological Argument does not give us any more reason to suppose that there's a God than does the Ontological Argument and the Argument to Design. Even so, the grounding intuition of the Cosmological Argument, that there's something about the universe as a whole or any set of universes that needs an explanation and that there wouldn't be about a decision in the mind of God to create a universe, is an intuition that many, if not most, people have at some time had, something that no doubt explains the prima facie appeal of the Cosmological Argument. This raised the suspicion that perhaps the very having of this intuition, the truth of which is incompatible with physicalism, is itself evidence in favour of the falsity of physicalism and thus supportive of theism (and of course a whole host of other supernatural views).

This then turned our attention to the Argument from Religious Experience. Here we found that there was potential for progress, that this and other 'seemings' do have to be accepted as evidence in favour of the existence of God, although what I called irreligious and atheistic experiences have, by the same token, to be taken as evidence against the existence of God. We have to bear in mind not just our own experiences, if any, but the collective experiences of all persons. Obviously investigating these issues would require much introspection and consideration of a wealth of material outside the field of the philosophy of religion. Although I did not provide any of this material, I suggested that an investigation into it would reveal that there is a preponderance of testimony in favour of there being a realm that lies beyond and explains the physical world (and which would indeed lie beyond and explain an infinite number of infinitely variable physical worlds); this realm is not malevolent and nothing is more important for one's ultimate fulfilment than orientating oneself to it properly. However (and again I stated it rather than argued for it), the testimony of humanity is too various to conclude anything beyond this. If I'm right about this, religious experience reveals that we have good reason to believe physicalism to be false, but it doesn't reveal that we have good reason to prefer any one religious view over any other.

I then turned to look at the Argument from Reports of Apparent Miracles, as an attempt to close this gap. I focused on Hume's arguments and concluded that, despite their flaws, they had given him the potential for a limited success. Unless the testimonies to the miracles of one religion are of greater quantity or quality, or have greater exterior evidence in their favour than those of others, Hume's Contrary Miracles Argument shows that it is not rational to prefer one religion over another simply on the basis of the miracle reports it contains. However, it is worth observing that this is of course quite compatible with its being overall reasonable to prefer one over another on the basis of other features. Importantly, Hume fails to show that it is always unreasonable to believe in the occurrence of miracles on the testimony of others. Thus—again depending on the results of a consideration of a wealth of material outside the philosophy of religion—an Argument from Miracles may be a good argument for the existence of God or, failing that, contribute positively to a good cumulative-case argument for the existence of God. And it may be—if the testimonies to the miracles of one religion are of greater quantity or quality—that there's enough evidence out there to mean that we have good reason to prefer one religious view over the others.

So, the Ontological Argument; the Argument to Design; and the Cosmo-logical Argument do not provide us with any reasons at all for thinking that it is true that there's a God. The Argument from Religious Experience and the Argument from Reports of Apparent Miracles *might* provide us with reasons for thinking that it's true that there's a God. These reasons could not, even in principle, constitute a good argument for the existence of God in the sense of an 'airtight' proof that there's a God. They could, however, in principle—perhaps in isolation or perhaps only in combination—constitute good arguments or a good argument for the existence of God in the sense of making it more probable than not that there's a God. I have to leave my conclusion as to the worth of these arguments as a 'could in principle' conclusion, as whether or not these arguments do in practice provide these reasons depends on whether or not the right sorts of testimonies and experiences are forthcoming, something that is beyond the scope of this book to establish, although I've ventured some of my own—unsupported—claims about what this investigation would reveal.

This is by no means an exhaustive list of all the arguments people have put forward or a fortiori might put forward as purporting to lay out evidence for believing that 'There is a God' is true. But these arguments are those that strike me as most prima facie plausible and those that enjoy most widespread support. It also looks as if other arguments that people have or might put forward must share their essential features with them. They'll either start from determinate experience, from some feature of the world; or they'll start from indeterminate experience, from the mere fact that there is a world; or they'll start from pure categories, a priori, from the concept of God. I hope to have laid out the reasons that *mutatis mutandis* might be employed to show that arguments that start in either of these last two ways are not ways of collecting evidence of the existence of God. I also hope to have shown how certain variants of arguments that start in the first of these ways may in principle be good ways of collecting evidence for the existence of God.

Now it is time to look at the most important argument that purports to give us a reason to believe that there is no God, the Problem of Evil.

12

The Problem of Evil

In this chapter, I'm going to look at *the* argument against the existence of God, the Problem of Evil. Why am I calling the Problem of Evil 'the' argument against the existence of God? Have I already covered some? Did you miss me doing so? Have you inadvertently skipped a chapter or two?

Just as Kant divided arguments for the existence of God into three kinds: those that begin from determinate experience; those that begin from indeterminate experience; and those that begin from pure categories a priori, so one could divide all arguments against the existence of God into three kinds too: those that begin from determinate experience, which will be versions of the Problem of Evil, if evil is understood in a broad enough sense; those that begin from indeterminate experience, from the mere fact that there is a universe; and those that begin from pure categories a priori, i.e. those that seek to show that there is some incoherence in the concept of God.

I say that the Problem of Evil is *the* argument against the existence of God because I think I've already covered arguments from pure categories a priori, i.e. any argument that would seek to establish the incoherence of the concept of God, in my first five chapters, where I argued that 'There is a God' made sense. One might argue for the non-existence of God from indeterminate experience, i.e. from the mere fact that there is a universe, by relying on the principle that if there were a God, he would have good reason not to create any universe at all. However, given our analysis of what it would mean to be perfectly good, one may dismiss such arguments very quickly: it does not seem at all plausible to say that God (were he to exist) would have been under an obligation to create no universe whatsoever or that it would have been good for him to create no universe whatsoever. To whom could he have been under this obligation? For whom could it have been good? *Ex hypothesi*, there would have been nobody else around and he could hardly be said to be obliged to himself not to create or to harm himself by bringing others into existence.

The only sort of argument against the existence of God that's left is thus some version of an argument that starts from determinate experience, that starts from some feature of the world that there is prima facie reason to suppose the theistic God would not have wanted to create, a feature that is, in other words, what we might call 'evil' if we allow the word 'evil' a rather stretched sense, to include anything that is in any sense bad. It is important to stress the breadth of this use of the word 'evil', since evil in the everyday sense suggests malevolent intention, something that does not follow from the wider sense operative here, where as well as moral evils (bad things for which agents other than God are morally culpable, e.g. murders) there might be natural evils (bad things for which no agent other than perhaps God is morally culpable, e.g. deaths due to disease). Taking evil in this the broadest of senses then, the existence of evil in the world seems—at least prima facie—good evidence that there is no God, indeed it seems overwhelming evidence that there is no God.

1. **God is by definition omnipotent and perfectly good.**
2. **Evil is by definition that which is to some extent and in some respect bad.**
3. **God, being omnipotent and perfectly good, could never be compelled or have any reason to bring about or allow to be brought about something that was to any extent and in any respect bad, i.e. evil.**
4. **So, if there were a God, then there would be no evil.**
5. **There is evil.**
6. **So there is no God.**

Presented thus, the Problem of Evil is a deductively valid argument. The premises don't just make the conclusion—number 6—probable; they make it certain. So the theist—committed as he or she is to denying number 6—must deny one or more of the premises.

Numbers 1 and 2 are definitional claims; the first is—as we have seen—true of the theistic God: omnipotence and perfect goodness are constitutive of the theistic conception of God. The second reports the rather stretched sense of 'evil' operative in the argument. In an argument one may define one's terms however one wishes, so there's nothing to be argued with there. The theist can't deny 1 or 2.

Number 3 looks very plausible, at least initially. Evil things are precisely things that there is good reason not to bring about or allow to be brought about, they are in some respect and to some extent bad. We've seen already, in discussing God's perfect moral goodness, that God always does that which he has most reason to do. Surely then the definition of evil assures us that he'll never find himself with good reason to bring about anything evil and his omnipotence assures us that he'll never find himself having to allow any evils to occur.

Number 4 is a sub-conclusion: it follows from 1, 2, and 3. So the theist can't deny 4 unless he or she has more basically denied one or more of 1, 2, and 3.

Number 5 is pretty obviously correct. If you think you don't believe it, ask someone to assist you with your philosophy of religion by punching you as hard as they can in the most sensitive bits of your body: that'll soon change your mind. Remember that we're taking evil in a broad sense to include anything that is in any sense bad and, as such, suffering physical pain is certainly an evil.

Given numbers 1–5, the conclusion that there is no God, number 6, drops out deductively.

The premises and the deductive validity of this argument are more obviously correct than is its conclusion, that there is no God. In other words, it looks as if the Problem of Evil is a good argument for the non-existence of God. Is there any way for the theist to show that it's not good after all? I shall argue that there is. In fact, I shall argue that the existence of evil does not even support the claim that there is no God. My strategy will be to look at what God's perfect goodness requires of him in his creation and show that this is much less than the proponent of the Problem of Evil (as an argument supporting atheism) supposes.[1]

◆ ◆ ◆

The traditional theistic picture has God entirely unconstrained—perfectly free—in what world he creates. But, as we have seen, God's perfect freedom differs from our imperfect freedom in that it entails that he cannot do that which he ought not to do and, further, he must always do the best thing for his creatures (whenever there is a best) or one of the joint best (whenever two or more are equally good and none better). It has seemed to some to follow from this that if there were a God, he would have created the best world that is logically and metaphysically possible (if there is a best of all possible worlds) or one of the joint best (if there are two or more equally good and none better). And if we were to accept the principle that one cannot be morally justified in doing a particular thing if there is something better that one knows about and could equally well do, we'll have to conclude that if there were no best (or joint best) of all possible worlds, God—to preserve his perfect goodness—would have to do nothing, create no world at all.[2] If we accepted this argument, then we'd have to conclude that the theist is committed to this world's being the best or joint best of all possible worlds. But in fact we shouldn't accept this argument, though some theists (notably Leibniz) have accepted it. It doesn't work because God's perfect goodness entails only that he do the best (or joint best) *if there is one for his creatures.*

Prior to the creation of a universe, there were, *ex hypothesi,* no creatures around for whom the question of God's doing the best or joint best could even arise; there was no creature who could either benefit or suffer from the continuing absence of a universe or from its creation. In particular we, as not yet existing, were not in a better or worse state than we are now—a state the improvement or diminution of which God could effect by bringing us into existence. We were not in a better or worse state prior to the creation of the universe *not* because we were in the same state, but because we were not in *any* state—we did not yet exist. And although it might be good or bad for those who do not yet *but will* exist if one does or fails to do certain things for them (e.g. put some money aside or fail to put some money aside for their education), it cannot be good or bad for them to bring them into existence. God cannot then be said to have had a reason for creating a world stemming from his perfect goodness towards his creatures. His perfect goodness is a matter of his perfectly fulfilling the demands of love *towards his creatures* and, prior to his creating a universe, there were no creatures who could make any such demands of him.[3]

The most analogous earthly situation I can think of is that of the choice, which I imagine most couples face, of whether or not to have a child. If one were to specify carefully various conditions (that there are no health risks involved in the potential mother conceiving; that having a child would not be financially ruinous to the couple or in some other way reduce their ability to meet their obligations; etc.), then it seems reasonable to suppose that there is no obligation and nor would it be better either to produce or to refrain from producing a child: they ought to be morally indifferent. They cannot show love to their 'possible child' by their decision to conceive or not to conceive, to make that possible child actual. It is not supererogatory if they do or if they do not have a child.

Imagine now a drug becoming available. It costs nothing; has no side effects; and the consumption of it affects one's gametes such that the more of the drug one takes, the healthier, more intelligent, etc. any child conceived is. With the arrival of this drug, no couple comes under an obligation and nor does it become better for them—a supererogatory act—to refrain from having any child at all just because it is now true of any child that they do have that they could always have had 'one better' by taking more of this drug. So, by analogy, even if it were true that for any possible world, God could always create a better, it would not follow that his perfect goodness would compel him not to create any world. It might be helpful in driving this latter point home were I to introduce you to Leibniz's ass, a hypothetical donkey that is a close cousin of a more famous donkey, Buridan's ass.

Buridan's ass was a donkey that, finding itself equidistant from two equally nourishing bales of hay, reasoned correctly that it had no more reason to eat one rather than the other. It then went on to conclude that the only reasonable thing for it to do was eat neither; it thus starved to death. Leibniz's ass was a donkey which found itself equidistant from an infinite number of bales of hay, such that for each of these bales of hay there was one more nourishing. It thus reasoned correctly that of any particular bale of hay it might eat it had less reason to eat that bale than it did to eat another. It then went on to conclude that the only reasonable thing for it to do was to eat none; it thus starved to death.

So, if there is a best of all possible worlds, God is not under an obligation and neither is it supererogatorily good for him to create it, for prior to his creation there are no creatures to whom he can have obligations or be supererogatorily good. If there is no best of all possible worlds, God is not under an obligation and neither is it supererogatorily good for him to create nothing just because for any world he does create it is *ex hypothesi* true that he could have created one— indeed, an infinite number—better. So far, it's looking as if God's perfect goodness doesn't constrain him in what world he creates at all. May we conclude at least that God's perfect goodness would have compelled him to create any creature he did create in the best of all possible worlds for it (if there is a best) or in one of the joint best (if there are two or more that are equally good and none better)? An affirmative answer to this question is much more plausible, at least initially (in a moment, I'll argue against it).

If a donkey found itself equidistant from any number of bales of hay but one of those bales was the most nourishing bale possible (or two or more were joint 'most' nourishing), the donkey would be less than fully reasonable if knowing of this it then chose to eat any bale other than this one (or one of these ones). By contrast, some have held that even if there is a best or joint best of all possible worlds for a certain creature, God's perfect goodness necessitates only that if he chooses to create that creature, he must choose which world to create that creature in from among those worlds that are 'good enough', a world's being good enough if in it that creature leads a life that's not so bad that it would have been better for it if it had never existed. But this does not seem plausible to me because, for the reasons sketched previously, the notion of a creature's being potentially better off (or worse off) if it had never existed seems confused. It's as confused as speaking of the brother that I never had being taller, less tall, or the same height as the sisters that I do have. The brother that I never had is not on the height scale at say zero feet and zero inches; he is not on the height scale at all. Thus his height cannot be compared with the heights of the sisters that I do actually have and who—being actual—do indeed have particular heights on this scale. Of course I can say things like, 'Had I had a brother, the chances are that he would have been taller than either of my sisters', but, as it is, the brother that I never had is not taller than, less tall than, or the same height as my sisters for he doesn't exist at all. Similarly, the brother that I never had is not less well off than, better off than, or as well off as the sisters that I do have. So any creature that does exist is not better off, worse off, or enjoying the same level of wellbeing as if he, she, or it had never existed.

If there is a best of all possible worlds for a particular creature, while God would have been morally indifferent about whether or not to create that creature at all, it seems then as if we should say that if he does create that creature, he has reason to create it in that world rather than any other; and if there are joint best worlds for it, if he creates that creature, he has reason to create it in one of those rather than any other.

Of course, even if we were to say this, we still could not directly conclude that theism is committed to this world's being the best or joint best of all possible worlds for each of us. Perhaps for any creature (that actually exists), whatever world it might exist in, there's always a possible world that that creature could have found itself in instead and that would have been better for it than that world. As we've already seen from considering the case of parents who could take a drug to 'improve' what sort of child they conceived and Leibniz's ass, if this were the case, then God's perfect goodness would not dictate that he not create this creature. His perfect goodness only dictates that he do the best or joint best for his creature where one is possible. It might be then that there is no best or joint best of all possible worlds for us and thus God's perfect goodness left him with carte blanche not just over whether or not to create us at all but over what world to create us in having decided to create us. Matters would be rather as they would be with a more acute version of Leibniz's ass. Although sadly Leibniz's ass did not realize it, he had carte blanche over which bale of hay to eat. But if there is a best or are joint bests of all possible worlds for us, then while God would still be able, without deviating from perfect goodness, not to create us at all, it would prima facie seem that we should say that he did not have carte blanche over the issue of in which world to create us. Why? Because, as we have just seen, he has good reason to create each of us in the world that is the best (or a joint best) of all possible worlds for us if there is one (or more than one joint best). That theists view the world as God's creation might therefore seem to commit them to its being the best or joint best of all possible worlds for each of its creatures or there being no best or joint best of all possible worlds for those of its creatures for whom it's not. But in fact, I'm about to argue, it doesn't commit theists to even this. We can start to see this by asking ourselves this question:

Does the fact that God's perfect goodness entails that if there is one, he must create the best or joint best of all possible worlds for his creatures mean that he must create each and every creature that is actually created in what is for each of them considered in isolation the best or joint best of all possible worlds (if there is such a world), or does it entail that for possible worlds each of which contains a given set of creatures, if he creates that set of creatures he must create them in the best or joint best of all possible worlds for this set of creatures considered as a totality (if there is such a world)? I shall maintain that it is only the latter and that he could do the latter without doing the former. This being so, we may conclude that God's perfect moral goodness does not dictate that he create any creature he does create in the best (or one of the joint best) of all possible worlds for it even if there is a best world or are joint best worlds for it. His good reason to create a particular creature in what is for it the best or joint best of possible worlds could be outweighed or balanced by good reasons to do the same for other creatures.

Consider two possible universes, A and B, in each of which live two creatures, P and Q. In universe A, creature P has freedom to do that which isn't the best that he could do for Q and freedom even to do certain things that he oughtn't to do to Q. We've already seen that having this sort of freedom is in itself a good thing for P. To have this freedom over Q necessitates P having more power than Q in certain respects and Q not having certain powers. For example, if P is going to have the freedom to insult Q, Q can't have the power to stop himself being insulted merely by willing it. In universe B, their roles are reversed: Q has power over P to the same extent and in the same respects as P has it over Q in world A. If these are the only differences between the universes, we may say that A is then a better universe for creature P than B to a certain extent, *e*, but it is not so good for Q and world B is better for Q than A but less good for P by the same extent, *e*. Of course God could create P and Q in two different universes, but he cannot—of necessity—create them in two different universes yet give them this freedom to influence one another; their having the freedom to influence one another necessitates their being in the same universe. Let's now suppose for the sake of argument that A is the best of all possible universes for P and B is the best of all possible universes for Q. Given what we have said earlier, these facts give God a reason to create P in A rather than anywhere else and to create Q in B rather than anywhere else, but of course it is logically impossible that God act on both these reasons and these reasons are equally strong, their strength being determined by e. What would his perfect goodness dictate that he do then? Create neither? If it did dictate this, it would dictate that he ought never to create any universe in which one or more creature had freedom to affect one or more other creature for good or ill. But that seems wrong. Imagine this:

You are a donkey-herder. Your herd is small. You have only two donkeys, P and Q. One day you find yourself with your two donkeys equidistant from two bales of hay. Bale A would be slightly better (to a certain extent, e) for donkey P than bale B and slightly less good (to the same extent, e) for donkey Q than B; bale B would be slightly better (by e) for Q than bale A and slightly less good (by e) for P than A. You cannot herd P to bale A and Q to bale B; you have to choose between the two bales. Should you have never let yourself get into such a situation in the first place? It doesn't seem at all obvious that you were under an obligation not to allow yourself to get into such a situation. Indeed it seems obvious that you weren't. There's a weakness in the analogy, in that if you don't take your donkeys to some bale, they'll both starve. So let's remove that dis-analogy by supposing you're a potential donkey-herder; you're about to choose whether or not to (non-ultimately of course) create a set of donkeys. You find yourself knowing that for any set of donkeys that contains more than one member that you create, you will one day face such a choice. Should you therefore create one or no donkeys, thus ensuring you never get into a situation such as that described, where you have to do something less good than you could do for one of your donkeys? It's not obvious that you shouldn't, especially if creating two or more donkeys would give each donkey a good—e.g. the pos-sibility of donkey friendship—that it would not have been able to have had it been created on its own.

We've already seen that for finite creatures (though not for God) the freedom to be less than perfect in two ways (doing less than the best we could and less than we ought for someone) is a power; it's something that it's good for us to have. Of course, as we've also seen, it's not the only thing that is or would be good for us to have, the ability to avoid being insulted by others simply by willing it would be an ability it would be good to have. So, God's perfect goodness would not dictate that he not create either world A or world B, even though each of these worlds has as a feature that it is not the best of all possible worlds for all of the creatures in it and there are *ex hypothesi* best of all possible worlds for each of its creatures. If the good of freedom to be less than perfect to one another required creating creatures in a world with some evils, then God's perfect goodness might allow him to create a world in which there were the evils necessary for it. (It could not compel him to do so as he'll always remain perfectly free to create no world whatsoever, but remain instead the sole existent thing.)

Not all evils are brought about by agents acting freely in blameworthy ways. As well as cold-blooded murders, there are deaths due to disease or accident. How are these, what we might call 'natural evils' in contrast to 'moral evils' to be explained on theism?

◆ ◆ ◆

My argument is that natural evils are a necessary result of there being free creatures living in a world governed by natural laws and that natural laws are necessary for there to be a world with agents who enjoy the freedom to be less than perfect to one another. Natural evils are the inescapable accompanying features of natural laws, natural laws being the necessary means to the good of this sort of freedom.

Suppose, for example, that P wishes to exercise his freedom to choose to do what he knows is less than the best he could do for Q. In fact he knows it's something that he shouldn't do to Q. It's causing Q to suffer ten minutes of excruciating agony just because he doesn't like the cut of Q's jib. Either P will get his wish—in which case Q will find that natural facts less than perfectly serve his interests; Q will find himself without enough power to stop P—or Q will be able to block P's malevolent intention—in which case P will have his interests less than perfectly served by natural facts; P will find he doesn't have enough power to harm Q as he'd like. If one agent is to have the freedom to choose to do evil to another, then that agent must have more power than the other in the relevant domain. And the fact that one agent has more power than another must be the result of facts that are not themselves within the power of those agents to determine, i.e. they must be natural facts. One can say then that natural evils are a foreseen but unintended necessary consequence of creating free creatures in a world with natural laws, natural laws being necessary for there to be free creatures able to choose to affect one another for good or ill. Natural laws provide the arena within which significantly free agents may interact, and a necessary feature of that arena is natural evil.[4]

So, our freedom to be less than perfect requires natural evils as well as moral evils. This in itself might not be of comfort to the theist. That there are those who suffer in any system of interrelating free creatures God might create doesn't mean that he's morally justified in creating a system of interrelating free creatures who suffer to the extent that some creatures in this world suffer. Perhaps, while his creatures having the freedom to affect one another in this way is itself a good, it's not a good that's good enough to justify the sorts of evils that we actually have in this world, the level of suffering that some of its inhabitants undergo. And perhaps—even if it is good enough to justify this—God doesn't have the right to create a system where some suffer to this extent.

Let's turn to address ourselves to these worries. To do so it will be helpful to introduce the notion of a good 'compensating' for an evil.

The notion of a good compensating for an evil is a rather tricky one and not just for the epistemic reason that it may not always be obvious whether a good really does compensate for an evil. It's also tricky because the compensating good may not be the same sort of good as the evil is evil and thus may not be said to outweigh it in any even-in-principle-quantifiable way. This will be easier to understand if I give another example.

Suppose you have a choice to make. You can become a sculptor or you can become a painter. Suppose also that you know (don't ask me how you know this) that if you choose to become a sculptor, you will become a truly great sculptor—on a par with Phidias or Henry Moore—but you'll suffer from the occasional bruised finger as your hammer goes awry during your chiselling. You also know that if you choose to become a painter, you will become a truly mediocre painter, with slightly less bruised fingers than you'd have had if you'd become a sculptor. You also know that apart from these differences each life will be the same for you.

If this was the choice that faced you, I think we would all agree that the physical pain of a few bruised fingers would be outweighed by the greater good of your being a truly great sculptor and not just outweighed for others: it would be outweighed for you too. Your being a great sculptor, even though it would mean being someone who suffered the physical pain of an above-average number of bruised fingers, would be a better life for you to lead than your being an average painter with a lesser number of bruised fingers. So the good of being a truly great sculptor is a greater good than the evil of a few extra bruised fingers is bad, but being a great sculptor isn't a physical pleasure which can be straightforwardly weighed against the physical pain of the bruised fingers. So, although there is a sense in which being a truly great sculptor compensates for the physical pain of some extra bruised fingers, this is a sort of compensation that can't be represented as an outweighing on some common scale.

Now one could in principle become a great sculptor without bruising any fingers and even if that never happens in practice, it's not the bruising of the fingers that makes one a great sculptor anyway—it's having a set of skills that one develops while, as a matter of fact, bruising a few of one's fingers along the way. The bruising of one's fingers is a contingently accompanying feature of a contingent means to the end of becoming a great sculptor. Let me suppose for a moment though that actually having had a few more than average bruised fingers is physically *necessary* for being a great sculptor for some reason—perhaps you just can't hold your tools properly unless your body has in some sense instinctively learnt how by doing actions that must bruise its fingers more than most. If some reason like that did obtain, then having bruised fingers would be a physically necessary accompanying feature of what was as a physically necessary matter of fact the only means to the end of becoming a great sculptor. In that case then we'd say that the good end of being a great sculptor would justify the bad features accompanying the means; it would compensate for them. Of course, even then, the accompanying evil to the only means of becoming a great sculptor wouldn't be a *logically* or *metaphysically* necessary accompanying feature to the only logically or metaphysically possible means to that end—God could have miraculously given you this instinctive ability to hold your tools without your having learnt it in the 'School of Hard Knocks' as it were. Nevertheless, the example serves to illustrate the point that a certain good can compensate for a certain evil when that evil is either a means to it or an accompanying feature of that means and that this compensation need not be a matter of giving one a greater amount of the same sort of thing that the evil has deprived one of.

Consider now this story: Once upon a time, a little fawn—let's call him 'Bambi'—got caught in a thicket in a forest. Bambi struggled for a while, but in the end realized that he could not get out of the thicket on his own. Not to worry. He waited for his friend, the rabbit Thumper, to bounce playfully along (as was his habit) and help him out. Unfortunately, that day Thumper was bouncing happily in another part of the forest and a forest fire had broken out near to Bambi. Bambi yelped as loudly as he could, trying to summon Thumper's help; but sadly Thumper was far away and the fire was getting closer. There was nothing the panicking Bambi could do; he struggled wildly to escape, but to no avail; the fire reached him and slowly started to burn him alive. Eventually, Bambi died in excruciating pain; nobody ever discovered his body. All the other animals in the forest lived such carefree lives that they didn't even think about where Bambi might have got to; even Thumper simply bounced playfully about as he always had done. The End.

The fire certainly wasn't the means to an overall good end for Bambi and if nobody ever discovers what's happened to Bambi and nobody even thinks about his absence, then it can't produce any effect on anybody else; *ipso facto*, it can't be a means to any good effect for anybody. So the forest fire burning Bambi to death isn't a means to any good end that compensates for it. But this does not mean that it itself cannot be compensated for.

Just because Bambi suffered an evil that was uncompensated for in this world does not mean that he suffered an evil that was uncompensated for full-stop. As we've seen, on theism, there is another world, after this one, in which these loose ends are tidied up. There's something rather pleasingly airtight about this move. Unless there is some conceptual absurdity in maintaining that God could arrange for Bambi to enter a heaven after this life, on theism there's every reason to think it's true that he does arrange for him to do so; and surely then we cannot have any reason to believe that in this heavenly realm there couldn't be compensating goods. Heaven is, after all, of infinite duration. Whatever someone suffers in a finite pre-mortem life, it has to be possible that they be compensated for it eventually in an infinitely extended post-mortem life. I conclude then that any evil a creature suffers in this world could be compensated for by God in the next. Of course, to establish that any evil that befalls a creature in a finite life could be compensated for by God in an infinite afterlife is not to show that all the evils in the world are necessary as means to those compensating goods. In our example, God could have arranged for Bambi to get into Heaven—and so have the goods that, as it is, constitute the compensation—after a quick, painless death, these heavenly goods thus not being needed to compensate him for anything, they being bonuses. Wouldn't that have been better for him? It pretty obviously would have been. If the theist were committed to there being no evil in the world that is not necessary as a means to a good end that compensates for it, theism would thus be untenable. However, the theist is—as we have seen—not committed to this. He or she is committed to there being no evil in the world that is not necessary as a means to a good end that compensates for it or as an accompanying feature of such a means. Bambi's death was not a means to any good end, for Bambi or anyone else, but it was a consequence of the laws of nature operative in the universe in which he lived, the laws of nature being necessary as means to the good of the freedom of the creatures in that universe to be less than perfect to one another. To have this sort of freedom requires, as we have seen, natural laws—i.e. laws that operate independently of any creature's will—and these laws must thus give rise to natural evils, suffering for which no agent (other perhaps than God himself) is responsible. The only question that can remain, then, is whether God has the right to create a universe where creatures like Bambi suffer to the extent that Bambi does as a result of natural laws, the operation of which is for the greater good of creatures as a whole. Would God's moral perfection compel him not to create a world where creatures suffer in this way as a result of the system? We are not talking of whether he has the right to create a universe in which he himself uses some creatures merely as a means to the end of the freedom of others (for Bambi isn't used as a means to anybody's end) but of whether he has the right to create one where he allows nature to 'take its course' and thus generate the suffering of Bambi, suffering that is a foreseen but unintended consequence of the laws of nature that he creates as necessary as the means to the end of the freedom of some of his creatures.[5]

◆ ◆ ◆

Consider this situation: you are a teacher in charge of a group of schoolchildren at playtime. We've established that it is good for these children to have freedom to do less than the best that they can for one another and indeed to do what they should not do to one another. That being so, you have reason to stand in a corner of the playground and let them invent and play their own games with one another, rather than ceaselessly stop them from interfering with one another and organize them 'for their own good'. Let's suppose you allow that reason to guide you. You stand to one side. Now and again, you notice that some of the children are choosing to use the autonomy you've generated to invent games that involve some of them suffering to some, limited, extent. There are, one might say, 'victims' of your laissez-faire system. Let's take an example: one of the children is chosen by mob rule to be piggy in the middle for some game. This is a role that is considerably less fun than the other roles, indeed it involves positive suffering: the child thus chosen suffers to some extent as a result of your system. Perhaps the child's character is developed in helpful ways by this experience; but, then again, perhaps it is not. Let's suppose that it is not and that neither is there any other greater good for the child or the children in general that comes from his or her suffering in this way on this occasion. You watch this happen. You maintain your distance. You do not intervene. Such eventualities are—after all—a foreseen but unintended consequence of the laissez-faire system that you've adopted. This child's suffering is not itself a means to a greater good that compensates for it. You've not used this child as a means to anything, but you have allowed the child to suffer when you could have stopped it.

Did you have the right to allow this to happen? Well, I suggest that the answer to this question depends on a number of things. One of these is how much suffering the child has actually undergone. If the game you allowed the children autonomy to develop had been a William-Golding-esque one involving the piggy in the middle being killed, then obviously you should have intervened; you'd have done something wrong in allowing the children in your charge to have *that much* freedom and power over one another. If, on the other hand, the suffering was of a relatively minor sort—a sort that would all be forgotten about within five minutes or so of the start of the next lesson—then, it strikes me, the answer is that you wouldn't have done anything wrong in taking this laissez-faire attitude, in allowing this child to suffer to the extent that he or she did. The child could have had a better playtime, but he or she has no cause to complain to you as a result of this.

So, our question must be, 'What determines how much evil you have the right to allow creatures in your system to suffer?'

I suggest that there are three relevant factors.

First, it depends on how good the overall effect of your system is. If it's really very good indeed that these children have the amount of freedom your system provides, then that will make it more morally justifiable for you to have allowed those who suffered in your system to suffer when you could have intervened. If, on the other hand, it's not that important whether or not those in your system have the level of freedom it provides, then that will make it less morally justifiable for you to have remained distant when one of them suffered as a result of your having given others the level of freedom you had given them. You could have intervened; stopped the suffering; and not thereby deprived anybody else of anything that valuable. So that's one factor.

Secondly, it depends on your capacity and intention to provide compensation for those who suffer in your system. If you know that after playtime is over you will compensate those who've suffered, that will make it more morally justifiable for you to allow them to suffer to the extent that you have. Conversely, if you know that you will not compensate sufferers for the suffering they've undergone, that will make you less morally justified in allowing them to suffer to this extent.

Thirdly, it depends on whether or not the people in question have refused to participate in your system. If, knowing of the sort of laissez-faire attitude you were going to adopt, the children had all agreed to be participants in the system, that would make you more morally justifiable in subjecting them to it. Conversely, if, hearing of the sort of system you were going to adopt, a child had asked you if he or she could stay inside this playtime, that would make you less morally justified in throwing that child out into the playground anyway.

◆ ◆ ◆

Let me leave those three factors on the table for a moment or two and turn to consider things from the child's perspective.

Imagine now, then, that, rather than being the teacher, you're a child. On arriving at school one day, you're greeted by the headmaster. 'Today,' the headmaster tells you, 'is a special day. You have a choice of which playground to play in. There are a number of playgrounds. In each playground the supervising teacher will adopt a certain level of this laissez-faire approach. In playground one it's zero. Each child is completely controlled in their every movement by teaching assistants, who guide the children's limbs inside the cotton-wool suits that every child wears. No child ever has freedom to be less than perfect in his or her relations with others, but then again, of course, there's nobody who suffers to any extent as a result of the choices of others. Playground one guarantees those children who reside in it that they won't suffer as a result of the system in the sense relevant here to any extent whatsoever. In playground two, there's a little bit of freedom. Every ten minutes, each child is taken out of their cotton-wool suits and allowed ten seconds in which they can act as they wish; thus, occasionally, one of these children uses their autonomy to punch another. Playground three has a bit more autonomy and thus offers a bit more danger of suffering than does playground two. And so on.'

'There's another feature of the meta-system we're running today', says the headmaster. 'Each person who suffers will be compensated for any suffering after playtime is over. So, those who've been in playground one won't need any compensation. Some of those who've been in playground two by contrast will have suffered as a result of the system there and thus they will need some compensation, but on average not as much as those who've suffered in playground three and so on. I want to stress, though, that no child—whichever playground they've been in—will leave school at the end of the day having suffered in a way that he or she will think has not been adequately compensated for.'

You thank the headmaster for apprising you of his meta-system and consider which playground you'll sign yourself down for.

Is the only playground it would be rational for you to choose to play in playground one?

I think the answer to that is 'no'. I'll justify that negative answer later. Before I do so, I want to speak to what I imagine are a large number of you who are growing rather impatient with my analogy for another reason.

◆ ◆ ◆

There's a crucial difference between my headmaster analogy and our case. God didn't ask any of us whether we'd mind being put into the universe he'd created. The headmaster—as it were—didn't ask us to choose a playground at the start of our school day; he just threw us into one, this one.

Someone might object, then, that even accepting that the first condition is met (that overall the level of freedom we enjoy really is worth the level of suffering necessary for it) and that the second condition is met (God can and does provide all of us with sufficient compensation for our sufferings in an afterlife), the third condition isn't met, God didn't ask us beforehand if we would be willing participants in the system he was about to create. That's a crucial disanalogy between God and the headmaster case. And this shows that God didn't have the right to put us into this world. It is indeed true that there's this disanalogy, but there's another crucial disanalogy. God couldn't—of necessity—have asked us in advance of our existence whether or not we'd be willing to suffer the evil that our existing in this world would entail for the simple reason that we didn't exist in advance of our existence. Does this let him off the hook, morally speaking, with regard to the third condition?

Can we find an analogy to guide our moral intuitions here? I think we can. The analogy is again the choice of whether or not to have children.

Ours is a world where there is a significant risk that any children we bring into existence will suffer. We can't guarantee that the system is overall worthwhile; or that they're going to get enough compensation if they suffer as a result of it; and we can't ask our children before they're born whether or not they're willing to be born into the world on these terms. Nevertheless, we do not regard ourselves as generally under an obligation *not* to have children. We certainly don't regard ourselves as under an obligation not to have children simply because we can't ask them in advance of having them whether or not they're willing to be born. So, I conclude that God not—of necessity—being able to act as the headmaster does, and ask us in advance of our existence whether or not we're prepared to take the risks that existence will bring, *does* let him off the hook morally speaking with regard to the third condition.

God's let off the hook with regard to the third condition and he can easily satisfy the second; as we've already observed, any finite amount of suffering a creature undergoes in this world must be capable of compensation ultimately in an infinitely extended afterlife, something that we saw in the first half of the book God must—if he exists—extend to all creatures to whom it would be good to extend it. The only question that remains, then, is whether the level of freedom to be less than perfect that we enjoy is overall worth the suffering it entails. How to answer this question?

Unfortunately, the answer that one gives to this question will depend entirely upon the probability one has previously assigned to theism. If one is asked by one's host at a dinner party whether one would like to try a dish that is certainly different from anything else one might have later and that some people enjoy even though others violently dislike, one's answer might reasonably depend on whether this dish is being offered to one as an option for the hors d'œuvre or for the main course. If one is told that it is an option for the starter and one is assured that the taste (if it is found to be unpleasant) may be washed away very quickly by the drink accompanying the main course, one would no doubt try it. If, on the other hand, one is told that the dish is an option for the main course (and there will be no desert), one would be more reasonable in refusing. It is not that one would be more risk-averse, just that the risk would be greater in relative terms, for what it was relative to would be smaller. Similarly then, if one sees the suffering of this world as a prelude to an infinite afterlife of perfect fulfilment in God's presence, the chance to enjoy a freedom that we will not be able to enjoy when directly exposed to God in Heaven will be judged worth the suffering that accompanies it. However, if one sees this world as all that there is, one's judgement will differ. It seems then that the mere existence of evil cannot be taken as in itself evidence against the existence of the theistic God for it would only be so on the hypothesis that there is no compensating afterlife, a hypothesis that is false on theism precisely because of God's omnipotence and perfect goodness.

◆ ◆ ◆

Let me tell you a bit about some ground-breaking technology that's been installed in the spine of the book you're holding.[6] (If you're not actually holding it, pick it up.)

This book is linked up—via the internet—to a computer that is running a programme called 'The Best Life You Could Lead'. If you squeeze the book as hard as you can between both hands, then it will painlessly implant into your hands electrodes that will then send signals to your brain meaning that the ideas you have can be shaped by the programme on the computer. You will be immediately plunged into a virtual reality world. You won't realize this, because your virtual-reality world will start off by being very much like the real world. It will seem to you that you decided *not* to squeeze the book (or perhaps that you did squeeze it but nothing happened) and that you're still sitting in the room reading it, etc. But after a few moments *in the virtual-reality world* (not in the real world), a good friend will rush in through the door to tell you that you've won the lottery. In the real world of course, no such thing will be happening— you'll just be sitting with the book in your hands, a rather fixed expression on your face, oblivious to your surroundings, a source of curiosity for anybody who might wander in.

Back in the virtual-reality world, it won't seem strange to you that you've won the lottery. You won't be able to choose to reflect on whether or not this is all 'too good to be true', because the computer will have implanted a false memory of your having bought a ticket (if such is needed) and it will suppress—or rather redirect—your reasoning. Your freedom to do less than is maximally conducive to your own happiness will be eliminated—painlessly, immediately, and totally—from that moment on because the computer can guide you through the virtual world more effectively, in the sense of more optimally for your happiness, than you'd be able to guide yourself. So it is that in the virtual world it will seem to you that you've chosen to leap up; hand out glasses of champagne to your friends and family (who've all appeared); and—over the next few weeks—use your winnings to make investments that by the end of the month have given you enough political power to unite all governments and bring world peace. You'll believe yourself to have found cures for all diseases and released a number one cover version of *Sitting on Top of the World*. Of course, all this will only be happening in the virtual world. In the real world, what will have happened is that I'll have hooked-up your body to an intravenous drip at one end (feeding you nutritious fluid) and a catheter at the other (removing waste products). For the rest of your life, as in the virtual world you go from strength to strength, in the real world you'll just be getting more and more dusty, and those who use the room will have to change the nutrition and waste bags that lie beside your body every week or so.

As you decide whether or not to squeeze the book, there's no need to worry that your friends and family might not be happy seeing you hooked up in this way to the virtual-reality machine: I've got books for them too. If you decide to squeeze it, I'll get them to squeeze books of their own so that they'll be in their own virtual-reality worlds, worlds where they'll think that they themselves are world leaders; pop stars; or whatever.

Assuming you believe all this, is it irrational for you not to squeeze the book? If you asked me, I would answer this question negatively; I would say that it's pretty obviously not irrational for me to think that freedom is worth it.[7] I may hazard that all of you reading this will agree with me in giving the question this negative answer. But we can easily imagine people differing from us in this regard; indeed, we can imagine that if our own lives were going much worse than they are, we would give the question a different answer.

Consider for example being on the torturer's table, about to be subjected to torture for twenty-three and a half hours a day for the rest of your life, with merely a half-hour slot each day in which you might freely pursue your own objectives. If you were then offered the choice of squeezing the book and thus avoiding the twenty-three-and-a-half-hours-a-day torture by renouncing any further freedom, it would seem to me pretty obviously irrational not to squeeze the book, to think that a half-hour-a-day's worth of freedom isn't worth the suffering that it would involve. Now imagine reducing the proportion of the days ahead that you will spend on the torturer's table until we reach the cut-off point where it becomes a matter of indifference to you whether or not you squeeze the book. It is perhaps strange to posit that there is a cut-off point— rather than that the matter becomes indeterminate—but let's try not to worry about that. Once we've settled on an approximate amount that would more or less balance the corollary freedom, imagine being told that suffering a slight but non-negligible amount of torture more than this (five minutes per day say?) was actually the only way to secure freedom for the rest of humanity. That fact would, I suggest, decisively tip the balance of reasons in favour of your not squeezing the book. The good of humanity as a whole would compensate for this extra suffering befalling you as an individual. Of course, it wouldn't compensate you personally for it; it would compensate the aggregate of people that is 'the system as a whole' for your suffering. This being so, it might well be that the sacrifice was not one it would be reasonable for you to accept (unless you were assured that you personally would be compensated for having made it in an afterlife). But whether or not it's prudent or would be overall reasonable for you to choose to make this sacrifice in the knowledge that you would actually happen to have in the situation we're trying to imagine, it remains the case that your making this sacrifice would, overall, be better than your not doing so. Overall, a system where you were forced to undergo this sacrifice would be worth it, and so I suggest that if the sufferers in a system are indeed going to be compensated for their suffering and if, were they to have been fully informed beforehand, they would have reasonably chosen to participate in it (for they would have seen that overall the system that entails their suffering is worth it) but one is not able to ask them beforehand as they have yet to be created, one is morally justified in creating such a system.

If all this is right, God's perfect goodness then allows him to create universes with all sorts of evil in them. If there are creatures for whom there is a best or joint best of all logically possible worlds, he might yet create such creatures in worlds that aren't the best or one of the joint best of all possible worlds for them. He might allow creatures to suffer in ways that produce no good for them whatsoever and produce no greater good for anyone else either. The only thing his perfect goodness prevents God from doing is creating a world of creatures who suffer to an infinite extent at a given time or a world of creatures such as Tantalus and Sisyphus, who are destined to suffer to some finite extent for ever. An infinite amount of suffering can never be compensated for (even by God) either as regards the individual creature who has suffered from it or as regards the system as a whole. But it is obvious that ours is not a world in which creatures can suffer to an infinite extent at a given time or one in which there are immortal creatures destined to suffer for ever (well, it's perhaps not obvious that it's not the latter, but we've certainly no reason to believe it is—how many immortal sufferers have you ever come across (again, note that a denial of the traditional doctrine of Hell seems necessary for this point to go through)?). On theism, as we have seen, after our finite lives here an infinite life awaits us hereafter. For every creature who suffers, there will come a day when they say that as individuals their suffering has been more than adequately compensated for and on which they will be able to see how their suffering fitted into a greater whole that was overall worth it. On that day, even those who were broken on the wheels of the machine as they turned will thank God for it.

◆ ◆ ◆

As I recall, Herodotus tells a story of the Barbarian despot, Xerxes, talking with a general in his court about his plans to invade Greece. Xerxes asks the general how many men he thinks the Greeks would need to muster before they would dare to oppose him in battle. The general asks Xerxes whether he wants an answer that will please him or the truth. Xerxes asks for the truth. The general tells him that if the Greeks have ten thousand men, then ten thousand will fight him; if they have only a thousand, then a thousand will take to the field; if they have only a hundred, then still those hundred will stand before him. Xerxes cannot believe this, for he plans to invade with the largest army the world has yet seen. If these Greeks were under the iron control of a tyrant, such as himself, he reasons, then perhaps they might go forward, even against impossible odds, from their fear of that tyrant and his lash. But these Greeks, he has heard, are free men and freedom is the end of discipline. The general replies that the Greeks are indeed free, but this is only because they have a master whom they respect more than they could fear any tyrant. This master is their duty. This they listen to and this they obey. And what it commands is ever the same: not to retreat in the face of barbarism, however great the odds; rather, to advance against it; to stay firm in their ranks; and to conquer or die.

A world without evil would be a world where we could turn every sword into a ploughshare; it would be a world where we never needed to fight because it would be a world where there was never anything worth fighting. A world with terrible barbarians is a world where there are people worth fighting; it is a world where we need swords as well as ploughshares; and it is a world where it's open to us to choose either to go forward into battle against the barbarians like free Greeks or meekly acquiesce to them as would the craven slaves of a barbarian despot. We are free to choose to be heroes or villains, to sacrifice ourselves or to save our own skins, to do our duty or to shirk it.[8]

Would a life without any evils at all be better than a life filled with such choices? It would certainly be easier—but then a life in the virtual world I've just described is easier than a life in the real world and I don't think you think it'd be better for you to go into that virtual world. Playground one is not the only reasonable choice. Would a life with *more* terrible evils than there are in our world and thus more such choices be better than a life with less evils, but of course less of this sort of freedom as a result? Is playground number infinity the only reasonable choice? As one goes up in playground numbers one gets more and more of this sort of freedom, but of course one gets more and more evil as a result. However, if this evil is compensated for across the system by the good of the corollary freedom and each sufferer will individually ultimately be compensated for his or her suffering in an afterlife, then—as this freedom is a good—it would seem that one should say 'Yes', playground infinity is the only rational choice. However, in fact here my analogy breaks down again—there is no playground infinity that God might have created. Of necessity, any creatures God could have created would have been creatures with a finite amount of freedom (in virtue of his necessary omnipotence, no creature can be as free as him). So it is that if theism is right, God was faced with a choice to create nothing; to create a world with no such freedom but no evil (Heaven straight away); or to create a world with a finite amount of this freedom and thus evil, a world in which he compensates everyone for their suffering in an afterlife (a world like ours, with Heaven afterwards). That our experience gives us reason to believe that if he exists, he has chosen the latter does not—I suggest—give us any reason to believe that he doesn't exist.

I conclude then that the argument from the existence of evil to the non-existence of God cannot be rendered as a good deductive argument; nor can it be rendered as a good inductive argument; nor again does evil inductively support the claim that there is no God. The occurrence of evil in the world provides us with no reason whatsoever to think that there's not a God.

◆ ◆ ◆

It is sometimes objected that to offer a 'solution' to the Problem of Evil in the manner that I have done in this chapter is to blunt our awareness of the evil or at least to blunt our motivation for combating it, either of which would provide a moral reason to object to the very process of undertaking a theodicy such as that sketched in this chapter.[9] This charge may be sustainable against some theodicies, but it is not sustainable against the one I have outlined. As we have seen, all that theism commits one to saying is that overall the system as a whole is worth it. Reconciling the existence of evil in the world with the existence of the theistic God in the manner sketched need not therefore diminish our awareness of particular instances of evil or remove our motivation for seeking to combat them. The theodicy sketched is compatible with accepting that in the actual world there are lots of evils that are completely gratuitous, that don't lead to any good end at all; there are lots of evils which are partially gratuitous in that even though they lead to a good end which could not, even in principle, have been achieved without them, lead to a good end which isn't good enough to compensate for the evils that produce it; and there are lots of evils that are dispensable, which is to say that even though they do lead to some good end which compensates for them, the good end in question could in principle have been achieved without them. We might very well be under an obligation or it might be a supererogatory good for us to remove some or all of these evils. In short, to justify God in the face of evil is not to justify evil in the face of God and, if we are conceptually clear-headed, neither will justifying God in the face of evil erode our motivation for fulfilling our obligations and performing supererogatory good acts to combat evil. If theism is right, there will come a time when every sword may safely be turned into a ploughshare, but if theism is right, that time is not yet. For now, we are called to act as free Greeks.

As I think it would be needlessly evil for me not to do so, I find myself motivated to tell you where I think all this leaves us. I'll do so in the next chapter, having looked at the nature of faith.

Conclusion

I want to finish by exploring the question, What is the relationship between having the belief that there's a God and having faith in God?

FAITH

One could understand having the belief that there's a God and having faith in God as one and the same thing. Let me call this the 'Faith is Belief That' theory.[1]

I'm going to conclude that faith is in part a matter of belief that there's a God, but that faith in God isn't just a matter of believing that there is a God—there's more to it than that. Before I can do that, I need to meet two arguments that people sometimes use to argue that faith doesn't have anything to do with belief-that. They both start from the undoubted fact that the theistic religions commend faith—one is praised for having faith and blamed for not having it.

The Faith is Belief That theory has to accommodate the fact that faith is commended and in doing so the Faith is Belief That theory needs to commit itself to two claims. First, the Faith is Belief That theory is committed to it being good to believe that there is a God. Only if it were good to believe that there is a God would it make sense to commend someone to the extent that they had acquired and maintained that belief. Secondly, the Faith is Belief That theory is committed to it being the case that whether or not one believes that there's a God is something that one can oneself affect by an act or acts of one's will. Only if it was within one's own power to acquire and maintain the belief that there is a God would it make sense to commend someone for acquiring and maintaining that belief. One can cast doubt on both these two claims and thus cast doubt on the Faith is Belief That theory.

First, I'm going to look at reasons for thinking that the Faith is Belief That theory isn't right because belief that there is a God does not seem to be—even on the truth of theism—such a good thing.

If we accept that believing the truth is in itself a good thing, then it seems that we'll have to accept that if there is a God it would indeed be a good thing to believe that there is. But is it plausible to maintain that it would be as good a thing as faith is undoubtedly perceived to be by the adherents of Judaism, Christianity, and Islam? If it were not, then that'd be a blow to the Faith is Belief That theory. Of course, it wouldn't be a fatal blow; it could be that the theory was right and it was just that adherents of Judaism, Christianity, and Islam had an overinflated view of how good it was to have the belief that there is a God. So an argument against its being a very good thing to believe that there's a God can't prove that the Faith is Belief That theory is wrong; at best it can show that it can't be rationally subscribed to by Jews, Christians, and Muslims if they're not prepared to downgrade their estimation of how good a thing it is to have faith in God. Let's see, though, if we can find an argument that can do even that.

There is a village in Devon called 'Brampford Speke'. I'll hazard that you didn't believe that before I mentioned it. But let's suppose I showed you sufficient evidence of its existence to convince you. If we accepted that true beliefs are in themselves good things to have, then we'd have to say that I'd have benefited you to at least some extent by giving you this belief. But by how much would I have benefited you? Not much, you might reasonably think; I'd have benefited you more had I given you twenty pounds. So, having the true belief that there's a village in Devon called Brampford Speke is, I suggest, a good thing for you, but it's not very much of a good thing. Why think that if there's a God, then belief that there's a God will be a much better thing than belief that there's a village in Devon called Brampford Speke? On the Faith is Belief That theory it'd have to be quite a bit better to justify all the commendation that faith receives in the theistic religions. Well, someone might plausibly argue that if there's a God, then he is more important on some absolute scale than villages in Devon because he's our benefactor and this entails a duty of gratitude towards him for us. So, if there's a God, then believing that there is a God is a better thing than believing that there is a village in Devon called Brampford Speke. We've seen that such a suggestion is plausible, but just how much better than believing that there's a village in Devon called Brampford Speke can the theist consistently maintain it is to believe that there's a God?

If there's a God, then he could make his existence a lot more obvious to us than he has done. Indeed, if there is a God, then he could reveal himself to each of us in a direct and overwhelming way, convincing us beyond any shadow of a doubt that he exists. This is, after all, precisely what will happen according to theism at the Last Judgement. To the extent that it was a good thing to believe that he exists, God would have a good reason to bring it about by these means— or others—that we believed that he exists, so the fact that many people don't believe that he exists is, one might argue, good reason on the truth of theism to suppose that it can't be that good to believe that he does. So—the argument goes—the theist can't believe that it's actually that good to believe that there's a God and thus if the theist clings to the claim that faith is something very good to have, he or she will have to abandon any account of faith that equates having faith with having the belief that there is a God, i.e. he or she will have to abandon the Faith is Belief That theory. You won't be surprised to learn that I don't think that this argument works; we've already seen the reasons why.

To the extent that God allows his existence and character to become manifest to a finite agent he detracts from that agent's freedom to choose to be less than perfect. The more uncertainty there is about the existence of God, the more it's possible for us to have a free choice between good and bad, right and wrong. It's not implausible to suggest that it's worth our while missing out on the good of knowing with absolute certainty that there is a God at least for the duration of our lives on earth if we will have that good in the afterlife. On theism, this is precisely what will happen.

The (it was argued irrefragable) principle that if it seems to someone that x, then that's in itself a good (albeit capable of being overruled) reason for that person and anyone they tell about it to believe that x, both renders the argument from religious experience and the argument from reports of apparent miracles potentially good arguments for theism, and renders the argument from atheistic experience and irreligious experience potentially good arguments for atheism. This alerts us then to the need for the defender of any religion to explain how his or her religion being true is compatible with—and perhaps ideally not even reduced in probability by—the fact that it seems to the majority of humanity that it's not true. This problem is particularly obvious for theists. Every Jew, Christian, and Muslim believes that his or her variant of theism is more true than any of the others; that all the monotheistic religions are more true than the non-monotheistic religions; and that all religions are more true than physicalism. However, each believes in a good God, a God who would surely therefore wish *all* his creatures to have the right religious beliefs rather than what the Jew, Christian, or Muslim must see as the alternatives: rough approximations (the Jew, Christian, or Muslim may see his or her own religion as a more or less rough approximation to the truth; he or she *must* see the variants of monotheism that are not his or her own as even rougher ones, otherwise he or she would convert); mostly false beliefs (non-monotheistic religions fail, he or she presumably thinks, to be even 'rough approximations'); or completely false beliefs (physicalism). Thus theists must address what we might call 'The Problem of Other Religions and Physicalism':[2] any variant of theism the truth of which is inconsistent with (or even merely rendered less probable by) the existence of/quantity of/variety of other religions and/or physicalism is threatened given that people do subscribe to a variety of religions and physicalism. But we have seen the solution provided by the variant of theism that commended itself to us as the most defensible on independent grounds in Part I, the version on which one's ultimate salvation is not determined by the accuracy of one's pre-mortem metaphysics. On theism, it was argued, one should conclude that all will ultimately find salvation, however wildly erroneous or non-existent their religious views during their earthly lives and thus, while accuracy in these views is very important—they are, after all, very important matters—it's not, quite literally, a matter of life and death. It is not at all improbable, then, on the variant of theism that we saw was most plausible, that large numbers of people would not be theists during their earthly lives in order to provide for us freedom of the sort described above; of course, given that on theism it is good to be a theist, it is probable on theism that any who use this freedom to choose to seek God out will be rewarded by finding him and to this point we will return in a moment.

At this stage we may observe that these reasons are sufficient for rejecting the first argument for thinking that the Faith is Belief That theory isn't right, i.e. the argument that as faith is so highly commended, it has to be something it is very good to have and the fact that we don't all believe that there's a God when if there is a God he could easily make us believe that he exists is a reason to suppose that it can't actually be that good to believe that there's a God. I've argued that God might have good reasons for allowing us not to believe that he exists (in this life) even if it would be very good indeed for us to believe that he exists, just as he might have good reasons for allowing us not to be perfectly good towards one another (in this life) even if it would be very good indeed for us to be perfectly good towards one another.

◆ ◆ ◆

The second reason one might advance for rejecting the Faith is Belief That theory is that beliefs-that are not under the direct control of the will and thus, one might argue, the having or lacking of them is not the sort of thing for which one could reasonably be praised or blamed. Allow me to consider this argument at greater length.

I'll give one million pounds to anybody reading this who is not in Brampford Speke if they can make themselves believe—even for a moment—that they are in Brampford Speke without going there. If you're not in Brampford Speke, do you want to believe that you are? If you believe my offer is a genuine one, then very probably the answer to that is 'Yes', you do. One million pounds would be quite handy and a fleeting false belief that you are in Brampford Speke wouldn't be too inconvenient. So why is it that you cannot make yourself believe that you are in Brampford Speke without going there? Is it just a quirk of your psychology that you can't do that? In other words, is it logically contingent that beliefs-that are not under the direct control of the will? It is not. As we've already seen, your beliefs-that are your beliefs about what the world is like. If you chose to try to acquire a particular belief-that simply because you would get some money as a result of doing so, then you'd know that you were choosing to try to acquire a belief-that by a mechanism other than one that made it more likely that you were acquiring a true belief-that than a false one, i.e. by a mechanism other than one that in some way put your beliefs-that in touch with the way the world is. But if you knew that that was how you were going to acquire a particular mental state, then you could not think of whatever mental state you got yourself into as a result as a belief-that, for you'd know that that mental state was not related to how the world is and your beliefs-that have to be mental states that you believe are related to how the world is in a way that makes them more likely to be true than false. You can't regard some mental occurrence of yours as a belief that you are in Brampford Speke while you realize that you have no truth-tracking reason for having that mental occurrence, for you can only take as your beliefs-that mental occurrences that you take to have some truth-tracking relation to the world, that's what makes those mental occurrences beliefs-that, rather than something else.

So beliefs-that cannot be acquired by direct acts of the will. Does this kill off the Faith is Belief That theory? No, it does not. For there are all sorts of things that cannot be acquired by direct acts of the will, but which one can nevertheless be commended for having acquired, for example knowledge of the philosophy of religion. You can't just decide, 'I'm going to acquire knowledge of the philosophy of religion'; sit there; will yourself to do so; and make it happen. You have to read books, think about the issues, and so on. But that you can't acquire knowledge of the philosophy of religion by direct acts of the will doesn't make it unreasonable for an examining body to commend you for having acquired it; or indeed to censure you if you show that you haven't acquired it. Beliefs-that about the philosophy of religion can be acquired by indirect acts of the will. You can acquire them by reading books, etc. and you can directly will yourself to engage in these activities.

◆ ◆ ◆

Having found no reason to reject the Faith is Belief That theory, I want to turn to consider another view of the nature of faith, what we might call the 'Faith is Belief In' theory. I'm going to argue that we should believe in a composite view—the Faith is Belief In and Belief That theory.

Consider this sentence:

I believe that the government has a policy of encouraging people to think of university education as simply training for the 'job market' beyond, but I don't believe *in* this policy.

This sentence makes sense. In fact, not only does it make sense, it's true. What am I saying about myself when I utter it? Well, I'm saying that although I believe that a certain thing (in this case a policy) exists, I do not believe that it *should* exist. Believing *that* is an intellectual commitment; believing *in* is a moral or existential commitment, a trusting in one person, course of action, or set of ideals, rather than another. I find myself unable to make a moral commitment to the government's policy because of a prior commitment that I've made to something that I perceive to be diametrically opposed to it—genuine education. Thus, although I am (painfully) aware that this policy exists, I do not to any extent believe in it. Indeed, it would not be inaccurate to say that while I am firmly convinced that it exists, I passionately *dis*believe in it.

So belief-that does not require belief-in. One can believe that something exists while not believing in it to any extent; in fact one can disbelieve in it. Does belief-in require belief-that? Can one believe in (or disbelieve in) something while not believing anything about it? One cannot, for the simple reason that one's belief-in (or disbelief-in) has to have some sort of belief-that associated with it to act as the handle by which it grabs the thing that one's believing in (or disbelieving in) and makes sure it's that thing that one's believing in (or disbelieving in) rather than something else or nothing at all. One cannot make a commitment to something one has no beliefs about; otherwise how could one know it was *that* one was making a commitment to rather than its opposite? How could it be that that *was* what it was that one was making a commitment to? So, there's this asymmetry: belief-that does not require any belief-in but belief-in requires at least some belief-that. This is why, if you are attracted to the Faith is Belief In theory, you'll have to combine it with the view that Faith is Belief That. Beliefs-in require beliefs-that, and thus if faith is a matter of belief-in, it must also be a matter of belief-that.[3]

Belief-in may sustain itself at a particular level while the certainty of the relevant belief-that vacillates. Take my belief-in the cause of opposing the displacement of the concept of education in people's minds by that of training: if a week or so goes by without anyone in power pushing forward the programme of attacking universities who busy themselves with an alternative vision, my belief that this is the government's policy might wane. I'd maybe think that it was more likely that I'd fallen asleep in a Faculty meeting (not entirely improbable) and had suffered some nightmare. But while my belief that there's something to oppose here might thus wax and wane, my belief-in opposing it (if it does indeed exist) might remain unchanged in its strength.

Given this, we can see that it won't be possible to believe in God without believing, in at least a vacillating way, that there is a God, but it may be possible to believe that there's a God yet not believe in him. If there's a Devil, then he believes that there is a God with much less vacillation than any of us, but he passionately *dis*believes in God; he's committed himself to quite another set of ideals and objectives. Of course believing that there's a God—a being who is, among other things, omnipotent and perfectly good—while not believing in him, i.e. while not making a moral or existential commitment to him, must be irrational. But then finite agents can be irrational, sometimes wilfully so. Very intelligent people can decide to commit themselves to the wrong things: *Delivering the course in the most efficient manner* (whatever that means) can replace *Education* as a goal of a Faculty, even a philosophy Faculty; *The Faculty's Research Assessment Exercise rating* can replace *Thinking the very best that can be thought.* The same can happen in religious matters too, where—on theism—it's even more dangerous. One can believe that there's a God, yet prioritize other things above him: one's own religion and its trappings;[4] and so on. The name for this tendency is 'idolatry' and religious idolatry is of course, on theism, the worst sin possible for it lies at the root of all other sins.

Faith in God then is a combination of believing that there's a God and believing in him. It is not possible to believe in God while not believing that he exists, but it is possible (albeit supremely irrational) to believe that he exists yet not believe in him. Of course, given that it's supremely irrational, one can only fail to believe in him owing to not being absolutely convinced that he exists. (The Devil then, after all, must be prone to at least some uncertainty.) As I've previously argued, a perfect revelation of God's existence would remove from one the possibility of not having faith in him. On the truth of theism, not believing in God will lead inevitably to idolatry, which is making one's ultimate moral or existential commitment to something less worthy than God, putting one's ultimate trust in something less trustworthy than one could have put one's trust in. Faith in God is the opposite of idolatry. It's no surprise, then, that, from a theistic point of view, one is commended for having faith. Having faith represents the 'turning' of oneself to God's will that lies at the root of all one's other obligations, and that will make the Last Judgement heavenly rather than hellish. (Remember though that as I use the term 'hellish' it doesn't imply *everlasting* punishment.)

I've argued that the strength of one's belief in God might remain unchanged even while one's certainty that there is a God vacillated. I now want to look at what level of belief-that is required as a 'minimum' before one can reasonably have faith in God. I'm going to argue that as long as you believe that it's more probable than not that there's a God, that is sufficient for you to be reasonable in believing in him and thus have faith in him.[5]

◆ ◆ ◆

Suppose that as you'd turned this page, I'd come into the room in which you read it with an open bottle of champagne, offering you a drink to celebrate you being about to reach the end of the book. You'd read the rest of it diligently, so you'd felt that you deserved (or perhaps, rather, *needed*) at least one drink. No sooner had you drained your glass than a man in police uniform had rushed in. He'd slapped me in handcuffs as he'd told you that I'd poisoned the drink I'd just given you and that unless you immediately drank the antidote that he'd brought with him, you'd die. I'd looked astonished and told you, 'Don't trust him! He's not really a policeman; I recognize him from the paper as a notorious poisoner. He's no doubt trying to poison you with what he's calling the antidote. Don't drink it.' What would it have been most reasonable for you to have believed and done?

I could alter the details of the story to 'balance it' in the following way. If it struck you as obvious from the story as I've presented it so far that you should have believed me rather than this supposed policeman, I'd add details of the following kind: as you'd looked at the putative policeman, you'd become pretty sure that you'd recognized him as someone you'd seen a photograph of in the local newspaper under a story about him being the new beat officer for your area. If it struck you as obvious from the story as I initially presented it that you should have trusted this putative policeman rather than me, then I'd add another sort of detail instead: as you'd looked at him, you'd become pretty sure that you'd recognized him as someone you'd seen a photograph of in the local newspaper under a story about him being a dangerous prisoner, recently escaped from a local lunatic asylum. Let me suppose then that I've tinkered around with the details of the story until I've got it such that—given the evidence—it would have been not in fact balanced, but rather slightly more reasonable for you to have believed that I was telling the truth rather than that this supposed police-man was. It would have been slightly more reasonable for you to have believed that the drink that I had given you was not poisoned and that the drink the 'policeman' was handing to you was poisoned, rather than the other way around. Given that, is there anything or anybody that or whom we could describe it as having been reasonable for you to have believed-in, which or whom you should have made an object of what I've been calling a moral or existential commitment, an object of your trust? Well, yes, pretty obviously: me. If it was slightly more likely that I was telling the truth than it was that this supposed policeman was telling the truth, it'd be more reasonable for you to put your trust in me, to follow my instruction and not drink his putative antidote than to follow his and drink it. Judging that it's just slightly more probable that I was telling the truth than that this 'policeman' was would make it reasonable for you to put your faith in me. If it had been balanced fifty/fifty, then it wouldn't have been *un*reasonable for you to put your faith in me or for you to put your faith in the putative policeman, but it wouldn't be positively reasonable either. As it was, it was—only slightly—unreasonable to put your faith in the 'policeman'. It was—only slightly—positively reasonable for you to put your faith in me.[6]

Let me apply this then to the case of God.

It certainly wouldn't be reasonable for you to perform actions that only ultimately make sense on the assumption that there's a God (for example, sing songs of praise to him in church on Sundays) if it is overwhelmingly clear that that assumption is false. But the case of the existence of God is not—I've argued—like that. My poison analogy purports to show that if the probability that there's a God can be raised just above the fifty/fifty point, it becomes unreasonable not to have faith in him. If it stays at the fifty/fifty point, then it looks as if it wouldn't be *un*reasonable to have faith in him, but it wouldn't be unreasonable not to either, to put one's faith in something else. If it can be lowered just below the fifty/fifty point, it looks as if it will become unreasonable not to have faith in something else, to commit oneself to some other ideology or set of ideals. But perhaps not—if the probability that there's a God is still greater than the probability of any other competing hypothesis.[7]

◆ ◆ ◆

I want to conclude by considering a rather unusual argument for its being unreasonable not to have faith in God. I'm going to approach this argument somewhat indirectly, so please bear with me.

Consider this situation: you find yourself at a horse race and you are choosing where to place your one-pound bet. For some reason, you *have* to place a bet, so no reasonable moral objections to gambling per se are going to be relevant. It's literally a two horse race, between horse A and horse B. Horse A and horse B each look as likely to win as one another from the form and so on. You approach the bookmaker and ask him what odds he's giving. He tells you something rather strange.

He's not offering odds as such, because he too can't see any way of deciding which horse is most likely to win. He can, however, offer you some choices. If you put your money on horse A and horse A wins, he'll give you one million and one pounds, so—as he'll have taken your pound off you initially—you'll be one million pounds up on the deal. If you put it on horse A and horse A loses, he'll have taken your pound off you and you'll get nothing in return, so you'll be a pound down. If you put it on horse B and horse B wins, he'll have taken your pound off you but he'll give it back, so you'll come out evens; if you put it on horse B and horse B loses, he'll have taken your pound off you and you'll get nothing in return, so you'll be a pound down again. Furthermore, if you put it on horse B and horse B loses, he'll punch you in the face repeatedly. Rather odd, I know, but it's my example, so I can do with it as I choose. You look back at the two horses and you look again at their form; and their jockeys; you name it; and you still can't tell which is more likely to win. You have to place a bet. Where would it be rational for you to put your money?

Surely the answer is on horse A. Even though you have no more truth-directed reason to believe that horse A will win rather than horse B, you have reason provided by the pay-offs that the bookmaker has set up to act as you would do if you did have truth-directed reason to put your money on horse A. If you put it on horse A, then—worst-case scenario—you'll be a pound down and—best-case scenario—you'll be a million pounds up. If you put it on horse B, then—worst-case scenario—you'll be repeatedly punched in the face and—best-case scenario—you'll come out evens.

Now let's alter the situation. Again, you find yourself at a horse race. It's a two-horse race between horse A and horse B. You study the form and so on and have no more reason for doing so to believe that horse A will win than you do to believe that horse B will win; and you have no more reason to believe that horse B will win than you do to believe that horse A will win. So far then, it's the same as before. You take out your pound coin; approach the bookmaker; and ask him what odds he's giving. He tells you something even stranger than he told you before.

You can't place bets on which horse will win; you have to acquire a belief-that concerning which horse will win. There are no odds, but the following pay-offs. If you believe that horse A will win and horse A does win, then he'll give you one million pounds. If you believe that horse A will win and horse A doesn't win, then he'll give you no money at all. If you believe that horse B will win and horse B does win, he'll give you no money either. And if you believe that horse B will win and horse B does not win, he'll repeatedly punch you in the face. You are about to protest that beliefs-that are not under the direct control of the will and as you have no more truth-directed reasons to believe that one horse will win rather than the other that there's thus no way you acquire either of these beliefs-that. Pre-empting this, the bookmaker points to a hypnotist who has set up his booth next to the bookmaker's. The hypnotist tells you that for a mere pound he can hypnotize you to believe anything and of course remove from you the memory that you've been to see him so that you can retain that mental state as a belief-that. He tells you that you've never been disappointed by his services in the past. 'That's because I've never met you before in my life,' you say. 'That's what you think,' he says. He points to a photograph on the wall of his booth, one of many under a sign that says 'Previous Satisfied Customers'. The photograph shows you smiling broadly while leaving his booth. You have no recollection at all of its being taken or indeed of ever having been in his booth before.

What would it be rational for you to do? Surely the answer is that it would be rational for you to pay the hypnotist in order that he might hypnotize you into believing that horse A is going to win.

◆ ◆ ◆

Now I turn to consider a situation where you have no more reason to believe that there's a God than you have to believe that there's not and no more reason to believe that there's not than to believe that there is, what I've called the fifty/fifty position. What should you believe? Either you are going to believe that there's a God or you're not: it's a two-horse race. (To make it a two-horse race, you'll notice that I've put believing that there is a God on one side and neither believing that there is a God nor believing that there is not a God in with believing that there's not a God on the other side. In the traditional terminology, I've put theism on one side and agnosticism with atheism on the other.) Given what I've argued previously, that although it is possible to believe that there's a God yet not believe in him it's obviously irrational not to believe in him if one believes that he exists, I can say then that for rational people it's a two-horse race between having faith in God and not having faith in God. If you're in the fifty/fifty position then, by definition, you don't think there's any truth-directed reason to have faith in God, but perhaps there are some non-truth-directed reasons to have faith in God.

Let's consider these two possibilities in order. First then, suppose that you do end up believing that there's a God and—being rational—you consequently believe in him. This—I've established—is equivalent to your having faith in God. Having faith in God is something that almost all the adherents of the various theistic religions are agreed increases your chances of getting into Heaven and enjoying an eternity of bliss. That's the potential upside of having faith in God then—an increased chance of an infinite bliss. The potential downside is that you may miss out on a few worldly pleasures. If you become a Jew or a Muslim, you'll miss out on the pleasures of bacon sandwiches; if you become a

Christian, perhaps you'll spend your Sunday mornings in church rather than in bed listening to light entertainment shows on Radio Four. In short, it doesn't seem that you'll miss out on much. So, having faith in God is rather like believing that horse A will win in my previous examples; if your horse comes home—if there is a God—you're more likely to get a reward that is far greater than your stake money. If you have faith in God and there isn't a God—if the other horse comes home, as it were—then you lose only your stake money, which wasn't much anyway. Now let's consider the possibility that there is a God and that you don't have faith in him. Almost all the major theistic religions are agreed that not having faith in God is a pretty sure-fire way of ending up in Hell, which is an eternity of torment. That's the potential downside; what's the potential upside? You may gain a few more worldly pleasures, for example bacon sandwiches here and there or listening to those radio programmes, i.e. the upside is not much. Nobody's biggest regrets on their deathbed are that they didn't have many bacon sandwiches or listen to enough light entertainment shows on radio. If there's a God and you don't have faith in him, you stand to lose infinitely more than you stand to gain. Not having faith in God is then like believing that horse B will win. If you are starting from the fifty/fifty position, then having faith in God offers you what you must view as a fifty/fifty chance of increasing your likelihood of infinite bliss and a fifty/fifty chance of missing out on a few worldly pleasures needlessly; and believing that there's not a God offers you what you must view as a fifty/fifty chance of increasing your likelihood of infinite torment and a fifty/fifty chance of not missing out needlessly on a few worldly pleasures. What is it rational to do in these circumstances? You have to play the odds, but—especially when the odds are (as far as you can tell) evens—you also have to look at the potential gains and losses of your options. Obviously, you have to get yourself to have faith in God. You should start looking for a hypnotist; and you should start looking for one quite quickly, for—as someone wiser than I once put it—you never know the day or the hour when your soul will be demanded of you. Death can happen any time and what can happen any time could happen today, could happen now.

What are we to make of this argument, which in its original form usually goes by the name of 'Pascal's Wager'?

◆ ◆ ◆

It might seem that to accept the conclusion of a Pascal's-Wager-type argument, one will have to accept that the possibilities, their probabilities, and their pay-offs are more or less as I've suggested. One will have to believe that it's possible that there's a God; and one will have to believe that if there's a God and one has faith in him, this is more probably going to increase one's chances of getting plus infinity than it is going to decrease one's chances of getting plus infinity relative to one's not having faith in him. If one thought that it is impossible that there's a God, then Pascal's Wager could offer one nothing. But I've argued that it's not impossible that there's a God. That's what my first chapters, establishing the coherence of the theistic conception of God, were about. So I think I can sweep that worry aside. If one thought that if there is a God, it is just as likely that he will punish those who have faith in him and reward those who do not as that he'll reward those who do and punish those who do not, then again a Pascal's-Wager-type argument could offer one nothing. So if there is a God, which is more likely out of these two? That he'll reward those who have faith in him and punish those that don't or that he'll reward those who don't have faith in him and punish those that do? Well, *out of these two*, I'd say it is pretty obviously the former—that he'll reward those who have faith in him and punish those who don't. God is of necessity good; faith involves believing that there's a God, something that, if there's a God, is a true belief. It's good to believe the truth; and it's bad to punish people for having done good things; so if there's a God and he's going to reward and punish people differently after their death on the basis of whether or not they've had faith in him, he's not going to punish those who've had faith in him for doing so; if he's going to punish anybody for whether or not they've had faith in him, he's going to punish those who didn't have faith in him.

But of course one might argue that God needn't punish or reward people for whether or not they've had faith in him at all. We've seen earlier that while on theism there is indeed a sense in which those who have not yet turned to God will find the Last Judgement more punishing than those who have, this punishment will be a self-inflicted realization of their own shortcomings and—as these shortcomings will not be infinite—they will not find it infinitely punishing. And, on theism, everlasting bliss awaits all of us beyond this judgement. In other words, it's most implausible to insist that the pay-offs for having faith in God and not having faith in God are as supposed by the Pascal's-Wager-type of argument that I've been discussing to date. If one becomes convinced by the sorts of considerations that I sketched earlier that if there is a God, then everybody will eventually get into Heaven anyway (whether or not they've had faith in him during their earthly lives), then the non-truth-directed reason for having faith in God that a Pascal's-Wager-type argument would enjoin upon us is weakened. It's weakened, but not entirely destroyed. And a weak reason for doing something is still a reason for doing it.

If there's a God, then it is, after all, bad not to have faith in him, and that means that those who haven't had faith in him will as a result be in receipt of *some* more punishment, *ceteris paribus*, than those who have had faith in him. It's not reasonable to think that it will be an infinite punishment, but it might be reasonable to think that it will be a punishment great enough to outweigh the inconveniences (if any) that having faith on this earth would bring. And in fact faith on this earth doesn't bring any great inconveniences; rather, the opposite: it brings benefits. Don't studies show that people who have faith in God have healthier and happier lives than those who don't?[8] Isn't it very plausible to suggest that these studies show that having faith in God brings much more happiness than is lost by not having the odd bacon sandwich or not listening to light entertainment shows on radio? I don't have time to look at these studies here; a thorough investigation of them would belong more properly to the psychology or perhaps sociology of religion. But if the evidence of these studies is that (putting aside for a moment whether or not there's a God) those who have faith in God benefit overall in this world to a certain extent, then as (if there's a God) we may be sure they will not suffer from having had faith in him in the next world, so we may say that there's overall a Pascal's-Wager-type non-truth-directed reason for us to do what increases our chances of having faith in God.

Should you then drop this book like a hot stone and rush to a hypnotist whom you'd pay to get you to believe that there is a God (and of course to make you forget that the only reason you had your resultant faith in God was because you'd been to see that hypnotist)? No. Because there's an alternative: prayer. As Kenny puts it:

There is no reason why someone who is in doubt about the existence of God should not pray for help and guidance on this topic as in other matters. Some find something comic in the idea of an agnostic praying to a God whose existence he doubts. It is surely no more unreasonable than the act of a man adrift in the ocean, trapped in a cave, or stranded on a mountainside, who cries for help though he may never be heard or fires a signal which may never be seen.[9]

Rather than rushing out to a hypnotist, one could then rush out to a synagogue, church, or mosque and utter a prayer there. There's no need to rush anywhere actually. One could say a prayer wherever one happens to be sitting at the moment. (Remember, if there is a God, then he's omnipresent.) What sort of prayer should one utter? Well the precise words wouldn't matter, as long as the content was a request addressed to God to the effect that he help one have faith in him.

Suppose then that you start to pray. Every night before you go to sleep, you get on your knees by your bed; clasp your hands together; and start speaking, addressing your comments to God. Each night you simply pray as follows, 'God, please help me have faith in you.' You then wait to hear any reply, asking yourself the following, 'Do I sense any answer?' If you do, you consider whether it is something that you incline to think of as revelatory of the presence of God or indicative of his absence and, if you don't, you consider whether you've listened enough to hear any answer that might have been given. You do this each night for a week. You start from the fifty/fifty position, i.e. you start on the first night thinking that it is equally likely that there is a God as that there's not. What, on this first night, should you think about the process of prayer? Should you think that it is a process that's likely to instil in you a true belief about whether or not there's a God or should you think of it as a form of self-hypnosis that might indeed instil in you a true belief about whether or not there's a God but has in itself nothing to do with the truth?

If there's not a God, then coming to believe that there is as a result of prayer isn't a process that has arrived at truth, quite the opposite: it's a form of self-hypnosis that has induced a false belief, a false belief that isn't too harmful and may indeed be beneficial, but a false belief none the less. But if there is a God, then though coming to a belief that he exists as a result of prayer could perhaps still be called a form of self-hypnosis, in fact there's a God 'behind' this and indeed all other natural processes, ensuring in this case that the belief in him that it produces is a true belief. If there's not a God, then coming to believe this as a result of praying and hearing nothing by way of reply, or sensing the absence of such a being by way of reply, produces a true belief. And if there is a God, then coming to believe that there's not as a result of praying and hearing nothing by way of reply, or seeming to sense the absence of such a being by way of reply, is producing a false belief. Being at the fifty/fifty position, you thus judge that praying is likely to be a truth-directed process of belief acquisition via the considerations outlined earlier in the discussion of the argument from religious and irreligious experience.

Now, whether or not one thinks there's a God, one will admit—I hazard—that praying to God that he help one have faith in him will—as a matter of fact—increase one's chances of ending up believing that there's a God and thus, if one's reasonable, having faith in him. After a few nights praying like this, it's thus statistically likely that you'll come to the belief that it's slightly more probable than not that there's a God. Although statistically unlikely, it's possible, however, that you'll have received no answer to your prayer; you'll have had the absence of any experience which you'd incline to describe as if of God. It's also possible, though even more unlikely, that you'll have experienced the absence of God. Nothing you can have experienced then will have given you any reason to believe that this process of praying to God that if he exists he reveal himself to you is not truth-directed. Just the opposite; anything you've experienced and even the absence of an experience will have simply increased your estimation of the reliability of this process in putting you in touch with ultimate metaphysical truth. You'll find yourself locked into what you'll have to consider an episte-mically virtuous spiral of prayer, one that ever increases your faith in God or that ever increases your certainty that he does not exist. If the latter, it would be slightly odd to continue to call the process prayer, rather than meditation or some such, for 'prayer'—like 'conversation'—seems to suppose assigning at least a 50 per cent probability of there being a person listening to one. But this is just a terminological quibble. Your experience or absence of experience will lead you reasonably to conclude that this process (be it best called prayer or meditation) is truth-directed. Unlike your situation with the hypnotist at the race-track then, there'll be no need for you to forget about how you've come to your resultant faith in God or confidence in his non-existence. Only if the experiences were variable (e.g. for a few nights it seeming to you in response to your prayers as if there was a God, for the next few its seeming to you as if there was not) might this confidence in the process be undermined. But this variation would over time itself be a reason to favour atheism, for if there were a God, he would have good reason not to allow the process of prayer to yield such results.

What follows from all of this, then, is that, as well as thinking a bit more about the philosophy of religion, we should think a bit more about comparative religion; the psychology of religion; the sociology of religion; and theology. And, having thought about them for a while, we might very well conclude that the only reasonable course is to stop doing so and to start to pray.[10]

Endnotes

INTRODUCTION

1. This way of defining religions is of course contentious; everything in this area is. One contentious implication might be that Platonism would count as a religion on this understanding; however, this does not seem objectionable to me: Platonism, it strikes me, obviously *is* a religion; it's just not one that anyone subscribes to (although elements of it have found their way into religions that people do subscribe to). I confess to almost total ignorance of Theravada Buddhism; perhaps it has no ontological commitment to the existence of some explanatory supernatural realm; if that is so, then it doesn't seem counter-intuitive to me to suggest that it's not a religion once we see that claiming that it's not a religion doesn't commit one to claiming that it can't nevertheless be a 'philosophy of life', i.e. a way of looking at the world that natural science describes and a set of practices and rituals that accompany this way of looking at it. On my understanding of the essence of religions, all religions naturally spawn philosophies of life in this sense (if—unlike Platonism—they are actually taken up by people), but not all philosophies of life are based on religions; as I say, I know little of Theravada Buddhism, but Marxism would definitely be an example of a philosophy of life that is not based on a religion. See also later note on the expansion of the notion of physicalism.
2. This is not to deny that physicalism became an intellectually available 'option' in the West's popular culture in the latter part of the twentieth century in a way that it had never been in any culture previously; however, it is still, at the start of the twenty-first century, an opinion chosen only by a tiny minority.
3. Even having given myself this restricted scope, I shall omit or pass quickly over some topics that other lines of argument would find more central to their path; an overview unhampered by the requirements of having to pursue an argument across the field is given by M. Peterson et al. (eds.), *Philosophy of Religion, Selected Readings* (OUP, 2000), a work that I recommend to you.
4. J. Locke, *An Essay Concerning Human Understanding*, 'Epistle to the Reader' (OUP, 1975), 6.
5. For an introduction to a quite different style of philosophy of religion, one could do a lot worse than read Stephen Mulhall's *Faith and Reason* (Duckworth, 1994); indeed, one could hardly do better.

CHAPTER 1

1. Of course any actual theists that you come across will believe that God has more properties than this (if they're Christians, for example, they'll believe that God was incarnate in Jesus and that his death atoned in some way for the sins of humanity) and these other properties—given that it's belief in them that distinguishes the adherents of one of the monotheistic religions from the adherents of another—will often feature

more 'up front' in theists' self-descriptions of their beliefs. No one, well no one outside a philosophy faculty anyway, would describe themselves as a 'theist'; they'd describe themselves as a Jew, Christian, Muslim, or some such; and when you asked them what it is they believed, they'd thus naturally find themselves talking about what they believe in contrast to believers in one of the other monotheistic religions. Despite their being the worthy subject of much philosophical discussion, I'm not going to address here any of the religious doctrines peculiar to the various monotheistic religions; I'm going to be focusing on what unites them, not what separates them.

2. There are various sorts of necessity (and possibility). There's logical or conceptual necessity (and possibility); metaphysical necessity (and possibility); and physical necessity (and possibility), to name but three. The logically or conceptually possible is that a full description of which does not involve a contradiction. Thus it is logically or conceptually possible that all bachelors be happy and it is logically or conceptually impossible that all bachelors be married. Metaphysical necessity (and possibility) is a more contentious notion. For the moment an example will have to suffice. (Sadly, it has to be a contentious one as there are no non-contentious metaphysical necessities.) It is metaphysically impossible for H. G. Wells's *The Time Machine* to be a true story. It's not logically or conceptually impossible as there's no contradiction (or at least there needn't be) in a complete description of an incident of going back in time, but nevertheless it's impossible for such stories to be true and the impossibility of their being true does not derive from the laws of nature that happen to be operative in our universe, as it would do if we were talking of the impossibility of building a spaceship that could accelerate to the speed of light. (A fuller description of and argument for the existence of metaphysical necessities is given in my discussion of the divine property of necessity.) The physically possible is that which is consistent with the laws of nature and the initial or boundary conditions of the universe; the physically necessary is that—if anything—which is entailed by these. The essential properties of God are both logically or conceptually necessary properties of God and metaphysically necessary properties of him. It's logically and conceptually impossible that God not have all these properties if he exists for they form part of the definition of God and given that one of these properties, which we'll come to in due course, is that he exist of metaphysical necessity, so it's metaphysically impossible that he not have these properties. We will come to this more fully in Chapter Three.

3. This isn't quite how the Doctrine of Divine Simplicity would have been understood by Aquinas, its most famous exponent; for him it amounts to the claim that in God the nine properties that I have given separately may in fact be identified with one another—God's omnipotence is his omniscience, is his eternality, etc. Further, God can be identified with this property.

4. Genesis 18: 22 and following.

5. A very interesting discussion of the matter of just how much or little is lost if theists abandon attributing the property of personhood to God is given by Hugh Rice in his *God and Goodness* (OUP, 2000), *passim*.

6. One might say that any concept that admits of borderline cases is, by definition, a vague one. This strikes me as a good—if one might say 'technical'—definition of vagueness, but it leaves my substantial point unaffected. I accept that the concept of personhood remains vague in this technical sense then (it admits of borderline cases),

but I claim that it is plausible to say that it is not vague in the non-technical sense employed in the main text and indeed everyday life (in that it admits of non-borderline cases too). In order to see this latter parenthetical point then, in lieu of any other obviously non-borderline case of personhood, I encourage the reader to consider himself or herself.

7. D. Dennett, 'Conditions of Personhood', which occurs as ch. 14 of his book *Brainstorms* (Harvester, 1981).

8. However, it is not unnatural to describe someone as having various beliefs even when in dreamless sleep. Imagine stumbling across the Pope while he is deep in dreamless sleep. On being asked of him, 'Does this man believe in God?', it would be most natural to reply 'Yes', even if one supposes him to be genuinely unconscious—i.e. having no conscious mental happening whatsoever—at the time. Having a belief then does not seem to necessitate holding the belief in question before one's attentive mind while affirming it or some such; rather, having a disposition to affirm it if put in the right circumstances, e.g. if woken up and asked the relevant question, suffices. If so, then even the majority of dreamless sleepers have beliefs.

9. If it really is unacceptable not to count foetuses and severely mentally retarded human beings as persons, I'll have to withdraw slightly, to the position that these psychological properties are sufficient (though not necessary) for personhood. This tactical withdrawal wouldn't affect the overall strategic shape of my argument (indeed it might represent an advance on another front, see below), though—in the light of the considerations presented in the main text—I see no reason to make it, at this stage. I put the 'at this stage' caveat in here as there are a couple of questions one might reasonably raise: since human beings have varying levels of personhood properties, doesn't the view presented in the main text imply that one ought to think of them as having varying levels of moral significance? And isn't it obvious that one oughtn't to do this? Assuming that the right answer to the second question is 'Yes', the view in the main text looks as if it might be in trouble: while it would only imply that the answer to the second question were 'No' were one to combine with it the view that degree of possession of personhood qualities determines degree of moral significance, what looks like the only alternative, a 'pass mark' view (that once one's over a certain level of personhood qualities, one gets complete moral significance and any increase in personhood qualities from then on doesn't entitle one to more), seems equally problematic as some severely retarded human beings have only the same level of personhood qualities as obviously non-personal, morally-insignificant things. To get out of this, it strikes me, one would have to engage in the sort of metaphysical 'derivation' I've tried to avoid for ease of presentation by staying at the level of these properties, a 'derivation' that might indeed ultimately lead one to think that the only view that provided one with all the answers one's ethical intuitions told one to want was the soul view. Despite the tenor of the main text (especially in what follows about indeterminacy), I'm not myself actually unsympathetic to those who find themselves compelled to travel down this road. I do have a strong ethical intuition that all humans have equal moral significance, equal then regardless of how low they fall on the personhood property scale (it's most implausible to me to suggest that a murderer of a mentally disabled child does something *less* bad than a murderer of a member of a philosophy faculty). And I have an equally strong intuition that the painless death

of any non-human animal is always in itself less bad than the painless death of a human. This tendency on my part then might be labelled—especially by those who would disagree with it—speciesism. The only way to make speciesism defensible, it strikes me, is indeed to subscribe to the soul view.

10. This way of presenting the case displays a tendency to treat the indeterminacy as ontological, not epistemic; whether or not this is the right way of treating it depends on the result of the metaphysical investigation spoken of at the end of the previous section and in the preceding note.

11. Alert readers with an interest in moral philosophy will have spotted that there's a link here between the essence of personhood and 'integrity' objections to consequentialism.

12. Alert readers with an interest in moral philosophy will have spotted that there's a solution to the problem of amoralism in here.

13. See also J. A. T. Robinson, *Exploration into God* (SCM, 1967) and A. Thatcher, 'The Personal God and a God who is a Person', *Religious Studies* 21 (1985), for attempts to make sense of such a claim.

14. Compare G. Jantzen, *Becoming Divine: Towards a Feminist Philosophy of Religion* (Manchester University Press, 1998).

15. It must be confessed that there is some difficulty in the notion of directness as employed in the direct knowledge criterion and the direct control criterion. The rough idea is that if, for example, I am trying to move a butterfly that is presently underneath a bell jar by sliding the jar along, taking the butterfly with it, then I must move my hand towards the jar. Unless I am in some way disabled, this will be direct; I won't need consciously to move anything else first in order to move my hand. Then I'll move the jar, less directly in virtue of first having had to move my hand. Then the butterfly will move as a result, an even less direct result of my basic action in moving my hand. I submit that we all have a rough intuitive grasp on the notion of directness employed here, a grasp sufficient for the argument of the main text to proceed. But it must be conceded that the analysis of this notion is difficult. It is tempting to analyse the directness spoken of here as a matter of proximity to the beginning of the causal chain leading to the result in question. However, were one to give in to this temptation, various implausible consequences would follow. One would have to conclude that nothing could count as one's body on complete determinism, and we surely don't want the fact that we have bodies straightforwardly to entail the false-hood of complete determinism. (Of course this would be a metaphysical rather than logical entailment and Substance Dualists might have little to fear from it, indeed they might have an argument for Substance Dualism to gain from it.) Personally, I think that a more promising line of analysis would be to think of the directness as a matter of what one first needs—consciously—to do. Even this though would not be without its problems. When driving a car, one probably doesn't think things like, 'Right, first I must move my hands in order to move the steering wheel, in order to get the car to turn to the right.' At most one thinks things like, 'I must move the car to the right' and quite often one doesn't even think things like that. Minutes of a car journey and relatively complicated manœuvres can be accompanied by no conscious thought at all on the part of the driver. On the analysis of directness suggested and the account propounded later, the car as a whole would have to be counted as

an—albeit temporary—extension of one's body for such periods, something that also seems prima facie counter-intuitive. I incline on balance to accept it.

16. Of course, also of interest to us qua philosophers is whether it's metaphysically possible that this happen, but this is one of the questions which, for ease of presentation of my main argument, I am trying to keep 'bracketed'.

17. A substance dualist might, of course, say that persons such as you and I are 'essentially incorporeal substances' or some such, but—assuming the usual interactionist version of substance dualism—as these 'essentially incorporeal substances' causally interact in the direct sort of way with relatively discrete bits of matter, so he or she should say that we're not incorporeal at the moment; of course, he or she may maintain that it's metaphysically possible that we could become such, because our essential part is immaterial and there's no metaphysical necessity meaning, for example, that this part will cease to exist on the destruction of our bodies.

18. There are a number of fascinating case studies of this. The most famous is Morton Prince's *The Dissociation of a Personality* (Longmans, 1905). For a first-rate discussion, one would be well advised to look to Kathleen Wilkes's *Real People* (Clarendon, 1988), especially ch. 4.

19. For a good attack on the coherence of such a suggestion, see J. C. A. Gaskin, *The Quest for Eternity* (Penguin, 1984), 109 ff.

20. It is not clear whether this alone will be sufficient to demarcate theism from pantheism, the view that God is the universe. It may be that the theistic understanding of God's ontological independence from the universe as implied by the divine property of necessity and indeed creatordom (both of which we will come to in a moment) would need to be drawn on here to put clear blue water between them.

CHAPTER 2

1. The correct answer to my mathematical question is approximately 684,171,000, 000,000,000,000,000,000,000.

2. As I recall it, Kryptonite actually removes Superman's super powers, rendering him mortal, but it does not itself kill him. My apologies to aficionados who find my playing fast and loose with such details an annoyance.

3. This is a bit quick. There are some questions that will require other considerations too. For example, it is quite possible that this state of affairs obtain: you freely choosing to continue reading this book despite having had your attention drawn to some of its deficiencies by its author; I hope that this is a state of affairs that you're going to bring about. Could God bring this about? To answer this would obviously require an analysis of what you freely choosing something amounted to and whether or not it was possible that someone could make someone else freely choose something; if they could, then God could; if they couldn't, then God couldn't.

4. For some interesting variations on the theme that omnipotence should be understood in terms of having the most power that it is possible to have see T. Flint and A. Freddoso, 'Maximal Power', in A. Freddoso (ed.), *The Existence and Nature of God* (Notre Dame, Ind., 1983); J. Hoffman and G. Rosenkrantz, 'Omnipotence Redux', *Philosophy and Phenomenological Research* 49 (1988), and E. Wierenga, *The Nature of God* (Cornell University Press, 1989).

5. The approach to omnipotence taken here has some parallels with the view that we should take as basic God's being perfectly good and allow this to limit the powers that God has. But if—as I argue—not all abilities are powers, rather than a proper understanding of maximal excellence or some such leading us to put limits on God's powers, a proper understanding of the nature of powers and liabilities (as mutually exclusive and exhaustive subsets of abilities) might allow a proper understanding of omnipotence and an understanding of how this entails perfect goodness. See G. Schlesinger, 'On the Compatibility of the Divine Attributes', *Religious Studies* 23 (1987), and cf. A. Kenny, *The God of the Philosophers*, ch. 7 (OUP, 1979), and T. Morris, 'Maximal Power', in A. Freddoso (ed.), *The Existence and Nature of God* (Notre Dame, Ind., 1983). For a sustained attack on my approach, see W. Morriston, 'Are Omnipotence and Necessary Moral Perfection Compatible? Reply to Mawson', *Religious Studies* 39 (2003); and W. Morriston, 'Power, Liability, and the Free Will Defence, Reply to Mawson', *Religious Studies* 41 (2005).

6. Most philosophers find it useful to draw a distinction between sentences, propositions, and statements that they might explicate somewhat like this: consider a situation in which the sentence 'The current king is bald' is uttered in the reigns of different kings: we might say that in each case different statements are made because different kings are referred to, but, in as much as the sense of 'The current king is bald' remains unchanged at the different dates of utterance, we might say that the proposition expressed is the same. Now consider a situation in which the sentence 'The current king is bald' is uttered during the reign of King Tim the First, and the sentence 'The previous king was bald' is uttered during the reign of King Tim the Second, where King Tim the Second comes to the throne immediately after King Tim the First. Here we might say that two distinct sentences have been used to make the same statement (King Tim the First has been referred to on both occasions and the same thing has been said about him) but, in so far as the two sentences are evidently not synonymous, we might say that two distinct propositions have been expressed.

   In short then, a sentence is a series of words bounded, when written, by full stops etc., and can be distinguished at the token level (one instance) and the type level (more than one instance with the same typography). The same type sentence may not always be used to express the same proposition. A proposition is what is expressed by a meaningful declarative sentence, such that two token declarative sentences with the same meaning may be said to express the same proposition, but perhaps not necessarily make the same statement. A statement is what the proposition expressed by a meaningful declarative sentence states, such that if two propositions attribute the same properties to the same objects, they make the same statement. For further discussion of these issues, see E. J. Lemmon, 'Sentences, Statements and Propositions', in B. Williams and A. Montefiore (eds.) *British Analytical Philosophy* (Routledge & Kegan Paul, 1966) and S. Wolfram, *Philosophical Logic* (Routledge, 1989).

   Some distinction such as this is essential if we are to solve the problem of how God can know what I know when I know that *I* am *here now*. Truths that a creature can say about itself using the idiom of the first person and indexicals such as 'here' and 'now' God knows, though he himself does not of course access these truths through the same sentences or propositions; ergo, it must be statements that ultimately carry truth.

7. I shall later nuance this understanding of God's goodness, but for present purposes nothing is lost by this simplification.

8. This argument (and some of what follows) assumes a particular understanding of what it is to be 'genuinely free', one which is usually called 'Libertarianism', not to be confused with the political ideology of the same name. Libertarianism is the 'consensus' view among theists in general and certainly among temporalist theists; as such, we may assume it for the purposes of this argument. But a temporalist who was willing to abandon the claim that we are free in this sense could, of course, avoid this argument for extending divine ignorance (though, by the argument of the previous paragraph in the main text, he or she would still need to posit some divine ignorance). See C. Campbell, *In Defence of Free Will* (Allen & Unwin, 1967); R. Sorabji, *Time, Creation, and the Continuum* (Duckworth, 1983); J. Kvanvig, *The Possibility of an All-Knowing God* (Macmillan, 1986); A. Plantinga, 'On Ockham's Way Out', *Faith and Philosophy* (1986), and J. R. Lucas, *The Future* (Blackwell, 1989), for imaginative and different treatments of this problem.

9. If God atemporally knows that you will give a copy of this book to your best friend, then he could have made it the case that a prophet 500 years ago predicted that you would, but either he'd have left it as a possibility that this prophet might go wrong (in which case you could retain the ability to do other than as prophesied) or he'd have removed the possibility of error and thus removed your ability to do other than as prophesied. The atemporalist can admit, in other words, that an atemporal God could remove his creatures' freedom and that he would have to do that (to at least some extent (he'd have no need to limit it over other things irrelevant to the prophecy)) if he wanted to make a prophecy an infallible one. But this does not seem problematic. God's ability to give a prophet a piece of infallible foreknowledge of your actions does not interfere with your freedom in performing those actions as long as he doesn't exercise that ability. The only problem arises if one in effect puts an infallible and omniscient 'prophet' inside time and earlier than your action, as one does if one views God as temporal and everlasting.

10. See e.g. B. Leftow's very thorough *Time and Eternity* (Cornell University Press, 1991). But contrast A. Padgett, *God, Eternity and the Nature of Time* (St Martin's Press, 1992) and R. Swinburne, *The Christian God* (OUP, 1994).

11. Genesis 6: 6–8 reads, 'The Lord saw that the wickedness of man was great in the earth, and that every imagination of the thoughts of his heart was only evil continually. And the Lord was sorry that he had made man on the earth, and it grieved him to his heart. So the Lord said, "I will blot out man whom I have created from the face of the ground, man and beast and creeping things and birds of the air, for I am sorry that I made them." But Noah found favour in the eyes of the Lord.' A certain sort of literal-minded believer in this story could of course use it as 'evidence' that not only could the God of traditional theism bodge things up, he does bodge things up. But then of course this sort of believer would have difficulty in giving a religiously satisfactory interpretation of the end of the story, where God promises never to do anything similar again. God's promise would be as if a policeman were to promise never to arrest a certain man again. From the moment of the promise onwards God and the policeman have to keep their fingers crossed that mankind/the man won't do anything that will put them in the 'awkward' position

where their only options are either breaking their promises or keeping their promises yet knowingly doing less than they ought. For recent discussions see Clark Pinnock et al., *The Openness of God: A Biblical Challenge to the Traditional Understanding of God* (InterVarsity Press, 1994).

12. C. Taliaferro (ed.), *Contemporary Philosophy of Religion* (Blackwell, 1998), 219; this is an adaptation from his formulation in *God, Time and Knowledge* (Cornell, 1989), 197.

13. Apart from an eschewing of extreme Kantianism, nothing else is required of our understanding of goodness for my argument to work, as my argument shows how a temporal God might do something that doesn't just fail to be good (on any plausible non-Kantian understanding), but is actually in itself bad (on any plausible non-Kantian understanding), indeed morally disastrous.

14. See John Sanders, 'Why Simple Foreknowledge Offers No More Providential Control than the Openness of God', *Faith and Philosophy* 14 (1997).

15. See e.g. Boethius, *The Consolation of Philosophy* (Penguin, 1969), v. 6.

16. See E. Stump and N. Kretzmann, 'Eternity', *Journal of Philosophy* 78 (1981), 429–58 for an elaboration of this criticism.

CHAPTER 3

1. I use the word 'wishes' to bypass the issue of whether or not a 'desire-satisfaction theory of action' is right—roughly, a theory that states that one always does whatever one believes will satisfy one's strongest desire. The claim that if free, one always does what one wishes, is intended to allow for the truth of such a theory, but also to allow for its falsity as in a case where—as one might put it—one wished for the sake of duty to act contrary to all one's desires. The claim that freedom simply is the power to bring about what one wishes seems to be refuted by certain examples of people who have very restricted abilities but wishes that are equally or slightly more restricted. However, the claim that freedom requires the ability to do what one wishes is far more plausible and is all that's needed for my argument.

2. The property that I call God's perfect goodness is sometimes called 'omnibenevolence', literally all-good-willing. As God is not restrained in acting on what he wills by a lack of power or by ignorance, his omnibenevolence quickly necessitates his omnibeneficence, literally all-good-doing. But neither of these terms quite captures the fact that not only is everything that God does good, he never fails to be anything but perfectly good, so I prefer the term 'perfect goodness' to describe this feature of the theistic concept of God. The understanding of perfect goodness argued for in the main text immediately raises some important questions. It might seem to entail that God will create the best possible world if there is one. And if there isn't a best possible world—not just because there are ties, but because there are infinitely many possible worlds, each one better than the last, what then—if anything—does God's perfect goodness entail he do? These issues are treated separately in Chapter Twelve.

3. This is a simplification. One could do something supererogatory for a 'cause', e.g. the spread of communism, without having the good of any individual in mind, indeed, as this example shows, while thinking of the good of any individual as subservient to this cause.

4. This example may seem needlessly confusing for another reason: in it the 'rightful owner' of the money is so repellent and you are so needy that it isn't at all clear that on *any* prima-facie plausible account the right thing to do is give him back the money. Would the example not be better if I made the rightful owner a nicer person, so that it then presented a simple contrast between self-interest and the interests (or rights) of others? Unfortunately, I can't do this. The less serious and pressing I make the threat to you and the less well-off I make the rightful owner, the less it will seem obviously, overall, reasonable for you to keep the money. Similarly, but less obviously, on some prima-facie plausible accounts the *nicer* I make the rightful owner, the less it will seem right for you to give the money back. This is because there's some plausibility in the suggestion that if you could reasonably believe that the rightful owner would have given you the money were you to have explained your position to him and asked him for it, you are morally justified in keeping it even in a situation where you do not explain yourself to him and ask him for the money. In order to 'head off' this objection to the example being one of a conflict between what it is, overall, reasonable to do and what it is morally right to do at the start, I thus make the threat to you great; the need of the rightful owner for the money small; and the rightful owner very mean.

5. This might not be immediately obvious. If one's ultimate enjoyment of everlasting life is not contingent on one's being perfect in this life (as it isn't on any plausible theistic view, not just the version I endorse in a later chapter), then it might seem that it could be reasonable to prefer present (immoral) enjoyment to present (moral) misery. (One might be reminded of Augustine's famous prayer: 'Lord, make me chaste. But not yet.') But it is not in fact objectively reasonable if, as I later argue will be the case on theism, in the Last Judgement one's culpable failures to be less than perfect will be terribly exposed as one stands before God. From that rightfully shamed perspective, one will correctly judge of every peccadillo, however gratifying it was at the time, that it wasn't worth it.

6. This is not to deny that there might be some things that would be good and that one might thus reasonably want but that can't be brought about, even by an omnipotent being, without acting immorally. On theism, it would have been good for Nietzsche to have loved God for the duration of his earthly life, but—let's suppose what is not implausible—that it would have been bad for God to have intervened directly to make Nietzsche do so, for such an intervention would have required a violation of Nietzsche's autonomy, something that in itself would have been bad. There seem to be three possibilities. First, it could be that the good of Nietzsche's loving God throughout his earthly life outweighed the bad of the violation of his autonomy that would have been required had God intervened (in which case God's not intervening to make Nietzsche love him would have been immoral). Secondly, it could be that they were balanced (in which case God ought to have been morally indifferent about whether or not to so intervene). Thirdly, it could be that the badness of the intervention would have been greater than the goodness of the consequence it brought about (in which case it would have been immoral for God to intervene). There is nothing in this that prevents God doing whatever it is that perfect goodness demands of him, although from the fact that Nietzsche obviously didn't love God throughout his earthly life, we may infer that the theist is committed to the first one of these three possibilities not being actual.

7. One might think that there's a difficulty raised for the divine attribute of perfect freedom by the conception of freedom that we have allowed to guide us thus far (on which for genuine freedom it has to be possible for an agent to do otherwise than he or she actually does) when we commit ourselves to claiming that God is of necessity perfectly good. But in fact the ability to do otherwise is quite compatible with being necessitated to do what is morally perfect once the nature of God's moral perfection is appreciated, that God must do the best (or joint best) for his creatures wherever there is one. Prior to the creation of a world, God's perfect goodness dictates nothing as to what he must do (for there are no creatures); every possibility is open to him. Once he has created a universe, then it still dictates nothing if he has created one with no creatures or creatures for whom there is no best (or joint best) and of course if he hasn't created such a universe, that itself will be the result of his informed choice not to do so. We shall return to, and slightly nuance, these points later in discussion of the Problem of Evil.

8. For a more detailed account of the property of necessity, with which I am in essentials in agreement, see J. Hoffman and G. Rosenkrantz, *The Divine Attributes* (Blackwell, 2002), ch. 4.

CHAPTER 4

1. The Sadducees, a Jewish religious sect at the time of Jesus, traditionally did not hold that God offers us everlasting life, so it would be safer to say that the vast majority of theists agree on this last point. However, as the majority among theists who do think that God offers us everlasting life is so vast, I allow myself to talk of 'all theists', supposing this in the main text.

2. There doesn't seem to be any impossibility in God's allowing his angels (if there are any) power to create ex nihilo in the sense of out of no pre-existent matter, but they would still be dependent on him for their having this power, so they would not be the ultimate creator of anything they so created. If we understand 'ex nihilo' in 'creation ex nihilo' as meaning 'from nothing' in the sense of dependent on nothing, then the traditional phrase 'creation ex nihilo' has the same meaning as my 'ultimate creation'.

CHAPTER 5

1. See J. Shaw's 'The Application of Divine Commands', *Religious Studies* 35 (1999) for an excellent discussion of some other reasons why God might reasonably wish to change the moral status of certain actions.

2. For example, D. Z. Phillips, *Death and Immortality* (Macmillan, 1970), *passim*, and A. Flew, *The Presumption of Atheism* (Elek/Pemberton, 1976), ch. 9.

3. In a Gallup survey of the early 1980s, 67 per cent of Americans were revealed to believe in life after death and even 53 per cent of those who said they were not involved in any regular religious activity said they nevertheless believed in life after death (G. Gallup, *Adventures in Immortality* (McGraw Hill, 1982), 201, 202). Ten per cent of (English) atheists believe in immortality according to one survey (D. Martin, *A Sociology of English Religion* (Heinemann, 1967), 102).

4. From henceforth, I shall be using the word 'death' to mean clinical death.

5. E. Hirsch, *The Concept of Identity* (OUP, 1982), ch. 1, and A. Quinton, *The Nature of Things* (Routledge & Kegan Paul, 1973), 63 ff., for example, both take engine disassembly to be a case of the engine going out of existence and then coming back again.

6. One complication is that the parts used by one person may well be used by another—a particular problem in the case of cannibals whose body parts, we may imagine in a limiting case, could all be parts previously belonging to others, their victims. How could God resurrect both the cannibal and his or her victims? An obvious answer is to say that he could do it sequentially. Consider this analogy. Imagine my using a certain number of Lego bricks to make a model plane; I then disassemble it to its component bricks and use all of them to make a model car; I then disassemble the car into its component bricks again. According to the view we're currently operating with, if I then were to rearrange the bricks in exactly the same way as they were initially arranged, this would be for me to recreate the plane. If I were then to break the plane up again and rearrange them in exactly the same way that they were subsequently arranged, this would be for me to recreate the car. Thus—with an infinite temporal extension ahead of me—I could perform these tasks an infinite number of times, giving each of the plane and the car an everlasting if gappy 'life'. Now obviously these lives would never overlap with one another. Could God give the cannibal an everlasting life in which he or she met his or her victims? I myself don't see why not on this theory—although this is more contentious. Suppose I rearrange the bricks into the plane. I then take one brick from the plane and put it to one side, replacing it on the plane with another brick qualitatively identical to the first. This would not, I suggest, destroy the identity of the plane. I then repeat this process until in the end my plane is made up of entirely different bricks from those that originally composed it, leaving a pile of bricks to one side, a pile of bricks that is now liberated from being used to constitute the plane so that they may be used to recreate the car, a car that can then exist simultaneously with the continuing plane. That the plane could survive the gradual—and in the end total—replacement of its parts in this way is the more contentious claim on which the possibility of God being able to reunite cannibals with their victims depends on the physicalist theory we are considering.

7. This means relative to a frame of reference incorporating both Earth and Alpha Centauri.

8. In the literature, people who take this view are reluctant to actually make this stipulation, as they think that precisely in virtue of us knowing all the above we must know what matters—hence to make such a decision is, at best, superfluous and, at worst, likely to distract us from what really matters.

9. Realism as a general policy on the nature of the constitution of the identity of all things seems unnecessarily pessimistic as to our chances of explaining identity and change and none have held to it. On the other hand, anti-realism as a general policy on the constitution of the identity of all things seems necessarily self-refuting; even the most ardent anti-realist must allow his explanations to stop somewhere if he is ever to finish presenting them and hence to provide explanations at all. If the identity of a and b, if it is to be ontologically grounded at all, is to be grounded in relations among things that are distinct from a and b, let us call them c and d, then we might ask what the identity of c and d is to be grounded in and, by the principle just given, if it is to be grounded in anything at all, it must be in relations among things of a different type

again, e and f. Thus, either the regress is infinite or circular or some identities must be taken as in themselves primitive, ungrounded, and inexplicable; in either of the first two cases no satisfactory explanation of the 'higher' identities will have been given at all by making reference to the 'lower' ones. Therefore, there must be some ontologically primitive identities assumed in any theory of the identity of persons or anything else.

10. This is basically the scenario described by J. Hick, in *Death and Eternal Life* (Collins, 1976), ch. 15 and elsewhere, as implied by the truth of the doctrine of bodily resurrection.

11. Presumably imperfections will be removed.

12. The argument for substance dualism from realism, as sketched briefly in the main text, relies on a transition from what is perceived to be logically possible to what we thus have good reason to believe is metaphysically possible. The only principle that the substance dualist will need to rely on to make this move is that apparent logical possibility is necessarily prima facie good reason to believe in metaphysical possibility. This principle must be accepted for any argument against him or her to proceed: therefore, he or she cannot be denied it. The substance dualist argument has this structure: 'That x is logically possible is good reason to suppose that x is metaphysically possible; thought experiments establish that x is logically possible and therefore that there is good reason to believe x is metaphysically possible; the metaphysical possibility of x implies the truth of substance dualism; therefore we have good reason to suppose that substance dualism is true.' Or, more specifically, given that (1) it seems logically possible that we might know all the physical and psychological facts yet not know the person fact, then (2) we have good reason to believe that the physical and psychological facts aren't the person fact; the two are metaphysically separate; and given (2), then (3) persons have an immaterial part, a soul substance, with which they are to be essentially identified. To reject the modalities the substance dualist relies on to make his case as even logical possibilities seems precipitate in the face of our pre-reflective intuitions in favour of realism. While Margaret Wilson writes that 'the fact that we can conceive that p does not entail that p is even [logically] possible: all that follows (at best) is that we have not yet noticed any contradiction in p' (M. Wilson, *Descartes* (Routledge & Kegan Paul, 1978), 191), it is notable that if the principle underlying this conclusion were, in fact, adhered to by Wilson as a necessary condition for epistemic justification, she could never arrive at any conclusion as to what is, in fact, possible and (hence) what is, in fact, actual. (Shoemaker makes the same point in his '*On an Argument for Dualism*', C. Ginet and S. Shoemaker (eds.), *Knowledge and Mind* (OUP, 1983, 248.) The substance dualist can legitimately respond to any threat to (1) along these lines with the charge that if we cannot use our intuitions to judge of logical possibility, then we are in very poor epistemic shape indeed. It seems a principle of rationality to accept that, after suitable consideration, if something seems to a subject to be logically possible, then *ipso facto* he or she has good reason to believe that it is logically possible. (See my later discussion of the Principle of Credulity in the main text.) Whatever charge of unsuitability in degree of reflection is then levelled against the substance dualist he or she can rebut by considering the matter further. The thought experiment of your travelling to Alpha Centauri seems to establish that it is not logically impossible that people might go wrong, even knowing all the physical

and psychological facts, about whether or not you've survived. Presumably then it is the step between (1) and (2) that is the best point at which to direct some fire. A physicalist might, it seems, simply deny that the step between (1) and (2) is justified, asserting that we are, in fact, to be entirely identified with some physical element whether or not we ever realize this and hence start to say it—there *is* a correct percentage of a certain area of physical stuff (presumably some section of our brains) that is us—and thus that (1) while, perhaps, expressing an epistemic possibility does not express any more of a metaphysical possibility than is expressed by pointing to a sample of what is, in fact, water and saying 'I could know everything about that stuff with regard to it's being H_2O, yet not know that it was water; therefore being water can't be simply being H_2O.' This would seem to be the position of D. M. Armstrong. (he asserts that 'disembodied existence seems to be a perfectly intelligible supposition' in his *A Materialist Theory of the Mind* (Routledge & Kegan Paul, 1968), 19.) However, this move will not ultimately work either, I think. The surrendering of the ground of logical possibility to the substance dualist will ultimately lead to total capitulation by the non-substance-dualist or overt dogmatism. The opponent of substance dualism will need, if he or she allows substance dualists onto his or her logical land, to hastily (and it will seem dogmatically) erect his or her own *de re* modalities to stop them crossing easily from that ground surrendered to them onto that, which he or she wishes to reserve for himself or herself, of metaphysical possibility. Setting up these metaphysical necessities where he or she does will then be overtly dogmatic as the thought experiments accepted by both parties as establishing that it is logically possible that one might know all the physical and psychological facts yet not know the personal facts (it was this acceptance that prompted the non-substance-dualist to allow the substance dualist onto the ground of logical possibility in the first place) would seem to be necessarily good evidence that this is metaphysically possible as well, whatever science may discover in the future—simply because our realist tendencies tend to make us think that science (metaphysically) *could* always be going wrong. In reply to 'This is just an instance of the Masked Man Fallacy,' the substance dualist can, it seems, reply 'It might be, but what more reason could one have for believing that it's not?' Of course, in so far as we don't have realist tendencies, then we have the easy anti-realist solution to the problem of how we might survive our deaths as discussed in the main text.

13. Most often, a person does not die before the human body with which he or she is associated undergoes certain biological changes, e.g. heart stopping. But this is not universally the case. Consider again the definition of personhood elaborated in Chapter One. On this account, what happens when someone moves into a persistent vegetative state is that they lose all interest in life in the very extreme sense of losing their personhood; the person dies but the body continues. When we say that if death is the end, it is bad for the person, we should be clear then that it is not biological death but personal death to which we refer. It may be worth pointing out that this does not imply certain things it might be taken to imply. It does not imply that we have carte blanche over how we treat patients in persistent vegetative states as, after all, they are not persons. It does not imply that we can, for example, keep them alive simply to be used as organ banks for those humans who are still people. Remember the discussion of how things that are not persons may still count morally. Perhaps we

cannot show the patient who is a human body in a persistent vegetative state due respect if we treat him or her as an organ repository for patients who are people. Perhaps we can. The account elaborated here commits one to neither alternative on these or the host of other fraught issues in this area. See James Rachels's book *The Ends of Life* (OUP, 1986) on these issues.

14. Some—such as Bernard Williams ('The Makropukos Case: Reflections on the Tedium of Immortality', *Problems of the Self* (CUP, 1973))—are impressed by the thought that, even if some sort of afterlife might be good for people, an *everlasting* afterlife would of necessity become undesirable for anyone enduring it. 'Nothing less will do for eternity than something that makes boredom unthinkable. What could that be? Something that could be guaranteed to be at every moment utterly absorbing... If, lacking a conception of the guaranteedly absorbing activity, one tries merely to think away the reaction of boredom, one is no longer supposing an improvement in the circumstances, but merely an impoverishment in his consciousness of them', (ibid. 95). Williams's argument deserves a much fuller treatment than I can give it here. Two points, however, may be made briefly. First, worshipping God in the full glory of the beatific vision is precisely the sort of guaranteedly absorbing activity that Williams demands. Of course—and this is a point that I return to in the main text—it is difficult for us in our fallen pre-mortem state to describe that vision in such a way as to make it obvious to us in our fallen pre-mortem state why it would be guaranteedly absorbing for all eternity. The news delivered by John Newton in the famous words, 'When we've been there ten thousand years, bright shining as the Sun, we've no less days to sing God's praise, than when we first begun,' I admit, is not entirely welcome to me with the level of enthusiasm I can currently muster for hymn singing, even John-Newton-hymn singing. But this failure is a failure of character and imagination (and very probably musical ability) on my part, not an incoherence or implausibility in the doctrine; indeed the failure on my part and resultant difficulty is precisely what one would expect on theism. This moves me on to the second point. Secondly then, it is not obviously true that thinking away the reaction of boredom to a situation in someone is always to posit an impoverishment in his or her consciousness of it. As anyone who has taught philosophy will know, students can get bored even when the subject matter does not by any means warrant it. This is a deficiency in them (and perhaps reveals that one's not done all that one might qua educator). To remove someone's capacity for *inappropriate* boredom is not to suppose an impoverishment in his or her consciousness of the object that he or she might otherwise find boring; rather it is to suppose an improvement. I do not have educated musical tastes and as such I would find an opera by Gilbert and Sullivan much less boring than one by Wagner. However, I am quite prepared to assent to Mark Twain's claim that Wagner's music is a lot better than it sounds. If, as Twain's way of putting it well captures, I can't now really imagine how that could be, I'm prepared to think that that's precisely because I am not musically educated; not being musically educated I wouldn't expect to be able to envisage what it would be like to be transformed into the sort of person who could listen to Wagner without getting relatively bored except by rather artificially 'thinking away' the boredom. But—however artificial—I can think this reaction away and I realize when I do so that—assuming the truth behind Mark Twain's aphorism—were

such a change to be effected in me, I would have been quite the opposite from being impoverished in my appreciation of what it was I was hearing.

15. Luke 15: 11 ff.

16. Dante, *The Divine Comedy*, the final stanza of 'Paradise' in the translation by Dorothy L. Sayers and Barbara Reynolds (Penguin, 1986).

CHAPTER 6

1. There's an uncontroversial principle that might look like the simplicity principle that I rely on here. According to this uncontroversial principle, a hypothesis that is simpler by committing itself to less is more likely to be true than one that is more complicated by committing itself to more. For example, a hypothesis that at least one Ninja monkey was involved is more likely to be true than the hypothesis that exactly one Ninja monkey was involved, as the first is entailed by the second but not vice versa. However, this sort of relative 'simplicity' is obviously nothing more than relative lack of specificity in the hypotheses being considered. The more controversial simplicity principle that I rely on is one by which of two equally specific hypotheses, the first that exactly one Ninja monkey was involved and the second that exactly two Ninja monkeys were involved, the first, in positing less entities, is simpler than the second and thus more likely to be true.

2. A. Plantinga, 'Reason and Belief in God', in A. Plantinga and N. Wolterstorff (eds.), *Faith and Rationality: Reason and Belief in God* (Notre Dame, Ind., 1983), 17.

3. The argument in the main text for deviating from the consensus among those who discuss the issue of belief in God being properly basic by saying that it is a necessary condition of a belief being *properly* basic that it be true, is terribly brief; the argument surrounding it to the effect that for anyone who's heard of agnostics and atheists, the belief in God can't be properly *basic*, which also deviates from the consensus opinion among those who discuss the issue of belief in God being properly basic, is even more brief. There are two points that might be helpfully added to smooth the furrowed brows of those who have been driven to reading this endnote. First, against this consensus, I would contend that there's something epistemically improper about continuing to hold a belief basically when one is presented with evidence against it. There's truth in the Humean claim that the wise (i.e. epistemically proper) proportion their belief according to the evidence. Secondly, there's something psychologically impossible about not behaving in the way that this Humeanism would encourage us to think is epistemically proper (at least in the case in point). Let me illustrate both points by reference to an example.

Suppose the police arrive at your door one day and show you evidence that you robbed a bank the day before; this is evidence so substantial that it would convince any juror beyond reasonable doubt of your guilt. You are flabbergasted, as you happen to have what you would—at least initially—describe as a very clear recollection of spending the whole of yesterday visiting a museum on the opposite side of town from the bank. We are free to hypothesize that the belief that you'd been in the museum for the whole of yesterday was, certainly before the police arrived, a basic belief for you (i.e. it wasn't based on any other beliefs, beliefs that might be expressed by your saying to yourself something like, 'I have an apparent memory impression of buying a ticket for the museum and seeing at the time that it had yesterday's date on it; therefore (given the general reliability of my memory et al.), the probability is that I was buying that ticket and thus visiting the museum yesterday.'). The police arriving at your door and presenting all this contrary evidence does not, so some would argue, oblige you to seek out evidence or arguments to rebut the evidence that they present; neither need it of psychological necessity motivate you to do so; thus your belief that you spent yesterday in the museum can remain properly basic. But both the claims supporting this conclusion seem manifestly implausible to me. First, it strikes me that however high your initial confidence in your belief that you spent yesterday at the museum, you *should* be more doubtful of it than you were prior to having this evidence presented to you. (To think otherwise is to subscribe to a form of a Humean prejudice that we will locate in his treatment of testimony to the occurrence of miracles, where one thinks it proper to bury some factual beliefs so deep in the foundations of one's noetic structure that one rules out the possibility of their ever being undermined by contrary testimony or other evidence.) Secondly, not only should you be, but also you just *would* be more doubtful, although I confess that a certain noetic inertia to which we are all subject (we are just lazy) means that this depends on the substantiveness of the evidence. Let's make the evidence really substantive, so it overcomes that inertia. Imagine the police showing you CCTV footage which seems to show someone who looks exactly like you robbing the bank. Furthermore, the footage has audio; you hear a voice exactly like yours coming from the person who looks exactly like you. This voice says to camera, 'After this crime, I'm going to be brainwashed by an accomplice so that I lose all memory of my committing it and instead have an apparent memory of spending today in a museum across the other side of town. Ha, ha, ha!' Is it really psychologically *possible* that this wouldn't make you question, even slightly, your initial confidence that you were in a museum across the other side of town yesterday (unless of course you were a Lockean about personal identity)? Even if no amount of contrary evidence could ever force you—in order to remain rational—to replace your belief that you were visiting the museum yesterday with the belief that you were robbing the bank yesterday (and it strikes me that there could be evidence substantial enough to do that), it strikes me as obvious that any evidence should and substantial evidence certainly would downgrade your certainty in your initial belief to at least some extent and—more importantly here—cause you to place it in relation to other beliefs you have, making that initial belief no longer basic for you even if you still held it. If you still held it, you'd start to back it up with other beliefs, e.g. that this sort of brainwashing was more improbable than someone faking video footage, etc. A self-selection effect will mean that those reading an endnote to a chapter halfway through a book entitled 'Belief in God' must similarly have overcome any initial noetic inertia over the project of considering the grounds, reasons, or lack of them for their belief that there is a God; their belief that there isn't a God; or their failing to form a belief either way.

CHAPTER 7

1. If you want to read his version, you'll be helped by knowing that it's in his book, *Proslogion*, ch. 2 ff. This is available in translation in a number of places, one of them is in *St Anselm's Proslogion*, translated by M. J. Charlesworth (Notre Dame, Ind., 1979).

2. For a much fuller treatment of the notion of possible worlds and this version of the ontological argument, see P. Van Inwagen, *Metaphysics* (OUP, 1993), ch. 5. This is a first-class book all round, and to be recommended in its entirety.

   Later on, I expand the notion of physicalism slightly in such a way that this characterization of physicalists' beliefs would not of necessity be true. I draw attention to this at the time in another endnote.

3. But see A. Plantinga, *The Nature of Necessity* (OUP, 1974).

CHAPTER 8

1. If you want to read it in its original version, you'll be helped by knowing that it's at the very beginning of his book, *Natural Theology* (available in a number of editions, one of which is SPCK, 1837).

2. There's another family of arguments that might be thought of as variants of the Argument to Design, yet that deserve to be given special treatment in that it's a feature of our minds rather than (or in addition to) the world outside them that is held up as evidence of an extra-universal designer, God. This thought finds expression in different forms in C. S. Lewis, *Miracles* (Macmillan, 1970), ch. 3; R. Taylor, *Metaphysics* (Prentice Hall, 1992), ch. 10; R. Walker, *Kant* (Routledge, 1978), ch. 11; and A. Plantinga, 'An Evolutionary Argument against Naturalism', *Logos* 12 (1991); *Warrant and Proper Function* (OUP, 1993), ch. 12; and 'Naturalism Defeated' (unpublished paper, available at http://www.homstead.com/philofreligion/files/alspaper.htm, accessed 29 March 2005). A collection of essays focused on Plantinga's version of the argument, but of relevance to the whole field, may be found in J. Beilby (ed.), *Naturalism Defeated?* (Cornell, 2002). (There's an interesting parallel argument in R. Swinburne, *Epistemic Justification* (OUP, 2001), ch. 2, to the effect that one cannot explain the value of true—in contrast to useful—belief on a physicalist account of the mind, a parallel argument because it's just a physicalist account of the mind that Swinburne thinks is directly threatened by it.)

   It is difficult to generalize, but we may say that each of these versions of the Argument to Design suggests that on physicalism (or—sometimes—on anything other than theism), the probability of our minds being reliable (or reliable in a particular area the defender of physicalism is committed to seeing them as reliable in) is either inscrutable; low; lower than it would be on the falsity of physicalism; or lower than it would be on the favoured religious hypothesis. (Obviously one might combine some of these conclusions in various ways, e.g. one might argue—as does Plantinga—that it's either low or inscrutable.) Now, in addition to the quite general considerations deployed in the main text, there are a variety of things the physicalist might say in response to this argument in its various versions. Perhaps the first move for him or her to make is to suggest that on physicalism, which is quite compatible, one might (at least prima facie) imagine, with the theory of evolution by natural selection, those creatures with more reliably true-belief-acquiring minds would be more likely to survive longer and thus procreate than those with less reliably true-belief-acquiring minds; thus they'd be more likely to send true-belief-acquiring-behaviour-inducing traits down the generations. For example, a caveman with the true belief that the sabre-toothed tiger ahead of him was something that it would be good to run away from would have been more likely to survive the encounter and procreate than one with the false belief that the sabre-toothed tiger ahead of him was something that it would be good to poke with a stick. Over time then, we'd expect to have 'bred into us' true-belief inducing mechanisms. There's no reliability 'left over' after we've told the right version of this evolutionary story. Now, against this, the proponents of the argument agree among themselves that there's some reliability left over, but they divide over how much and where this left-over reliability is. Some might accept that this sort of story is sufficient for explaining some true-belief-inducing mechanisms, e.g. that it would explain why we've had true beliefs in the past or perhaps have them about sabre-toothed tigers, but argue it couldn't explain why we'll continue to have true beliefs in the future (the future can't yet have been relevant to evolution) or why we have true beliefs about certain other things, e.g. metaphysics, perhaps especially what is on his or her opponent's view the truth of physicalism; true beliefs about these things can't convey an evolutionary advantage. (See Walker.) Alternatively (or in addition), the proponent of the argument might maintain that evolution selects for behaviour, which isn't of necessity positively correlated to any extent at all with true belief. A caveman with the false belief that the sabre-toothed tiger ahead of him was something it would be good to poke with a stick but who also falsely believed that the best way to poke something with a stick was to run away from it would also have survived our imaginary encounter. (See Plantinga.) The opponent of the argument thus has to render plausible the suggestion that his or her evolutionary story doesn't, after all, leave any reliability left over and the best way to maintain this is, it strikes me, to concede that true beliefs in some areas and/or in some situations aren't positively adaptive (in evolutionary terms) but that these areas and/or situations are few and far between and thus we might expect on physicalism a general true-belief-inducing faculty to be positively adaptive and to spill over cognitive reliability into these odd areas and situations, giving us true beliefs there too. (This won't alone be sufficient to meet Walker's argument, for which a full discussion of the problem of induction, specifically why we have more reason to believe all emeralds are green rather than grue, would be required. See D. Stalker, *Grue!* (Open Court, 1994). See also J. Foster, *The Divine Lawmaker* (OUP, 2004).) My apologies to aficionados of these arguments, for whom this discussion will have been painfully brief. I refer interested readers to the discussions in Beilby, *Naturalism Defeated*.

3. Romans 1: 20.
4. As one has to posit at least one being, so it might seem simplest to posit an infinite number of such beings. However, there cannot be an infinite number of infinitely powerful beings; thus simplicity it could be argued will ultimately lead one to posit one being of infinite power rather than an infinite number of beings each of which has a finite amount of power, for the latter hypothesis would leave one with an infinite number of unexplained facts about the finitude of each being. But see my later 'multiverse hypothesis'.
5. A very readable introduction to the subject is Richard Dawkins's *The Selfish Gene* (OUP, 1976).
6. It is tempting to see an impermeable division between the biological story and the planetary one, but the Game of Life suggests otherwise. See Martin Gardner, 'The Fantastic Combinations of John Conway's New Solitaire Game "Life"', *Scientific American* 223 (1970).

7. See J. Barrow and F. Tipler, *The Anthropic Cosmological Principle* (OUP, 1986). See also John Leslie, *Universes* (Routledge, 1989), for a different treatment of this; and Hugh Rice, *God and Goodness* (OUP, 2000).

8. A detailed account is given by Richard Swinburne in his book *The Existence of God* (Clarendon, 1979), 64 ff.; or the 2nd edn. (Clarendon, 2004), 66 ff.

9. Some philosophers are very sceptical that this question can meaningfully be asked. See e.g. Bede Rundle's determined attack on the question in *Why There Is Something Rather Than Nothing* (OUP, 2004).

10. Compare A. O'Hear's very interesting 'Epicurean Objection to Swinburne', in his *Experience, Explanation and Faith* (Routledge & Kegan Paul, 1984), 135–43.

11. It may be worth observing that, contrary to the thrust of the argument in the main text, manoeuvring in this way against the Argument to Design may yet force one (on certain assumptions) to posit some extra-universal order and thus accept that there's a sound Argument to Design for the existence of an orderer. For while it is true that the infinite number of infinitely variable universes hypothesis could explain the fine tuning of the laws of nature, there are (arguably three) other features of these laws that it is less obviously true it could explain: the laws of nature are simple; they are beautiful; and they are universal in scope (pushing miracles aside for the moment). Given that we survive long enough to reproduce, someone might argue that we could not but be able to understand and predict the world around us to some extent; it's thus impossible for us to observe a universe of which we cannot form at least some understanding. However, our current understanding of the laws of nature far outstrips what is on any account plausibly required for us to survive and reproduce. After all, lower animals survive and reproduce without even a folk-scientific understanding of the laws of nature and plants survive and reproduce without any understanding at all. Secondly, physicists are agreed that the laws of nature that our universe operates according to are beautiful. Simplicity and beauty are closely connected in ways we need not examine if we accept for the sake of argument that these may not be two separate points, but, as a sign of how pervasive and deep beauty is supposed to be by physicists, it is notable that the elegance of a physical theory is universally taken by physicists to be in itself evidence of its truth. Thirdly (or secondly if we group simplicity and beauty together then), there could have been more exceptions to the laws than there seem to be; it wouldn't have hampered us greatly had the law of gravity, for example, failed to operate every so often arbitrarily in a relatively confined location and then re-established itself. As it happens though, it is exceptionless. Again, it's arguable how separate a point this is—consistency contributes to simplicity and beauty. Again, we need not decide this here, as we can run these facts (if separate facts they be) together for the purposes of our discussion. Grouping them together, then, we may say that our situation is rather as if we have been let into a room the door of which we know will only be unlocked if there's something tolerably comprehensible by way of literature in it; and we find, when we enter, not simply something tolerably comprehensible, but a simple, beautiful, and maximally consistent work of literature. Of all those sets of laws of nature that would be conducive to life in the broad sense necessary for us to observe them, many, it seems, are not as simple, beautiful, or exceptionless as are the laws of nature in our universe. The fact that our laws have this feature (these features) thus needs

explanation. From these points, it looks then as if there may yet be scope for an argument, not from the fine tuning of the laws of nature, but from their simplicity, beauty, and/or universality, to an extra-universal orderer.

Now one could locate this extra-universal explanation by positing a law of 'supernature', which selects from among the infinite set of infinitely variable *possible* universes a subset (perhaps still infinite?) of universes that are actual. But this would be an instance of order itself in that it would distribute the probabilities unevenly across these possibilities and have a preference for simple, beautiful, and exceptionless sets of laws of nature. What exists as a result of this law of supernature, one might say, is still a set of variable universes, but they are variable *within the parameters imposed by them all having to obey relatively simple, beautiful, and universal laws*. On the one hand, this, it could be argued, would still be positing a (perhaps still infinite?) set of things all of which were similar to the one thing we know exists already—our universe—and as such it would have simplicity on its side when put up against the theistic hypothesis as an explanation of the order in our universe. But, on the other hand, in contrast to the multiverse hypothesis discussed in the main text, it would be a hypothesis that would leave an instance of order unexplained—admittedly, order at such a high level (beyond even the laws of nature) that one could not have had any experience that would give one reason to believe that it was a sort of order for which there needed to be an explanation—and if one's already accepted that one has reason to believe that order in mental stuff does not need to have an explanation, then one has reasons of simplicity telling against it (and in favour of the theistic hypothesis); it'd be simpler to say that there was only one sort of unexplained order, order in mental stuff, rather than that there were two, one in mental stuff and one in the principles that dictate the parameters within which the infinite set of actual universes is created from the larger infinite set of possible universes. And the theistic hypothesis could, with this argument for substance dualism 'in the bag', be fairly represented as positing one more of something we know exists already, a self-ordering mind, so the fact that the alternative is positing an infinite number of things of a sort we know exists already (universes governed by relatively simple, beautiful, and universal laws) offers it no comparative advantage. Thus it might seem that a good argument for substance dualism on independent grounds could yet render the Argument to Design, construed as an argument from the simplicity, beauty, and/or universality of natural laws, a good argument for the existence of God; failing that, it could yet render it an argument that could contribute something to a good cumulative case argument for the existence of God.

Let's turn back to the second objection to the fine-tuning version of the Argument to Design that I discussed and see how it applies to this version, for in the main text I implied that it was in itself fatal. Would God have good reason to create a universe the laws of nature of which were simple, beautiful, and universal in scope? Again, one might find it hard to see any reason that he could have had, but this is not by any means to surrender the point that given that minds can do arbitrary things for which there is no explanation (if this has been given), an argument that left us with brute inexplicability in a mind might nevertheless seem more acceptable than one that left us with brute inexplicability elsewhere. And it's not in fact *as* hard to see what reason God might have to create a universe with people in it as one with relatively simple, beautiful, and universal laws as it is to see what reason he might have to create a universe with people in it at all. A universe with people in it who can understand (the laws are simple); take pleasure in (they're beautiful); and make plans concerning (they're universal, so the world around them doesn't do arbitrary things) seems to be a universe where the people in it are better off than one they can't understand (the laws are complicated); can't take pleasure in (they're ugly); and can't plan (they're not universal). It might seem, then, that, given that God had arbitrarily decided to create a world with people in it, he would then have a good reason to create it with simple, beautiful, and universal natural laws.

I want to make two brief points. The first one is that the chief danger for this version of the Argument to Design, it seems to me, lies in the fact that its defender will need to make simplicity, beauty, and universality not necessary for people, but just good for them; if it were actually necessary, then this would collapse this version of the argument back into the fine-tuning version, which we have already seen reason to reject. This, I fear, cannot be done. But justifying this fear of mine would take a long time, so let me suppose for the sake of argument that it is misplaced, that we could indeed be reasonable in believing that of all those sets of laws of nature that would be conducive to life in the broad sense necessary for us to observe them, many are not as simple, beautiful, or exceptionless as are the laws of nature in our universe. Then it strikes me, this should be of no ultimate comfort to the theist, for the 'solution' to the Problem of Evil that I shall later present will be simultaneously undermined in so far as this Argument to Design is supported, because there are all sorts of things that would be good for people that God patently hasn't given us (to keep us in this realm, we're not, for example, all born intuitively aware of the laws of physics). If this second point of mine is right, then, regardless of whether or not my fear that this version of the Argument to Design must ultimately collapse into the fine-tuning version is misplaced, the overall support for the conclusion of my book will remain unaffected. Strengthening the Argument to Design as an argument for the existence of God in this way will be strengthening the Problem of Evil as an argument against the existence of God. Despite our having reached it by a somewhat circuitous route, this is not at all a surprising conclusion. The more one allows that features of the natural world could be evidence in favour of God's existence, the more one should allow that features of it could be evidence against.

CHAPTER 9

1. It's reprinted in full in Bertrand Russell, *Why I am not a Christian and Other Essays on Religion and Related Subjects* (Unwin, 1979), ch. 13.
2. I take it that those who would claim that the laws of nature are metaphysically necessary may be taken to fall into the first camp here; according to them, it's a brute fact that these laws rather than some others, others that are logically possible, must be actual.
3. It might be thought that this doesn't follow if we take the 'this' to refer to the infinite set of infinitely variable universes. If our intuitions as expressed so far in the paragraph in the main text to which this is a note are right, this multiverse is a contingent aggregate made up of contingent universes. We earlier argued that, *pace* Copleston, as long as each member of an aggregate of contingent things is explained, *ipso facto*

the aggregate is explained (there's no contingency 'left over' as we put it) and we also suggested that it is sufficient in explaining our particular universe to appeal to the aggregate (recall the end of the main text's previous paragraph: 'Question: Why does this particular universe exist? Answer: Because every possible universe exists'). This naturally raises the thought: can we then answer the question, 'Why does this multiverse (every possible universe) exist?' with 'Because particular universe 1 exists; particular universe 2 exists; particular universe 3 exists; etc., ad infinitum,' and thus leave nothing unexplained, the existence of every particular universe being explained in terms of the multiverse and the existence of the multiverse being explained in terms of the existence of every particular universe? It seems not, as, despite what we said earlier against Copleston's point, there is a contingency 'left over' in the case of this example (just as there was in fact in the one we used against him: the contingency that people read books at all), in this case the contingency is that there are universes at all. To see this 'meta-contingency', consider this: you enter a bookshop one day, looking for a rather obscure book on the philosophy of religion. The man behind the counter senses your diffidence as you approach and, before you can speak, tells you that you won't be disappointed; he'll have whatever book it is that you're after. You ask for a copy of 'Belief in God' by T. J. Mawson. He goes through a back door and, before it has even had time to close on him, returns with a copy in his hand. You look surprised. 'Allow me to explain how I happen to have a copy,' he says, 'In this shop, every book that is possible is actual. Furthermore, I can search my shelves infinitely fast. Thus, I can always instantaneously provide for my customers whatever book they wish for. You asked for 'Belief in God', *et voilà!*' He slaps it down on the counter with a flourish, adding, 'It's the same price as all my books, an infinite number of pounds. (I have high overheads.)' You apologize and explain that, as you only have a finite amount of money, so you will not, after all, be purchasing the book. He looks understanding, telling you, 'I get a lot of that.' Before you leave, you ask him: 'While I can see, given your pricing strategy, how it is you're able to keep them, may I ask how it is that you happen to have such a collection of books in the first place?' He replies, 'It's really quite simple. Perhaps it will help me explain it to you if I mention that each book has a number (it helps me find them quickly). Thus, I have book 1; I have book 2; I have book 3; etc., ad infinitum. The aggregate that is my collection of books is nothing more than the sum of its parts and, as I have all the parts, so *ipso facto* I have the aggregate.' You look increasingly puzzled. 'Yes,' you say, 'but how is it that you happen to have, say . . .', you look on the spine of the copy of 'Belief in God' on the counter and notice that it happens to be number 278,949, '. . . number 278,949 here?' he looks puzzled in turn. 'Well I just explained that fact to you when I brought it out. In this shop, every book that is possible is actual; book 278,949 is possible, so it's actual. And I have every book that's possible, because I have books 1, 2, 3, 4 etc. ad infinitum.' So far, let us allow, he has indeed explained everything you have asked for an explanation of, at least once. But now let's suppose you shift tack: 'Why a bookshop, rather than, well let's say, a hotel? Why an infinite number of books rather than an infinite number of hotel rooms?' Now, it seems, you have alighted on a contingent fact that he's yet to explain. Perhaps he doesn't need to explain it (perhaps it would be satisfactory for him to say, 'Well, that's just a brute fact'), but if he is to explain it, he needs to step outside the facts of which he's already made mention.

In fact, this is what he does. He replies, 'Well, a Mr Hilbert runs the local hotel. And if you knew how accommodating it is, you'd see that there's really no need for a second.'

4. Readers may have noticed that I'm relying on a slightly broader notion of physicalism than that I introduced at the beginning of the book in making my 'things are even worse' point. I started by defining physicalism as the view that the physical universe that we find ourselves in is all that there is; there's nothing beyond it that explains it. I'm now counting as a physicalist view the view that there's an infinite number of infinitely variable such universes beyond this one and that this multiverse explains the existence of our universe. The other substantial points made in the main text (and the rejection of the Cosmological Argument as a good argument or as possibly contributing to a good cumulative case argument) do not rely on this. However, I make this extension of the understanding of physicalism as it seems to me the right way to go in order to preserve the mutually exclusive and exhaustive distinction between the physicalist view and the religious, for it strikes me that the person who posits an infinite number of infinitely variable universes has a metaphysically rich 'world-view', but his or her world-view is not a religious one. If this is the right way to go, we need some way of characterizing what it is that religious people qua religious people believe in that's not simply an 'extra-universal explanatory entity', because the multiverse this type of physicalist believes in is that sort of thing too; the difference, I suggest, is that the physicalist either posits no explanation of the physical universe or an explanation in terms of something essentially similar (more physical universes) for which there's no explanation; the religious person posits something qualitatively different, in the case of the theist, a God, for which there's no explanation. It's this difference that makes Ockham's razor dictate that a pysicalist explanation of the order of the universe in terms of a multiverse of the sort described in the main text be preferred over a theistic (or indeed any other religious) explanation. (Or at least it dictates it on this evidence alone; there may be other evidence that leads one to prefer the theistic account; we'll come to that later.)

5. F. Darwin (ed.), *Life and Letters of Charles Darwin* (John Murray, 1888), i. 316 n. But see Darwin's own assessment of the possibility of using such a feeling as a reason for a belief, ibid. 312. See also e.g. J. J. C. Smart in A. Flew and A. MacIntyre (eds.), *New Essays in Philosophical Theology* (SCM, 1955), 46.

CHAPTER 10

1. I've adapted it rather freely from H. G. Wells's *The Country of the Blind*, which is reprinted in a number of editions of his works, most commonly collected under the title *Short Stories*, but sometimes collected under the title *The Time Machine and Other Short Stories*.

2. See D. Hay and A. Morisy, 'Reports of Ecstatic, Paranormal, or Religious Experience in Great Britain and the United States—A Comparison of Trends', *Journal for the Scientific Study of Religion* 17 (1978). The willingness of people to admit to such experiences depends on the style of investigation, a more intimate personal conversation bringing forward more claims than a traditional poll. See D. Hay, ' "The Biology of God": What is the Current Status of Hardy's Hypothesis?', *International Journal for the Psychology of Religion* 4 (1994).

3. First edn. 254 ff., 2nd edn. 303 ff. Cf. W. Rowe, 'Religious Experience and the Principle of Credulity', *International Journal for Philosophy of Religion* 13 (1982); G. Gutting, *Religious Belief and Religious Skepticism* (Notre Dame, Ind., 1982); C. Davis, *The Evidential Force of Religious Experience* (Clarendon, 1989); W. Alston, *Perceiving God* (Cornell University Press, 1991); K. Yandell, *The Epistemology of Religious Experience* (CUP, 1993); and J. Gellman, *Experience of God and the Rationality of Theistic Belief* (Cornell University Press, 1997).

4. Cf. J. Gellman, *Experience of God and the Rationality of Theistic Belief* (Cornell University Press, 1997), ch. 3. And see also his *Mystical Experience of God: A Philosophical Inquiry* (Ashgate, 2001).

5. On the other hand, people might have non-truth-directed incentives for believing in God, e.g. their having the belief that if God exists, they'll be rewarded for believing in him and if he doesn't, they won't lose out on much, if anything. We'll return to these points in the last chapter.

6. That I need to add this last premise, that you also think that there's contingency in the universe, may be seen to make whether or not this argument counts as an Argument from Religious Experience or a revivified Cosmological Argument a 'nice' question; however nice though, nothing of substance turns on it. The important point is to avoid double counting it.

7. William James's *The Varieties of Religious Experience* (e.g. Fontana, 1960) is the *locus classicus* and a good starting point for such an investigation. A first-rate discussion of the argument is given by Caroline Franks Davis in her book *The Evidential Force of Religious Experience* (OUP, 1989); she reaches a similar conclusion to me, but that's not the only reason I think it's a first-rate discussion.

8. Cf. A. O'Hear, *Experience, Explanation and Faith* (Routledge & Kegan Paul, 1984), ch. 2.

CHAPTER 11

1. It's in the standard edition of the Enquiries, entitled *Enquires Concerning Human Understanding and Concerning the Principles of Morals*, ed. Selby-Bigge (Clarendon, 1989), 115. All the quotations from Hume in this ch. come from ch. X of his first Enquiry, the chapter devoted to miracles.

2. Although note that it does not require that a miracle be performed by a benevolent someone as I have glossed it. Having introduced such a gloss, I shall actually follow Hume on this point in the main text and not incorporate it being caused by a benevolent someone into the revised definition of miracle that I offer. See my 'Miracles and Laws of Nature', *Religious Studies* 37 (2001), for a more detailed discussion of the inadequacies of Hume's definition of miracles.

3. This parenthetical clause is important as without it one runs the risk of making miracles impossible by mere stipulation; they are in danger of being defined as exceptions to exceptionless regularities.

4. I intend this to be taken as a simplified 'place holder' for something along the lines of 'When your brain has undergone changes x, y, z, it can never again perform processes a, b, c', where x, y, z specify changes that are clearly on the 'dead' side of clinically dead and processes 'a, b, c' are processes the performing of which would clearly place one on the alive side.

CHAPTER 12

1. There is one qualification to my conclusion. Atheistic and irreligious experiences are evils on theism (for they mislead those who have them about important issues) and, as argued for previously, these evils do indeed provide good reason to believe theism false; indeed it's because they provide these reasons that they are evils on theism. These experiences then escape my 'solution' to the Problem of Evil and ought to be taken—for the reasons previously articulated—as reasons to believe that there is no God. By a similar argument, the prima-facie plausibility of the Problem of Evil to people is in itself an evil that escapes my solution to it, i.e. my showing that the Problem of Evil isn't ultimately plausible—somewhat surprisingly, perhaps—doesn't undermine the claim that the fact that it initially appears plausible (to many, if not most) is a reason to suppose that there's no God.

2. Although in Leibniz's sense of possible world, he couldn't help 'creating a world', if only the one in which he alone exists, I am using world in this context to refer to whatever it is, if anything, that is genuinely created by God in the sense described earlier.

3. Cf. Adams's treatment of this problem in R. M. Adams, 'Must God Create the Best?', *Philosophical Review* 81 (1972). See also W. Rowe, 'Can God be Free?', *Faith and Philosophy* 19 (2002).

4. See my 'The Possibility of a Free Will Defence for the Problem of Natural Evil', *Religious Studies* 40 (2004), and D. Basinger, 'Evil as Evidence Against God's Existence', in M. Peterson (ed.), *The Problem of Evil: Selected Readings* (Notre Dame, Ind., 1992).

5. Cf. W. Rowe, *The Philosophy of Religion* (Dickenson, 1978), 88 ff.

6. Cf. R. Nozick's 'Experience Machine' in his *Anarchy, State and Utopia* (Basic Books, 1977).

7. Of course, it may be that there are things that this machine deprives one of other than freedom and that is the loss of these that grounds this choice. If you're worried that you'll have less true beliefs in the machine too, don't be; that can easily be amended. The computer will pack your brain full of the contents of the *Encyclopaedia Britannica*, so you'll actually have more true beliefs in the virtual world than you'd have in the real world. The machine might even be able to give you more true beliefs about your current life (e.g. by packing in a million about the biological happenings in your stomach or some such), but it seems that it couldn't provide you with the real satisfaction of many of your desires (unless it changed the desires to be simply desires for the feeling that would accompany believing that you were doing various things), for in the machine you wouldn't really solve the problems of the world, you would just appear to yourself to have done so. Related to this, the machine can't give you genuine achievement (as opposed to the sense of genuine achievement) or genuine relationships (as opposed to the illusion of genuine relationships); these latter two losses, it seems to me, are ones that it's impossible to hypothesize away by altering the details of the machine, so the 'argument from the pleasure machine' isn't a conclusive one in favour of us valuing freedom.

8. Cf. J. Hick, *Evil and the God of Love* (Harper & Row, 1977), 327–8.

9. See e.g. C. Mesle, *John Hick's Theodicy: A Process Humanist Critique* (Macmillan, 1991).

CONCLUSION

1. For a painstaking discussion of the relationship between belief-that and belief-in see H. H. Price, 'Belief "In" and Belief "That" ', *Religious Studies* 1 (1965). In this article, Price is predominantly concerned with trying to show that belief-in is not reducible to belief-that. As the discussion in the main text makes clear, I am sympathetic to his general thrust, although I don't see the need to deny that a reduction might be successful. One might say that either belief-in is not reducible to belief-that, as Price suggests, or that it is, but that the criteria by which one can satisfy a claim to believe in something are whether one's actions do in fact show a tendency to do that thing/support that cause/etc. The criteria for it being the case that one believes that something is true are that one has a particular attitude towards a statement, i.e. a tendency to affirm it when put in the right circumstances, and so on. The criteria for it being the case that one believes in something are that one has a particular attitude towards an action/ideal/person and so on, i.e. a tendency to perform that action/strive to live up to that ideal/respect that person, and so on. As long as this point is granted, nothing of significance turns on whether or not Price's main contention is right. See also A. Kenny's very good discussion in *What is Faith?* (OUP, 1992). There is also much of interest in Paul Helm's recent and very nuanced *Faith with Reason* (OUP, 2000).

2. Sometimes the Problem of Physicalism is hived off from the Problem of Other Religions and given separate treatment under the title 'The Problem of Divine Hiddenness'; see e.g. J. Schellenberg's *Divine Hiddenness and Human Reason* (Cornell, 1993) and D. Howard-Snyder and P. Moser (eds.), *Divine Hiddenness* (CUP, 2001). As my discussion of the evidential force of irreligious experience earlier makes clear (and my conclusion will underscore), I believe the structure of the argument from divine hiddenness to the non-existence of God to be inductively valid and thus that it is a potentially good argument against the existence of God. The Problem of Other Religions as then left behind is itself the subject of a dedicated body of literature, foremost among which is J. Hick's *An Interpretation of Religion* (Palgrave Macmillan, 2004) and Peter Byrne's *Prolegomena to Religious Pluralism* (Macmillan, 1995). For a very perceptive discussion of Hick's view see C. Insole, 'Why John Hick Cannot, and Should Not, Stay out of the Jam Pot', *Religious Studies* 36/1 (2000); for a less perceptive analysis of Byrne's, see my ' 'Byrne's' Religious Pluralism', *International Journal for Philosophy of Religion* (forthcoming) Hick responds to his critics in his *Dialogues in The Philosophy of Religion* (Palgrave Macmillan, 2004).

3. See also R. Trigg's rather fine *Reason and Commitment* (CUP, 1973).

4. Amongst theists, to prioritize one's own religion and its trappings above the God whom it describes and for whose worship it purports to act as the most suitable vehicle is the form of idolatry that it is easiest for those who make conscious efforts to avoid idolatry to fall into. It is also one of the most pernicious forms of idolatry, lying as it does at the root of all intolerance between the adherents of the world's various religions. The theist must always remember that it is not one's beliefs about God that are the proper object of worship and praise: it is God himself. So, when Cupitt claims that, 'Religion forbids that there should be any extra-religious reality of God' in his *Taking Leave of God* (p. 96) he is, if this account is correct, idolatrous—it is idolatrous

to think of God as merely existing internal to one's religion. If one is a Jew, Christian, or Muslim, the only view of one's religion that is compatible with one retaining it is the view from which it is seen as one's response to a God who exists outside it. The debate between realists and anti-realists is a debate between different philosophers of religion; it is not a debate among the religious, the religious already being committed by their being such to seeing anti-realism as idolatry. Compare Keith Ward, *Holding Fast to God* (SPCK, 1982) with Cupitt's work. Peter Byrne, *God and Realism* (Ashgate, 2003) is also very perspicacious and indeed perspicuous on this. My own attempts to address this topic may be found in my 'Religions, Truth, and the Pursuit of Truth: A Reply to Zamulinski', *Religious Studies* 40/3 (2004).

5. In fact I think that as long as you believe that the God hypothesis is more probable than any alternative, even if the probability you assign it is less than 50 per cent (i.e. you think a disjunction formed of all the alternatives is more probable than it), you may nevertheless be reasonable in having faith in God, but I rest content with arguing directly for the more minimal claim in the main text.

6. A slight modification to the story yields a different moral. Suppose that the chance of what the 'policeman' calls the antidote being poisoned is known to be zero, whereas the chance that the original champagne being poisoned is known to be small but not zero, say 5 per cent. In these circumstances, it would be rational to take the antidote, that is, to put your faith in the putative policeman. See also my previous note and later discussion of Pascal's Wager.

7. See previous two notes.

8. See, e.g. L. Francis, 'Religion, Neuroticism, and Psychotism', in J. Schumaker (ed.), *Religion and Mental Health* (OUP, 1992).

9. A. Kenny, *The God of the Philosophers* (Clarendon, 1979), 129.

10. In getting to the end of my argument, it occurs to me that it might be useful to direct interested readers to a couple of books that go over the same ground that I have attempted to cover, but go over it in as different a direction as possible. On this score, as well as for their general merits, both W. Rowe's *Philosophy of Religion* (Dickenson, 1978) and N. Everitt's *The Non-Existence of God* (Routledge, 2004) commend themselves.

Bibliography

ABRAHAM, W., *An Introduction to the Philosophy of Religion* (Englewood Cliffs: Prentice-Hall, 1985).
—— and HOLTZER, W. (eds.), *The Rationality of Religious Belief* (New York: Oxford University Press, 1987).
ADAMS, M. M., *Horrendous Evils and the Goodness of God* (Ithaca, NY: Cornell University Press, 1999).
—— and ADAMS, R. M. (eds.), *The Problem of Evil* (Oxford: OUP, 1993).
ADAMS, R. M., 'Must God Create the Best?', *Philosophical Review* 81 (1972).
—— 'Divine Necessity', *The Journal of Philosophy* 80 (1983).
—— *The Virtue of Faith* (Oxford: OUP, 1987).
ADLER, J., *Belief's Own Ethics* (Cambridge, Mass.: MIT, 2002).
ALSTON, W., 'Does God Have Beliefs?', *Religious Studies* 22 (1986).
—— *Divine Nature and Human Language* (Ithaca, NY: Cornell University Press, 1989).
—— *Perceiving God* (Ithaca, NY: Cornell University Press, 1991).
ANSELM, *St Anselm's Proslogion*, M. J. Charlesworth (trans.) (Oxford: Clarendon 1965).
AQUINAS, *Summa Theologica* (London: Blackfriars, 1963).
ARMSTRONG, D. M., *A Materialist Theory of the Mind* (London: Routledge & Kegan Paul, 1968).
BADHAM, P., *Christian Beliefs About Immortality* (London: Macmillan, 1976).
BARNES, J., *The Ontological Argument* (London: Macmillan, 1972).
BARROW, J., *Theories of Everything* (Oxford: OUP, 1991).
—— and TIPLER, F., *The Anthropic Cosmological Principle* (Oxford: OUP, 1986).
BASINGER, D., *Religious Diversity* (London: Ashgate, 2002).
—— and BASINGER, R., *Philosophy and Miracle* (Lewiston: Edwin Mellen, 1986).
BEATY, M. (ed.), *Christian Theism and the Problems of Philosophy* (Notre Dame, Ind.: University of Notre Dame Press, 1989).
BEILBY, J. (ed.), *Naturalism Defeated?* (Ithaca, NY: Cornell University Press, 2002).
BOETHIUS, *The Consolation of Philosophy*, V. Watts (trans.) (Harmondsworth: Penguin, 1969).
BRUMMER, V., *Speaking of a Personal God* (Cambridge: CUP, 1992).
BYRNE, P., *Prolegomena to Religious Pluralism* (London: Macmillan, 1995).
—— *God and Realism* (Aldershot: Ashgate, 2003).
CAHN, M., and SCHATZ, D. (eds.), *Contemporary Philosophy of Religion* (Oxford: Clarendon Press, 1982).
CAMPBELL, A., *In Defence of Free Will* (London: Allen & Unwin, 1967).
CASTANEDA, H. N., 'Omniscience and Indexical Reference', *The Journal of Philosophy* 64 (1967).
CHAPPELL, T., 'Why God is not a Consequentialist', *Religious Studies* 29 (1993).
—— 'Why is Faith a Virtue?', *Religious Studies* 32 (1996).
CLARK, S., *How to Live Forever* (London: Routledge, 1995).
—— *God, Religion and Reality* (London: SPCK 1998).

CLIFFORD, W. K., 'The Ethics of Belief', *Lectures and Essays* (London: Macmillan, 1879).

CRAIG, W., *The Cosmological Argument from Plato to Leibniz* (New York: Barnes & Noble, 1980).

—— *The* Kalām *Cosmological Argument* (New York: Harper & Row, 1980).

—— 'God and Real Time', *Religious Studies* 26 (1990).

—— 'A Swift and Simple Refutation of the *Kalam* Cosmological Argument?', *Religious Studies* 35 (1999).

CROWDER, C. (ed.), *God and Reality: Essays on Christian Non-Realism* (London: Mowbrays, 1997).

CUPITT, D., *Taking Leave of God* (New York: Crossroad, 1981).

—— *The Sea of Faith* (Cambridge: CUP, 1984).

DANTE, *The Divine Comedy*, Dorothy L. Sayers and Barbara Reynolds (trans.) (Harmondsworth: Penguin, 1986).

DARWIN, F., (ed.), *Life and Letters of Charles Darwin* (London: John Murray, 1888).

DAVIES, B., *An Introduction to the Philosophy of Religion* (Oxford: OUP, 1993).

DAVIS, C., *The Evidential Force of Religious Experience* (Oxford: Clarendon, 1989).

DAVIS, S., *Logic and the Nature of God* (Grand Rapids, Mich.: Eerdmans, 1983).

DAWKINS, R., *The Selfish Gene* (Oxford: OUP, 1976).

DOUVEN, I., 'Review of Belief's Own Ethics', *Ars Disputandi* 3 (2003).

DRAPER, P., 'Pain and Pleasure: An Evidential Problem for Theists', *Nous* 23 (1989).

DESCARTES, R., *The Philosophical Writings of Descartes*, J. Cottingham, R. Stoothoff, and D. Murdoch; and A. Kenny (vol. iii) (trans. and eds.) (Cambridge: CUP, 1984–91).

DENNETT, D., *Brainstorms* (Brighton: Harvester, 1981).

DEVINE, P., 'On the Definition of Religion', *Faith and Philosophy* 3 (1986).

DURRANT, M., *The Logical Status of 'God'* (London: Macmillan, 1973).

EDWARDS, P., *Immortality* (New York: Macmillan, 1992).

EVERITT, N., 'Substance Dualism and Disembodied Existence', *Faith and Philosophy* 17 (2000).

—— *The Non-Existence of God* (London: Routledge, 2004).

FISCHER J.,(ed.), *The Metaphysics of Death* (Stanford, Calif.: Stanford University Press, 1993).

—— 'Foreknowledge and Freedom: A Reply to Gale', *Faith and Philosophy* 19 (2002).

—— (ed.), *God, Foreknowledge and Freedom* (Palo Alto, Calif.: Stanford University Press, 1989).

FLEW A., (ed.), *Body, Mind, and Death* (New York: Macmillan, 1964).

—— *God and Philosophy* (London: Hutchinson 1966).

—— *The Presumption of Atheism* (London: Elek/Pemberton, 1976).

—— *God, Freedom, and Immortality* (Buffalo: Prometheus Books, 1984).

—— and MACINTYRE, A. (eds.), *New Essays in Philosophical Theology* (London: SCM, 1955).

FLINT, T., 'Middle Knowledge and the Doctrine of Infallibility', *Philosophical Perspectives* 5 (1991).

FORREST, P., 'An Argument for the Divine Command Theory of Right Action', *Sophia* 28 (1989).

—— *God without the Supernatural: A Defence of Scientific Theism* (Ithaca: Cornell University Press, 1996).

FOSTER, J., *The Case for Idealism* (London: Routledge & Kegan Paul, 1982).

—— *The Immaterial Self* (London: Routledge, 1991).

—— *The Divine Lawmaker* (Oxford: OUP, 2004).

FREDDOSO, A. (ed.), *The Existence and Nature of God* (Notre Dame, Ind.: University of Notre Dame Press, 1983).

GALE, R., 'Mysticism and Philosophy', *Journal of Philosophy* 57 (1960).

—— *On the Nature and Existence of God* (Cambridge: CUP, 1992).

—— 'Divine Omniscience, Human Freedom, and Backward Causation', *Faith and Philosophy* 19 (2002).

GALLUP, G., *Adventures in Immortality* (New York: McGraw Hill, 1982).

GARDNER, M., 'The Fantastic Combinations of John Conway's New Solitaire Game "Life"', *Scientific American* 223 (1970).

GASKIN, J. C. A., *The Quest for Eternity* (Harmondsworth: Penguin, 1984).

—— (ed.), *Varieties of Unbelief* (London: Macmillan, 1989).

GEACH, P., *God and the Soul* (London: Routledge & Kegan Paul, 1969).

—— *Providence and Evil* (Cambridge: CUP, 1977).

GELLMAN, J., *Experience of God and the Rationality of Theistic Belief* (Ithaca, NY: Cornell University Press, 1997).

—— 'On a Sociological Challenge to the Veridicality of Religious Experience', *Religious Studies* 34 (1998).

—— *Mystical Experience of God: A Philosophical Inquiry* (London: Ashgate, 2001).

GINET, C., and SHOEMAKER, S. (eds.), *Knowledge and Mind* (Oxford: OUP, 1983).

GOODCHILD, P. (ed.), *Difference in the Philosophy of Religion* (London: Ashgate, 2003).

GUTTING, G., *Religious Belief and Religious Skepticism* (Notre Dame, Ind.: University of Notre Dame Press, 1982).

HARDY, A., *The Spiritual Nature of Man: A Study of Contemporary Religious Experience* (Oxford: Clarendon 1979).

HARRISON, J., *God, Freedom and Immortality* (London: Ashgate, 1999).

HARTSHORNE, C., *The Logic of Perfection* (LaSalle, Ill.: Open Court, 1962).

—— *Anselm's Discovery* (LaSalle, Ill.: Open Court, 1965).

HASKER, W., 'Must God Do his Best?', *International Journal for Philosophy of Religion* 16 (1984).

—— *God, Time and Knowledge* (Ithaca NY: Cornell University Press, 1989).

—— 'The Necessity of Gratuitous Evil', *Faith and Philosophy* 9 (1992).

—— 'Swinburne's Modal Argument for Dualism: Epistemically Circular', *Faith and Philosophy* 15 (1998).

HAY, D., ' "The Biology of God": What is the Current Status of Hardy's Hypothesis?', *International Journal for the Psychology of Religion* 4 (1994).

—— and MORISY, A., 'Reports of Ecstatic, Paranormal, or Religious Experience in Great Britain and the United States—A Comparison of Trends', *Journal for the Scientific Study of Religion* 17 (1978).

O'HEAR, A., *Experience, Explanation and Faith* (London: Routledge & Kegan Paul, 1984).

HEDLEY, D., 'Pantheism, Trinitarian Theism and the Idea of Unity: Reflections on the Christian Concept of God', *Religious Studies* 32 (1996).

HELM, P. (ed.), *The Divine Command Theory of Ethics* (Oxford: Clarendon, 1979).

—— *Eternal God* (Oxford: OUP, 1988).

—— *Faith with Reason* (Oxford: OUP, 2000).

HENRY, D., 'Does Reasonable Nonbelief Exist?', *Faith and Philosophy* 18 (2001).

HERSHENOV, D., 'The Metaphysical Problem of Intermittent Existence and the Possibility of Resurrection', *Faith and Philosophy* 20 (2003).

HICK, J., *Arguments for the Existence of God* (London: Macmillan, 1971).

—— *God and the Universe of Faiths* (London: Macmillan, 1973).

—— *Death and Eternal Life* (London: Collins, 1976).

—— *Evil and the God of Love* (London: Macmillan, 1977).

—— (ed.), 'Religious Pluralism', *Faith and Philosophy* 5/4 (1988).

—— *An Interpretation of Religion* (London: Palgrave Macmillan, 2004).

HILL, D., *Divinity and Maximal Greatness* (London: Routledge, forthcoming).

HIRSCH, E., *The Concept of Identity* (Oxford: OUP, 1982).

HOFFMAN, J., and ROSENKRANTZ, G., 'Omnipotence Redux', *Philosophy and Phenomenological Research* 49 (1988).

—— —— *The Divine Attributes* (Oxford: Blackwell, 2002).

HOUSTON, J., *Reported Miracles: A Critique of Hume* (New York: CUP, 1994).

HOWARD-SNYDER, D. (ed.), *The Evidential Argument from Evil* (Bloomington, Ind.: Indiana University Press, 1996).

—— 'In Defense of Naïve Universalism', *Faith and Philosophy* 20 (2003).

—— and MOSER, P. (eds.), *Divine Hiddenness* (Cambridge: CUP, 2001).

HUGHES, C., *On a Complex Theory of a Simple God* (Ithaca: Cornell University Press, 1989).

—— 'Miracles, Laws of Nature and Causation', *Proceedings of the Aristotelian Society*, supp. vol. 66 (1992).

HUME, D., *Dialogues Concerning Natural Religion*, R. H. Popkin (ed.) (Indianapolis, Ind.: Hackett, 1980).

—— *Enquiries Concerning Human Understanding and Concerning the Principles of Morals*, L. A. Selby-Bigge (ed.) (Oxford: Clarendon 1989).

INSOLE, C., 'Why John Hick Cannot, and Should Not, Stay Out of the Jam Pot', *Religious Studies*, 36 (2000).

—— and HARRIS, H., (eds.), *Faith and Philosophical Analysis: The Impact of Analytical Philosophy on the Philosophy of Religion* (London: Ashgate, 2005).

JAMES, W., *The Varieties of Religious Experience* (London: Fontana, 1960).

JANTZEN, G., *God's World, God's Body* (Philadelphia: Westminster, 1984).

—— *Becoming Divine: Towards a Feminist Philosophy of Religion* (Manchester: Manchester University Press, 1998).

JORDAN, J., *Gambling on God: Essays on Pascal's Wager* (Lanham, Md.: Rowman & Littlefield, 1994).

—— 'Pascal's Wager Revisited', *Religious Studies* 34 (1998).

KANT, I.,*Critique of Pure Reason*, N. Kemp Smith (trans.) (New York: St Martin's Press, 1965)

KENNY, A., *The God of the Philosophers* (Oxford: OUP, 1979).

—— *What is Faith?* (Oxford: OUP, 1992).

KENYON, J., 'Doubts About the Concept of Reason', *Proceedings of the Aristotelian Society* (1985).

KOEHL, A., 'Reformed Epistemology and Diversity', *Faith and Philosophy* 18 (2001).

KRETZMANN, N., 'Omniscience and Indexicality', *Journal of Philosophy* 63 (1966).

KERR, F., *Theology After Wittgenstein* (Oxford: Blackwell, 1988).

KVANVIG, J., *The Possibility of an All-Knowing God* (London: Macmillan, 1986).

LEFTOW, B., 'God and Abstract Entities', *Faith and Philosophy* 7 (1990).

—— *Time and Eternity* (Ithaca, NY: Cornell University Press, 1991).

—— 'On a Principle of Sufficient Reason', *Religious Studies* 39 (2003).

LEIBNIZ, G., *The Monadology and Other Philosophical Writings*, R. Latta (trans.) (Oxford: OUP, 1925).

—— *Theodicy*, E. M. Huggard (trans.) (London: Routledge & Kegan Paul, 1951).

LESLIE, J., *Value and Existence* (Oxford: Blackwell, 1979).

—— *Universes* (London: Routledge, 1989).

LEWIS, C. S., *The Problem of Pain* (London: Geoffrey Bles, 1940).

—— *Miracles* (London: Macmillan, 1970).

LEWIS, D., *Counterfactuals* (Oxford: Blackwell, 1973).

—— *On the Plurality of Worlds* (Oxford: Blackwell, 1986).

LOCKE, J., *An Essay Concerning Human Understanding* (Oxford: OUP, 1975).

LUCAS, J. R., *The Freedom of the Will* (Oxford: Clarendon 1970).

—— *A Treatise on Time and Space* (London: Methuen, 1973).

—— *The Future* (Oxford: Blackwell, 1989).

MACKIE, J. L., 'Evil and Omnipotence', *Mind* 64 (1955).

—— *The Miracle of Theism* (Oxford: Clarendon, 1982).

MALCOLM, N., 'Anselm's Ontological Argument', *The Philosophical Review* 69 (1960).

MARTIN, C. B., *Religious Belief* (Ithaca, NY: Cornell University Press, 1959).

MARTIN, D., *A Sociology of English Religion* (London: Heinemann, 1967).

MARTIN, M., *Atheism* (Philadelphia: Temple University Press, 1990).

—— *The Case Against Christianity* (Philadelphia: Temple University Press, 1991).

McCLOSKEY, H. J., 'God and Evil', *The Philosophical Quarterly* 10 (1960).

McGHEE, M., 'The Locations of the Soul', *Religious Studies* 32 (1996).

McKIM, R., *Religious Ambiguity and Religious Diversity* (Oxford: OUP, 2001).

McNAUGHTON, D., *Moral Vision* (Oxford: Blackwell, 1988).

MAVRODES, G., *Belief in God* (New York: Random House, 1970).

MAWSON, T. J., 'The Problem of Evil and Moral Indifference', *Religious Studies* 35 (1999).

—— 'Miracles and Laws of Nature', *Religious Studies* 37 (2001).

—— 'God's Creation of Morality', *Religious Studies* 38 (2002).

—— 'Omnipotence and Necessary Moral Perfection are Compatible: A Reply to Morriston', *Religious Studies* 38 (2002).

—— 'How a Single Personal Revelation Might Not Be a Source of Knowledge', *Religious Studies* 39 (2003).

—— 'The Possibility of a Free Will Defence for the Problem of Natural Evil', *Religious Studies* 40 (2004).

—— 'Religions, Truth, and the Pursuit of Truth: A Reply to Zamulinski', *Religious Studies* 40 (2004).

MESLE, C., *John Hick's Theodicy: A Process Humanist Critique* (London: Macmillan, 1991).

MESSER, R., *Does God's Existence Need Proof?* (Oxford: Clarendon, 1993).

METCALF, T., 'Omniscience and Maximal Power', *Religious Studies* 40 (2004).

MITCHELL, B., *The Justification of Religious Belief* (London: Macmillan, 1973).

—— (ed.), *The Philosophy of Religion* (Oxford: OUP, 1986).

—— *Faith and Criticism* (Oxford: Clarendon, 1994).

MOLINA, L., *On Divine Foreknowledge*, A. Freddoso (trans.) (Ithaca, NY: Cornell University Press, 1988).

MOORE, A., *Realism and Christian Faith: God, Grammar, and Meaning* (Cambridge: CUP, 2003).

MORRIS, T. V., *Anselmian Explorations* (Notre Dame, Ind.: University of Notre Dame Press, 1987).

—— *Divine and Human Action* (Ithaca, NY: Cornell University Press, 1988).

—— *Our Idea of God* (Downers Grove: InterVarsity Press, 1991).

—— and MENZEL, C., 'Absolute Creation', *American Philosophical Quarterly* 23 (1986).

MORRISTON, W., 'Must the Beginning of the Universe have a Personal Cause?', *Faith and Philosophy* 17 (2000).

MORRISTON, W., 'Are Omnipotence and Necessary Moral Perfection Compatible? Reply to Mawson', *Religious Studies* 39 (2003).

MULHALL, S., *Faith and Reason* (London: Duckworth, 1994).

MURRAY, M., 'Three Versions of Universalism', *Faith and Philosophy* 16 (1999).

MURPHY, B., 'Are God's Hands Tied by Logic?', *Ars Disputandi* 3 (2003).

MURPHY, M., 'Divine Command, Divine Will, and Moral Obligation', *Faith and Philosophy* 15 (1998).

NIELSEN, K., *An Introduction to the Philosophy of Religion* (New York: St Martin's Press, 1982).

NOZICK, R., *Anarchy, State and Utopia* (New York: Basic Books, 1977).

OPPY, G., *Ontological Arguments and Belief in God* (Cambridge: CUP, 1995).

—— 'On "A New Cosmological Argument"', *Religious Studies* 36 (2000).

PADGETT, A., *God, Eternity, and the Nature of Time* (New York: St Martin's Press, 1992).

PALEY, W., *Natural Theology* (London: SPCK, 1837).

PASCAL, B., *Pensées* (A. J. Krailsheimer, trans) (Harmondsworth: Penguin, 1966).

PENELHUM, T., *Survival and Disembodied Existence* (London: Routledge & Kegan Paul, 1970).

—— (ed.), *Faith* (New York: Macmillan, 1989).

PETERSON, M. (ed.), *The Problem of Evil: Selected Readings* (Notre Dame, Ind.: University of Notre Dame Press, 1992).

—— HASKER, W., REICHENBACH, B., and BASINGER, D. (eds.), *Philosophy of Religion, Selected Readings* (Oxford: OUP, 2000).

PHILLIPS, D. Z., *Death and Immortality* (London: Macmillan, 1970).

—— *Faith and Philosophical Enquiry* (London: Routledge & Kegan Paul, 1970).

—— *Religion Without Explanation* (Oxford: Blackwell, 1976).

—— *Wittgenstein and Religion* (New York: Macmillan, 1993).

PIKE, N. (ed.), *God and Evil* (Englewood Cliffs, NJ: Prentice-Hall, 1964).

—— *God and Timelessness* (London: Routledge & Kegan Paul, 1970).

PINNOCK, C., et al., *The Openness of God: A Biblical Challenge to the Traditional Understanding of God* (Downers Grove: InterVarsity Press, 1994).

PLANTINGA, A., *God and Other Minds* (Ithaca, NY: Cornell University Press, 1967).

—— *The Nature of Necessity* (Oxford: Clarendon Press, 1974).

—— *God, Freedom and Evil* (Grand Rapids, Mich.: Eermans, 1974).

—— *Does God Have a Nature?* (Milwaukee, Wis.: Marquette University Press, 1980).

—— 'How to be an Anti-Realist', *Proceedings and Addresses of the American Philosophical Association* 56 (1982).

—— 'On Ockham's Way Out', *Faith and Philosophy* 3 (1986).

—— 'An Evolutionary Argument against Naturalism', *Logos* 12 (1991).

—— 'Naturalism Defeated' (1994), unpublished paper, available at http://www.homstead.com/philofreligion/files/alspaper.htm, accessed 29 March 2005.

—— *Warrant: the Current Debate* (Oxford: OUP, 1993).

—— *Warrant and Proper Function* (Oxford: OUP, 1993).

—— *Warranted Christian Belief* (Oxford: OUP, 2000).

—— and WOLTERSTORFF, N. (eds.), *Faith and Rationality: Reason and Belief in God* (Notre Dame, Ind.: University of Notre Dame Press, 1983).

POJMAN, L., *Philosophy of Religion* (New York: McGraw-Hill, 2000).

PRINCE, M., *The Dissociation of a Personality* (London: Longmans, 1905).

PRICE, H. H., 'Belief "In" and Belief "That"', *Religious Studies* 1 (1965).

—— *Belief* (London; George Allen, 1969).

—— *Essays in the Philosophy of Religion* (Oxford: Clarendon, 1972).

PUTNAM, H., *Realism With a Human Face* (Cambridge, Mass.: Harvard University Press, 1990).

QUINN, P., *Divine Commands and Moral Requirements* (Oxford: Clarendon, 1978).

QUINTON, A., 'The Soul', *Journal of Philosophy* 59 (1962).

—— *The Nature of Things* (London: Routledge & Kegan Paul, 1973).

RACHELS, J., *The Ends of Life* (Oxford: OUP, 1986).

REICHENBACH, B., *The Cosmological Argument: A Reassessment* (Springfield: Charles Thomas, 1972).

—— *Evil and a Good God* (New York: Fordham University Press, 1982).

—— 'Omniscience and Deliberation', *International Journal for Philosophy of Religion* 16 (1984).

RESCHER, N., *Pascal's Wager* (Notre Dame: University of Notre Dame Press, 1985).

RICE D. H., *God and Goodness* (Oxford: OUP, 2000).

ROBINSON, H., *Matter and Sense* (Cambridge: CUP, 1982).

—— (ed.), *Objections to Physicalism* (Oxford: Clarendon, 1993).

ROBINSON, J. A. T., *Exploration into God* (London: SCM, 1967).

ROWE, W., *The Cosmological Argument* (Princeton, NJ: Princeton University Press, 1971).

—— *The Philosophy of Religion* (Belmont, Calif.: Wadsworth, 1978).

—— 'Religious Experience and the Principle of Credulity', *International Journal for Philosophy of Religion* 13 (1982).

—— 'Can God be Free?', *Faith and Philosophy* 19 (2002).

RUNDLE, B., *Why There is Something Rather Than Nothing* (Oxford: OUP, 2004).

RUSSELL, B., *Why I am not a Christian and Other Essays on Religion and Related Subjects* (London: Unwin, 1979).

SANDERS, J., 'Why Simple Foreknowledge Offers No More Providential Control than the Openness of God', *Faith and Philosophy* 14 (1997).

SCHELLENBERG, J., *Divine Hiddenness and Human Reason* (Ithaca, NY: Cornell University Press, 1993).

SCHLESINGER, G., 'On the Compatibility of the Divine Attributes', *Religious Studies* 23 (1987).

SCHUMAKER, J., (ed.), *Religion and Mental Health* (Oxford: OUP, 1992).

SCOTT, M., 'The Morality of Theodicies', *Religious Studies* 32 (1996).

—— 'Seeing Aspects', *International Journal for Philosophy of Religion* 44 (1998).

—— 'Framing the Realism Question', *Religious Studies* 36 (2000).

—— and MOORE, A., 'Can Theological Realism be Refuted?', *Religious Studies* 33 (1997).

SENNETT, J., 'Is There Freedom in Heaven?', *Faith and Philosophy* 16 (1999).

SENOR, T., 'Divine Temporality and Creation Ex Nihilo', *Faith and Philosophy* 10 (1993).

SHAW, J., 'The Application of Divine Commands', *Religious Studies* 35 (1999).

SHERRY, P., *Religion, Truth and Language Games* (London: Macmillan, 1977).

—— *Spirit, Saints and Immortality* (London: Macmillan, 1984).

SLOTE, M., *Goods and Virtues* (Oxford: Clarendon, 1983).

SMITH Q., and CRAIG, W., *Theism, Atheism and Big Bang Cosmology* (Oxford: Clarendon, 1993).

SOBEL, J., *Logic and Theism* (Cambridge: CUP, 2004).

SORABJI, R., *Time, Creation, and the Continuum* (London: Duckworth, 1983).

SOSKICE, J. M., *Metaphor and Religious Language* (Oxford: OUP, 1984).

SPRIGGE, T. L. S., *The Vindication of Absolute Idealism* (Edinburgh: Edinburgh University Press, 1983).

STACE, W., *Time and Eternity* (Princeton, NJ: Princeton University Press, 1952).

STALKER, G., *Grue!* (Chicago: Open Court, 1994).

STUMP E., and KRETZMANN, N., 'Eternity', *Journal of Philosophy* 78 (1981).

SUDDUTH, M., 'Can Religious Unbelief be Proper Function Rational?', *Faith and Philosophy* 16 (1999).

SWINBURNE, R., 'The Argument from Design', *Philosophy* 43 (1968).

—— *The Concept of Miracle* (London: Macmillan, 1970).

—— 'The Argument from Design—A Defence', *Religious Studies* 8 (1972).

—— *The Coherence of Theism* (Oxford: Clarendon, 1977).

—— 'Natural Evil', *American Philosophical Quarterly* 15 (1978).

—— *The Existence of God* (Oxford: Clarendon, 1979).

—— *Faith and Reason* (Oxford: Clarendon, 1983).

—— *The Evolution of the Soul* (Oxford: Clarendon, 1986).

—— *The Christian God* (Oxford: Clarendon, 1994).

—— *Providence and the Problem of Evil* (Oxford: Clarendon, 1998).

—— 'The Modal Argument is Not Circular', *Faith and Philosophy* 15 (1998).

—— *Epistemic Justification* (Oxford: Clarendon, 2001).

TALIAFERRO, C., *Consciousness and the Mind of God* (Cambridge: CUP, 1994).

—— (ed.), *Contemporary Philosophy of Religion* (Oxford: Blackwell, 1998).

TAYLOR, J., 'Kalam: A Swift Argument from Origins to First Cause?', *Religious Studies* 33 (1997).

TAYLOR, R., *Metaphysics* (Englewood Cliffs, NJ: Prentice-Hall, 1992).

TENNANT, F. R., *Philosophical Theology* (Cambridge: CUP, 1928–30).

THATCHER, A., 'The Personal God and a God Who Is a Person', *Religious Studies* 21 (1985).

TILGHMAN, B. R., *An Introduction to Philosophy of Religion* (Oxford: Blackwell, 1993).

TRIGG, R., *Reason and Commitment* (Cambridge: CUP, 1973).

—— *Rationality and Science* (Oxford: Blackwell, 1993).

VAN INWAGEN, P., *An Essay on Free Will* (Oxford: Clarendon Press, 1983).

—— *Metaphysics* (Oxford: OUP, 1993).

—— *God, Knowledge, and Mystery* (Ithaca: Cornell University Press, 1995).

WILLIGENBURG, T. VAN, '*P*, but I Lack Sufficient Evidence for *p*', *Ars Disputandi* 3 (2003).

WAINWRIGHT, W., 'God and the Necessity of Physical Evils', *Sophia* 11 (1972).

—— 'Mysticism and Sense Perception', *Religious Studies* 9 (1973).

—— *Mysticism* (Madison, Wis.: University of Wisconsin Press, 1981).

—— *Philosophy of Religion* (Belmont, Calif.: Wadsworth, 1988).

WALKER, R., *Kant* (London: Routledge, 1978).

WARD, K., *Holding Fast to God* (London: SPCK, 1982).

—— *God, Chance and Necessity* (Oxford: Oneworld, 1996).

WIERENGA, E., 'Intrinsic Maxima and Omnibenevolence', *International Journal for Philosophy of Religion* 10 (1979).

—— *The Nature of God* (Ithaca, NY: Cornell University Press, 1989).

WILKES, K. V., *Real People* (Oxford: Clarendon, 1988).

WILLIAMS, B., *Problems of the Self* (Cambridge: CUP, 1973).

—— and MONTEFIORE, A. (eds.), *British Analytical Philosophy* (London: Routledge & Kegan Paul, 1966).

WILLIAMS, T., and VISSER, S., 'Anselm's Account of Freedom', *Canadian Journal of Philosophy* 31 (2001).

WILSON, M., *Descartes* (London: Routledge & Kegan Paul, 1978).

WOLFRAM, S., *Philosophical Logic* (London: Routledge, 1989).

WOLTERSTORFF, N., *Divine Discourse: Philosophical Reflections on the Claim that God Speaks* (New York: CUP, 1995).

WYNN, M., 'From World to God: Resemblance and Complementarity', *Religious Studies* 32 (1996).

—— *God and Goodness: A Natural Theological Perspective* (London: Routledge, 1999).

YANDELL, K., 'Religious Experience and Rational Appraisal', *Religious Studies* 8 (1974).

—— *The Epistemology of Religious Experience* (Cambridge: CUP, 1993).

ZAGZEBSKI, L., *The Dilemma of Freedom and Foreknowledge* (New York: OUP, 1991).

—— 'Omniscience and the Arrow of Time', *Faith and Philosophy* 19 (2002).

ZIMMERMAN, D., 'The Compatibility of Materialism and Survival: The 'Falling Elevator' Model, *Faith and Philosophy* 16 (1999).

Index